George Washington Julian, Joshua Reed Giddings

The life of Joshua R. Giddings

George Washington Julian, Joshua Reed Giddings

The life of Joshua R. Giddings

ISBN/EAN: 9783337733346

Printed in Europe, USA, Canada, Australia, Japan

Cover: Foto ©ninafisch / pixelio.de

More available books at **www.hansebooks.com**

THE LIFE

OF

JOSHUA R. GIDDINGS

BY

GEORGE W. JULIAN
AUTHOR OF "POLITICAL RECOLLECTIONS"

CHICAGO
A. C. McCLURG AND COMPANY
1892

TO THE MEMORY OF

𝔐𝔶 𝔚𝔦𝔣𝔢,

LAURA GIDDINGS JULIAN,

THIS LIFE OF HER FATHER

IS AFFECTIONATELY DEDICATED.

PREFACE.

IN the following pages I have dealt with the chief facts in the public life of JOSHUA R. GIDDINGS. Its importance centres entirely in his warfare against Slavery. To this he dedicated himself with absolute singleness of purpose and the whole strength of his nature. It seems to have been his predestined work; for he was drawn to it by every fibre of his heart and every prompting of his judgment and conscience. It was this fervor of spirit and perfect concentration of energy which armed him with his power, and enabled him to link his name imperishably with a cause which vitally involved the fortunes of the Republic and the progress of liberty throughout the world.

That such a life should be fitly commemorated, will not be disputed. Interesting sketches of his career have been given to the public, but as yet no adequate life of the man has appeared. Whether I have produced this in the volume now submitted, I must leave my readers to determine. I have made an honest endeavor, and this was prompted by several considerations. I was personally acquainted with Mr.

Giddings during the greater part of his public service, and have long been familiar with his anti-slavery labors; my relations to his family gave me free access to his private correspondence and other papers of interest and value in the preparation of such a work; and it was the wish of his surviving relatives and friends that I should undertake it. While I have written in sympathy with my subject, I trust it will be found that I have not slighted the duty of discrimination, or seriously failed in the endeavor to deal fairly and impartially with the famous men and stirring events of a grand epoch.

G. W. J.

IRVINGTON, IND.,
    January, 1892.

CONTENTS.

CHAPTER I.

Ancestry and Early Life. — Pioneer Trials and Hardships. — Military Experience. — Teaching School. — Choice of the Legal Profession. — Marriage. — Children 11

CHAPTER II.

Success at the Bar. — Sent to the Ohio Legislature. — Partnership with Benjamin F. Wade. — Business Troubles and Failing Health. — Election to Congress. — The Slavery Question 27

CHAPTER III.

DECEMBER, 1838, TO MARCH, 1839.

Personal Journal. — Last Session of the Twenty-fifth Congress. — Scenes and Incidents. — Growing Domination of Slavery. — Development of Character 46

CHAPTER IV.

MARCH, 1839, TO MARCH, 1841.

The "Amistad" Case. — The Twenty-sixth Congress. — The Famous New Jersey Election Contest. — The Slave-ship "Enterprise." — The Harrison Campaign. — Nomination of Birney. — Speech on the Florida War . . . 73

CHAPTER V.

MARCH, 1841, TO DECEMBER, 1842.

Meeting of the Twenty-seventh Congress. — Trial of John Quincy Adams. — The Case of the "Creole," and Censure of Giddings. — Letters from Mr. Chase. — The "Pacificus" Papers. — Weary of Public Life 102

CHAPTER VI.

DECEMBER, 1842, TO DECEMBER, 1844.

Second Session of the Twenty-seventh Congress. — The Twenty-first Rule. — Southern Intolerance. — Claim of West Florida Slaveholders. — Claim for Slaves lost in the Coastwise Trade. — Speech. — Encounter with a Southern Bully. — Annexation of Texas. — The Twenty-eighth Congress. — Presidential Canvass of 1844. — Position of Mr. Clay. — His Letters. — Attitude of Giddings. — Friendship of Adams and Himself . . 140

CHAPTER VII.

DECEMBER, 1844, TO MARCH, 1847.

Last Session of the Twenty-eighth Congress. — Repeal of the Gag-rule. — Insolence of Southern Members. — General Jessup as a Slave-trader. — Mr. Calhoun's New Argument for Annexation. — The Measure consummated. — First Session of the Twenty-ninth Congress. — The Oregon Question. — The War with Mexico. — Minor Questions. — Last Session of the Twenty-ninth Congress 171

CHAPTER VIII.

MARCH, 1847, TO DECEMBER, 1848.

Novel State of Parties. — Correspondence. — Meeting of the Thirtieth Congress. — Struggle for the Speakership. — Controversy with Winthrop. — Other Questions. — Death of Mr. Adams. — Speech on General Politics. — Escape of Slaves on the Schooner "Pearl." — Mob in Washington. — Speech. — Hope H. Slatter and Rev. Mr. Slicer. — The Claim of Hodges. — Campaign of 1848. — Letter to Truman Smith. — Effect of the Free-Soil Movement 206

CHAPTER IX.

DECEMBER, 1848, TO MARCH, 1851.

Second Session of the Thirtieth Congress. — Slavery and the Slave-trade in the District of Columbia. — The Pacheco Case. — The Ohio Senatorship. — Address of Southern Members. — The Effort to establish Slavery in California. — Meeting of the Thirty-first Congress. — The Speakership. — Defence of the Free Soilers. — Speeches. — Work of this Congress 258

CHAPTER X.

MARCH, 1851, TO MARCH, 1855.

Effect of the Compromise Measures. — Meeting of the Thirty-second Congress. — Agitation to prevent Agitation. — Encounter with Stanley. — The Welcome of Louis Kossuth. — Death of Mr. Clay. — Slave Claim of Watson. — Speech on the Compromise Measures. — Presidential Nominations of 1852. — The Second Session of the Thirty-second Congress. — Claim of William

Hazzard Wigg. — Meeting of the Thirty-third Congress. — The "Amistad" Case. — Repeal of the Missouri Compromise. — The Case of the "Black Warrior." — Second Session of the Thirty-third Congress 286

CHAPTER XI.

MARCH, 1855, TO MARCH, 1859.

The Congressional Vacation. — Meeting of the Thirty-fourth Congress. — State of Political Parties. — The Speakership. — Election of Banks. — Birth of the Republican Party. — Letters from John Brown. — Speech on the Deficiency Bill; on the Assault on Sumner. — The Philadelphia Convention and its Platform. — Last Session of this Congress. — Speeches. — Letters from John P. Hale. — The Dred Scott Decision. — Work in Vacation. — First Session of the Thirty-fifth Congress. — The Lecompton Constitution and the Crittenden-Montgomery Amendment. — Diary of Giddings. — The English Bill. — Speech on "American Infidelity." — On the African Slave-trade. — Nomination of his Successor. — Letters from Friends. — Voice of the Press. — Second Session of the Thirty-fifth Congress. — Farewell Speech. — Testimonials 320

CHAPTER XII.

MARCH, 1859, TO MAY, 1864.

The "Exiles of Florida." — The John Brown Raid. — The Lecture Field. — Scene in the Chicago Convention. — Campaign of 1860. — Letter to Hon. Thomas Ewing. — Another Literary Venture. — Appointed Consul-General to Canada. — Correspondence with Sumner. — Life in Montreal. — The Reciprocity Treaty. — Further Correspondence. — Declining Health. — "History of the Rebellion." — Death 365

CHAPTER XIII.

CHARACTERISTICS.

Personal Traits. — Devotion to Family. — Friendships. — Fondness for Athletic Sports. — Religious Principles. — Political Foresight. — Moral Earnestness. — Practical Qualities as a Reformer. — His Place in History . . . 396

APPENDIX.

PACIFICUS: THE RIGHTS AND PRIVILEGES OF THE SEVERAL STATES IN REGARD TO SLAVERY; *being a Series of Essays published in the " Western Reserve Chronicle" in* 1842 415

INDEX. 463

MR. GIDDINGS,

AT THE AGE OF TWENTY-EIGHT.

(From an Old Portrait.)

THE LIFE

OF

JOSHUA R. GIDDINGS.

―・―

CHAPTER I.

Ancestry and Early Life. — Pioneer Trials and Hardships. — Military Experience. — Teaching School. — Choice of the Legal Profession. — Marriage. — Children.

THE ancestors of JOSHUA REED GIDDINGS were English, and their descendants are now to be found in almost every section of the Union. They are industrious, enterprising, and thrifty, and their influence has always been on the side of education and progress, and of civil and religious liberty. They are noted for their devotion to the principles of morality, and it is their boast that no one of the name has brought disgrace upon the family by violating any criminal statute. They are generally found in the humbler walks of life; but their genealogy is honored by famous names, including those of Nathaniel Hawthorne and Rufus Choate,[1] while several of the name have served their country in the halls of Congress and other conspicuous positions. They are equally remarkable for their patriotism, as shown by the record of their service in the French and Indian wars, the American Revolution, the War of 1812, and the late War for the Union.

[1] The Giddings Family, by Minot S. Giddings, published in 1882.

The family is not less noted for its pioneer spirit, which brought its first emigrants from the Old World to New England, and sent their descendants to the western frontier, where they took the lead in planting civilization in the wilderness.

The first of the name who came to this country was George Giddings, who settled in Ipswich, Massachusetts, in 1635. He emigrated from St. Alban's, Hertfordshire, and was a man of property and position. From 1661 to 1675 he was selectman for the town, and for a long time a ruling elder of the first church. He had a strong will, as is shown by the record of a long lawsuit, which he carried through all the courts for the purpose of establishing a principle. Of his son John and his grandson Thomas, through whom the descent of Joshua R. is traced, very little is known. The latter removed to Lyme, Connecticut, about the year 1725. His son Joshua settled in Hartland, Connecticut, in 1756. He was a man of influence, holding many town offices, and was a prominent member of the Congregational church. He had five sons, three of whom served in the Revolution, Joshua, the fourth son, being with Arnold on Lake Champlain. This last-named Joshua removed in 1773 to Tioga Point, now called Athens, Bradford County, Pennsylvania, where he married Submit Jones, who died in 1785, leaving three children. He afterwards married Elizabeth Pease, of Enfield, Connecticut, a descendant of John Pease, who settled on Martha's Vineyard in 1635. Of this marriage there were four children, the youngest of whom was Joshua Reed, born Oct. 6, 1795. Six weeks after his birth his parents removed to Canandaigua, then near the western limit of civilization, and afterwards holding its place as the chief town of western New York.

In the winter of 1805 the elder Joshua resolved to go farther west, and he and his eldest son visited Wayne Township, in Ashtabula County, Ohio, in search of a new home. Here he selected a large tract of land, which he secured in exchange for his Canandaigua farm; and having built a cabin, cleared a little patch of ground, and planted a garden and small cornfield, he awaited the coming of his family in the spring of 1806. The journey was toilsome and difficult, and was made in a farm wagon, which also conveyed the household goods, and was drawn by four oxen. On June 16, just as they were crossing the Ohio and Pennsylvania line, a total eclipse of the sun left them in darkness and compelled them to camp in the woods. They were several weeks on the way, but at last reached the centre of Wayne Township, where they found the cabin already prepared for them, and were welcomed by the father and son.

Here the battle of life for young Giddings was to be fought. Ohio had been admitted into the Union only three years before. The country was a wilderness, inhabited by Indians and wild beasts; but it was to be the nursery and training-ground of Western Reserve character and manhood. The story of his early years strongly resembles that of Lincoln's, barring the difference between life in Kentucky and on the Western Reserve. It has been the fashion to dwell upon the straitened circumstances which have so often darkened the early lives of public men, and thus to appeal to popular sympathy while contrasting their famous achievements with the obscurity of their early struggles. The people of fifty years ago were very familiar with the story of "Corwin, the wagoner boy," and of "Ewing, the salt-boiler of the Muskingum." A little later, the admirers of Henry Clay appealed to the popular heart by picturing him as "the mill-boy of the slashes," while still later, Abraham Lincoln was paraded as "the rail-splitter of Illinois." This style of biography is now out of date; and it never had any better justification than the demands of campaign politics. It is not probable that any of the famous men referred to ever felt the need of sympathy in their early struggles. Each formed a part of the pioneer community in which his lot was cast, and simply did his co-operative share in the work of the family, while all were ready to face their trials and privations bravely, if not joyfully.

But frontier life always has its charms, and these were not lessened when New England Puritanism was transplanted to the wilds of northeastern Ohio. It was the birth of the Western Reserve, and the forerunner of a broader and better type of humanity than that of New England itself. The area of this famous Reserve is about five thousand square miles, and its population may now be estimated at six hundred thousand. "No other five thousand square miles of territory in the United States," says Hinsdale, "lying in a body outside of New England, ever had, to begin with, so pure a New England population," and "no similar territory west of the Alleghany mountains has so impressed the brain and conscience of the country."[1] This is due, in part, to the fact that these pioneers emancipated themselves from the religious dogmatism and inveterate political conservatism in which they had been reared. Congregationalism on the Reserve was no longer an established religion, while Federalism gradually relaxed its hold upon the people. From the beginning the spirit of reform was in the air, and the people gradually outgrew their provincialism, while holding fast their fundamental principles.

[1] The Old Northwest, p. 388.

The settlement of this region by such a community marked an epoch in American civilization. "Puritanism," says Bancroft, "was religion struggling for the people." These pioneer settlers brought with them their love of liberty and respect for law. They believed in the sacredness of human rights because they accepted Christianity as "the root of all democracy." They had no respect for any distinctions resting upon property, color, or race. They had among them men of education, who took the lead in founding common schools, academies, town-libraries, and debating-clubs, while churches sprang up in every direction, in evidence of the common zeal for religion. Through toil and self-denial they sought the establishment of well-ordered Christian homes, which they valued as the basis of society and the foundation of the state. Industry, frugality, endurance, courage, and hardihood were demanded by the situation, and these virtues were never found wanting. Their lives were necessarily primitive. They were obliged to subdue the earth and make the forests and streams tributary to their wants, and this was literally a struggle for existence; but they were ready for it, and entered upon it with strong will and irrepressible courage. Flax had to be raised and hatchelled, and spinning-wheels and looms constructed for its manufacture into clothing. Sheep had to be introduced, and their wool spun and woven into winter garments. Houses and barns had to be provided, and roads and bridges constructed. Game and fish had to be supplied in abundance while the forests were being felled and the soil fitted for tillage. Maple-sugar had to be manufactured, and nameless miscellaneous drudgery performed.

In nearly all this work the boy of ten years did his part. His training was physical and altogether practical, and his naturally vigorous constitution became thoroughly developed. He grew with the growth of the community of which he was a member, and was never found wanting in any task. In the use of the axe he became an expert, and before he was grown he could chop and put up six cords of wood in a day. No man better understood the use of the shot-gun and rifle. In the wrestling-match and the foot-race he was second to none. He was a recognized athlete, growing to the height of six feet two inches, broad-shouldered, compact, and well-proportioned. It must not be understood, however, that his moral training was neglected, for his father was a devout Presbyterian, who thoroughly imbued his children with his own moral and religious principles.

Nor was his education forgotten. He had learned the alphabet in school in Canandaigua, and on beginning life in Ohio he soon taught himself to read and write. No systematic education was then possible, and his entire school attendance from first to last was only a few weeks. He was obliged to learn what he could in the little snatches of time which the constant pressure of his active duties permitted. There were no libraries, and books were exceedingly few; but his appetite for reading was ravenous, and he devoured every newspaper, pamphlet, or book he could lay his hands on, no matter how ancient or dog-eared. He read such books of travel, biography, poetry, fiction, and theology as he could pick up, and his mental digestion was as remarkable as his appetite. A copy of Lindley Murray's Grammar which fell in his way was thoroughly studied, and he also became interested in mathematics. He studied late at night by the firelight in his father's cabin, or at springtime by the blazing light of the sugar-camp; and yet in this desultory and handicapped struggle for self-education he laid a substantial foundation for the career which awaited him.

But at the age of sixteen the regular course of his life was suddenly interrupted by the War of 1812, which startled the country and cast its shadow over the Northwest. The settlers on the Western Reserve were in a state of commotion. The Indians in that region left their wigwams to join the enemy, whose ravages on the Maumee were reported. General Hayes commanded a regiment of soldiers composed of men residing in Trumbull and Ashtabula counties. Giddings joined this regiment, which marched to the Huron; and on September 25 Major Frasier, with a detachment of about one hundred and fifty men, was ordered to proceed as far as Lower Sandusky. At that place there had been a stockade erected for the defence of the people dwelling there, which, having been deserted upon the surrender of General Hull, remained unoccupied till Major Frasier took possession. It became known as Fort Stephenson. From this point a scouting-party was sent out upon the peninsula in quest of provisions which had been left at Sandusky, and a body of Indians, estimated at forty-seven, was discovered on the farm of one Ramsdell, at Two Harbors, on the shore of the lake. The news of this discovery found the forces at Camp Avery so reduced by exposure and sickness that they were able to muster but two guards, consisting each of two relieves, so that each man was actually compelled to stand at his post one fourth of the time. Mr. Giddings was on duty at the time the news reached camp, and in an account of the situation he says: —

"When relieved from my post at a little before sunset I found them beating up for volunteers. I soon learned the cause, and without going to my quarters I joined the small party who were following the music in front of the line of troops. According to my recollection, there were in all sixty-four who volunteered to share the dangers of the enterprise. We were dismissed for thirty minutes to obtain our evening meal. It was between sunset and dark when we again assembled at the beating of the drum and prepared for our departure. Daylight had fully disappeared before we shook hands with our companions-in-arms and marched forth in the silent darkness of the night."

The little company, under command of Captain Cotton, advanced by boats that night, steering for what was then called the Middle Orchard, on the shore of the bay, nearly opposite to Bull's Island, not far from the point where the enemy had been discovered. Two battles were fought that day, with the loss of twelve men and their boats. The enemy stripped and scalped two of our dead who were left on the field, and the scalping-knife of the Indian chief Omick was found plunged to the hilt in the breast of one of them. This chief resided in Wayne township, and Giddings had known him for years. The Indians now deserted the peninsula, and these two battles, the first that were fought in Ohio during the War of 1812, have been overlooked by all the historians of the war; but Mr. Giddings himself wrote a detailed account of them in 1843, which forms an important contribution to the history of that war and to the annals of the Western Reserve. His service lasted five months, at the end of which he was mustered out and returned to his home. It tested his strength and endurance on the march, his good conduct in camp, and his courage in the face of danger. It taught him the value of discipline and self-reliance. It gave him a better knowledge of himself and of human nature, and new ideas of life and incitements to thought.

During the progress of the war the Reserve was

several times menaced, but no other conflicts followed, and there was no occasion for any further military duty by Giddings. This was fortunate for his father, who sorely needed his help; for the title to the lands in which he had invested his all failed, and the family was again thrown upon its resources and obliged to renew the hard struggle with poverty on another tract. Giddings was the youngest of four brothers; and while he manfully did his part in this struggle, he availed himself of every possible opportunity to push forward the work of self-education. He was now nearly eighteen years old, and his thirst for knowledge constantly increased. In a fragment found among his papers, referring to this period, he says that from his childhood he had accustomed himself to earnest thinking, and that at an early age he had been led to study the idioms of our language and the philosophy of arithmetical rules. As he found his mind constantly enlarged by new ideas and increased knowledge, he determined to know more than he could ever hope to do as a day laborer. He keenly felt the shackles which bound him, and longed for untrammelled liberty to think and act for himself. His diligence in study was noticed by the people of his neighborhood, and it soon became understood that he was a scholar. He was known to be a student, and they quite naturally took his scholarship for granted.

It was not surprising, therefore, that at the age of nineteen he was called upon by his neighbors to teach school. He frankly pleaded lack of qualification; but the plea was not accepted, and he entered upon the work. This was fortunate for the children of the vicinage, who greatly needed instruction, and equally fortunate for the teacher. He was stimulated in his work by the desire to keep in advance of his scholars, while he constantly refreshed his memory of what he had previously learned. He applied himself to his new vocation with all the ardor that had marked his outdoor labors. He resumed his study of mathematics, besides more completely mastering the use of the English language. His teaching, of course, was confined to the winter months, for he held his place in all the hard work of clearing the land and cultivating the soil during the season; but his work as a teacher seems to have inspired him with a burning desire to pursue his studies more systematically, and to master them more thoroughly.

At this time the Rev. Harvey Coe was settled as a minister at Vernon, in Trumbull County. He had been liberally educated, and according to the custom of that day, had a room appointed for the use of such young men as desired to obtain the benefits of his instruction. They boarded with him, or with neighbors near by, and at stated hours visited him at his rooms. Under the instructions of this country parson, Giddings now devoted himself to mathematics and Latin, and continued his studies nine months, when he resumed the business of teaching, which he prosecuted during the school season for four years, attending to his farm duties in the summer. The education thus acquired was necessarily fragmentary and unsystematic; but his strong grasp of mind, tireless industry, and unquenchable zeal gave a remarkable thoroughness to his work, and increased confidence in himself as the time approached when he must deal with the vexed question of a business for life.

In the autumn of 1818 he returned to his home at Williamsfield, and his friends and neighbors were anxious to know his intentions and plans for the future. He told them frankly that he had decided upon the study of the law. This was a great surprise to them. He had lived with them from childhood, and toiled with them in the fields. He had never enjoyed the means of obtaining even a common-school education, and they regarded his course as the effect of a vain desire to defeat the designs of Providence, according to which they believed that people born in humble life should be content with their lot. They ridiculed his theory that success and distinction in the profession could be obtained by diligence. They told him he could not make a lawyer, and that by changing his habits he would lose his love of labor, while he could not make a living by his profession. Only two of his neighbors encouraged him in his ambition; these were his brother-in-law, Nathaniel Coleman, and Anson Jones, who were both men of education, and regarded as the most influential citizens of the township.

In spite of all dissuasions, Giddings was unwavering in his purpose; and seeing this, several of his friends and two of his brothers offered him pecuniary aid in prosecuting his studies. In December he left his father's home on foot to begin the study of law under Elisha Whittlesey, Esquire, of Canfield, in Trumbull County. Mr. Whittlesey was a lawyer of eminence, and several of the distinguished lawyers and famous men of northern Ohio studied in his office. He was subsequently a member of Congress sixteen consecutive years, being the immediate predecessor of Mr. Giddings; and he afterwards served many years as First Comptroller of the Treasury. The distance from Williamsfield to Canfield was forty miles, and Giddings carried his own baggage, consisting of three shirts, two pairs of stockings, four white neckcloths, and two pocket-handkerchiefs. He had also seventeen dollars in cash. He had now defined to his own satisfaction his future course. He saw his pathway unmistakably before him, and he determined to bend all his energies to the accomplishment of his purpose.

In the village of Canfield he was a stranger to every one but his preceptor, whom he had met before; but he soon became acquainted, and was greatly pleased with the society of the village. He was invited to the houses of the best citizens, and his temperate habits, diligence in study, and correct deportment brought him into general favor. He entered upon the study of law with great spirit. At all hours of the day he was to be found in the office, sweeping it out and building the fire before sunrise, and continuing his studies till late at night.

Soon after he came to the village, he made his first essay in public speaking. The young men of the place had formed a lyceum, at which important questions of government and state policy were discussed. William A. Whittlesey, a nephew of his preceptor and a graduate of Yale College, was a fellow-student of Giddings, and they were both invited to join the lyceum, which they did, and at the next meeting arrangements were made for the two young men to take the lead in debate on opposite sides of the question. Whittlesey held the decided advantage over his opponent in the matter of educational qualifications; but in the opinion of the large audience who had assembled to hear the debate, Giddings acquitted himself admirably, and the two young men, who had had no previous intimacy, now became attached friends. This friendship continued during life, and they served together many years later in the lower branch of Congress.

It was not long after this that these students began to find employment in the small litigation at all times carried on in country towns before sheriffs' courts and justices of the peace. They were generally on different sides, and often travelled many miles to attend these courts, charging their clients five dollars, which they found quite convenient in paying for their board and supplying themselves with pocket-money. At this time Elisha Whittlesey was engaged in an extensive business, and Giddings was often sent to different counties to look after the affairs of his employer. This enabled him to extend his acquaintance and make friends among the people. During the second year of his study he began to look forward to his admission to the Bar, and his preceptor suggested to him that whatever business might come to him from that time he might enter in court in the name of Mr. Whittlesey, and on his admission he could substitute his own name as attorney and receive the fees. Of this kind offer he gladly availed himself, and at the first term of the court after his admission he entered a list of more than thirty causes in his own name.

According to the custom of that day, the preceptor was required to propose for the consideration of the Bar the names of such young men as he desired to have admitted to an examination, and secure their unanimous consent to present these names to the judges of the Supreme Court. In observance of this custom, Mr. Whittlesey presented the names of Joshua R. Giddings and William A. Whittlesey as candidates for examination. Two objections to Giddings were made, — first, that he had not received the proper literary training; and second, that the sphere in which he had been reared was not such as to entitle him to associate with members of the Bar. To these objections the friends of Giddings replied that his literary training would be tested by the examination proposed; and that as to association, it would have to be mutual, or it could not exist. They urged that the only question for the Bar to pass upon was his moral character and legal knowledge, and not the sphere in which he moved. The objections, however, were strongly urged by two members of the Bar, who were quite aristocratic in their feelings, and warm words were exchanged; but seventeen out of nineteen members voted for the admission of Giddings to an examination, and Mr. Whittlesey was instructed to give him the necessary certificate. Of this opposition he was never informed till after his admission. At the examination he acquitted himself to the entire satisfaction of the judges, and by some of the oldest members he was pronounced the best *theoretical* lawyer of the county at the time. One week after his admission, which occurred in February, 1821, he appeared before the Court of Common Pleas of Ashtabula with a list of cases which might well have awakened the pride of a lawyer who had been years in practice.

While yet a student, Giddings was married to Miss Laura Waters, of Trumbull County, — a young woman of more than common intelligence and worth. She was the daughter of Abner Waters, who had removed from Granby, Connecticut, to Ohio in 1816. To the eye of worldly prudence the wisdom of his marriage at this time would have seemed at least debatable. He had not yet entered the threshold of his profession. Without the help of friends he could not buy a library. If, during the first few years of his practice, he could earn more than enough for his own support, he would need it in preparing for the responsibilities of marriage. Miss Waters was likewise poor, earning her livelihood by teaching. But their marriage was the special concern of nobody but themselves, and the sequel vindicated their action. The practice of Giddings proved remunerative from the beginning, and his young wife contributed her earnings as a teacher to the purchase of a law library. They began housekeeping in Wayne Township upon his father's farm, and he built an office in the adjoining village of Williamsfield, where he began his professional career.

Eight children were born to them, three of whom died in infancy. Of the remaining five, the eldest was Comfort Pease, who was born Jan. 7, 1820. He is a farmer, and resides in the vicinity of Jefferson.

The second son, Joseph Addison, was born Feb. 17, 1822. He began life as a lawyer, and was subsequently elected judge of the Probate Court of his county. For a number of years he edited "The Ashtabula Sentinel," of which his father was corresponding editor during the greater part of his congressional term, and he was vice-consul at Montreal at the time of his father's death. He resides on the old homestead at Jefferson.

The eldest daughter, Lura Maria, was born Sept. 24, 1825, and died Aug. 23, 1871. She was among the early workers in the anti-slavery reform, and was thoroughly devoted to her father, whom she accompanied to Washington during several sessions of Congress. She was also with him in Montreal at the time of his death. She was a woman of more than ordinary endowments, and possessed admirable traits of character; and during the last years of her life she took the lead in the erection of a beautiful monument to her father, which fitly commemorates a daughter's devotion, and the public services of him whose likeness it bears.

Grotius Reed, the youngest son, was born June 21, 1834, and died in 1867, on his thirty-third birthday. He began the practice of law in 1860, but on the breaking out of the Rebellion he raised a company of men for the war, and was unanimously elected captain. He was soon afterwards appointed major in the Fourteenth Regiment of United States regulars, and assumed command at Fort Trumbull, Connecticut. He was subsequently ordered to New Orleans as a general mustering and disbursing officer, where he mustered in the first two colored regiments raised in Louisiana. From this position, at his own request, he was relieved and ordered to the field, where he distinguished himself for his bravery in the battles of Chancellorsville and Gettysburg, for which conduct he was publicly complimented. An injury received by the falling of his horse while in command of the first brigade of regulars in the New York riots unfitted him for field service during the remainder of the war, and he died at Macon, Georgia, while in command of the military post at Savannah.

The younger daughter, Laura, was born May 19, 1839. She was the favorite child of her father, and largely inherited his qualities. Like her sister, she shared his society in Washington during a portion of his Congressional service, and in Montreal afterwards. On Dec. 31, 1863, she was married to George W. Julian, of Indiana, and died March 31, 1884, at her home in Irvington, in that State.

The wife of Mr. Giddings was born Jan. 19, 1798, and died Nov. 15, 1864, surviving her husband a little less than five months. She was noted for her piety, her complete consecration to the service of her husband and family, and her faithfulness to duty in all the relations of life.

CHAPTER II.

Success at the Bar. — Sent to the Ohio Legislature. — Partnership with Benjamin F. Wade. — Business Troubles and Failing Health. — Election to Congress. — The Slavery Question.

IN his famous speech on Conciliation with America, in 1775, Burke says the study of law "renders men acute, inquisitive, dexterous, prompt in action, ready in debate, full of resources." Among the causes which kept alive the spirit of independence in the Colonies, he names their familiarity with English law, which enabled them to "augur misgovernment at a distance, and snuff the approach of tyranny in every tainted breeze." The political career of Giddings recalls these passages and aptly illustrates their force. Whoever will read the Congressional debates from 1838 to 1858, in which he took a considerable part, will see how well his legal training served him in discussing the constitutional relations of slavery to the government, and with what admirable readiness and skill he parried the assaults and exposed the sophisms of the slaveocracy. It thus happened, quite unwittingly to Giddings himself, that during the seventeen years of his professional life, beginning with his admission to the Bar in 1821, and closing with his election to Congress in 1838, he was arming himself for his great battle with the slave-masters, which ended only with his retirement from public life in 1859.

His entry upon the work of his profession, as we have seen, was singularly unpretentious. He was not long, however, in finding out his mistake in locating in Williamsfield, and the following year he established himself in Jefferson, the shire town of the county, where he resided during the remainder of his life. It is difficult now to realize the condition of the country and the state of society in northern Ohio seventy years ago, when he entered the profession. Ashtabula and the adjacent counties were sparsely populated, and the courts were held in rough loghouses. The people generally lived in rude huts or cabins, and were nearly all poor. The whole aspect of affairs in this border life was raw and aboriginal. The vast litigation since created by our railway system and other forms of corporate property was not dreamed of by the people of that generation. As little did they dream of the marvellous increase of wealth through commercial development which was to open new fields for the lawyer, and offer him large fees for his services in important causes. The Bar of that day had to content itself with a country practice and small fees, because cities and great causes were unknown.

But such a country practice had its advantages. It dealt with small cases, but with a great variety of questions, while the lawyer of to-day usually devotes himself to a special branch of his profession or to a particular class of cases. The practice of Giddings also brought him into contact with all classes of men, and thus acquainted him with human nature and broadened his mind. It is easy to see that in such ways as these he constantly trained and invigorated his faculties, and prepared himself for the leadership in politics which awaited him. It must be understood, too, that although his cases were comparatively unimportant and his fees small, the legal principles involved were substantially the same as those arising in controversies in which great interests are at stake. The schooling thus acquired was of inestimable value, giving him at once a ready familiarity with legal principles and a practical knowledge of men and their affairs.

At this time the jurisdiction of the Court of Common Pleas included five or six counties, in which its sessions were held three times in each year. The Supreme Court was composed of four judges, and was also a Circuit Court, with a jury, sitting in each county once a year, and reserving cases to be heard by the four judges *in banc*. Giddings, with his chief professional brethren of the county, joined the presiding judge of the circuit in his journey on horseback to the different courts, which were always largely attended by the people.

Lawyers at that time commanded more genuine respect from the public than they now receive, and the potency of oratory and personal magnetism was greater than at present. To the people of that day there was something fascinating and theatrical in a trial in court. The stalwart form of Giddings and his great strength singled him out for general observation and special comment. He was not remarkable for volubility of speech. He often hesitated for a word, and generally waited for it; but sometimes he would persist in having it at once, when he would close his eyes very tight, and compel it.[1] He had but one gesture in speaking, and that was with both arms and clenched fists, as if determined to hammer his ideas into his hearers; but with his clear common-sense, perfect mastery of the

[1] A. G. Riddle, in "Bart Ridgely."

main points of his case, and his knowledge of the jury, he was a formidable advocate, and had few, if any, rivals at the bar. He studied his cases thoroughly, and knew how to elicit the facts from the witnesses, while his tact, perfect self-possession, and unfailing good-nature did him excellent service, and tempered the asperities of his professional work.

Early in his practice Giddings became connected with some important cases which greatly aided his reputation. One of these was the famous malpractice case of Williams *vs.* Hawley, which attracted more attention than any ever litigated in Ashtabula County. The wife of Williams was thrown from her horse and her ankle dislocated, the outer bone of the leg protruding about half an inch. The surgeon, Dr. Hawley, laid the bone open along the perpendicular line some four inches, and then, prying the ligaments aside, sawed off two and a half inches from the lower end of the bone, thus rendering her a cripple for life. He was a man of great wealth, high professional reputation, and surrounded by influential friends; while the husband of the woman was a poor farmer without the means to carry on a lawsuit. Dr. Hawley had sued him for his bill, which the farmer thought exorbitant, and desired to reduce on the trial. Giddings, after carefully acquainting himself with the case, advised him to bring suit against the surgeon for damages for malpractice. The professional reputation of Dr. Hawley was thus involved, and he prepared himself for a most resolute and stubborn fight. All the physicians of the vicinity were his witnesses, and every possible effort was made in his defence; but the plaintiff obtained a verdict for five hundred dollars.

The defendant appealed the case to the Supreme Court, and in this second trial John C. Wright, of Cincinnati, then famous as a lawyer, was retained for the defendant, and the evidence of the most noted physicians of New York and Philadelphia was introduced. The case was far more vigorously and elaborately contested on both sides than before, and the popular interest in it was lively and wide-spread. Mr. Wright spoke five hours in behalf of his client, during which the court, jury, and spectators were frequently convulsed with laughter by his wit, humor, and sarcasm, while not a muscle of his solemn face was moved. The tide seemed to be strongly in his favor. Giddings occupied only two and a half hours in his closing speech. The attempt to laugh his case out of court seemed to inspire him with redoubled courage and fervor, and throwing aside his notes, he devoted his argument to the simple facts of the case, which he analyzed with great skill. He made it perfectly clear from the testimony that Mrs. Williams had been made a cripple for life by the professional misconduct or stupidity of the defendant, and that he should be adequately punished by a verdict for damages. He had the close attention of the jury and all present from the beginning to the end of his speech, and the absolute seriousness of the discussion was in noted contrast with the effort of Mr. Wright. The jury brought in a verdict of five hundred and seventy-five dollars for the plaintiff, while the vociferous plaudits of the people aggravated the disappointment of the defendant and his counsel.

The defendant then prayed an appeal to the court *in banc*, and made such representations touching the popular feeling in the case in Ashtabula County, and urged such technical grounds for setting aside the verdict, that it was done, and a change of venue was ordered to Trumbull County. After a continuance of one year it was again brought to trial; but this time there was no laughter or levity. The case was argued at length, and after the retirement of the jury and a reported disagreement, involving the charge of bribery of one of the jurors, they were discharged, and the cause continued till the following term. At that term the case was again argued before another jury, and the plaintiff obtained a verdict for nine hundred dollars. Judgment was entered upon this verdict, and the triumph of Giddings was complete. The litigation had lasted six years, and it does not appear that he ever received any compensation from the plaintiff; but the value of his triumph was worth more to him than any fee at that time would have been.

Giddings was more especially successful in criminal cases, and his practice in such cases was quite as extensive as that of any lawyer in northern Ohio. He often declared that some of his clients were convicted of crimes of which he thought them innocent, and that in every such instance he believed he suffered more mental anxiety during the trial than the victims who sat by his side.

Soon after the trial in the civil suit just mentioned, his moral courage and professional ability were subjected to a severe test. A young woman was murdered in the Kirtland woods, in Geauga County. A man named Barnes, a pedler with a wagon, was seen to enter the forest immediately after the girl on the same road. The people of the vicinity were unanimously of opinion that he was the murderer. Before the examining court many circumstances conspired to show his guilt. The friends of Barnes were anxious to obtain the services of Giddings; but politicians declared it would be fatal to the reputation of any man to defend one so obviously guilty. This determined his course, for he declared he would not live in a community that believed him capable of being swayed by such considerations. After consulting with Barnes, Giddings came to the conclusion that he was innocent; but on account of the highly exasperated feeling against his client, he availed himself of his legal privilege of selecting the Supreme Court as the tribunal for the trial, by which means it was postponed ten months.

When this court convened, however, the popular feeling seemed to have increased, and the friends of the murdered girl employed Hon. Sherlock J. Andrews, a distinguished lawyer of Cleveland, to assist the attorney for the State. Barnes was penniless; and although Giddings was now assigned for his defence, the law at that time allowed him no compensation. The trial proceeded, and after elaborate argument on both sides, the jury rendered a verdict of Not guilty. The friends of Barnes rushed from the crowd and overwhelmed Giddings with their expressions of gratitude, which he often declared was the richest reward he ever received for defending any man. Barnes lived several years afterwards, and it finally appeared by the testimony of a convict in the penitentiary that he was innocent; and Barnes himself on his death-bed, when assured that his recovery was impossible, denied all knowledge of the murder.

These cases were followed by important suits in Buffalo and the western counties of New York and Pennsylvania, in one of which Millard Fillmore was the opposing counsel. Large interests were involved in this case, and Giddings succeeded by his tact and vigilance, greatly to the mortification of Mr. Fillmore, who prided himself on his skill and assiduity in the preparation of his cases.

While in the full tide of his professional success, Giddings was announced as a candidate for representative in the Ohio Legislature. This was done without his consent or knowledge, and he had no disposition to be drawn into politics at this time, as it would seriously interfere with his business. His friends, however, urged him to make the race, and so did his relatives, except his mother, who remonstrated against his entering into political life. After much hesitation he determined to enter the canvass, but with the public avowal that he would not consent to another election. He engaged in the contest with great zeal, and in his journal of that date he relates that his anxiety for success completely filled his mind till the election; but that afterwards he so felt the responsibility of his position that he would have made almost any sacrifice to escape it. He says that the difficulties of travel were then such that it required a week to reach Columbus from Jefferson. In the organization of the House he was made chairman of the Committee on Military Affairs. No exciting questions came before the Legislature at this session, and although he took an active part in urging certain judicial reforms, the chief advantage of this brief legislative experience was the knowledge of parliamentary law which it gave him. He declined a renomination, but two years later he became a candidate for the State Senate, and failed of an election, this being the only time he was ever defeated at the polls.

In 1831 he formed a partnership with Benjamin F. Wade, of Ashtabula County, then a young lawyer of much promise, who, like himself, had studied under Elisha Whittlesey. It was a profitable partnership for both parties, and their business rapidly extended over the counties of Ashtabula, Trumbull, and Geauga. Mr. Wade had only recently been admitted, and his lack of self-confidence for a time kept him in the office in the preparation of cases, so that Giddings had the management of business in the courts. Wade, however, was not long in coming to the front, and the practice of the firm became one of the largest in the State. Their earnings far exceeded the demands of their simple village life, and in an ill-fated moment both entered into large land purchases, principally in Toledo, being carried away by the fever of town-lot speculations. Giddings counted himself so rich as to warrant his retirement from practice, and in 1836 dissolved his partnership with Wade, his place being filled by Rufus P. Ranney, who had been a student in the office.

But his bright prospects were suddenly blighted by the great financial panic which followed. The price of land declined alarmingly, and purchasers were made bankrupt. The result was that Giddings found himself a poor man at the age of forty, while his troubles were seriously aggravated by his failing health. A distressing form of dyspepsia and an irregular action of the heart, which greatly troubled him in his later life, made his condition wretched; he believed his splendid constitution was fatally undermined. Hypochondria followed, and for months in succession he kept up his fight with Giant Despair. His physician advised him to travel, and he set out on horseback, passing through the State of New York to Hartford and Enfield in Connecticut, where he visited relatives of his mother by the name of Pease. On his return he visited sundry points in the West, including the then infant city of Chicago. In the light of subsequent events the following extract from a letter to Mrs. Giddings, dated Chicago, July 20, 1837, may interest the reader: —

"I arrived here last evening. My health and spirits have improved in travelling. I find this to be much more of a city than I had expected. There are said to be between seven and eight thousand inhabitants now, whereas there were about one hundred four years since. There are now large and spacious brick buildings, for the accommodation of all kinds of business, where there was not even a *frame* building four years since. There is a fine harbor crowded with shipping, and the bustle of business constantly salutes the ears of the inhabitants. I have seen much of the Western country, and certainly I have been highly pleased with my present tour. Never until yesterday did I see a *boundless* prairie, where in any one direction the eye cannot rest on hill or mountain, forest-tree or shrub, or bush or water, — where one vast ocean of prairie, of unlimited extent, presented itself to view. The prospect was boundless and cheerless. It seemed that by some means Nature had been disrobed of her forest mantle, and now lay reposing under a rich vesture of green herbage, dotted and bespangled with innumerable flowers and blossoms of the most gaudy hue. I wish you could have seen it; it gave me a feeling of solemnity. The view, though beautiful, was solitary. Occasionally a lark or blackbird would start up before us, flitting along and trying to find a limb or twig or fence to alight upon; but finding none, its weary wings would again guide it to the bending grass. Now and then a prairie hen would start suddenly from the ground, and whirring through the air for a distance, dive amid the waves of green herbage and disappear from the view. These winged creatures alone appeared to be at home amid this lovely, this lonely, this majestic scene.

"Well, I have seen so much that I intend to see more. I assure you that I have felt quite at home for two days past while eating pone and pork in the woodman's shanty, and I never slept sounder than the night before last, although I had neither bed nor mattress, pillow nor blanket. I would certainly like to spend one or two months in rambling through the Western wilds, and I believe nothing would be better for my health than to travel, live poorly, and sleep on the floor or ground as occasion should require."

His travels so improved his health and spirits that he returned to his practice, forming a partnership with Flavel Sutliff, a clever young man whose promising career was suddenly terminated two years later by insanity. The retirement of Giddings from the Bar for so short a time did not greatly interfere with his business, and the new firm was at once overrun with important cases. But his professional career was suddenly cut short forever by unexpected events. Elisha Whittlesey, who had served his district in Congress for sixteen years, was appointed by President Van Buren

Fourth Auditor of the Treasury, and resigned his seat in the Twenty-fifth Congress in the midst of his term. For the place thus vacated, Giddings became a candidate, his Whig competitors being Hon. Ralph Granger and Hon. Horace Wilder. He received the nomination, and as the Democrats were in a hopeless minority in the district, his election was assured. Thus the way was opened for his historic career in Congress and the great work of his life.

Before attempting to follow Giddings in his anti-slavery labors, it will be well to clear the way by a brief summary of important preliminary facts. Slavery in the American colonies was not of their seeking. It was thrust upon them by a foreign hand, and was utterly repugnant to their principles, and alien to their spirit and policy. In all the colonies, unless we except Georgia and South Carolina, the evil was endured, but never embraced. It existed in Virginia forty years before it received any legal recognition. Hostility to slavery was manifested in Pennsylvania by some German Quakers as early as the year 1688. This was followed by the official condemnation of it by the Yearly Meeting of Friends for the colonies of Pennsylvania and New Jersey in 1696. The New England Quakers took similar action against the slave trade in 1715. Two prominent Quakers, Ralph Sandiford and Benjamin Lay, wrote against slavery in 1729 and 1737; and they were followed by Anthony Benezett and John Woolman, whose services largely aided the complete emancipation of the Society of Friends from the evil in the colonies in which they labored. A vigorous effort was made to save the colony of Georgia from the scourge of slavery by General Oglethorpe, who had the co-operation of John Wesley; but slavery finally triumphed. The stand taken by Wesley and Whitefield is well known, and Jonathan Edwards and Dr. Samuel Hopkins belonged to the same class of thoroughgoing abolitionists.

Hostility to slavery and the slave trade so increased in the colonies that those of New England, New Jersey, Pennsylvania, and Virginia petitioned the Throne for the abolition of the foreign traffic, and their Legislatures passed laws against it; but the parent country turned a deaf ear to their wishes. As the era of independence approached, the anti-slavery tide reached its flood, as was shown by the non-importation resolves of the Continental Congress of 1774, and the concurring action of the separate colonies. In 1775, the year before Thomas Paine electrified the country by his "Common-Sense," he wrote an anti-slavery article which appeared in Bradford's "Pennsylvania Journal," in which he predicted the separation of America from Britain, and expressed the hope that our gratitude for the event might be shown by "an Act of continental legislation which shall put a stop to the importation of negroes, soften the hard fate of those already here, and in time procure their freedom." During the Revolutionary War and up to the year 1789 slaves escaping from one colony to another became legally free.

The champions of independence were the chief foes of the slave trade and slavery, while the revolutionary movement had its strongholds where the slave population was smallest and the institution was in a state of decline. Indeed, it is safe to say that in a very important sense independence had its genesis in the anti-slavery opinions and labors which preceded it; and this honor ought freely to be accorded to the abolitionism of the colonial period. It is true that the struggle for independence was political; but it is equally true that its basis was the inborn rights of man, or, as Madison phrased it after the struggle was over, "the rights of human nature." It was the religious conviction that liberty is the birthright of all men which inspired the anti-slavery zeal of the colonists and prepared them to rebel against the power which asserted the right to bind them in all cases whatsoever.

This view is well supported by historic facts. In the year 1774 the Pennsylvania Abolition Society was formed, of which Benjamin Franklin was for years the president. John Jay was the president of a similar society in New York, organized a few years later. Abolition societies were formed in Maryland, Virginia, New Jersey, Delaware, Rhode Island, and Connecticut. At the beginning of the Revolutionary struggle, and during its continuance, the churches were all anti-slavery. In 1784 the ordinance of Jefferson, prohibiting slavery after the year 1800 in all "the territories ceded already or to be ceded by individual States to the United States," only failed by an accident, while three years later the famous ordinance forbidding the introduction of slavery in all territory then under the jurisdiction of the National Government was adopted by the unanimous vote of the States then represented in Congress, including Georgia and the Carolinas. At that time slavery had already been abolished, or measures were soon afterwards to be taken for its abolition, in seven of the States, while in the six remaining it was understood to be in course of inevitable decay. The new Constitution provided for cutting off the foreign supply, the source of its life, while private emancipations were going on in all the States under the prevailing spirit of liberty, which had gathered new life in the struggle for independence. The Constitution made concessions to slavery. The foreign traffic was not to be interdicted prior to 1808. Fugitive slaves were to be surrendered, and three fifths of the slave population counted in the basis of representation.

With these qualifications, slavery was a State institution with which it was neither the right nor the duty of the National Government to intermeddle, either to help or hinder it; and the concessions named, were only agreed to because of the assurance everywhere felt that the evil was to have only a transient sufferance, a brief hospitality pending the adoption of measures for its peaceable but total extirpation; and this bargain with slavery never would have been made if the framers of the Constitution could have foreseen that the power thus abetted would treacherously demand perpetuity, and assert its absolute political supremacy in the government. Mr. Madison declared it to be wrong to admit in the Constitution "the idea that there can be property in man;" and on this ground its framers studiously omitted the words "slave," "slavery," and "servitude" from its text. They referred to slavery by circumlocution and innuendo, turning upon it an averted face, and shying away from it as a profane thing, while reluctantly granting it a temporary tolerance.

The anti-slavery spirit of the times was so dominant that in the year 1791 Granville Sharpe, the head and front of English abolitionism, was made a doctor of laws by the University of William and Mary in Virginia. The cause of emancipation was then supported by public opinion, and only opposed by a diminishing fraction of society. It was as easy to be an abolitionist then as to be in favor of prison reform or the improvement of the condition of the aborigines. Slavery had not yet become a great political and moneyed power. It was not supported by formidable ecclesiastical backing. It attempted no social outlawry. It was not pre-eminently a respectable institution. The men who sought its abolition were not obliged to encounter brickbats and unmerchantable eggs. The age of martyrdom was yet in the distance, and no one dreamed of the dispensation which was to startle the civilized world in the following century, and drench the land in blood.

In the entire history of human progress it would be difficult to find a more curious chapter than that which records the complete miscarriage of the hopes and expectations of the founders of the government touching the fortunes of slavery in the United States. Its ascendency finds a partial explanation in the invention of Whitney's cotton-gin, in 1793, — making the production of cotton exceedingly profitable, through the breeding of slaves for its cultivation, — and in the acquisition of Louisiana in 1803, opening to slavery an immense area of fertile soil in latitudes remarkably adapted to the growth of this plant. But slavery began to play the master prior to these events. The concessions made to it in the Constitution gave it a new birth. In the debate in Congress in 1790 on the anti-slavery petition headed by Dr. Franklin, Southern members exhibited the same spirit of domination which marked their discussions in later times; and one of them intimated that the lives of certain members who favored the doctrines of the petition would be endangered should they happen to be found in certain Slave States. In the same year a treaty was concluded with the Cherokee Indians by which Georgia slaveholders were enabled to recover their fugitive slaves who had fled to the Spanish province of Florida, and providing a perpetual annuity of fifteen hundred dollars as compensation to said Indians for their services in the recapture of such fugitives. This treaty, negotiated by

Washington, and ratified by the Senate, was the first exercise of the treaty-making power under the government; but it was unauthorized by the Constitution, which made no provision for the recovery of fugitives escaping into a foreign State.

The power of slavery was strikingly illustrated in the passage of the Fugitive Slave law of 1793. It was enacted in secret session. It is not known who introduced the measure, nor what reasons were urged in its favor, nor whether it was debated. It was not authorized by any express provision of the Constitution, and so far as it imposed duties upon State magistrates it was unconstitutional, and was afterwards so declared by the Supreme Court of the United States. By its perfectly unguarded provisions, the free colored people of the Northern States were exposed to the Southern kidnapper for nearly three quarters of a century, and thousands of them were carried into bondage; but it passed the House of Representatives by a vote of forty-eight to seven, and its repeal was impossible prior to the Civil War.

In 1797 the Quakers of North Carolina emancipated their slaves. The Legislature of the State passed an Act authorizing their re-enslavement. The victims of this outrage petitioned Congress for redress, and the House of Representatives, by a vote of fifty to thirty-three, *refused to receive the petition*. This question gave rise to a debate in which, for the first time, threats were made to dissolve the union if Congress should persist in discussing the question of slavery.

When the District of Columbia was created by cessions from Virginia and Maryland, Congress acquired the sole and exclusive jurisdiction over it, and in 1801 proceeded to re-enact the slave codes of those States for its government, and thus nationalized slavery and the traffic in slaves therein. Congress had no power to do this, because the Constitution expressly provides that no person (under Federal jurisdiction) shall be deprived of life, liberty, or property without due process of law.

The Act of Congress of 1807, prohibiting the foreign slave trade and branding it as piracy, made ample provision for the coastwise trade between the border States of the North and the cotton States of the South, — a traffic far more barbarous and cruel than the piratical trade with Africa. The Constitution conferred no power upon Congress thus to legislate for slavery.

The cases cited show the unmistakable trend of the National Government towards slavery in the earlier and better days of the Republic, and it steadily grew stronger. Florida was purchased in the interest of slavery, and received into the Union as a Slave State, in palpable contravention of the anti-slavery policy of the ordinance of 1787. Three large Slave States were carved out of the Territory of Louisiana and admitted into the Union, thus again stretching the compromises of the Constitution over a large region which the founders of the government believed they had no right to acquire. The National Government assisted in expelling the red man from seven or eight States of the South at the cost of many millions, so that the white man could enter with his peculiar institution where otherwise it was forbidden. The Government carried on two disgraceful Florida wars at the bidding of the slave-catchers of Georgia and South Carolina, and these national slave-hunts cost the country at least forty millions of dollars. The Missouri struggle in 1820 plainly revealed the fact that slavery had become a great political power, while the abolition societies, once so flourishing, had been disbanded or had lost their spirit. Slavery expurgated our literature, mutilated the school-books of our children, rifled the mails, and trampled upon the right of petition and the freedom of debate, while it controlled our foreign diplomacy and all the departments of the government.

The startling political apostasy which had been gradually nearing its climax was accompanied by a like apostasy in the churches, which at last became the bulwarks of the slave power; and that power was finally interwoven with the whole fabric of American society and institutions. The church and the state joined hands with it as the new trinity of the nation's faith. It made and unmade politicians. To oppose it was to confront mobs, persecution, and sometimes death. It was to give up reputation, honor, ease, and all the prizes of life which worldly prudence or ambition could covet. It was to take up the heaviest cross yet fashioned by this century as the test of Christian character and heroism. Such was the appalling outcome of the concessions made to slavery as embodied in the Constitution of 1789. Instead of opening the way for "liberty throughout all the land to all the inhabitants thereof," as the fathers of the government so confidently anticipated, these concessions, in the words of John Quincy Adams, made "the propagation, preservation, and perpetuation of slavery the vital and animating spirit of the National Government." The slaveholders so willed it, and they never intermitted their purpose; and the Northern States acquiesced.

It was in this epoch of slave-holding arrogance on the one hand, and Northern cowardice on the other, that Joshua R. Giddings took his seat in the lower branch of the Twenty-fifth Congress, in December, 1838. Slavery had not yet found its way into politics. The Liberty party and the Free Soil party, which succeeded it, were not organized till years afterwards. Giddings was a Whig, and his Whig constituents were hostile to slavery; but as yet they had formulated no well-defined method of resisting its usurpations. The Abolitionists were few, and everywhere misunderstood and hounded by the mob. The people of the non-slaveholding States were asleep, while the slave oligarchy was meditating new schemes of aggression, and stealthily plotting their complete subjugation. The right of petition and the freedom of debate had been stricken down in the House of Representatives two years before. Lovejoy had been murdered in Alton the year previous for refusing to surrender the freedom of the Press to pro-slavery ruffians; Pennsylvania Hall had been burned by a Philadelphia mob only a few months before.

The same spirit of lawlessness had prostituted the mail service of the United States as a means of silencing the voice of freedom. Up to this time Giddings had devoted himself to his profession, and had not seriously examined the relations of the Federal Government to slavery, and the rights and duties of the Free States respecting it; but he had now become profoundly interested in the subject through the speeches of Theodore D. Weld, one of the most eloquent of the early Abolitionists, who had spoken at Jefferson and other points in northern Ohio the year before. Under this awakening, Mr. Wade and himself had taken the lead in forming an anti-slavery society, which at first contained only four members. This was the beginning of his warfare with slavery. He was now to confront it on the floor of Congress, and as an earnest, conscientious, and brave man to define his position and maintain it.

CHAPTER III.

DECEMBER, 1838, TO MARCH, 1839.

Personal Journal. — Last Session of the Twenty-fifth Congress. — Scenes and Incidents. — Growing Domination of Slavery. — Development of Character.

DURING the first session of his congressional service Giddings kept a private journal, in which he made a daily record of his impressions about men and affairs. It was intended only for the amusement of his family and particular friends; but there are passages in it which properly belong to the story of his political career, and they are all the more valuable because they relate to the formative period of his public life, and lay bare the real thoughts of the man.

He left his home for Washington on the 24th of November, 1838. His journal describes the tedious journey over the Alleghanies as it was made at that time; and after reaching Frederick City on the 29th, we find this entry: —

"This morning, soon after breakfast, we were joined by a number of Members of Congress who had travelled night and day without any stopping except to eat their meals. Among them I was introduced to a gentleman by the name of Crockett, — a name familiar to most of our American people, for I think few among us are ignorant of the biography of David Crockett, his father. The son appears to possess few of the leading traits of character which distinguished his father. He seemed to be a modest, unassuming man, and is said to be very amiable in his character and disposition. He spoke with great veneration and affection of his father. In company with him I was introduced to Mr. Senator Smith, of Indiana, a man of plain, blunt manners, about forty-five years of age, stoutly built, and with no attempt to play the gentleman. He is a man of plain common-sense, and a lawyer by profession. He somewhat distinguished himself in a speech on the Sub-treasury bill two years since. Thomas Corwin, of Ohio, also formed one of the company. He is a man of middle size, well built, with dark complexion and black eyes. He was born in the lower walks of life, and up to the time he was two-and-twenty, probably never thought of rising from obscurity. In 1812 he was a wagoner in the Northwestern army. At that time, it is said, his unrivalled wit and the brilliancy of his imagination used to draw around a lazy throng during the long evenings, and he then prided himself as much probably on attracting the notice and admiration of teamsters and soldiers as he now does on standing forth as one of the most brilliant orators in the councils of the nation."

Mr. Giddings gives the following description of the ride over the Baltimore and Ohio Railroad to Washington: —

"At eleven o'clock about one hundred and twenty passengers, seated in three cars, carrying from forty to sixty passengers each, started upon the Baltimore and Ohio Railroad for Washington. The cars are well carpeted, and the seats cushioned. We had also a stove in each car, which rendered them comfortably warm. Thus seated, — some conversing in groups, others reading newspapers, and some, from loss of sleep in travelling, sleeping in their seats, — we were swept along at the rate of fifteen miles per hour. At the usual time our candles were lighted, and we presented the appearance of three drawing-rooms filled with guests travelling by land. At about seven o'clock we arrived at Washington City. The moment we stopped we were surrounded on every side with runners, porters, hackmen, and servants, — one calling to know if you would go to Gadsby's, another if you would go to Brown's, another if you would take a hack, etc. They are a source of great annoyance, which the police ought to prevent."

On Saturday evening of December 1 Mr. Giddings attended a caucus of the Whig members of the House, of which he says: —

"I was pleased with the talent, foresight, and acumen exhibited by the leaders of our party; Sergeant of Pennsylvania, Bell of Tennessee, and Evans of Maine are among the leaders."

He was sworn in, with other members, December 3, and in his entry of that evening we find the following: —

"I this day for the first time had an opportunity of observing many of the distinguished men of the nation, and I confess I was disappointed in their appearance. There was not that dignity of carriage about them which I expected. Among them was John Q. Adams, formerly President of the United States, and now a Representative from Massachusetts. He was, strictly speaking, educated a politician, and has continued in political life from his youth up to this time. He is said to have spent more than twenty-eight years of his life at foreign courts. He has held many responsible offices under the government, and is said always to have acquitted himself with honor. He is about five feet eight inches in height, very bald, with low forehead, and nothing about the shape of his head that indicates unusual talent; yet his physiognomy has something of an intellectual appearance. He is truly regarded as a venerable personage."

This sketch of Mr. Adams is noteworthy as the prelude to a friendship between these men which was to be as lasting as life. Adams was to be the mentor and inspirer, and Giddings the faithful and trusted disciple. Henceforward they were to stand side by side and shoulder to shoulder in battling for the rights of man. The influence of the elder over the younger man was undoubtedly great, and his position in the House was singularly unique and commanding. It is safe to say that no other man in the nation could have filled his place and done his work. His patriotism and personal integrity were unquestioned and unquestionable. His long and distinguished public service at home and abroad gave him a prestige which no other man of his time possessed. His great ability was conceded, and his knowledge unsurpassed. His courage was perfect, and only equalled by his combativeness, while his power of invective was unrivalled. His love of justice was a passion, and his hatred of slavery inborn and heartfelt. He could not be seduced by popular applause, nor moved a jot by popular obloquy. In politics Mr. Adams was absolutely independent. He began his life in the Federal party; but when he found it taking a false position, he abandoned it, and provoked the wrath of his old friends by accepting office under Mr. Jefferson. Later in life, when the Republican party, since called Democratic, swerved from what he considered its true course, he allied himself with the Whig party; but he always defied its discipline. He characterized Northern Democrats as "the consistent Swiss guards of slavery," and Northern Whigs as "the languid, compromising non-resistants of the North, afraid of answering a fool according to his folly." To the Whig party he was a burden, always putting himself in the way of harmony between its Northern and Southern sections, while the Whig Press of the Union, with rare exceptions, condemned him. Such was the remarkable man raised up by Providence to stand in the breach and bid defiance to the slave-masters. He was now in the white heat of his fight for the right of petition and the freedom of debate. I believe any other man would have been silenced, and that thus the ascendency of the slave power would have been indefinitely prolonged. Giddings caught his spirit, and valiantly seconded his labors while he lived; and when the old hero and patriarch rested from his toils, his mantle fell upon his beloved disciple.

Returning to the journal, we find the following entry on December 4: —

"I also learned to-day that a resolution was passed at the last session of the present Congress appropriating to each member certain books, to the number of some sixty volumes, and of the value of from five to ten hundred dollars; and being a member of this Congress, the question is now in my mind whether I ought to take the books. In this way some forty to fifty thousand dollars of the public funds have been extracted from the public treasury and given to members by way of perquisites over and above their compensation. Now, if the pay of members is not sufficient, I would raise it. If it be sufficient, why take more, without letting the people know it? But the members seem to think it of little importance."

The entry for December 7 touches the same question of public economy.

"The House convened at the usual hour, and having been in session twenty minutes, adjourned over to Monday, leaving two whole days, in which much business might be transacted. It is, however, said to be a custom which cannot be done away with. But however long the custom may have existed, I think it ought to be broken up. There are thousands of people who have claims on the government, and who have spent much time and money to obtain at the hands of Congress that which is their just due, and are now pining in poverty, while Congress uniformly says it has not time to attend to it. At the close of the last session it is said that sixty bills were lost which had passed the Senate, because the House had not time to pass them. And yet we can throw away days at a time without doing anything."

In his entry of December 8, he describes a visit to President Van Buren.

"On entering, we saw the President sitting at a circular table engaged in conversation. On seeing us he arose, and interchanging salutations with the other gentlemen, with whom he was acquainted, I was then presented to him. He conducted the whole ceremony with great politeness and ease, and inviting us to seats, resumed his former situation and engaged in the most familiar conversation with the whole company. During the conversation I had an opportunity of viewing the phrenological conformation of his head and features. He is small of stature, has a low forehead, is very bald, with eyes sunk far back in his head. His general appearance is not prepossessing. Indeed, to a casual observer he would present the appearance of a man of ordinary character; nor do you see any evidence of extraordinary intellect until you look him squarely in the face, when you are at once impressed with his shrewdness and intelligence. He converses fluently and rapidly. His room is fitted up in a plain and becoming style. A neat mahogany book-case, filled with miscellaneous works, two circular mahogany tables, eighteen or twenty chairs, with a large mirror over the mantelpiece, and a common sofa, constitute the paraphernalia of his receiving apartment."

The reader who remembers the story of Mr. Van Buren's White House extravagance, as circulated by the Whigs in 1840 with such damaging effect, may be surprised at these statements respecting his household furniture.

In his diary of December 11, Giddings refers to the proceedings in the House on the introduction of Mr. Atherton's gag resolutions. There was great excitement, but the rules were suspended for the purpose of receiving them; and Mr. Atherton, who rose to argue them, demanded the previous question, which was carried. The resolutions passed the next day by a vote of 126 yeas to 73 nays. This was the first important measure on which Giddings gave a vote. He had no opportunity to speak, and it is not likely that at this early stage of his congressional service he desired to enter into the discussion of a matter so momentous. But the effect of these proceedings must have been of service in preparing him for future action.

"*Thursday, December* 13. — An amusing incident occurred in the House to-day. Ex-President Adams, who is a violent opponent of the present administration, takes great delight occasionally in showing his want of respect for the officers of government. The Yeas and Nays were ordered on a vote about to be taken, and when his name was called, he arose and commenced an argument. This was entirely out of order, and members from different parts of the House began to call him to order, as did the Speaker also. The cries of 'Order!' became louder and more boisterous. The Speaker called louder and louder for 'Order! *Order!* ORDER!' but Mr. Adams continued speaking, as though a perfect silence existed around him. The uproar increased, and the Speaker, rising from his chair, in great agitation and excitement, with stentorian voice called on the House to assist him in enforcing the rules. Amid this tumult Mr. Adams suddenly dropped into his chair, and the uproar instantly ceased, before the Speaker had fully pronounced his desire for assistance. As Mr. Adams sat down, convulsed with laughter, Waddy Thompson, from South Carolina, possessing much ready wit, and being himself willing to raise a laugh at the expense of the Speaker, stepped up to where Mr. Adams sat, and with great shrewdness of manner said, in reply to the Speaker's request: 'I am here, Mr. Speaker; I am ready to help. What shall I do?' The manner and tone of voice with which he spoke were perfectly inimitable, and threw the whole House into a roar of laughter."

The entry of December 14 is a notable one. It shows that Giddings had been at school, and that he was rapidly getting his lesson.

"It is a fact, which every man of observation must see, by spending a few days in the Representatives' Hall, that there is a vast difference in the character of the members from the North and South. During this week every person present must have witnessed the high and important bearing of the Southern men, — their confident and bold assertions, their self-important airs, their overbearing manner; while the Northern men, even on the subject of slavery, are diffident, taciturn, and *forbearing*. I have myself come to the honest conclusion that our Northern friends are in fact afraid of these Southern bullies. I have bestowed much thought upon the subject. I have made inquiry, and think we have no Northern man who dares boldly and fearlessly declare his abhorrence of slavery and the slave-trade. This kind of fear I never experienced, nor shall I submit to it now. When I came here I had no thought of participating in debate at all, but particularly this winter. But since I have seen our Northern friends so backward and delicate, I have determined to express my own views and declare my own sentiments, and risk the effects. For that purpose I have drawn up a resolution calling for information as to the slave-trade in the District of Columbia, which, among other things, calls for the number of slaves who have murdered themselves within said district within the last five years after being sold for foreign markets, and the number of children who have been murdered by their parents during said time under the apprehension of immediate separation for sale at a foreign market, and the amount of revenue collected on sale of licenses to deal in human flesh and blood. I showed the resolution to several friends, who advise me not to present it, on two accounts: First, that it will enrage the Southern members; and secondly, that it will injure me at home. But I have determined to risk both; for I would rather lose my election at home than suffer the insolence of these Southerners. Mr. Fletcher, of Boston, is the only man that consents to my presenting the resolution. This morning a friend called on me to show me a scurrilous attack upon me in the government paper of to-day. I am in some doubt whether to call the public attention to it or not. However, it seems to render a full declaration of my sentiments both necessary and proper."

Under date of December 16, he speaks of Washington funerals.

" The respectability of the deceased is measured by the number of hacks that follow the hearse. Of course, a great number of empty hacks usually follows the procession. If a member of Congress dies, the usual procession is constituted of all the hacks in the city, which are employed to follow the hearse whether they have any passengers in them or not. A monument costing some three or four hundred dollars is also erected, and the whole expense is paid from the public treasury, including a hundred and fifty dollars to the landlord where the member dies. During the last session a member from Baltimore died, and his body was carried to Baltimore on the railroad for burial. All the cars owned by the company were put in requisition, and the members of the two Houses all took seats in the cars, followed the corpse to Baltimore, stayed over night, had their dinners and wines, lodging and breakfast, all at the expense of the nation. It was thought that the whole expense was not less than four or five thousand dollars. But if members can go to Baltimore at the public expense, I do not see why they may not take a trip to Philadelphia or New York, or even go to Boston, or west of the mountains. . . .

" *Tuesday, December* 18. — House met, and the subject of moving a petition respecting Haytien independence occupied the day. It is amusing and astonishing to see the views entertained by most of the members on the subject of abolition. At the South the general impression is that it is designed to create a general rebellion among the slaves, and have them cut their masters' throats. At the North they have no definite idea of the meaning of abolition, and Northern men appear afraid to come out and declare their sentiments. They seem to feel great delicacy on the subject. Instead of stating the question of abolishing slavery in the District of Columbia and the slave-trade between the States, they keep at a distance from the subject, and as yet no one has come forth and with plainness set forth the claims of the North, and all seem afraid to do so."

On the 21st, he sketches a speech by Mr. Wise, of Virginia, on a resolution of inquiry into the frauds committed by public officers in New York: —

"This was the first set speech I had ever listened to in Congress; but it was a fair specimen, I am told, of all speeches of that kind. Soon after he commenced, his political friends gathered around him, among whom were John Q. Adams, W. J. Graves, S. S. Prentiss, Rice Garland, Stanly, Willams, and in short, most of his personal and political friends, who took seats or stood in groups near him. He spoke slowly and with great composure, and would frequently stop to make inquiry of those around him on matters of which he did not possess the requisite intelligence. He was often happy in his satire, and during his long periods was helped by information and good hits by those around him, who, if they thought of a good idea, would remind him of it at his next period. In this way they helped him much, but did not disconcert him. He spoke of Secretary Woodbury in terms of severe reproach, and also of the President, Speaker, and nearly all the officers of the government. He spoke about six hours. The Representatives generally dined from four to five o'clock, and returned to hear the conclusion of his remarks. This is the way that most of the great speeches here are made, as I am informed. I think most of our lawyers of ordinary industry could do as well as these noted orators if they had the chance.

"*Monday, December* 24. — One of the candidates for the next Presidency, a man whose name and character are identified with the history of the nation, called to pay me the accustomed civilities observed in official life. His amiable manner and dignity of carriage, and his elevated bearing, make you feel at once in the presence of one who is your superior, while you feel perfectly at ease, as much so as though you were visiting with your equals, or those with whom you have long been familiar. He had but barely left my room when the carrier entered with my letters, among which was one from another candidate for the highest office within the gift of the people. I have no doubt that either will be willing to accept the office if elected."

The name of the first of these candidates is not given, but the second was William Henry Harrison, as the following letter will show: —

NORTH BEND, Dec. 15, 1838.

DEAR SIR, — . . . In relation to the subject of the Presidency, some surprise has been expressed by a few of Mr. Clay's friends that I, who was so ardent and so long a supporter of his for the chief magistracy of the Union, should consent to become his rival. My answer to this is, that I never for one moment entertained the idea of being a candidate for that office until I was brought forward under circumstances which made it impossible for me to decline. But there was and still exists another reason why I should not decline; viz., that I am in possession of facts that were convincing to my mind that Mr. C., if he were the opposition candidate, would very probably be defeated, while I had good grounds to believe that I would probably succeed. You may perhaps smile at this remark, and say that it is an opinion common to all candidates that their chance is the best, and not more likely to be true in this instance than in all the others. But as it is notorious that I never sought the office, more credit may, I think, be given to me when I assert that my opinion is founded upon facts, and not upon any vainglorious notion of the merit of my pretensions. I will mention one or two circumstances to give you an idea of the character of the information I possess which has led to the formation of the opinion above expressed. I am amongst the oldest and most extensively known of the Western pioneers. I have stood in the relation to many thousands of our citizens either as their commander or brother soldier. Now, it so happens that almost all of the pioneers and old soldiers of the West were on the side of the administration, brought over to that side by their attachment to General Jackson; and that attachment produced by his being himself one of the class to which it was their boast to belong. He out of the way, is there any difficulty in believing that they might be willing again to give their support to another of the same class, although of inferior pretensions, rather than to any one whose pursuits and course of life had no resemblance to their own? If I were to disclose the contents of some letters I have received, and some more circuitous verbal communications from some of the leaders of our opponents, it would surprise our friends and startle our enemies.

. . . .

I am, very truly yours,

W. H. HARRISON.

Hon. J. R. GIDDINGS.

Only the political portion of this letter is given, which shows how earnestly and plausibly the old general urged his claims. The tone of it towards Giddings personally is most friendly, and in striking contrast with that manifested a few years later, as we shall see.

"*Thursday, December* 27. — This morning on coming into the hall it was evident that some unusual expectation had been excited. The galleries were crowded to overflowing, and all the avenues to the hall were filled. Men and women, old and young, rich and poor, had turned out to hear the Mississippi orator, and no one who had obtained an eligible situation for hearing could be induced to leave it. Mr. Prentiss is not more than thirty-five years of age, and was born and educated in Maine. At the age of two-and-twenty he emigrated to Cincinnati, where he read law with Nathaniel Wright, Esq., of that city, after which he went to Vicksburg, Mississippi, where he commenced the practice of law and has since resided. He soon distinguished himself in his profession, and was elected to Congress in 1836; and his seat being contested, he then first brought himself into notice. He is truly one of Nature's most gifted sons. He is a Whig; and as the present system of the national administration was his theme to-day, high expectations were entertained of the intellectual treat he was to give the House and spectators. He did not disappoint his friends. During the entire session he either chained the audience in breathless silence, or convulsed them with laughter. His irony was of the most bitter kind, his invective solemn and impressive, and his eloquence lofty and commanding. For three hours the partisans of the administration sat in tortures, and writhed beneath his castigation. No one could, while hearing him, entertain any other feelings towards them than those of pity. When we returned for dinner we found our boarding-house in total confusion. Women and girls, blacks and whites, master, mistress, and servants, all had been to hear Prentiss, and all forgot that their boarders would want dinner until he closed his remarks.

"*Saturday, December* 29. — The subject of granting pensions came up in debate. That being a subject on which I thought myself possessed of tolerable information, and the attendance being thin, I ventured for the first time to address the House. I expected to be greatly embarrassed, and to have my voice tremble; but was surprised to find it full, and that I was able to make myself heard through the whole hall. I spoke but a moment, not intending to occupy time, but more for the purpose of trying my voice.

"*Monday, December* 31. — I received a note from Mr. Gales, requesting me to meet a few friends at his house at eight o'clock, but did not arrive till half-past eight. The company was composed of about one hundred Whig members of the two houses of Congress, with some five or six distinguished gentlemen of that party who happened to be in Washington. The company was select and very social. I took the earliest opportunity to engage in conversation with the venerable Ex-President Adams, during which he referred to his youthful adventures during the Revolutionary War, and stated that while going to France in 1778, at the age of thirteen years, on board an American frigate, they were chased and fired upon by a British ship, and he recounted the adventure with much glee and spirit. He said he crossed the Atlantic twice afterwards in a French ship during the war. He told me his age was seventy-two years in September last.

"Wishing to see and become acquainted with the great men of the nation, I was next introduced to Mr. Clay, of Kentucky. I had met him in 1822, but he has changed in appearance much since that time. He is very social and farmer-like in his conversation. I spent some half hour with him, during which we passed over many commonplace subjects, and discussed the advantages of Ohio and Kentucky, touching lightly on politics, when I discovered much hidden feeling beneath a cool, dispassionate exterior. I left him with a higher admiration for the man than I had previously entertained."

On New Year's Day Giddings joined the great throng that attended the customary public reception of the President, which he describes in detail. He then says: —

"Still one more call remained to be made. I had been invited to call on our venerable ex-President, and to his residence I now bent my way. In a retired mansion we found him and his lady surrounded by some dozen friends, who showed by their countenances and conversation that they had called in reality to pay their *respects* to this great man, whose name will hereafter fill the brightest page of American history. Here we met and saluted the aged statesman in a large and comfortable drawing-room, with his matronly lady, his sister, a daughter-in-law, and two grandchildren. We found him in the midst of a truly domestic circle. No noise or bustle interrupted that expression of goodwill which we all felt towards him. His countenance glowed with benevolence and kindness. We were introduced to the members of his family, sat a while, and after some pleasant conversation we left this interesting man, feeling that we had seen a specimen of true greatness united with genuine republican simplicity. Mr. Adams belongs to no local district, to no political party, but to the nation and to the people. He is elected by his district in Massachusetts, comes here with his family during the session of Congress, and keeps house by himself. While in the House he consults with no one, acts in concert with no one, and holds himself accountable to no one but the nation. He belongs as much to the former age as to this,—perhaps he may be said to be the connecting link between the former generation and the one now in active life."

On January 5, Giddings made his first regular speech in the House. As this effort brought him at once to the front as a man of courage and ability, it will be worth while to give his own account of the circumstances under which he made it:—

"*Friday, January* 4. — This day nothing occurred worthy of notice, except as its transactions connected myself with proceedings which may hereafter bring my name before the public. Mr. Jones, who claimed a seat here as delegate from Wisconsin, had been elected in 1836, served two years, as limited by the organic laws, and, at the expiration of his term, which was in October last, again appeared in the field as a candidate and was defeated. This defeat was mostly attributed to his connection with the duel in which Mr. Cilley fell last winter in this city. After his defeat he came here, and claimed to hold his seat in the House during the present Congress, urging that his time did not commence until December, 1837, and that the service and receiving pay in 1836 were all in his own wrong. I believe his object to be the travel fees from Wisconsin and his *per diem*, which amount to about two thousand dollars, and think he ought not thus to carry off the national treasure. I have tried to get some older member to introduce a resolution denying his right to compensation, which I know he has already drawn. But as no older member will do it, I have determined to take it upon myself, and thinking that justice to him required me to apprise him of my design, have written him a note stating my intention, and conveyed it through the medium of the post-office.

"*Saturday, January* 5. — I spent the whole morning in preparing to sustain the resolution which I intended to present to the House. I had yet many misgivings as to my success before that body, whether I should not be so much embarrassed as to be unable to proceed. Mr. Jones is a professed duellist; his conduct in the matter I considered disgraceful. If I spoke, I knew I should speak my mind as soon as I should became warmed with my subject. Many of the members I knew dared not speak as they thought, on account of Mr. Jones's duelling character. Of this I entertained not the slightest fear; all my apprehensions were lest I should not succeed as well as I intended in exposing what I deemed a gross abuse of the situation he held. I went to the House with fear and trembling. I had written Jones that I should bring forward the resolution, so now I could not retreat. The House was called to order, and the clerk was reading the journal. I had my resolution written, and when the clerk had finished reading, was on my feet with my resolution in my hand, and called the Speaker's name; but he responded to the call of Mr. Mason, who sent to the Chair a resolution almost in the very words of the one I held. I felt relieved from my embarrassment, and when the resolution was read, the Speaker remarked that he had a communication from Mr. Jones. The reading was called for. In it Mr. Jones stated that he had drawn his mileage and *per diem;* but on the evening previous had received a note from Mr. Giddings, which he therewith transmitted to the Speaker, together with the funds he had drawn from the treasury.

"When my name was mentioned, all eyes were turned upon me; I was a new member, and all seemed to look with astonishment at the course I had dared to take. Some of my friends came to me and inquired why I had done as I did; others appeared to think me too diffident to carry out what I had commenced, and came to me to encourage and urge me forward. General Mason took the floor, of course. While he was speaking, I was advised to withdraw, and let the older members manage the matter. When General Mason was through, I tried to get the floor, and failed. Mr. Bouldin, of Virginia, obtained it. I soon saw that he had no correct view of the subject, and felt somewhat emboldened. He spoke for half an hour, and when he ceased, I strove for the floor again; but Mr. Wise obtained it, and I saw that Mr. Thomas, of Maryland, — an old member, and one who spoke often, — was determined to get it next, and of course I knew he would get it, as he is the leader of the Van Buren party and a favorite of the Speaker. I went to him and requested the privilege of speaking before he did; this he refused, and I determined that if I followed him, he should hereafter be at least a little careful in throwing himself before me or in my way.

"My friends now came and urged me to insist upon having the floor; but, as I expected, Mr. Thomas obtained it. I took notice of his argument, and when he sat down I succeeded in getting the floor, and, to my utter surprise, found my voice full and clear. I felt a little embarrassment, but cared nothing for that while my voice should appear natural. Having made my introduction, I proceeded to answer the argument of Mr. Bouldin. I had hardly stated the position he had taken, when he saw the light in which I was about to place him, and at once requested the floor to explain. I yielded; he explained. I proceeded in my argument, but in less than five minutes Mr. Bouldin and Mr. Wise were both on their feet, wishing to explain. Cries of 'No! No!' were heard, but I yielded. By this time I had thrown off my embarrassment, and when they resumed their seats I let fall a good-natured joke which drew forth a burst of laughter. I proceeded to the argument of Thomas; he, too, was on the floor, and I refused to yield it. I proceeded; he again solicited the floor, and I yielded it. My friends now loudly remonstrated against my yielding the floor any more. Thomas explained and sat down. I proceeded, with a determination to scorch him for his want of delicacy in not permitting me to precede him in the argument. I took ample vengeance on him, and finally got through the argument with tolerable satisfaction to myself, and, I am told, to the satisfaction of my friends."

Commenting upon this speech, Giddings, on January 7, says, —

"A member of Congress, when he comes unknown to Washington, attracts little attention among his fellow-members. With citizens and officers of government, his official character is a sufficient recommendation to command their respect and constant attention. But with his fellow-members he attracts no attention whatever, until he makes some display of his powers, tact, or political management. I have now fairly made my *début*, and to-day I fancied myself, on entering the hall, greeted more warmly than heretofore; members who had previously barely paid the passing salutation now came to my seat, with great politeness inquired after my health, and many of them congratulated me upon the favorable reception of my speech. . . . I now felt that I had fairly entered upon the business of a member. I felt myself entitled to express my views more freely than I had heretofore done. Many of the most celebrated lawyers in the House and of the nation took occasion to express their high gratification at the manner in which I had 'used up' (as they said) the chairman of the Judiciary Committee."

This account of his first important appearance on the floor of the House foreshadows his future course. He had only been a member of Congress a little over a month, but his diffidence was giving place to self-confidence. He had become acquainted with members, and by comparing himself with them had learned to estimate himself. His strong individuality was revealing itself, and his associates must have perceived that a man of his positive qualities would make himself felt in behalf of whatever measure he might espouse.

On January 21, Giddings makes an interesting reference to Mr. Adams, who on that day addressed the House, stating that he had for a long time been in receipt of daily communications threatening his life, that his position was not understood by the nation, and that he wished the privilege of giving an *exposé* of his views. He says that Mr. Adams was evidently ill at ease, and that his solemn manner and the tones of his voice, now tremulous with age, so wrought upon the House that leave was granted him to make his explanation.

"His views as stated would compare with those of the Abolitionists generally, except that he declared himself not prepared to vote for the abolition of slavery in the District of Columbia. He said that he was prepared to abolish the slave-trade between the States, and to recognize the independence of Hayti. He said he would vote for the removal of the seat of government to some place where slavery did not exist, but he doubted whether that would be constitutional. He assigned no reason for any of his opinions, but stated generally that his opinion was not so fixed but that it might be altered on argument. His speech occasioned great sensation. It seemed to convince the South that he was not so great an enemy to them as they had supposed, and some of the Northern members appeared to think he was not so strongly opposed to slavery as they thought him to be. Others said that he had expressed the same views which they had always understood him to possess. Mr. Slade, of Vermont, who is the greatest Abolitionist in the House, seemed to be very apprehensive that the speech would have a bad influence on the subject of abolition. He drew up interrogatives to Mr. Adams, for the purpose of drawing from him further explanations, and submitted them to my inspection. This I considered useless, having no hope that Mr. Adams would make further disclosures of his views than he had made to the world. I am, however, fully of the opinion, from the language used by Mr. Adams and the cautious manner in which he expressed himself, that his want of readiness to abolish slavery in the District is not owing to any doubt as to the power of Congress to do so, nor to any other reason than a question as to the policy of such action.

"The difficulty that has often presented itself to my mind is that if Congress should pass a law to abolish slavery in the District, before it could take effect the slaves would all be taken out of the District, and the law would find none here to take effect upon. But if Congress should first pass a law prohibiting the taking of any slave out of the District, that would keep them here, and a law to abolish slavery would liberate from nine to ten thousand slaves. Of Mr. Adams's views, beyond what he has publicly expressed, I know nothing; but these thoughts have often run through my own mind, and I think them worthy of serious reflection by the philanthropic."

Mr. Adams's position on this question was offensive to some of the Abolitionists, and James G. Birney branded him as the enemy of freedom. Congress had legalized slavery and the slave traffic in the District by an Act which was unwarranted by the Constitution; for Congress had "no more power to make a slave than to make a king." It had nationalized these evils, which before were strictly local and sectional. The right of Congress to repeal its own legislation was constitutionally unquestionable, and the duty to exercise that right was imperative. The same government which had branded the foreign slave-trade as piracy had created and was sustaining in the capital of the Republic a more pitiless traffic than that on the high seas. The hesitation of Northern men to strike at this evil was one of the marvels of slave-holding domination. When the District was created by cessions from Maryland and Virginia, and afterwards, in 1801, when Congress accepted the cessions, these States anticipated the total abolition of slavery at no distant day. For forty-five years after the formation of the government, no question was raised as to the power of Congress to abolish the evil in the District. As late as the Twenty-fourth Congress, in 1834 and 1835, numerous petitions for its abolition were received, referred, and debated. The perfect union of the South on the basis of the sacredness and perpetuity of slavery was the development of a later time.

Six years after this speech of Mr. Adams he stated his position somewhat more definitely in an address to his constituents. He declared himself opposed to the immediate abolition of slavery in the District, because it would violate the principle of local self-government. The people of the District were unrepresented in Congress, and an Act of emancipation therefore would be " an Act of the most arbitrary and despotic character." He raised the further point that it would be evaded by the removal of the slaves pending its passage. Both these difficulties could have been met by providing compensation for slave-owners, as was done by several of the Northern States, and thus ridding the people of those States of their complicity with the evil. Mr. Adams expressed the further opinion that slavery in the District would die out of itself through the voluntary action of the slaveholders, and that the slave traffic would hasten the event. He thought that in twenty, or perhaps ten, years not a slave would be left in the District. He lived long enough to realize his mistake. Like Abraham Lincoln, he found instruction in the logic of events. Under the exasperating stress and friction of a steadily increasing Southern lawlessness during the last years of his life, he reconsidered his earlier opinions, and was undoubtedly ready to employ the whole constitutional power of the government on the side of freedom.

On January 29, Giddings speaks of the latitude

of debate allowed in Committee of the Whole, and says: —

"Seeing the wide range of debate, it struck me as a favorable place to bring forward the subject of slavery, upon which debate is prohibited in the House. For this purpose I digested and reduced to paper a plan for commencing an attack on the slave-trade in the District of Columbia."

He failed to obtain the floor, and was obliged to defer his attack.

"*Wednesday, January* 30. — This day Mr. Slade, of Vermont, came to see me, with an expression of great anxiety in regard to the exposition which Mr. Adams had made of his views concerning slavery. He appears to apprehend great results from these disclosures. Not feeling any very serious apprehensions on the subject, I told him that the opinions of Mr. Adams would pass off like the opinions of any other man; that I intended to give my own opinion as a counterbalance to that of Mr. Adams. He desired to know how I should bring the matter forward, and I told him. He was at first incredulous as to the feasibility of my plan, but soon agreed that I was correct, and before he left, promised to make an effort himself upon the same plan."

This is followed by the description of a scene well calculated to arouse Mr. Giddings's indignation and inspire him with renewed courage and zeal in the fight upon which he had entered.

"This day a coffle of about sixty slaves, male and female, passed through the streets of Washington, chained together, on their way south. They were accompanied by a large wagon, in which were placed the more feeble females and children of such tender years as to be unable to walk. A *being* in the shape of a man was on horseback, with a large whip in his hand, with which he occasionally chastised those who, through fatigue or indolence, were tardy in their movements. This was done in the daytime, in public view of all who happened to be so situated as to see the barbarous spectacle.

"*Monday, February* 4. — This being petition day, I had determined on raising a question as to the abolition of slavery in the District of Columbia. This I communicated to my friend Fletcher, who was incredulous as to getting up the question, but pledged himself to sustain me, provided I would get the subject before the House. At about three o'clock the State of Ohio was called for petitions. I obtained the floor, and after presenting some others on various subjects, I brought forward one for the abolition of slavery in the District of Columbia, and moved that it be referred to the committee on said District. The Chair, at this time occupied by Mr. Briggs of Massachusetts, decided that the petition must lie on the table. From this decision I appealed; and the Chair having stated the appeal, I obtained the floor and proceeded to argue the question of the prohibition of the petition by the resolutions of 11th and 12th of December. Mr. Garland, of Louisiana, called me to order. There was much uneasiness apparent among the members. The Speaker, Mr. Polk, resumed the chair, and desired me to state distinctly the motion I had made. This I did, when he pronounced me in order. I then proceeded with my remarks. I went on, mentioned the resolutions, and showed that they did not extend to the petition under consideration. After this, I pronounced the resolutions opposed to the Constitution, and *ipso facto* void, and proceeded to demonstrate that position."

Upon being reminded by the Speaker that he was out of order, and finding it impossible to proceed in the face of constant interruptions, Giddings withdrew his appeal, having accomplished his purpose in protesting against the gag rules of the House.

On the 7th of February Mr. Clay made his famous speech against the Abolitionists, in which he declared that "that *is* property which the law declares *to be* property," and that "two hundred years of legislation have sanctioned and sanctified negro slaves as property." It was one of the unfortunate speeches of his life; but he was looking forward to the Presidency, and had yielded to the persuasions of his Whig friends, who thought it necessary that he should clear himself of all suspicion of sympathy with the Abolitionists. The speech pleased Calhoun and his friends, but offended many of the best men in the Northern States. Giddings had been one of Mr. Clay's admirers, and would gladly have followed his fortunes;

but this now seemed morally impossible. In his journal of this date he says: —

"This afternoon, while I was engaged in the House, intelligence was brought to me that Mr. Clay had made an attack upon the Abolitionists; that he had made a long speech in which he had attacked them without mercy. Many Van Buren men came to me and endeavored to tantalize me about the attack Mr. Clay had made upon a large portion of the electors of my district. It was known among many Whigs that I had stepped forward to bring about a reconciliation between the Abolitionists and the friends of Mr. Clay. My friend Fletcher came to me and gave me a description of the speech. He stated that Mr. Clay had said substantially that Congress had no right to abolish slavery in the District of Columbia, unless it were necessary for the accommodation of Congress or the benefit of the people of the District. This was different from what I had before understood, and I knew would disappoint the expectations of the people I represent. I had publicly avowed my adherence to Mr. Clay for President in preference to Mr. Van Buren, and I felt that the speech would place me at home in an attitude unexpected by me and my friends. Before I left my seat, therefore, I despatched a note to Mr. Clay, demanding distinctly whether he believed Congress to possess the right of abolishing slavery in this District *when no other reason existed for it than mere benevolence to the human family.*"

The friends of Clay endeavored to induce Giddings to withdraw this note; but he refused, declaring that Mr. Clay had been very indiscreet, and had disappointed the expectation of his friends in Ohio, and injured himself. A zealous friend of Clay censured Giddings for thus criticising such a man, to which Giddings replied that he would allow no man, either Mr. Clay or any other, to ridicule or misrepresent his constituents, and that he should feel it his duty, on the first occasion which should offer, to disabuse the public mind of the false impression conveyed. The result was that Clay called to see Giddings in person, and finding him absent, repeated his call on February 12.

"Mr. Clay called upon me while in my seat to-day. I retired to the lobby with him. He spoke of the letter, and said he thought his speech was a sufficient answer to it. I called his attention to the one distinct point set forth in the letter, which did not appear in the speech. The conversation became dull, and with a cold invitation to call and see him, he left me."

On the 13th of February Giddings made his first anti-slavery speech. The occasion was a timely one. A bill had been introduced in the House providing for an appropriation of thirty thousand dollars to build a bridge over the east branch of the Potomac; and this was accompanied by sundry memorials of citizens of the District praying that no notice be taken of the anti-slavery petitions which had been presented to the House, and that such petitions be not received. These memorialists termed the petitioners "fanatics," and their petitions "seditious memorials." Here was an opportunity to strike a blow at slavery and the slave-trade in the District, and Giddings moved to strike out the enacting clause of the bill, giving his reasons therefor. He spoke in the midst of constant interruptions, and was finally compelled by the rulings of the Speaker to take his seat; but what he was permitted to say may properly be quoted here.

"But, sir, I will assign my reasons for believing that the seat of government will be removed. It is known, sir, that the slave-trade in its worst and most abhorrent forms is being carried on here to an alarming extent. [Here Mr. Giddings was called to order, but the Chair decided that he was in order.] We are told by some honorable gentlemen that the subject of its continuance cannot be discussed in the House; that a dissolution of the Union would follow as the inevitable consequence of any interference with the traffic on the part of Congress. On the other hand, I have come to the conclusion that Northern men, who have from their infancy been bred in the love of liberty, where every precept impressed upon their youthful minds, every principle of their matured years, has habituated them to think of the slave-trade with disgust and abhorrence, to contemplate it as only existing among barbarians and uncivilized nations, to look upon it with horror, — I say, sir, that it is my opinion that such men can never consent to continue the seat of government in the midst of a magnificent slave-market. I say it distinctly to the committee, to the nation, and to the world, that Northern men will not consent to the continuance of our national councils where their ears are assailed while coming to the Capitol by the voice of the auctioneer publicly proclaiming the sale of human, of intelligent beings. [Several gentlemen here called Mr. Giddings to order, and he was again sustained by the Chair.]

"I thank you, Mr. Chairman, for your cool and impartial decision of the question of order. I will remark that I was assigning my own reasons, not those of any other gentleman. I say distinctly that I have not commenced these remarks with feelings of unkindness to any man, or to any part of this nation. I have been induced to embrace the present opportunity by a deep and solemn sense of justice, which I think is due to the district which I represent, and to a large part of the Northern States. They, sir, feeling an honest abhorrence of the slave-trade, have sent in their petitions against it. I have myself presented the petitions of many thousands of Northern freemen on the subject; but their petitions have been disregarded, and the voice of American freemen in favor of liberty has been silenced. Their representative, sent here with authority to act for them, to speak their views, to express their wishes, has been bound, hand and foot, with a sort of legislative strait-jacket, so far as the subject of this slave-trade is concerned, and his lips have been hermetically sealed, to prevent him from a declaration of their views, and from demanding their rights. Sir, upon this floor I have heard gentlemen — honorable gentlemen — say that those citizens who have thus petitioned this House, would be hanged if found in Southern States.

"I pass any such remarks; they were made under feelings of excitement, and did not express the real sentiments of their authors. But, sir, while the voices of Northern freemen are silenced upon this floor, and their representatives here are not permitted to declare the sentiments of those who sent them, we are called upon to make heavy appropriations of their money for the benefit of this District. Many thousands of our people have endeavored to express to this House their views of the slave-trade as carried on here. We refuse to hear them; we treat their petitions with contempt; but in answer say, 'Your money shall be taken for the improvement of this city, although it be a slave-market; we will not hear your objections to the slave-trade, but we will tax you to build a slave-market.' This, sir, is wrong; it is palpably wrong.

"But, sir, I was saying that the appropriation was for the benefit of this District principally; it is to be made for the benefit of the people of this District: and what is their language to those whose funds are now sought to be appropriated? The language of the people of this District is expressed in their memorials, lately presented to both houses of Congress. In those memorials the free and independent citizens who petition us in regard to the slave-trade of this District are termed 'a band of fanatics;' their petitions are termed 'seditious memorials;' their efforts to stop the inhuman and barbarous practice of selling men, women, and children are termed 'foul and unnatural.' Congress is prayed, not only to refuse a reading or reference of these petitions, but we are requested not to receive such petitions.

"This, sir, is the language of the people of this District towards those whom I am supposed to represent, whose sentiments on this subject of the slave-trade I openly and unequivocally avow. I, sir, have been honored with the high trust of representing the people thus stigmatized, and I would deem myself unworthy of the trust if I permitted such language to pass unnoticed. Honorable gentlemen have presented the memorials of the people here in both houses of Congress, and have advocated the principles, repeated and enlarged upon the language used. Sir, under all this abuse I am asked now to contribute from the funds of the people thus abused, to the improvement of this city and for the benefit of those who thus assail their motives and stigmatize their acts. I object to the appropriation under these circumstances. I protest against it, and I repeat that while this state of things remains, I shall be opposed to all appropriations in this District not necessary for the convenience of government. I take my stand here. I now avow my firm determination to give my vote for no further appropriations for this District until the voice of these petitioners be heard and acted upon, and their prayers granted or refused. I say no appropriations except such as are really necessary for the comfortable continuance of the government.

"I want to be understood, and not misrepresented. It is the slave-trade to which I now allude, not to slavery. That is another subject. On that I may at some other time give my views; but let no man accuse me of now saying anything in regard to his right of holding his fellow-man as property, or of now saying anything concerning it. What I have said, and what I intend to say, will refer to nothing but the slave-trade. I intend to disarm my opponents of all cause in regard to the constitutional right or the power of Congress over the subject. I am aware of the feeling which gentlemen have on this subject, and I assure them of my intention not to say anything offensive to them, further than duty requires. I hope that, whoever may become excited, I may speak and act from the convictions of sober judgment. I once alluded to the statement of honorable gentlemen that we cannot interfere with the slave-trade in this District without a dissolution of the Union. This threat, sir, I beg leave to say, I disregard. I will leave that question to be discussed by those who deem the slave-trade in this District of more importance than the continuance of the Union. But should a dissolution take place, the appropriation now in question would surely be of little importance.

"I, sir, have alluded to the fact that, on the beautiful avenue in front of the Capitol, members of Congress, while on their way to the Capitol, during this session, have heard the harsh voice of the inhuman auctioneer publicly selling human beings. They have also been compelled to turn aside from their path to permit a cofile of slaves, males and females, chained to each other by their necks, to pass on their way to this national slave-market."

Here the speech of Giddings was cut short by the ruling of the Chair, as related in his diary.

"After I had spoken a few moments, Mr. Howard said he would call me to order. I demanded the question to be reduced to writing. The Chair decided that I had the right to have it so reduced, and from this decision Mr. Howard appealed. Much debate and confusion followed, several members speaking at the same time, each calling the other to order, and each insisting that he was right. Much excitement prevailed, and the House became a scene of perfect confusion and uproar. Some appeared to enjoy this much; among these the venerable ex-President laughed most heartily, and coming to my seat, advised me to insist upon my rights, not to be intimidated by the course taken by the Southern men. This confusion lasted about one hour; and, as I suppose, for the purpose of restoring order, the chairman, without taking the vote of the committee on the appeal, decided that I was out of order. . . . A vote was then taken on my motion and carried, the enacting clause of the bill being stricken out."

Giddings was now fairly launched on the angry sea of anti-slavery politics; he had entered upon his life-work; and although the Southern men had in this instance silenced him by their clamor, they saw clearly that he could not be subdued. His journal shows that several of the leading men of the South endeavored to insult him while in his seat; but he refused to have any altercation with them. Henceforth he was to encounter the wrath and scorn of the slave-barons and their Northern allies, and to come under the ban of social outlawry; but this only armed him with fresh courage and roused the spirit of defiance. His course had won the hearts of the best men in the House, and secured for him a recognition that compelled the respect even of his enemies.

Giddings's journal refers to occasional incidents which no doubt served as aids to his anti-slavery education. One of these is the following: —

"*Thursday, February* 14. In the evening we were alarmed by a thrilling cry of distress which continued for some minutes. It proved to be the outcry of a slave who was undergoing the chastisement of his master; and fearing he would die in the operation, broke from him and ran. He was pursued, knocked down, and pounded by the master and son till he appeared lifeless; and the spectators, interfering, were told that he was the property of his master, who had the right to kill him if he pleased. The master and his son then took him and dragged him through the street as they would have done a dead hog, to a stable, and there left him."

I give one further entry, dated March 2, which shows his native kindness of heart.

"An incident occurred, in my view, that illustrates the difficulty of obtaining justice from the government. A man named Nye has claimed about six thousand dollars from the government for several years, and has himself personally pressed the matter for some sessions past. During the last session Mr. Whittlesey, chairman of the Committee on Claims, reported against it, although the Senate had reported in favor of it. Mr. Whittlesey was looked upon as infallible authority on the subject of claims. Nye was put in jail for want of money, and suffered much. His claim again passed the Senate, and was referred to the House Committee on Claims. Nye himself wrote an able review of Whittlesey's report, and pointed out its errors; but many things intervened to prevent the committee from passing on it until to-day. I agreed with two or three others that we would get together and pass upon this claim, provided that it were possible to get a quorum to the committee-room. This we effected, and agreed to report the bill giving him his whole claim. This was done as late as two o'clock P. M. When we left the room, I was in front, and Nye was at the door. I told him we had agreed to report his bill for the amount claimed. He attempted to thank me, but tears choked his utterance, and I felt deeply myself, — so much so that I found tears running down my own cheeks; and unwilling that my weakness should be discovered, I averted my face to disguise my feelings from those passing by me in front. As I turned my face, my eye rested upon Mr. Chambers, our chairman, who, though a man of rough exterior, and who has been through many a bloody battle, was so wrought upon by Nye's feeling that he wept profusely."

At the close of this session the diary came to an end, and was not resumed till ten years later, and then only temporarily. This is deeply to be regretted, for if he had continued it during his long public service, it would have proved an interesting autobiography and a valuable contribution to the history of the anti-slavery conflict. As it was limited to the first session of his Congressional service, I have deemed it proper to make liberal extracts from it, as a revelation of the spirit, character, and purpose of the man. It anticipates his further achievements in the work of reform, and gives the key-note to his public life.

CHAPTER IV.

MARCH, 1839, TO MARCH, 1841.

The "Amistad" Case. — The Twenty-sixth Congress. — The Famous New Jersey Election Contest. — The Slave Ship "Enterprise." — The Harrison Campaign. — Nomination of Birney. — Speech on the Florida War.

THE growing rapacity of slavery furnished the Abolitionists with a new object-lesson in the summer of 1839. A Cuban slave-ship landed her cargo of Africans at Havana, in June, and after their imprisonment for a short time in the barracoons of that city, forty-nine of them were purchased by I. Ruiz, and three others by P. Montez, slave-dealers. A pass for these fifty-two persons was obtained from the governor by paying him the usual fee, which constituted a portion of his official perquisites, for permitting the foreign slave-trade to be carried on in that island. This pass was merely a license to Montez and Ruiz to transport certain *ladinos*, or legal slaves, naming them, from Havana to Principe, on the south of the island. The legality of their slavery was assumed, and as they had been thrown into prison on their arrival in Havana, they had no opportunity to speak in their own behalf. But as they had been stolen in Africa and brought to Cuba in violation of Spanish law and treaty stipulations, they were legally free. The negroes, however, were shipped on board the schooner "Amistad" about the 1st of July, and she sailed at once for her port of destination. The crew consisted of the captain, mate, and three sailors, and there were three passengers besides Montez and Ruiz and the negroes claimed by them.

When four or five days out, the Africans suddenly rose upon their oppressors, slew the captain and cook, and wounded two of the crew. The others surrendered, and the negroes took possession of the ship, holding Ruiz and Montez in subjection, who were now obliged to obey the men they had so recently called their "property." The crew and passengers were sent on shore, and Ruiz and Montez directed to guide the ship to Africa, whence their victims had been torn by slave-holding cupidity. The Spaniards, however, took advantage of the foggy weather and the darkness of the night, and heading the ship northwardly, came to anchor on the coast of Connecticut. Lieutenant Gedney, of the schooner "Washington," engaged on the coast-survey, took possession of the "Amistad" and cargo, claiming salvage on the negroes, whom he regarded as "property," while he permitted Montez and Ruiz to go at liberty. The slave-trade was thus brought home to the shores of New England and unveiled to the public view; while the love of liberty exhibited in the heroism with which these barbarians had obtained possession of the ship seems to have been totally unrecognized.

The Spanish minister demanded that these Africans should be sent back to Cuba and delivered up to the authorities of that island, to be punished for thus regaining their freedom; and the President of the United States took sides with the slave-dealers, and instead of setting the negroes free, ordered them to be seized and imprisoned under the authority of the United States, at the instance of the Spanish minister. The United States district attorney accordingly appeared on behalf of Montez and Ruiz, as well as of the Spanish minister, and the proceedings were had before the United States District Court for the State of Connecticut, while the friends of the negroes engaged eminent counsel in their behalf. Southern politicians now became excited and alarmed. The trial of this case before any slave-holding tribunal would have given them no concern; but its adjudication before a Connecticut court and jury was to be dreaded, although the President was anxious that the court should in some manner obtain a conviction of the Africans. This he demonstrated by sending an armed vessel to New Haven, pending the trial, with orders to carry these Africans to Cuba as soon as they should be delivered to the captain on board, sending secret directions at the same time to the attorney and marshal of the district to hurry the prisoners on board the ship as rapidly as possible after the decision of the court against them, without giving time to their counsel or friends to take an appeal. Mr. Adams, in the mean time, introduced resolutions in the House of Representatives calling on the President to inform Congress by what authority these persons, charged with no crime, were held in prison.

The knowledge of this transaction had now reached the public through the newspapers in every section of the Union, and the decision of the court was awaited with great interest and anxiety. After a patient investigation, judgment was given in favor of the prisoners, declaring that by the laws of God and man they were free.

This decision disappointed the Administration, and the district attorney appealed to the Circuit

Court; but failing here, the case was brought before the Supreme Court of the United States, and to the action of this tribunal the attention of the whole country was now directed. The "Amistad" case in all its details thus became the study of the people. The Administration dealt with the matter as a party question, while the opponents of slavery rallied to the work of rescuing these imperilled Africans from the clutches of pirates, and saving the country from public disgrace. The majority of the judges on the Supreme Bench were then slave-holders, and Baldwin, one of the judges from the Free States, was warmly in sympathy with slavery. With great unanimity the anti-slavery men of the country turned to Mr. Adams as the man to argue this cause before the Supreme Court. Every one conceded his ability, but it was especially desirable to have his great moral influence in the argument of such a cause before the court and the country. Notwithstanding his great age and the burdens of his long public service, he consented to defend these negroes. He did so with great reluctance, saying, "Oh, how shall I do justice to this case and to these men?" It was a great occasion and a great opportunity. The legislative branch of the government had become the instrument of slavery. The Executive had openly and actively espoused the claim of Ruiz and Montez, and had even endeavored to deprive their victims of the right to appeal to this tribunal. Giddings said, —

"The question was one which struck at the very existence of slavery. Were these degraded, ignorant, superstitious heathen entitled to life and liberty? Had the Creator endowed them with these prerogatives? These questions constituted the momentous issue to be tried. The court, clad in judicial robes; the distinguished Attorney-General and numerous members of the Bar; Governor Baldwin, acting as prisoner's counsel for the Africans, associated with Mr. Adams, who had long since left the Presidential chair with the honors and blessings of a nation; the vast audience, the solemn bearing and dignity of the court and officers, — all conspired to render the proceeding one of high moral sublimity."

Mr. Adams proved himself equal to his work. The great cause inspired him with unwonted strength, and there was perfect silence during his argument of eight hours' duration. His effort was honorable alike to his humanity and his patriotism. He had fought a good fight; and when, after full deliberation, the court pronounced his clients legally free, the measure of his satisfaction was complete. The decision was a severe blow to Van Buren's Administration and to the oligarchy he had so crouchingly served; but to have decided otherwise would have been a legal monstrosity,— it would have been the open espousal of a traffic which the nation had branded as piracy. And yet Charles J. Ingersoll, of Pennsylvania, Chairman of the Committee on Foreign Affairs in the House of Representatives, afterwards introduced a bill appropriating seventy thousand dollars for the payment of the piratical claim of Ruiz and Montez. The bill was accompanied by an elaborate report; but both received their quietus, after a masterly speech by Mr. Giddings, exposing the illegality and baseness of the claim.

When the Twenty-sixth Congress met, on the 2d of December, 1839, party spirit was rampant, party lines were strictly drawn, and the caucus was king. No member was expected to avow any doctrine or policy without its approval. The Democrats controlled all the departments of the government; but their ascendency in the House at this session was rendered uncertain by a contest of the seats of five members from New Jersey, who brought with them the regular gubernatorial certificate of their election. The clerk of the House, according to custom, called the members to order and began the roll-call. When he reached New Jersey, he called the name of one member from that State, and then said there were five other seats which were contested, and that not feeling authorized to decide the dispute, he would pass over the names of the New Jersey members, and proceed with the roll till the House should be organized, when the question could be decided. This apparent fairness was really an unwarranted assumption of power. It was his sole business to call the names of those persons who presented the customary formal credentials, having no right to take cognizance of the fact that the seats of such persons might be the subject of a contest. He was undoubtedly the servant of his party in this proceeding, for so evenly was the House divided that the admission or exclusion of these five members in the first instance would determine the political complexion of the body. The members holding the certificates were Whigs, and if the clerk could keep them out until the organization of the House should be completed, the Democrats would elect their Speaker and make up the committees.

This proceeding raised a fearful storm. The clerk said he could put no question, not even of adjournment, till the House should be formed, while his own election as clerk depended upon his course. The wrangle continued till the 5th of December, and threatened serious consequences, but was at last ended by the sudden consent of all parties that Mr. Adams should come to their relief. He accordingly addressed the House, and offered a resolution "ordering the clerk to call the members from New Jersey possessing the credentials from the governor of that

State." The question was now raised: "How shall the question be put?" "I intend to put the question myself," said Adams. Rhett, of South Carolina, opposed this, and offered a resolution that Williams, of North Carolina, be appointed chairman of the meeting; but Williams objected, and the name of Adams was substituted. There was nearly a universal shout in the affirmative, and Rhett and Williams conducted Adams to the chair. His service was difficult and stormy, and did not terminate till the 16th of December, when Hunter, of Virginia, was chosen Speaker.

This incident fairly indicates the spirit in which both parties entered upon the work of this session, and the reason why the question of slavery was less engrossing than during the previous Congress. Party was paramount in all things. The Presidential election was approaching, and members of both parties had an eye single to the struggle. On the subject of slavery the South acted as a unit, while Northern members of both parties deferred to their Southern brethren, who thus ruled their respective organizations. Mr. Adams was nominally a Whig, but in fact an Independent. Mr. Slade, of Vermont, was a Whig, had held office in the State Department during the Administration of Adams, and was an ardent supporter of his party; but he was an antislavery man from conviction, and generally a follower of Adams. Giddings had served only one session, and was regarded as a Whig of doubtful character, on account of his anti-slavery action. Another member now entered Congress as an avowed supporter of human rights. This was Seth M. Gates, of Genesee County, New York, a lawyer of reputation, of high moral character, and an unflinching supporter of what he believed to be right. These four members stood aloof from political parties when subjects involving moral principle or the rights of humanity were in issue. Many Northern Whigs sympathized with them, but none were ready to sustain them at the sacrifice of party allegiance.

At no time in the history of the government had the supremacy of slavery been so unquestioned as during this first session of the Twenty-sixth Congress. As soon as the committees of the House were announced, Mr. Wise moved a resolution declaring that whenever any petition, resolution, or paper should be presented touching the abolition of slavery or the slave-trade in the District of Columbia or in the Territories of the United States, the question of reception should be made, and that question laid on the table. This resolution was adopted by the House, and the right of petition and freedom of debate on the subject of slavery thus again suppressed. The Democrats charged the Whigs with favoring Abolitionism; and to counteract these efforts Mr. Clay again addressed the Senate on the subject in defence of his party against this charge, and was again complimented by Calhoun. In the Florida War, which was then in progress, bloodhounds from Cuba had been imported and employed by the Government in the work of capturing fugitive Indians and slaves. The Whigs denounced this, in the hope of making party capital out of it, but not upon anti-slavery grounds. Garrett Davis of Kentucky offered resolutions calling on the Executive to open negotiations with the British Government, and if possible obtain a treaty by which fugitive slaves should be surrendered, or their value paid to the master by the Government of England. The domestic slave-trade was becoming more profitable, and the vigilance of Mr. Calhoun was now shown in a case which invites particular attention in following the march of the slaveocracy towards supremacy.

A ship called the "Enterprise," built for the transportation of slaves from the District of Columbia to New Orleans and other ports far south, cleared from the port of Alexandria on the 22d of January, 1835, for the port of Charleston, with a cargo of slaves collected principally in the District of Columbia. Encountering severe storms, she was driven out of her course, and having suffered severely in her rigging, put into Port Hamilton, Bermuda, for repairs. According to the law of nations, the jurisdiction of every independent government is co-extensive with its own territory, and reaches a marine league into the sea. If a ship comes into the port of another nation she is boarded by the health-officer of the port long before reaching the shore; licensed pilots and revenue officers enter on board, call for bills of health, manifests, and information as to her cargo. The persons on board are amenable to the local laws. And such was the case with the slaves on board the "Enterprise" when they entered Port Hamilton. They were no longer subject to the local law of slavery, but under the protection of British laws, and were therefore free. The captain demanded of the local authorities their help in holding them in bondage; but as British laws recognized no such distinction as master and slave, no such help could be granted.

The slave-merchants returned to Washington and laid their complaints before General Jackson, who at once espoused their cause and demanded of the British Government compensation for the loss. To this demand the British minister replied that by the law of nations the ship, on entering Port Hamilton, became subject to British laws, and that there was in that port no law of slavery, and no British officer could recognize the right of one man to hold another as *property*. Smarting under this fling at the barbarism of slavery, Calhoun presented to the Senate three propositions, declaratory, as he said, of the law of nations.

The first asserted that "a ship or vessel on the high seas in time of peace, engaged in a lawful voyage, is, by the law of nations, under the exclusive jurisdiction of the State to which her flag belongs."

The second declared that "should such a ship be forced, by stress of weather or other unavoidable accident, into a friendly port, she would lose none of her rights pertaining to her on the high seas. On the contrary, she and her cargo, and the persons on board, with their *property*, and all the rights belonging to their personal relations as established by the laws of the State to which they belong, would be under the protection which the law of nations extends to the unfortunate under such circumstances."

The third asserted that "the brig 'Enterprise,' which was unavoidably forced by stress of weather into Port Hamilton, Bermuda, *while on a lawful voyage* on the high seas from one port of the United States to another, comes within the principles of the foregoing resolution, and that the seizure and detention of the negroes by the local authorities of that island was an act in *violation* of the laws of nations, and highly unjust to our citizens, to whom they belonged."

These propositions were briefly debated, and then referred to the Committee on Foreign Affairs; and in a few days reported back favorably, with slight amendments, by Mr. Buchanan. The report says, among other things, that "wherever the flag goes, the country is. In whatever distant seas or foreign ports, wherever the national flag floats, there is the nation."

This was a deliberate attempt to change the law of nations by resolution of the Senate, and the declared purpose was to nationalize an institution local to the States in which it existed, and borrowing its life from State laws. The resolutions were advocated by Calhoun, Clay, and Benton, who spoke of the claims of slavery in tones of injured innocence, and with an assumption which fairly implied that these novel and revolutionary doctrines were self-evident truths. They were opposed only by Mr. Porter, of Michigan, who had just taken his seat in the Senate. He was a lawyer by profession, and a man of character, but had attained no distinction as a statesman. He spoke well, but timidly, as if conscious that he stood alone, and suspected the soundness of his own opinions in confronting the united wisdom of so many eminent men. He moved to lay the resolutions on the table, and he alone voted for the motion, while every Senator from the Slave States, and Messrs. Allen and Tappan, of Ohio; Buchanan and Sturgeon, of Pennsylvania; Dixon, of Rhode Island; Hubbard and Pierce, of New Hampshire; Robinson and Young, of Illinois; Williams and Powell, of Maine, voted with the slave-holders; and Webster and Davis, of Massachusetts; Southard and Wall, of New Jersey; Wright and Tallmage, of New York; Ruggles, of Maine; Smith and White, of Indiana; and Knight, of Rhode Island, declined voting. The Senate was divided as follows: for the resolutions, 33; against them, 1; neither for nor against them, 10, with one vacancy and five absent. The resolutions were then adopted by 33 yeas, none voting in the negative.

Such was the humiliating record made by the Senate of the United States on the 15th of April, 1840. It will be read with amazement by coming generations. If any legal principle could then be regarded as absolutely settled, — settled by the law of nations, the common law, and the whole current of English and American decisions, — it was that slavery is the creature of positive law, and is confined to the territorial jurisdiction in which it exists. But the habit of submission to its demands had become so chronic, and it had so long fed upon the virtue of our public men, that the Senate, without one dissenting vote, repudiated this principle. But there were men in the lower branch of Congress who refused to wear the shackles of slavery, and did not spare the wretched sophistry of these Senate resolutions. In the admirable speech of Giddings already referred to, he thus deals with the logic of Calhoun and his retainers: —

"By the laws of Cuba the master may flog his slave, may sell him. Would the authorities of New York look on and see a Spanish slave-holder flog his slaves, or commit violence upon them? Would they listen to the shrieks of the slave in such a case, and remain silent? Is New York liable to be converted into a slave-market in that way? If the slave resist the violence of the master in Cuba, the master may shoot him down. If he do it at the wharf in New York, would the people there look on, with their arms folded, saying, 'It is done under the Spanish laws;' or would they say, in the words of this report, 'The act was committed in Spain, for Spain is at our wharf'?

"Agreeably to this doctrine, a Brazilian slave-ship fastens to a wharf in New York. The people of that city go on board, find the decks stowed full of emaciated, starving Africans, suffering all the horrors incident to that disgusting traffic. Those who appear too far gone to be regarded as profitable stock are thrown overboard while yet in life; those who exhibit signs of discontent are flogged; and those who resist are shot down, or murdered with a bowie-knife or cutlass. This is all done at the wharf, in plain view of the people. But the Brazilian flag floats at the mast. Brazil is there, and Brazilian laws are in force, and the people must permit these much-abused slave-dealers to be guided by their own sense of justice.

"Sir, suppose a slave-ship from South Carolina, or any other sister State, were to enter the port of Boston, from stress of weather. would the laws of Massachusetts lend their protection to the slave-dealers? If the slaves should rise in a body and come on shore in pursuit of their freedom, would the officers of that State, or the people of Boston, be bound to pursue such fugitives through the streets of that city? Or, if in pursuit of freedom they were to seek sanctuary in Faneuil Hall, that old cradle of liberty, would the good people of that patriotic Commonwealth seize them and drag them forth, replace them on board the slave-ships, and deliver them over to the tender mercies of piratical dealers in human flesh? If they were to lend their protection to the personal relations of those on board, as established by the laws of South Carolina, they must do this; yet I cannot believe that any slave-holding Senator, who gave his vote in favor of these resolutions, would advocate such doctrine before the country. Nor do I believe that any Northern Senator, who sat in silence when that vote was taken, would now publicly admit the correctness of such doctrines. It was a most unfortunate attempt of the Senate to change the law of nations. They overstepped the bounds of their power and of their influence. They will regret the vote. Their descendants, in coming time, will blush when they read the record of that act."

The Harrison campaign of 1840 was chiefly remarkable for its indescribable drollery and grotesqueness. Its talisman was "hard times" and "hard cider," and its rallying cry "Tippecanoe and Tyler too." It was a huge national frolic. The Whig candidate, singularly enough, was not a Whig, but was nominated solely on the ground of his availability. His followers avowed no principles whatever, and they tendered but one issue, and that was the necessity for a change of the national administration. The demand for this change was well founded, for the spoils system, inaugurated by Jackson, was completely in the ascendant, and the corruptions and defalcations of Van Buren's Administration called loudly for reform. But the mistake of the Whigs was in assuming that a change would be equivalent to a cure, thus begging the very question on which some satisfactory assurance was required. They did not perceive that a mere change of men, without any change of system, would be fruitless, and that the superior virtue and patriotism of the Whigs could not be taken for granted. But the cry of "hard times" had a wonderful potency, while the working-classes were constantly comforted by the promise of "two dollars a day and roast beef," if Harrison should be elected.

In the political whirlwind which swept over the country during this struggle, the question of slavery had little chance to be heard; and yet the logic of the situation called for the organized political action of anti-slavery men against the candidates of both parties, who were alike untrustworthy. Van Buren, as we have seen, had attempted to shelter the slave-trade under the national flag. He had taken sides with the enemies of the right of petition and the freedom of debate, in order to conciliate the South. He had stood by Jackson in his lawless interference with the mails at the bidding of slave-holders. He had fairly illustrated his character as "a Northern man with Southern principles."

General Harrison, on the other hand, was a pro-slavery Virginian. While Governor of Indiana Territory, he had repeatedly sought the introduction of slavery into that region through the suspension of the ordinance of 1787. He had joined hands with the South in 1820 on the Missouri question. He had no sympathy with the struggle of Adams and his associates against the gag and for the right of petition, and regarded the discussion of the slavery question as unconstitutional. He had declared that "the schemes of the Abolitionists were fraught with horrors upon which an incarnate devil only could look with approbation."

With such candidates it was easy to see why well-informed anti-slavery men could not support them, and why they should insist upon inaugurating the movement which was finally to triumph at the ballot-box. Indeed, political action against slavery had been clearly contemplated and provided for by the American Anti-slavery Society at its historic convention in Philadelphia, in December, 1833. Its platform declared that Congress "is solemnly bound to suppress the domestic slave-trade between the several States, and to abolish slavery in those portions of our territory which the Constitution has placed under its exclusive jurisdiction." Of course this would require the agencies of politics.

But the anti-slavery men of the country now divided upon the question of forming a political anti-slavery party. A large division of them, under the lead of Mr. Garrison, argued that such a party would compromise the moral power of the cause by entangling it with the evils of place-seeking and demagogism. The reply to this argument was that it proved too much. The logic of it condemned popular government itself, and thus sought to cure the vices of politics by abjuring political action altogether. It was further urged that moral power alone could not destroy slavery, and that other and diverse agencies were necessary, including the use of the ballot both as a duty and a necessity. If existing parties declined this duty, a third party seemed to be the only alternative, and could not be disowned on the plea that it would fall under the control of political mercenaries. It was an absurdity to suppose that in a government carried on by the ballot, slavery could be destroyed without political action.

The voting Abolitionists, accordingly, nominated for the Presidency Hon. James G. Birney, of Kentucky, a lawyer and a man of high moral character, who had emancipated his own bondmen, and openly avowed his hostility to the institution. There was, however, some disagreement respecting the timeliness of this nomination. A considerable number divided their votes between the regular candidates, the greater portion giving their support to General Harrison. This is explained by the fact that the record of the party candidates was not then understood as it is to-day, and that the overshadowing power of slavery strangely darkened the minds of men. The issue of slavery was a new one in our politics, and anti-slavery men themselves were often obliged to grope their way in the bewilderment of the times. The situation was fairly indicated by two letters to Giddings from prominent and representative anti-slavery men belonging to different sections of the Union. The first is from Dr. Gamaliel Bailey, editor of the "Philanthropist," at Cincinnati, and better known afterwards as the editor and publisher of the "National Era" at Washington, D. C. He was singularly well informed, conscientious, and clear-sighted, and few men rendered more effective service to the anti-slavery cause than did he during his labors of more than forty years. His lettter is dated Jan. 15, 1840, in which he says,—

"Much anxiety is expressed respecting the course we may think proper to take in regard to the nomination of General Harrison. So far I have kept silence; but I shall be compelled, I foresee, to say something. I think, on the whole, a tolerably fair case may be made out for the General. I had the pleasure of a visit from him the other day. He was in fine health and good spirits. I am inclined to think a defeat would not break his heart. He seems to be fully aware that the action of Abolitionists may to a great extent determine the result of the election. The interview, on the whole, made an impression on me favorable to the General's views on the great question of human rights. I hardly think that he would suffer himself, if elected, to be used by the slaveholding interest. However, he would require good advisers.

"As to the project of a separate political party, I think it will fail. Myron Holley's paper has been discontinued for want of support; so that the only papers now which advocate the measure are the 'Emancipator' and 'Massachusetts Abolitionist.' Lewis Tappan wrote to me that my article on the subject had given general satisfaction in New York. . . . I hope you will continue to furnish me with everything interesting connected with our cause."

This letter, like the one from General Harrison, of December, 1838, already quoted, reveals a strong disposition on his part to make fair weather with the Abolitionists, notwithstanding his intense hostility to their principles. He seems to have been conquering his prejudices, while at the same time conquering the prejudices of Dr. Bailey.

The other letter is from Lewis Tappan, of New York, and dated Feb. 17, 1840. As a pioneer and leader in the anti-slavery cause he was quite as well known as Dr. Bailey, and his equal in sagacity, courage, and fidelity to principle. He was a member of the executive committee of the American Anti-slavery Society, of which his brother, Arthur Tappan, was the first president. Among other things, he says,—

"It is quite possible the Abolitionists are inattentive to some of the signs of the times. They know well that Mr. Van Buren has pledged himself to the pro-slavery side of the question, and that the leading supporters of his Administration act in accordance with his base subserviency to the South. He acts upon the principle, many years ago avowed, that, by uniting the Democracy of the South with the Democracy of the North, or a portion of both, he could maintain his ascendency. The largest portion of his party, including some who have professed to be Abolitionists, are base enough to imitate him. This is one sign. Another is that the Whigs, though professing to be the friends of freedom of discussion, the right of petition, the cause of universal liberty, yet will not jeopard the principles of their party when they and abolition come in collision. The Whigs, it is true, opposed Johnson's execrable resolution, and so have the Van Buren men in the Legislature of this State; their constituents forced them to do it. But, my dear sir, if the Whigs are resolute for human rights, why did they nominate for President General Harrison, who has declared his opposition to such principles in unequivocal language? Why have they not rebuked Mr. Monroe, of this city, for his infamous speech on abolition? Why has Mr. Clay been suffered to denounce the friends of human rights in his place unrebuked? Why have Webster and Davis been dumb when liberty has been cloven down in the Senate? In a word, why has not the Whig party come out manfully in favor of the anti-slavery cause, sink or swim? Oh, it is because they execrate the cause, — that is, many of the leading papers and politicians. Look at the leading Whig papers in this city, for example. I have no more confidence in one party than in another on this question, although I acknowledge that the Whigs have been more friendly to us than the Van Buren men. If the union of the North on this subject is inevitable, as you think, why do not the leading men of the party openly and fearlessly announce the fact? If they do not speedily, a new political party will be formed, and that soon. I have done all I could to prevent it; but the tendency that way is strong, and perhaps irresistible. I fully believe that if the Whigs should honestly and courageously take this ground, they would have great accessions; but if they do not, they are ruined.

"I have thus very hastily given you my views, as you desired. It is a long time since I have been in the harness of party, and perhaps you may think I reason very foolishly. But I trust they are the reflections of an honest man, — one who is straightforward; for principles rather than men; for moral principles at all hazards, and for considering all other questions as subsidiary. If slavery continues, we are a ruined people. Destroy that, and there is some chance that we shall be a righteous and happy people."

It is not surprising that the votes of anti-slavery men throughout the country were divided and scattered in this canvass, when their leaders were unable to agree. It was a season of political chaos, prophetic of new formations out of which the truth was slowly to be evolved. This correspondence shows that Giddings was seriously considering the question of duty in the excitement and uproar of this memorable canvass; but, like his anti-slavery colleagues in the House, and the great body of his Whig constituents, he gave his support to General Harrison, who was elected by an overwhelming majority, and whose attitude towards the anti-slavery men, with whom he had been holding dalliance, was soon to be tested. Mr. Birney received only seven thousand votes. It was a small beginning, but it filled the slaveholders with alarm. They saw that it inaugurated abolitionism as a working force in our politics, and that it had come to stay; and whatever may be said in criticism of the mistakes or shortcomings of the Liberty party, or of the larger parties which succeeded it, the pregnant fact remains that the steadily growing power of organized political action at last drove the slave oligarchy into the madness of rebellion and self-destruction.

The second session of the Twenty-sixth Congress assembled under novel circumstances. The Democrats, who had long been in power, were soon to retire, and the responsibilities of the government were to devolve upon the Whigs. The question of slavery had not been an issue in the late national struggle, but there was still some feeling of curiosity as to the position which the incoming President might choose to occupy. Mr. Adams, on the first day of the session, gave notice of his intention to move a repeal of the "gag resolution," which was now known as the 21st rule of the House; but this was not accomplished. The continued suppression of the freedom of debate was keenly felt by Giddings and his associates during this session, and on Feb. 8, 1841, he proposed to test the extent to which they would be permitted to discuss subjects *collaterally* involving the question of slavery. He selected the Florida War as his subject, and so prepared his remarks as to give them a direct bearing upon a bill just introduced by Mr. Thompson of South Carolina, appropriating one hundred thousand dollars for the removal of certain Seminole chiefs and warriors west of the Mississippi.

Giddings obtained the floor after Thompson had spoken, and at once proceeded to develop the *cause* of the war, and the object of its continuance. He quoted the authority of Mr. Thompson, the Indian agent, to show that the Seminoles refused to go west, lest the negroes, who had so long resided with them, should be seized and enslaved by the Creeks; that the object of constraining the Seminoles to emigrate was to enslave them; and that to effect this piratical object the nation had been plunged into war. He denied that the Government was endeavoring to remove these Indians for the purpose of occupying their lands, and quoted the authority of General Jessup for the statement that "these lands would not pay for the medicines used by our troops while employed against the Indians."

These facts had never before been brought to the attention of the public, and they were very offensive to Southern members. Mr. Warren of Georgia called Giddings to order; but the chairman, Mr. Clifford, a Democrat from Maine, declared the remarks to be strictly in order. This gave him confidence, and Mr. Adams showed his interest in the discussion by leaving his seat and taking a position in front of the clerk's desk, where he watched every movement of Southern members, now gathered around Giddings, who proceeded to read further documents sustaining his position that the Florida War had been waged by the Government to aid the slaveholders in the capture of runaway slaves, and for the enslavement of Indians and negroes who were free. He showed that a large portion of the fugitives from Georgia, who fled prior to 1802, intermarried with the Seminoles, or Southern Creek Indians, and that the Government, by treaty in 1821, compelled the Creeks to pay for these fugitives; that the Creeks, supposing they had thus acquired a good title to them from the United States, claimed the wives and children of the Seminoles, who, however, finally refused to remove west, preferring to remain and fight the whites rather than hazard the loss of their wives and children by becoming again incorporated with the Creeks; and that the interests of the Florida slaveholders required that the Seminoles should be compelled to emigrate, which the United States undertook to accomplish. He further proved, by official documents, that $141,000, which rightfully belonged to the Indians, was paid to the slaveholders by the Government as compensation for the children of fugitive slaves *who would have been born to their masters if their parents had remained in servitude.*

Mr. Habersham of Georgia called him to order, on the ground that his remarks were not relevant to the bill. Giddings explained that he had no intention of discussing the question of slavery; that he did not expect to examine its merits or demerits, nor even to pronounce it right or wrong; and that he only intended to show that it constituted the cause of the

Florida War, while neither Congress nor the Federal Government had any authority under the Constitution to involve the people of the nation in a bloody war to support the institution.

He then read reports of the Indian agent to show that persons residing with the Seminoles, though born free, had been seized and enslaved by desperate men from Columbus, Georgia; that a number of men, headed by one Douglass, who kept a pack of bloodhounds, had invaded the Indian plantation, seized whole families of free colored persons, carried them to Georgia, and sold them as slaves. In reference to this he said, —

"Our army was put in motion to capture negroes and slaves. Our officers and soldiers became slave-catchers, companions of the most degraded class of human beings who disgrace that slave-cursed region. With the assistance of bloodhounds they tracked the flying bondman over hill and dale, through swamp and everglade, until his weary limbs could sustain him no longer. Then they seized him, and for the bounty of twenty dollars he was usually delivered over to the first white man who claimed him. Our troops became expert in this business of hunting and enslaving mankind. I doubt whether the Spanish pirates, engaged in the same employment on the African coast, are more perfect masters of their vocation. Nor was our army alone engaged in this war upon human rights. They merely followed the example of a class of land-pirates who are ever ready to rob or murder when they can do so with impunity."

Giddings proceeded to show by documentary evidence that the people of Florida understood the great object of the war to be the capture of fugitive slaves, and that the Government had lent itself to their services. He quoted an order issued by General Jessup declaring that "all Indian property captured from this date will belong to the corps or detachment making it," and showed by a letter from the general, written a few days later, that the word "property," as used in said order, meant "*negroes*, cattle, and horses." This order bears date Aug. 3, 1837. In reference to it Giddings said, —

"I think that history will record this as the first general order issued by the commander of an American army in which the catching of slaves is held out as an incentive to military duty. I mention this fact, and bring it to the consideration of the committee, with feelings of deep mortification. As an American I feel humbled at this act, which cannot be viewed by the civilized world otherwise than as dishonorable to our arms and nation. That this officer, intrusted with the command of our army and the honor of our flag, should appeal to the cupidity, the desire of plunder, and the worst of human passions, in order to stimulate his men to effort, is, I think, to be regretted by men of all parties in all sections of our country. Our national flag, which floated in proud triumph at Saratoga, which was enveloped in a blaze of glory at Monmouth and Yorktown, seems to have been prostituted in Florida to the base purpose of leading on an organized company of 'negro-catchers.' Sir, no longer is 'our country' the battle-cry of our army in their advance to victory, but 'slaves' has become the watchword to inspire them to effort. No longer does the war-worn veteran, amid the battle's rage, think of his country's glory and nerve his arm in behalf of freedom, but with eagle eye he watches the wavering ranks of the enemy, and as they flee before our advancing columns, he plunges among them to seize the sable foe, and make him his future slave."

Giddings next refers to another order of General Jessup, dated Sept. 6, 1837, declaring that "Seminole negroes captured by the army will be taken on account of Government and held subject to the order of the Secretary of War," and that the sum of twenty dollars from the public funds will be allowed to the captor of each fugitive. This order was approved by the Secretary of War on the 7th of October following. The people of the United States, through the efforts of their accredited officers, thus became the purchasers and holders of slaves, and the nation a slaveholding nation. Said Giddings,—

"In this manner we have been led on by slaveholding influences, step by step, until we find our government and nation involved in the crime of holding slaves. The people have been kept ignorant of these facts. No solitary voice has been raised to inform them of these violations of their rights, of the rights of humanity and of the Constitution, of this stain upon our nation's honor. It further appears that the people of the United States, — the laborers of Ohio and other free States, — have been compelled to contribute of their hard earnings to pay a bounty of twenty dollars for each negro captured and delivered to the white people as a slave."

In this connection he refers to the alacrity with which the commanding general entered into the business of slave-catching, as shown by his letter of May 25, 1837, directed to Lieutenant-Colonel Harney:

"If you see Powell [Osceola], tell him I shall send out and take all the negroes who belong to the white people; and he must not allow the Indian negroes to mix with them. Tell him I am sending to Cuba for bloodhounds to trail them; and I intend to hang every one of them who does not come in."

Of this letter Giddings says, —

"If the negroes had quietly suffered themselves to be trailed with bloodhounds, or supinely permitted themselves to be hanged for their love of liberty, they would have deserved the name of slaves. The expenditure of five thousand dollars for bloodhounds in Cuba was not, as has been supposed, for the purpose of trailing Indians. In this letter we have it officially announced that they were sent for and obtained for the purpose of *catching fugitive slaves*. I desire the people of this nation to understand distinctly that they are taxed for the purpose of maintaining and supporting slavery in the Slave States; that their treasure has been appropriated directly and publicly to that purpose; that our army — many of whose officers and soldiers were bred in the Free States and in the love of liberty — has been employed, by order of the commanding general, in pursuing and capturing fugitive slaves. Nor is that all. The freemen of the North are taxed for the purchase of bloodhounds to act in concert with our army in this disgraceful and disgusting mode of conducting the war."

This speech proved exceedingly exasperating to Southern members, and Giddings was frequently interrupted by questions of order and incidental debate, which consumed three hours; but he finally concluded what he desired to say. In his diary of this date, Mr. Adams says Giddings "proceeded step by step, citing his documentary proof as he went along, to the exquisite torture of the Southern duellists and slave-mongers, Georgians, Carolinians, and Virginians." Mr. Cooper of Georgia replied, saying that he regarded the speech as altogether aimed at slavery. He spoke of abolition as a "moral pestilence," to be condemned by all good men. He referred to Adams and Giddings as leaders in the Abolition ranks, while they were encouraged and cheered on by the Whig party; and he particularly charged General Harrison with encouraging Abolitionists, and thus involving the Whig party of Georgia in the odium of supporting the right of all men to liberty. He alluded to the case of a vessel from Maine that had carried a slave from Georgia, when the Chair called him to order.

Mr. Black of Georgia insisted that Giddings had made an anti-slavery speech, and that Mr. Cooper ought to be allowed to reply. Mr. Adams also interposed, saying the gentleman had made a pointed allusion to him, and he hoped to enjoy the privilege of replying. Mr. Wise of Virginia sustained Black, and on an appeal the House sustained him, and Cooper proceeded to arraign the authorities of Maine as Abolitionists. Black next obtained the floor, and at once arraigned Ohio for her cruelty to the colored people. He was called to order, decided to be out of order, but permitted by a vote of the House to proceed. He was nervously excited, declaring that he intended to be personally offensive to Giddings, and holding a copy of the Bible in his hand, read: "Thou hypocrite, first cast the beam out of thine own eye," as he pointed his finger directly at the object of his wrath. He assured the House that if the member from Ohio (Giddings) should come to Georgia, he would be hanged.

Mr. Downing, the delegate from Florida, next obtained the floor, and out-rivalled Black in vulgar assaults upon Giddings. Mr. Thompson of South Carolina was more refined in his language, declaring that the Whig party was not responsible for the course pursued by "the very obscurest of the obscure individuals belonging to that party.". Giddings replied that every member of Congress would select the position which he chose to occupy before the people; and he would inform the gentleman from South Carolina that he did not possess the power to designate the position which other members should fill in the public mind, although he must choose his own. He said he well understood the insult offered by the gentleman from South Carolina, but he could not resent it in the manner common among Southern gentlemen, as the people of the Free States would not permit their public servants to practise that barbarous mode of settling difficulties; and if they would, his own conscience would not permit it. But he would say to the gentleman, in the language of a military veteran who, after meeting the enemy in a hundred battles, happened to offend a young officer, who spat in his face, expecting to call out a challenge: "Could I as easily wipe the stain of your blood from my soul [wiping the spittle from his face with his handkerchief], *you should not live an hour.*" Mr. Alford of Georgia sprang from his seat, uttering profuse threats, and rushed towards Giddings with apparently hostile intentions; but when he arrived within a few feet of him, Governor Briggs of

Massachusetts stopped him, and persuaded him to return to his seat. To Mr. Downing no reply could be made consistent with self-respect; but when that gentleman next approached him with the ordinary salutation of friends, Giddings refused to give him his hand, assuring him that he was at liberty to address him on official business, but on no other pretence whatever.

This speech proved an invaluable agency in the political education of the people. It breathed a new life into the anti-slavery cause. The startling facts it embodied were for the first time dragged to light from their hiding-place among musty executive documents, and put on public duty. The curtain was lifted upon a frightful spectacle of maladministration, showing that the Federal Government, which was established to secure the blessings of liberty, had long been prostituted to the base purpose of upholding and perpetuating the curses of slavery. While it maddened the slaveholders by uncovering the record of their lawlessness and calling them to their reckoning, the people of the Free States were astounded at their own supineness in thus tamely submitting to Southern usurpation. They saw that custom and the insidious policy of gradual encroachment had made slavery their master, and that Jackson and Van Buren had only conformed to the fashion of the times in allowing it to dictate the entire policy of the Government respecting the Florida War. The speech was published in large editions, liberally scattered over the country, and could not fail to become a potent auxiliary in the cause of reform. Henceforward it was certain that the slaveocracy would be watched, while Giddings earned the gratitude of his country and of coming generations by this timely public service. It called forth the following letter from the venerable William Jay: —

NEW YORK, 623 Broadway, Feb. 22, 1841.

SIR, — I had the honor of receiving your letter at Bedford, West Chester County, the place of my residence, it having been forwarded to me from this city; but the document mentioned in it did not accompany it. The next day I left home for this place, where I expect to remain some weeks. I beg you to accept my thanks, not merely for your polite attention to myself, but also for your fearless exposure on the floor of Congress of the iniquities connected with the war in Florida.

May I ask the favor of you, sir, to forward to my present address another copy of the document in question, together with a report of your speech and of the debate to which it gave rise. Our New York papers seem indisposed to give the public full information on the subject.

I have the honor to be, sir, with very great respect,
Your obedient servant,
WILLIAM JAY.

The HON. MR. GIDDINGS.

General Harrison reached Washington on the day of this memorable debate, and when he heard of it expressed great dissatisfaction, declaring that he would relieve the Whig party of all odium brought upon it by the action of Giddings. When the latter called on the President-elect, on the following day, he met with such evidence of displeasure that he never afterwards repeated the call, although he had labored earnestly for the Whig cause in the previous canvass. Mr. Thompson, who had publicly insulted Giddings for maintaining the freedom of speech, was rewarded with a mission to Mexico, although South Carolina had given no vote for General Harrison. Giddings and his anti-slavery colleagues in the House were still further disappointed by the inaugural address of the President, the original draft of which was so offensive to the advocates of the right of petition and the freedom of debate that even Mr. Clay protested against it, and prevailed on the General so to modify it that it meant nothing, and was of course inoffensive. Such was the outcome of anti-slavery hopes and expectations touching the action of the new President.

CHAPTER V.

MARCH, 1841, TO DECEMBER, 1842.

Meeting of the Twenty-seventh Congress. — Trial of John Quincy Adams. — The Case of the "Creole" and Censure of Giddings. — Letters from Mr. Chase. — The "Pacificus" Papers. — Weary of Public Life.

THE Twenty-seventh Congress was convened in special session on the 31st of May, 1841. There was a Whig majority of forty in the House, and seven in the Senate; but as no principles had been avowed in the preceding canvass, and as John Tyler, who had now become President, had been chosen by the Whigs solely on the ground of his availability as a Southern man, it was not strange that the party now became divided into warring factions. John White of Kentucky was chosen Speaker, and after the House was organized, Mr. Adams renewed his efforts to abrogate the 21st, or gag, rule; but failed, as heretofore. He, however, was made chairman of the Committee on Foreign Affairs, while Giddings was placed at the head of the Committee on Claims. Mr. Wise complained of this, and said that Giddings would never report a bill to pay a master for the loss of his slave, if killed in the public service. Several members, seeing Giddings present, asked Wise to question him on the subject. "I will," said Mr. Wise; and turning to Giddings, said: "I will ask the chairman if he would report a bill to pay a master for the loss of a slave killed in the public service." Giddings replied: "I cannot say what the committee might do, but I should myself follow the precedents, which are uniform from the commencement of the government." Mr. Wise said he was aware that the precedents were against such payment, but they were wrong, and he was anxious to correct the error.

During this special session and the regular session which followed in December, Southern members became more and more irritable, and their Northern sympathizers more uneasy. The social relations of members were seriously disturbed, and the Florida War speech had so embittered the feeling towards Giddings that there were not probably a dozen slaveholding members who recognized him on the street or in the Hall of Representatives. This feeling extended in a less degree to Slade and Gates; but the position of Mr. Adams placed him beyond the reach of these puerile attempts, and he quietly devoted himself to the work of presenting anti-slavery petitions. They were of various kinds, and each provoked renewed hostility. One after another was laid on the table on motion of some Southern member; but he stood at his desk and patiently applied himself to his task, showing no sign of retiring from the conflict. Slade, Gates, and Giddings usually sat near him on these occasions, deeply concerned in what was passing; while Wise, Gilmer, Holmes, and others were on either hand, watching him with intense interest.

At length, on the 25th of January, 1842, he took from the file of papers before him the memorial of Benjamin Emerson and forty-five other citizens of Haverhill, in the State of Massachusetts, praying Congress to adopt immediate measures for the peaceful dissolution of the Union of these States, — first, because no union can be agreeable or permanent which does not present prospects of reciprocal benefits; second, because a vast proportion of the resources of one section of the Union is annually drained to sustain the views and course of another; third, because, judging from the history of past nations, if the present course be persisted in, it will overwhelm the nation in utter destruction." Mr. Adams moved the reference of this petition to a select committee of nine members, with instructions to report an answer to the petitioners, showing the reasons why the prayer of their petition cannot be granted.

The utter madness of Southern members in dealing with this petition can be most perfectly realized by keeping in mind a few significant facts. In the first place, Mr. Adams declared himself opposed to the object of the petition, and moved the appointment of a committee to report adversely, with their reasons therefor. In the next place, as Congress has power to propose amendments to the Constitution, it was perfectly legitimate for these petitioners to ask Congress to take measures for the peaceful reconstruction of the government as a means of escaping what they considered intolerable evils. In the third place, the howl which was set up against the introduction of this petition came from men who had repeatedly threatened to dissolve the Union, in order to redress their grievances,— not peaceably, as proposed in the petition presented by Mr. Adams, but by revolution and violence. Finally, the petition in this case was an exact copy of one presented some years before by South Carolina disunionists.

Mr. Hopkins of Virginia obtained the floor, and inquired of the Speaker if it would be in order to burn the petition in the presence of the House. Wise and Gilmer demanded that Mr. Adams should be formally censured, and Gilmer offered a resolution to that effect.

Southern members were completely carried away by the frenzy of their passions, and before the House adjourned, a caucus was called for that evening, to take measures looking to the trial and punishment of Mr. Adams. An effort was made to secure a meeting of Northern members who were willing to stand by him; but Northern Whigs generally replied that "it would look like a sectional quarrel." A few members friendly to him, however, convened that night at the room of Giddings. These were Slade and Young of Vermont, Calhoun of Massachusetts, Henry, Lawrence, and Simonton of Pennsylvania, and Gates and Chittenden of New York. Rev. Joshua Leavitt, of Boston, and Theodore D. Weld, of New Jersey, also attended, though they were not members, but zealous friends of Mr. Adams. These two gentlemen were appointed a committee to wait on him and inform him that they and the members convened would tender him any assistance in their power. At a late hour they repaired to his residence and stated the object of their visit. The old patriot listened attentively, and for a time was unable to reply, being apparently much affected. At length he stated that the voice of friendship was so unusual to his ears that he could not express his gratitude; but he would feel thankful if they would examine certain points to be found in the authors of which he gave them a list, and have the books placed on his desk at the hour of meeting the next day.

At that time Mr. Marshall of Kentucky, who had been selected by the Southern caucus to take the lead in the fight against Mr. Adams, introduced a series of resolutions, preceded by a long preamble, setting forth the "perjury and treason" to which Congress was invited by the petition. The last resolution declared "that the aforesaid John Quincy Adams for this insult, the first of the kind ever offered to the government, and for the wound he has permitted to be aimed, through his instrumentality, at the Constitution and existence of his country, the peace, security, and liberty of the people of these States, might well be held to merit expulsion from the national counsels; and the House deem it an act of grace and mercy when they only inflict upon him their severest censures for conduct so utterly unworthy of his own past relations to the State and his present position; this they hereby do, for the maintenance of their own purity and dignity; for the rest, they turn him over to his own conscience and the indignation of all true American citizens."

After a preliminary speech by Mr. Marshall, pretending to great moderation and fairness, Mr. Adams spoke briefly, causing to be read those passages in the Declaration of Independence which speak of the right of the people to alter or abolish their government when it becomes an insupportable burden, and reminding the slaveholders of their acts of usurpation threatening the liberties of the people. "If you had not violated the right of petition," said he, "you would never have seen this petition." Wise took the floor in reply, and was eager for the fight. He sent out the challenge, "Come on, Macduff, and damned be he who first cries, Hold, enough!" He spoke of Mr. Adams as "a white-haired hypocrite," and charged him with forsaking the friends of his father, and trampling on the ashes of the dead. He referred to him as one who, "in the fury of his apostate zeal, could prey upon the dead like the vampire." He declared that he was "dead as Burr, dead as Arnold," and that "the people would look upon him with wonder, would shudder, and retire." Mr. Marshall followed in an elaborate and able speech, but equally savage and remorseless in its spirit. Mr. Adams declined to enter upon his defence until the House determined whether it would consider the charges against him, which it decided to do by a vote of 118 to 75.

He now became the accuser, and arraigned the slaveholders at the bar of the nation for endeavoring to destroy the right of *habeas corpus*, of trial by jury, the freedom of the post-office, the liberty of speech, of the Press, and of petition. For the purpose of effecting these objects, he charged that they had formed a coalition with the Northern Democrats, and that if the rights of the Free States could not be otherwise protected, the petitioners were justified in asking for a dissolution of the Union. He charged South Carolina and other Slave States with seizing and enslaving free colored citizens of the Northern States, in violation of the Constitution. He exposed the effects of slavery upon the pecuniary interests of the country, comparing New York with Virginia, and contrasting the educational institutions of the Empire State with those of the Old Dominion; while he also contrasted the internal improvements, industry, and thrift of New York with the miserable highways, deserted plantations, dilapidated dwellings, and general poverty of Virginia. And he charged that a systematic effort was being made by the slaveholders to force the country into a war with England in order to maintain the African slave-trade.

"His manner," according to Giddings, "was calm and self-possessed; his voice clear and firm; his words measured; his venerable form erect under the weight of more than seventy years. There he stood, confronting a power which for more than half a century had controlled the councils of the nation." At times he was impassioned, and his invective unrivalled. He made no reply to Mr. Hopkins, who had suggested the burning of the petition, merely referring to him as "the combustible gentleman from Virginia." In reply to Wise, he referred to his connection with the duel in which Cilley of Maine had fallen, and pronounced him far more guilty than the man who pulled the trigger by which a brother member had been sent to find judgment. He declared that Wise had come to the House with his hands dripping with blood, and his face smeared with human gore; and that, with these evidences of murder upon his person, he had attempted to read moral lectures to members of the House. Giddings, in his account of the trial, says he was sitting near Wise at this time, and saw from his countenance the feelings which tortured him.

When Mr. Adams came to Marshall and his charge of high treason in presenting a petition, he suggested the propriety of his returning to Kentucky to *commence* the study of law. He made an allusion to his habits of immorality, and expressed an earnest desire that he might reform. He then proceeded to the work of torture. As he continued his remarks, he became more and more aroused, and drawing one arrow after another from his well-stored quiver, he sent them with unerring aim into the flesh of his victim, with no other apparent object than to see him writhe under the infliction. His eloquence became more glowing and his invective more impassioned, until his assailant was utterly demolished, and then he resumed his seat. A painful silence ensued. Marshall had been standing some thirty feet from Mr. Adams, his arms folded across his breast; but no effort could disguise the evidences of his humiliation. His cheeks were pale with emotion, and the whole contour of his face gave an expression of deep mortification. He declared afterwards that he would rather have suffered death than the torment to which he had been subjected. It was a chastisement as terrible as it was deserved, and it was not possible that he could ever forget it. On a subsequent occasion, when he entered the hall and found Mr. Adams replying with some severity to an attack by a member from Pennsylvania, Marshall, on learning the facts, replied, "Well, if he has fallen into Adams's hands, all I can say is, May God have mercy on his soul!" The trial continued from day to day, and the manifest strength and determination of Mr. Adams gave no promise of its speedy conclusion; while in answer to inquiries as to the time he would require to complete his defence, he intimated that it would be about ninety days.[1]

The slaveholders, seeing the tide turning against them under this arraignment of their own lawlessness, became weary of the spectacle and anxious to end it; and Mr. Gilmer proposed a compromise, by which further proceedings were to be abandoned, if Mr. Adams would withdraw the petition he had presented. This was indignantly refused. He defied the House, and spurned the proffered capitulation. He continued his defence, or rather his prosecution of the slaveholders, till the 7th of February, when, on motion of Mr. Botts of Virginia, the whole sub-

[1] Address of Mr. Giddings on the trial of John Q. Adams.

ject was laid on the table, by a vote of 106 to 93. Mr. Adams then proceeded to dispose of a budget of two hundred anti-slavery petitions, after which the House adjourned. On the 2d of March following, Giddings presented a petition from Austinburg, in Ohio, praying for a dissolution of the Union; but not a word was heard about censuring him, or the disgrace of the House, or the perjury or high treason involved in his act. The triumph of Mr. Adams was complete.

The interest in this famous duel between Mr. Adams and the slave-power seems to be heightened by time. That power was then lord of the ascendant, and Mr. Adams was dealt with as a felon and an outlaw; but he is now glorified as a hero and revered as a prophet. Slavery and its champions in 1842 have gone to their reckoning, and we survey their exploits from a new mount of vision. In the clear perspective of the past, the story of this outrage possesses more than the fascination of a romance. The following letter from Giddings to his wife, written while the trial was in progress, may therefore prove interesting to the reader. It is dated Feb. 6, 1842:

"Never in my life have I felt that the welfare of this mighty nation depended so much upon the efforts, courage, and determination of the friends of liberty as I have for the past week. Mr. Adams has spoken three days. He has won the friendship of the entire Whig party of the North, disarmed the Loco-focos of a portion of their hatred, conciliated the feelings of many, and has shown up the manner in which the slave interest has insidiously crept into our whole policy, subsidized our papers, poisoned our literature, invaded the sanctity of the post-office, degraded our patriotism, taxed the free labor of the North, frightened our statesmen, and controlled the nation. He is, I believe, the most extraordinary man living; but I cannot attempt a description either of him or his speech. Suffice it to say that he has made the entire South tremble before him. I have with my own eyes seen the slaveholders literally shake and tremble through every nerve and joint while he arrayed before them their political and moral sins. The power of his eloquence has exceeded any conception which I have heretofore had of the force of words or logic. He has, in my opinion, opened a new era in our political history. I entertain not the least doubt that a moral revolution in this nation will take its date from this session of Congress. I am confident that the charm of the slave-power *is now broken*. I may be too sanguine, — quite likely I am, — but such are my candid sentiments. The slaveholders naturally tremble lest their efforts shall raise a political revolution at once. Indeed, if the tone of some of the Eastern papers be taken as a criterion, they may well fear. Poor Marshall is literally 'used up,' and Wise acts like a maniac. Oaths and imprecations are thrown out by him constantly. The trial has excited such intense interest that the Senate has for a day or two been almost deserted. Senators sit in the hall during the whole day, listening to Mr. Adams. Lord Morpeth has been steadily there since the commencement of the conflict, a silent but interested listener during each day."

Few will now question the judgment of Giddings as to the effect of this triumph of the right of petition and the freedom of speech. It was the preconcerted and deliberate purpose of the slave-masters to make an example of the great ringleader of political Abolitionism. They meant to humiliate and crush him, and they did not doubt their ability to do this. Had they succeeded, the efforts of smaller and less famous men would have been fearfully crippled, if not fatally paralyzed. In the end freedom would have won; but the victory was gloriously anticipated by the matchless courage and resources of John Quincy Adams.

But the failure of this conspiracy against Mr. Adams was followed by a still more flagrant outrage. The champions of slavery were in no mood to profit by their experience, and this time their chosen victim was Giddings. The case concerned the foreign policy of the Government, and calls for some fullness of treatment. The Federal Constitution expressly grants to the General Government all jurisdiction over the subjects of commerce and navigation upon the high seas, and the power to define and punish felonies thereon. The States were thus denied any jurisdiction over these subjects, while every ship sailed under the national flag. In 1807 Congress passed a law regulating the coastwise slave-trade in vessels of over forty tons' burden, prescribing minutely the manifests, forms of entry at the custom-house, and specifications to be made by the masters of such vessels. This law for the protection and encouragement of the traffic in slaves between the slave-breeding and slave-buying States was unauthorized by the Constitution. The Federal Government had nothing to do with slavery save in the matters of taxation, representation, and the return of fugitive slaves, and this coastwise traffic had no reference to these subjects. The slaveholders had the right to drive or transport their slaves inland from one State to another, but they had no right to ask Congress for facilities of shipment by sea. This legislation, however, as we shall see, involved the nation in serious difficulties and complications. By the Treaty of Ghent, the British and American Governments pledged themselves to the Christian world to use their endeavors totally to abolish the traffic in slaves. They made no exceptions or reservations, and therefore the treaty fairly covered the traffic on our coast, as well as the foreign trade which had been declared piracy by England and the United States. Indeed, our domestic traffic was more inhuman and revolting than the foreign, inasmuch as its victims were comparatively civilized and Christianized men and women.

In passing around the peninsula of Florida, our

slave-ships were sometimes wrecked on British islands, and the slaves, by virtue of English law, became free. In these cases the slaveholder sought the co-operation of the English Government, notwithstanding its obligations under the Treaty of Ghent, and the subject was brought before Congress. In the year 1830 the ship "Comet" sailed from Alexandria, in the District of Columbia, with a cargo of slaves bound for New Orleans. She was wrecked on the false keys of the Bahama Islands, and the passengers and slaves carried by the wreckers to Nassau, in the island of New Providence, where the slaves asserted their liberty under British laws. The ship "Encomium," sailing, in 1834, from Charleston, South Carolina, with a number of slaves for New Orleans, was stranded near the same place, and the slaves became free. The ship "Hermosa," which sailed from Richmond, Virginia, in 1840, was wrecked on the British island of Abacco, whence the slaves were taken to Nassau, where they asserted their liberty.

Jackson and Van Buren zealously espoused the cause of the slaveholders in the two cases first named, and Mr. Stevenson, of Virginia, then representing our Government at the British court, asserted in his official correspondence that there is no distinction between property in "persons" and property in "things." He declared that our Government had "in the most solemn manner determined that slaves killed in the public service of the United States were to be regarded as property, and paid for as such." This statement was totally unwarranted by facts, and contradicted both by history and the records of the nation; but by these misrepresentations the British Ministry was led to pay for the slaves lost on board the "Comet" and the "Encomium," as they were stranded prior to the emancipation of the West Indian slaves. The Ministry, however, as we have seen, refused to pay for the slaves lost on board the ship "Enterprise," heretofore referred to, which ran into Port Hamilton, Bermuda, through stress of weather, in 1835, after the abolition of British slavery. This refusal was exceedingly offensive to the slaveocracy, and its hostility was still further stimulated by the loss of slaves on board the "Hermosa," already mentioned.

Senator Barrow of Louisiana presented the petition of certain insurance companies in that State, praying Congress to take measures for obtaining compensation from the British Government for the loss of the slaves on board the last-mentioned ship. He stated explicitly that the case might present the question of *peace or war with Great Britain;* and he declared that the people of the Southern States would be the last to submit to the principles of international law as construed by the authorities of the British Islands, and that if they continued to interfere with our commerce our navy would bombard their towns. Mr. Calhoun and other Senators concurred in the views of Mr. Barrow, but advised the parties concerned to await the action of the British Government in the case of the "Creole."

This ship had sailed from Hampton Roads on the 27th of October, 1841, with one hundred and thirty slaves on board, bound for New Orleans. On the 7th of November, the slaves rose against the officers and crew, and declared their right to freedom, taking possession of the deck of the ship at the same time. The alarm being heard below, one of the slave-dealers named Hewell, in attempting to shoot one of the men as he came on deck, was struck with a hand-spike and killed. The other slave-dealers, captain and crew, surrendered, and the people called "chattels" were thus suddenly transformed into free men and women, while the slave-dealers were as suddenly subjected to the power of their former bondmen. The mate was now ordered to steer the ship to Liberia; but being assured that their provisions and water would not last them half way, they consented to enter the port of Nassau, where, under British laws, they were free. They were, however, arrested and imprisoned. The captain of the "Creole" demanded them as criminals, to be brought back to the United States for punishment; but the authorities of the island refused until they should consult the Government at London. The slaves demanded their baggage; but the master of the ship declared that they had no baggage, that they were themselves the property of their masters, and of course could hold no property; but the British authorities compelled him to deliver to each negro his blanket and such clothing as he had possessed while on board.

The slave-dealers returned to the United States, and at once called on President Tyler for the interposition of the Government in obtaining compensation for their loss. The case was well calculated to test the principles and policy of both Governments. There was no law of the United States which authorized these traffickers in human flesh to hold their victims in subjection, and if there had been, it would not have imposed on these victims any natural or moral obligation to submit to being thus carried to the barracoons of New Orleans. The American and British Governments were bound by their solemn pledge in the Treaty of Ghent to abolish the traffic in slaves, and this pledge clearly enured to the benefit of the men who had been made free by English law.

The subject excited much interest on both sides of the Atlantic, and the Senate, by resolution, called on the President for the correspondence between our Government and that of England respecting the matter. In answer, the Executive transmitted to that body a copy of the instructions sent by Mr. Webster, our Secretary of State, to Mr. Everett, our minister at London. Says Mr. Webster, —

"The British Government cannot but see that this case, as presented in these papers, is one calling loudly for redress. The 'Creole' was passing from one port in the United States to another on a voyage perfectly lawful, with merchandise on board, and also with slaves, or persons bound to service, natives of America, and belonging to American citizens, and which are recognized as property by the Constitution of the United States in those States in which slavery exists.

"In the course of the voyage some of the slaves rose upon the master and crew, subdued them, murdered one man, and caused the vessel to be carried to Nassau. The vessel was thus taken to a British port, not voluntarily by those who had the lawful authority over her, but forcibly and violently, against the master's will, and with the consent of nobody but the mutineers and murderers.

"Under these circumstances, it would seem to have been the plain and obvious duty of the authorities at Nassau, the port of a friendly power, to assist the American consul in putting an end to the captivity of the master and crew, restoring to them the control of the vessel, and enabling them to resume their voyage and to take the 'mutineers and murderers' to their own country to answer for their crimes before the proper tribunal."

These efforts of the Senate and Executive to shelter the slave-trade under the national flag struck Giddings with the most profound astonishment. Senators had openly declared that the question might become one of peace or war with Great Britain if she did not consent to sustain this commerce in mankind in her ports. In the case of the "Enterprise," which came before the Senate in March, 1840, that body, by unanimous vote, had affirmed the principles now declared by Mr. Webster, who quoted that action of the Senate in support of his present position, and was complimented by Calhoun. No voice was raised in the Senate against this monstrous effort to nationalize slavery, while General Cass, our minister to France, was vehemently denying the right of England to visit American ships for the purpose of ascertaining whether slaveholding pirates were prosecuting their nefarious business under the shield of our flag.

And the case was aggravated by the wretched pretexts on which Mr. Webster sought to justify his cringing servility to the South. He declared that slaves "are recognized as property by the Constitution of the United States in those States in which slavery exists." No one better knew than himself that this is not true. In every instance the Constitution refers to them as "persons," and its framers unitedly acquiesced in the opinion of Mr. Madison, who "thought it wrong to admit in the Constitution the idea that there could be property in man." But if we concede that the Constitution does recognize slaves as property "in those States in which slavery exists," it certainly does not follow that they are so recognized *outside of those States*, and in countries in which it is forbidden.

Equally sophistical is the statement that the voyage of the "Creole" "was perfectly lawful." The foreign slave-trade was made piracy by both England and the United States; and although Congress had undertaken to regulate the traffic on our coast, it did not and could not legalize it on the high seas, or extend the law of slavery beyond the jurisdiction of the Slave States. But if the voyage had been perfectly lawful, it could not have affected the situation in the smallest degree. The ship might have been landed in Massachusetts, but the slaves would undoubtedly have been free, for the simple reason that slavery is always confined to the jurisdiction in which it exists.

Equally unwarranted was Mr. Webster's reference to these slaves as "mutineers and murderers." A mutineer is one in lawful subjection to superior authority who disobeys it. The slaves were free men under English law, and had a perfect right to defend their liberty; and they were not murderers, because they had an equal right to take life in self-defence.

All this is now perfectly understood; but in 1842 it was not allowed to reach the public. The Senate was a unit in the service of slavery, and in the House of Representatives all debate on the subject was prohibited by the 21st rule. Nothing could be done for the country, unless some way could be opened for the popular agitation of the question, and Mr. Adams was pre-eminently the man for the emergency. But he was exhausted by the labor and excitement of his protracted trial, while the committee of which he was the head was utterly hostile to his principles. Giddings, therefore, after conferring with his particular friends, prepared the following resolutions, which he hoped in some form to make available : —

"*Resolved*, That prior to the adoption of the Federal Constitution each of the several States composing this Union exercised full and exclusive jurisdiction over the subject of slavery within its own territory, and possessed full power to continue or abolish it at pleasure.

"*Second.* That by adopting the Constitution, no part of the aforesaid powers were delegated to the Federal Government, but were reserved by and still pertain to each of the several States.

"*Third.* That by the eighth section of the first article of the Federal Constitution each of the several States surrendered to the Federal Government all jurisdiction over the subjects of commerce and navigation upon the high seas.

"*Fourth.* That slavery, being an abridgment of the natural rights of man, can exist only by force of positive municipal law, and is necessarily confined to the jurisdiction of the power creating it.

"*Fifth.* That when a ship belonging to citizens of any State of this Union leaves the waters and territory of such State and enters upon the high seas, the persons on board cease to be subject to the laws of such States, and thenceforth are governed in their relations to each other by, and are amenable to, the laws of the United States.

"*Sixth.* That when the brig 'Creole,' on her late passage for New Orleans, left the jurisdiction of Virginia, the slave-laws of that State ceased to have jurisdiction over the persons on board, and they became amenable only to the laws of the United States.

"*Seventh.* That the persons on board said ship, in resuming their natural rights to liberty, violated no law of the United States, incurred no legal penalties, and are justly liable to no punishment.

"*Eighth.* That all attempts to regain possession of or to re-enslave said persons are unauthorized by the Constitution or laws of the United States, and are incompatible with our national honor.

"*Ninth.* That all attempts to exert our national influence in favor of the coastwise slave-trade, or to place this nation in the attitude of maintaining a commerce in human beings, are subversive of the rights and injurious to the feelings and interests of the people of the Free States, are unauthorized by the Constitution, and prejudicial to our national character."

These resolutions were submitted to Mr. Adams for his approval. He was perfectly frank in saying that he could not support the one which denied the right of the Federal Government to abolish slavery in the States, while he held the principle that in case of insurrection or war, the Federal Government might, under the *war power*, abolish it. To this Giddings replied that the resolutions, being presented *in time of peace, and having evident relation to a state of peace*, would not be regarded as applicable to a state of war, which operated to suspend the laws of the country and subject the people to despotic rule, in order to save the nation, and that making exceptions as to a state of war might obscure the doctrines and weaken the force of the several distinct propositions. To this Mr. Adams rejoined that the friends of slavery in future years and *during times of war* would quote these resolutions as denying the right of the Federal power to interfere with slavery even amidst domestic insurrection or foreign invasion; but he added, "I will cheerfully sustain all but that which denies this right of the Federal Government."

The resolutions, it will be seen, were in direct conflict with those presented by Mr. Calhoun in the case of the "Enterprise," and with the doctrine avowed by the Executive in the cases of the "Comet" and "Encomium," as well as that now asserted by Mr. Webster.

On the 21st of March, the State of Ohio was called, under the rules of the House, for resolutions. Giddings obtained the floor, and stated that he had prepared a series of resolutions in relation to a subject which had called forth some interest in the other end of the Capitol and in the country, and that he desired to submit them to the House for consideration, and would call them up for action upon the next day which should be devoted to the consideration of resolutions. He sent them to the Clerk's desk, to be read, with the expectation that they would be published in the newspapers and carefully considered by members, with a view to their action upon them the following week.

The reading attracted general attention, and a second reading was called for, during which they received the most profound attention. General Ward of New York inquired whether it was in order to demand the previous question. The Speaker replied in the affirmative, when Mr. Everett of Vermont moved to lay them on the table. His motion was rejected. Mr. Holmes of South Carolina, under great excitement, remarked: "There are certain topics, like certain places, of which it might be said,—

"'Fools rush in where angels fear to tread.'"

The demand for the previous question was seconded. Mr. Everett asked to be excused from voting, but took occasion to express his "utter abhorrence of the firebrand course of the gentleman from Ohio." Mr. Fessenden of Maine, and Mr. Floyd of New York, opposed any immediate vote upon the resolutions, while Mr. Cushing of Massachusetts, after reading them at the clerk's table, said: "They appear to be a British argument on a great question between the British and American governments, and constitute an approximation to treason on which I intend to vote no."

Mr. Fillmore of New York inquired if it was in order to ask Mr. Giddings to withdraw the resolutions. The latter did not desire to see members, in the excitement of the moment, commit themselves against principles which he believed would meet their approval in moments of cool reflection, and he withdrew the resolutions, saying he had only intended, on this occasion, to call attention to the subject, and ask a vote at some future day. Nothing could well have been more considerate or more studiously respectful than this action of Giddings; but Mr. Botts of Virginia at once obtained the floor, saying the withdrawal of the resolutions did not excuse their presentation, and he moved a suspension of the rules for the purpose of offering the following preamble and resolution: —

"*Whereas*, The Hon. Joshua R. Giddings, the member from the Sixteenth Congressional District of Ohio, has this day presented to this House a series of resolutions touching the most important interest connected with a large portion of the Union, now a subject of negotiation between the United States and Great Britain, of the most delicate nature, the result of which *may involve those nations*, AND PERHAPS THE CIVILIZED WORLD, IN WAR.

"*And whereas*, It is the duty of every good citizen, and particularly of every selected agent and representative of the people, to discountenance all efforts to create excitement and dissatisfaction and division among the people of the United States, at such time and under such circumstances, which is the only effect to be accomplished by the introduction of sentiments before the legislative body of the country hostile to the grounds assumed by the high functionary having in charge this important and delicate trust ;

"*And whereas*, Mutiny and murder are therein justified and approved in terms shocking to all sense of law, order, and humanity ; *therefore*, —

"*Resolved*, That this House hold the conduct of said member is altogether unwarranted and unwarrantable, and deserving the severest condemnation of the people of this country, and of this body in particular."

The rules were not suspended, and Mr. Weller, a Democrat from Ohio, then offered the resolutions as his own, and demanded the previous question. There was much excitement in the hall, and in answer to an inquiry of Mr. Holmes the Speaker stated that the previous question would not cut off Mr. Giddings from the right to be heard in his own defence. From this decision Mr. Fillmore of New York took an appeal, and the decision was overruled by a vote of 118 to 64. The House then adjourned.

Fully believing that he would be permitted to defend himself, Giddings spent the entire night in preparation, and before the meeting of the House on the next day he visited Mr. Adams for consultation. He found him greatly depressed. Mr. Adams told Giddings the House would not permit any defence to be made, that the vote would be taken without debate, and that appearances indicated the passage of the resolution of censure. Giddings replied that he had supposed the reflections of the night would convince members of the impropriety of *condemning a man unheard*. Mr. Adams answered: " You are not as familiar with the slaveholding character as I am. Slaveholders act from impulse, not from reflection; they act together from interest, and have no dread of the displeasure of their constituents when they act *for slavery.*"

On the meeting of the House Mr. Weller proposed to withdraw his demand for the previous question, provided Giddings would at once proceed in his defence, with the general understanding that the previous question should be called at its conclusion. Giddings refused to make any terms for the purchase of his constitutional rights, and asked for a postponement of the question for the purpose of enabling him to prepare his defence; but the vote was taken on seconding the demand for the previous question, which stood 77 in the affirmative to 70 in the negative. Weller now moved a suspension of the rules to enable Giddings to be heard; but the Speaker decided that as the House had ordered the previous question, it must be put before any other motion could be entertained. A proposition was now made to hear him by common consent; but as he was proceeding to speak, Mr. Cooper of Georgia objected, and he resumed his seat.

The champions of slavery were thus completely caught in the toils of their own violence. They recoiled at the shameless outrage in which they had too hastily involved themselves. The policy now urged by the whole force of parliamentary law to an immediate conclusion was to inflict a gross wrong upon a representative without permitting him throughout the proceedings of two days to utter a single word in defence or explanation of his course. By the application of the previous question, preceded by the reversal of the Speaker's decision, they had even deprived *themselves* of the liberty of permitting Giddings to speak before the execution of their sentence. As the truth dawned upon them they were frightened and confounded; but they saw no way by which they could extricate themselves. They had locked themselves in, and thrown away the key to their deliverance. By their own votes all the screws of parliamentary law had been tightened upon them while they still struggled in vain to escape. Mr. Triplett of Kentucky moved to suspend the rules to permit Giddings to speak; but the Speaker correctly decided that under the law of the House, confirmed by usage and repeated decisions, no such motion, nor any motion whatever, except to lay on the table or to adjourn, could be entertained. This he made so clear that, furious as they were in their dilemma, they sustained the Speaker's decision by a large majority. Mr. A. H. H. Stuart of Virginia then moved to reconsider the vote by which the previous question had been carried, in order to permit the House to retrace its steps; but this, too, the Speaker declared to be out of order, and the House again felt obliged to sustain him. After a motion by Mr. Adams to lay on the table had been negatived, the resolutions of censure were passed by a vote of 125 to 69.

In the mean time Giddings, while sitting at his desk, wrote the following note: —

To the Reporter of the Intelligencer:

When I rose so often during the confusion of business in the House this day, and was so often called to order, the last time by

Hon. Mark A. Cooper of Georgia, I had written out and desired to have stated to the House what follows: —

"Mr. Speaker, I stand before the House in a peculiar position. It is proposed to pass a vote of censure upon me, substantially for the reason that I differ in opinion from a majority of the members. The vote is about to be taken, without giving me an opportunity to be heard. It were idle for me to say that I am ignorant of the disposition of a majority of the members to pass the resolution of censure. I have been violently assailed in a personal manner, but have had no opportunity of being heard in reply; nor do I now ask for any favor at the hands of gentlemen, but in the name of an insulted constituency, in behalf of one of the States of this Union, in behalf of the people of these States and of our Federal Constitution, I *demand* a hearing in the ordinary mode of proceeding. I accept no other privilege; I will receive no other courtesy."

This note appeared the next morning in the current proceedings of the House.

When the Speaker declared the resolutions carried, Mr. Giddings rose, and taking formal leave of the Speaker and officers of the House, of his colleagues, of Mr. Adams, and a few other personal friends, passed out of the hall. As he reached the front door he found Senators Clay and Crittenden, who had been spectators of the scene just described. As Mr. Clay extended his hand he thanked Giddings for the firmness with which he had met the outrage perpetrated upon him, declaring that no man would ever doubt his perfect right to state his own views against the slave-trade, particularly while the Executive and the Senate were expressing theirs in favor of it. After resigning his office as a representative, Giddings left the city for his home.

Up to this date, nothing in the history of the government had so clearly illustrated the autocratic power of slavery over the nation as this action of the House of Representatives upon these resolutions of Giddings. The principles they affirm are simple truisms. No one now disputes them, and no one then ventured to controvert them. Mr. Botts, indeed, condemned them as ill-timed, while the question to which they related was the subject of negotiation between England and the United States, and some of the newspapers which warmly supported Giddings made the same objection, which, oddly enough, is also urged by Mr. Schouler, in his "History of the United States."[1] The objection utterly vanishes in the light of a few obvious facts. While the papers relating to the negotiation pending between the United States and Great Britain remained in the Executive archives, and no one knew what doctrine the President had advanced, or what demands he had made, neither Congress nor the people could discuss the questions involved, for the simple reason that they were ignorant as to what the official correspondence contained. It is equally true that the President was under no obligation to promulgate his views while in his opinion the interests of the country would be prejudiced by their discussion. All calls upon the President for information in such cases are made subject to his discretion; but if communicated and published, it becomes the legitimate subject of discussion by every American citizen. The people are the source of power, and their representatives have a perfect right to discuss all questions involved in the negotiations of the Government from the moment of their publication.

It was in accordance with this principle that Calhoun, on the 4th of March, 1840, offered a series of resolutions affirming the duty of the government to protect the slave-trade, the negotiations touching the matter having previously been furnished by Mr. Van

[1] Vol. iv. p. 427.

Buren, in response to a call of the Senate. Nobody proposed to censure him for introducing his resolutions pending the negotiations. They were fully discussed, and adopted by unanimous vote of the Senate. During the same session a member of the House of Representatives from South Carolina, as chairman of the Committee on Foreign Relations, made a report in which he alluded to the refusal of Great Britain to make compensation for the slaves who had been liberated from on board American vessels engaged in the slave-trade, as a cause of war. The matter was a subject of negotiation between the British Government and our own, and yet no one raised any question as to the propriety of his act. The subject of our Northeastern boundary was a matter of negotiation for many years, and during almost every session of Congress covering this period it was discussed, while no one questioned the propriety of such discussion. The plain truth is that this complaint of the *untimeliness* of the resolutions of Mr. Giddings was inspired by the fact that in the opinion of his accusers they were offered on the wrong side. No one can doubt that if he had taken sides with Webster and Calhoun, he would have been thanked for the timeliness as well as the wisdom of his action. The slaveocracy was publicly making the threat of war with England if she did not consent to co-operate with the United States in support of the traffic in slaves; and if, under such circumstances, the representatives of the people could be gagged, our system of government would have been ready for its epitaph.

The proceedings of the House in this case proved of great value in awakening the people to a consciousness of their danger. The anti-slavery Press published them in full, while many of the party papers noticed them. Public meetings were held in the principal cities of the Free States, which asserted the right of members of Congress freely to express their views, while the constituents of Giddings manifested their indignation in large public meetings, which fully indorsed his action and asked him to become a candidate for re-election. He was chosen by an overwhelming majority, and instructed to re-assert and maintain his doctrines. Within five weeks from the date of his censure, he resumed his seat in the House. His feelings at this time may be gathered from the following extract from a letter to his son, dated the 8th of May: —

"I arrived here on Wednesday evening, and was soon surrounded by friends, who certainly appeared glad to see me back. They had suffered greater anxiety than I had been sensible of. Father Adams said that it had the effect to improve his health as soon as he heard I was in the city, — and that was not long after I arrived, for there were enough to go with the intelligence, as all seemed to know that he felt extremely anxious on the subject. Andrews, of Cleveland, introduced me to the House. Many looked up with smiling faces, while others appeared to be perfectly dumfounded. I received many long and hearty greetings from those who had opposed my censure, and from some who voted against me. Governor Wallace, of Indiana, in particular, seized me by the hand, and in the most feeling manner acknowledged his error in voting to censure me, and assured me of his most heartfelt satisfaction at seeing me again in my place. Greetings and conversation occupied the whole of my time during the day."

The Committee on Foreign Affairs of the Senate, to whom the message of the President on the subject of the "Creole" and Mr. Webster's letter to our minister in London were committed, made no report upon those important state papers, and Mr. Calhoun ceased to call the attention of the country to these claims for slaves. The Senate forbore all further discussion of the subject, and neither the Secretary of State, nor President Tyler, nor his successor, Mr. Polk, took any further action respecting it. They seemed to have been silenced by the effort to silence Giddings. The case of the "Creole" also attracted attention in England, and the English Press re-published the proceedings in the House of Representatives, while the British ministry refused indemnity to the slave-dealers before the news of the censure of Giddings reached that country. In the mean time, Lord Ashburton was appointed Envoy and Minister Plenipotentiary for the purpose of settling existing international questions, except those arising from the release of slaves on British islands, including the case of the "Creole," as to which he was authorized to hold no correspondence. Such were some of the fruits of this latest crusade of the slaveholders against the freedom of debate.

But the vanquished party were not yet ready to give up the fight. They knew that Giddings was instructed to re-offer his resolutions, and that if thus presented, the House must adopt or reject them. But they could only be presented when the States were called for resolutions, which was on each alternate Monday, so that the men who had voted for his censure were able to control the business of the House and on each resolution day to carry a motion to proceed to other business. This they did during the remainder of the session and the whole of the last session of the Twenty-seventh Congress. Giddings therefore seized upon the first opportunity to vindicate in a public speech the doctrines avowed in his resolutions. Although he spoke with much plainness respecting the slave-trade and the officials who had encouraged that commerce, he was not called to order, but was listened to with respectful attention while reasserting the doctrines for which he had been censured sixty days before. The freedom of debate was substantially regained, although the Twenty-first Rule continued to hold its place in the manual for over two years afterwards.

While engrossed with the labors of this session, the question of organized anti-slavery action against both the Whig and Democratic parties was again pressed upon the attention of Giddings. The question was important, though it related only to the method of serving the great cause. During the previous year, Salmon P. Chase, then at the threshold of his political career, had taken the lead in organizing the Liberty party in Ohio, as a preliminary to the formation of a national party. This led to a correspondence between him and Giddings, in which the former, as will be seen, expressed himself with the clearness and vigor which marked his later utterances. On the 21st of January, 1842, he wrote, —

Hon. J. R. Giddings:

Dear Sir, — I am much indebted to you for your prompt answer to my letter. I do not wonder at your hesitation in regard to political action. The Liberty party is so small now, and there are so many circumstances calculated to discourage the hope of political action on principle by the masses of either party, that I am rather surprised that any men of distinguished political position should be willing to unite their destinies to those of the new party, than that so few should. And yet, when I reflect that the principles of this party are, incontestably, the precise principles of American liberty, and that unless they prevail, the country itself must perish, I cannot suppress the faith that a sure, though perhaps remote, triumph awaits it. I firmly believe also that if we can — and what is there to prevent this? — secure the balance of power in the Legislatures of the Free States and in Congress, we shall be able to accomplish immense good for the country, by checking the ruinous measures of one party, and aiding in carrying the beneficial propositions of another, without any bias in favor of either except what the measures proposed should from time to time produce. This of itself would do much to destroy the baneful spirit of partyism now so visible in all that is done in our State or national legislature. . . .

What good is to be gained by cleaving to the Whig party? I never expected it would hang together a year after General Harrison's election, and it is split up sooner and more irreconcilably than I anticipated. I do not believe that it is possible for any man, not even for Corwin, to be elected governor by the Whig party in this State next fall. And if we must be in a minority, why not be in a minority of our own, rather than in a minority of men who despise us or affect to do so? For my own part, I am more and more satisfied with the course I have taken and the position I have assumed. I feel satisfied that I am in the right, and that the expedient and the right are one.

You have no doubt seen, and I hope approve, of the address of the convention. You will see that it presents a broad platform on which all can stand, of both parties, who desire the deliverance of the country from the slave-power. You will notice also a resolution offered by Mr. Morris, calling for a national convention of the Liberty party. The reason why this was adopted was that some dissatisfaction is felt here in the West with the nominations of the national convention at New York, because that convention is regarded rather as a meeting of the national Anti-slavery Society than as a convention of the Liberty party. Besides this, it is thought that if Mr. Adams or Governor Seward would accept the nomination, great additional strength might be gained for the party. What do you think of this? Would either of those gentlemen accept? Would it be advisable to offer the nomination to either of them if they would? I suppose both of them are anti-slavery men to the extent of this address. Mr. Leavitt seems to apprehend danger from disturbing the present nominations. My fears, I confess, have an opposite direction. I fear it will be difficult to persuade any considerable body of the people to unite in the support of one so little known as Mr. Birney is, and who has seen so little of public service. Governor Seward, on the contrary, is for his age one of the first statesmen in the country, and Mr. Adams is perhaps the very first. . . .

Yours very truly,

S. P. CHASE.

On the 15th of February following, Mr. Chase again wrote, and more earnestly than before, urging the claims of the Liberty party, and the duty of antislavery men to rally to its support.

MY DEAR SIR,— I thank you for your two last very interesting letters. The nation is greatly indebted to you and other friends of freedom for the noble stand taken by you in regard to the right of petition. The country is beginning to awaken at length to the danger of slaveholding encroachments, and the time is rapidly drawing on, I trust, when the champions of freedom will have the place which of right belongs to them in the confidence and favor of a long deceived and oppressed, but now awakening, people.

I think, however, that it will be necessary to go to the bottom, and plant ourselves upon the rock of fundamental principles. It will not do to compromise any more. The principle must be established and acquiesced in, that the government is a non-slaveholding government; that the nation is a non-slaveholding nation; that slavery is a creature of State law, local, not to be extended or favored, but to be confined within the States which admit and sanction it. I hardly think the Whigs, as a party, are prepared to take this ground. The most they will do is to *tolerate* liberty. They will, in this quarter, hardly do that. They will not do it at all unless attachment to liberty is made subservient to party ends, and secondary to party obligations. There has been something said of nominating Judge King by the Whig party. I do not expect it, though he has been a distinguished, able, and influential Whig. Nor, to say truth, do I desire it. For such is the feeling of opposition to antislavery principles with many of the Whig party that thousands would vote for Shannon in preference to him; while many of the Democrats, who would otherwise support him, would be persuaded that the nomination is a Whig manœuvre, and would fall back into their party ranks. I should prefer, for one, to go into the battle with our own strength. We may be defeated now, but at the next election parties must divide on *principle*, and then we must triumph.

I will send, under cover, to your address a number of copies of our Liberty address, directed to various gentlemen in Washington, to whom I will thank you to have them delivered. Why cannot the members from Vermont, who accord in principle with the Liberty convention, go home and plant the standard of liberty upon the Green Mountains? I feel confident that the State would at once rally under it. Why submit any longer to the degradations so long endured? Why consent at all that the principles and rights of the Free States, — of the nation, indeed,

— shall be trampled upon, or, if recognized at all, recognized as a matter of grace and favor? I am tired of the cap-in-hand policy. I am unwilling to feel myself and my opinions to be contraband articles in my political party, only tolerated because not safely to be dispensed with. I cannot but think that you and they share these sentiments. Why not, then, act upon them?

Excuse me if I seem too earnest. It seems to me that there is now a glorious opportunity to restore the government to its original principles, and I cannot but hope that before the Congress rises, you and others will feel free to take the position of leaders of the Liberty party, and issue an address to the people which will be responded to throughout the land. I verily believe there are multitudes, even in Slave States, who would hail such a movement with joy. If Mr. Adams could be induced to take a part in it, how could his illustrious life be more brightened towards its close?

I have written him a letter, which I enclose. It is some years since I have seen him, and he has possibly forgotten me. He knew, however, my uncle, formerly Senator from Vermont, and perhaps also my uncle, the Bishop of Illinois, well. I want you to vouch for me, and to get for me, if possible, an *early* answer to my letter. It is principally upon the subject of slavery in the District, and the fundamental principles of the Liberty party. It does not, however, support any action such as is referred to above. It would not be fit for *me* to suggest a course to *him*. You can converse with him on the subject with propriety. I shall be glad to have you read my letter to him.

We are organizing our Liberty clubs in this county, and expect to make a respectable rally. Faithfully yours,

S. P. CHASE.

The letters of Giddings have not been preserved, but he disagreed with Chase as to the wisdom of this third-party movement, as the letters quoted imply, and he dealt with it fully, in concluding a series of essays prepared in the summer and autumn of this year, which he devoted to a patient and critical examination of the rights and privileges of the several States in regard to slavery. His purpose was to formulate a working theory of political action against the evil, while fully according to the Slave States their Constitutional rights. These timely and valuable essays first appeared in the "Western Reserve Chronicle" over the signature of "Pacificus."

The starting-point and fundamental idea of his exposition was that slavery is the concern of the States in which it exists, with which the Federal Government has no Constitutional right to interfere in any way. This was no new doctrine, for it had been held by the people of all parties for half a century. It was not a sectional doctrine, for both the North and South had espoused it; and it was not an anti-slavery doctrine, because the slaveholding States affirmed it.

Giddings laid hold of this principle as the basis and complete justification of his warfare against slavery, and he proposed to hold the slaveholding States to the strict logic of their own position. If the Federal Government had no constitutional right to abolish slavery, it had no constitutional right to support it. If the people of the slaveholding States had the right to be perfectly exempt from Federal interference with their peculiar institution, the people of the non-slaveholding States had the right to be entirely exempt from the guilt and expense of its support through Federal agency. If Congress had no more power to abolish slavery in South Carolina than it had to abolish free schools in Massachusetts, then South Carolina had no more right to ask Congress to legislate for slavery than it had to ask the Government of Brazil. There is absolute reciprocity of rights as between the slaveholding and non-slaveholding States; and the question is not at all affected by the compromises of the Constitution. The Free States agreed that three fifths of the slaves should be counted in the basis of representation, and that fugitive slaves should be delivered up. Beyond these concessions to slavery they had no duty to perform. They had no right to assert against it except the right to *be let alone*. Planting himself upon the Declaration of Independence, and the clause in the Preamble of the Constitution which declares that one of the purposes for which it was ordained was "to secure the blessings of liberty," Giddings summoned the people of all parties to the work of administering the government in accordance with the principle on which they professed to be agreed.

After setting forth with remarkable clearness the rights and duties of the people of the Free States touching the recapture of fugitive slaves, and the suppression of "domestic violence," he proceeds to point out in detail the multiplied instances in which the Federal Government, from its very beginning, had been prostituted to the service of slavery. He refers to the Act of Congress of 1801 legalizing slavery and the slave-trade in the District of Columbia, which it had no constitutional right to do; to the Act, equally unauthorized, regulating the coastwise slave-trade; to the espousal of the foreign slave-trade by the Federal Government, and its recognition of slavery as a national interest by compensating slaveholders for the loss of slaves made free under British laws; to the espousal of slavery by the Federal Government in lending itself to the recovery of fugitive slaves made free by Spanish law, and in compensating slave-claimants for their loss; to the prosecution of the Florida War, which had its origin in the unconstitutional interference of the Federal Government in behalf of slavery; and to the establishment of slavery and the slave-trade in Florida and other Territories of the United States, in violation of the Constitution, which makes free all places under the exclusive jurisdiction of the Government.

It is needless to follow Mr. Giddings in this branch of his subject, which he thoroughly explored, laying bare a mass of facts with which the country is now familiar, but which were then novel and startling.

The faithful and consistent application of this principle of Federal non-intervention with slavery was the controlling aim of his public life; and his interpretation of it invested it with the interest of a political discovery. In reply to those Abolitionists who sought the freedom of the slave through the dissolution of the Union, he said,—

"The very existence of slavery depends, not upon the Constitution, but upon its violation; not upon the support which our people are bound by the Constitution to lend it, but upon the support which has been extorted from them by violation of the Constitution. When the day shall arrive when Northern men will insist upon their rights, and refuse to contribute the substance acquired by their toil for the maintenance of Southern slavery, that scourge of our land will cease."

Giddings was right. He had found the clew to the riddle which had hitherto baffled solution. The destruction of slavery wherever found outside of the Slave States under Federal sanction, would have been fatal to its existence in those States; and as the slaveocracy was not content with its constitutional rights, but was determined to nationalize and eternize the curse, he proposed to defeat its baleful purpose by the weapons of the Constitution which it defied.

These essays were extensively published in the newspapers of the day, and in the following year were printed in pamphlet form and widely scattered over the Free States, under the frank of members of Congress. They undoubtedly exerted great influence in the creation of an anti-slavery public opinion in the Northern States, while they paved the way for the organized movement which triumphed in 1860; and they are worthy of preservation as an important contribution to the permanent literature of the anti-slavery conflict.[1] The debatable point in them was the conclusion, in which Giddings exhorts the opponents of slavery to rally under the banner of the Whig party, as the chosen instrument of reform. This was a mistake, and he himself acknowledged it a few years later, when that party perished in the shameful attempt to outdo its Democratic rival in the abjectness of its servility to the South. This mistake, however, was by no means generally apparent in 1842. The Liberty party failed to rally the people or to arrest public attention. Its doctrines were not clearly defined, and were generally misunderstood. The Whig party was extensively credited with anti-slavery tendencies, while the Democratic party was notoriously in sympathy with slavery. A party was needed which would marshal the intelligence and conscience of the country on that single question; but the formation of such a party was not the work of a day, nor could it be created by a few men. It had to grow, and was obliged to wait on the teaching of events.

In August of this year Giddings determined to retire from public life. He was weary of the strife which his attitude on the slavery question made inevitable. His natural love of peace and kindness of heart made him long for the rest and quiet of his own home, and he accordingly addressed the following note to his devoted friend, Henry Fassett, editor of the "Ashtabula Sentinel."

[1] See Appendix.

Mr. Fassett:

Please say to the electors of our Congressional District that it is not my intention to be a candidate for re-election. I have delayed answering many inquiries upon that subject, as I intended addressing the people of our district through the medium of the Press on my return from the present session of Congress; but that time has been so long delayed that I think duty requires me to inform our people of my determination.

This was a surprise and a disappointment to Mr. Fassett; he at once called about him a number of the most intelligent and faithful friends of Giddings, who earnestly and unitedly protested against his retirement, and finally prevailed upon him to reconsider his determination. But the subject was not dismissed from his mind, as will appear from a letter to Mrs. Giddings a few months later, in which he endeavored to persuade himself that he had already rendered service enough to justify his retirement. The absolute frankness of this letter, which was intended only for his own household, will interest the reader. He does not disguise the satisfaction he feels in referring to his achievements, while the general tone is that of a tired man longing for rest. It is a revelation of himself. I quote the following extract: —

"My opposers need not say, 'Oh that mine enemy had written a book!' for they have my views on slavery pretty fully expressed. Taking my speech on the Bridge question in 1838-39, my speech on the Florida War, my resolutions on the 'Creole,' my speech on the Army Bill, on the bill for the relief of the people of West Florida, and that on the bill for the relief of the owners of slaves on board the 'Comet' and 'Encomium,' and 'Pacificus,' and the world may understand my views tolerably well. This I have been anxious to bring about, and that object is now effected; so that, should I die to-morrow, or never again appear before the public in any way, I can lay my hand on my heart and say that in this respect I have endeavored to do my duty.

"It is therefore a great satisfaction to me now to look back over the scenes through which I have passed. They have surely been scenes of trial, of severe trial. My reputation and character at times I really apprehended would be trampled in the dust before the almost irresistible influence of slavery. Indeed, my life has been sought on account of my adherence to truth and justice. But I have been sustained and protected by that kind Providence which has always been round about me, and I now look forward to the time when I may lay aside the cares and responsibilities of public life, and making my bow to the people, I may be allowed to retire from the arena of strife and danger to the bosom of my family."

But he was again prevailed upon by friends to remain at his post of duty, and he perhaps yielded to their wishes the more readily from the fact that at this time he was receiving resolutions of thanks and congratulatory addresses from public meetings and societies in nearly every Free State, warmly commending the doctrines he had avowed in Congress, and the steadfastness with which he had maintained them. He saw that his labors, to which he had referred in the foregoing letter, were appreciated, and that the cause of freedom was advancing. He was no longer to stand alone. Eloquent lecturers were travelling and speaking in all the Free States, while such papers as "The Emancipator," "The Liberator," and "The Philanthropist" were doing excellent work for the cause. The time to lay aside his armor had not come, for he was in the midst of his fight.

CHAPTER VI.

DECEMBER, 1842, TO DECEMBER, 1844.

Second Session of the Twenty-seventh Congress. — The Twenty-first Rule. — Southern Intolerance. — Claim of West Florida Slaveholders. — Claim for Slaves lost in the Coastwise Trade. — Speech. — Encounter with a Southern Bully. — Annexation of Texas. — The Twenty-eighth Congress. — Presidential Canvass of 1844. — Position of Mr. Clay. — His Letters. — Attitude of Giddings. — Friendship of Adams and Himself.

AT the beginning of this session Mr. Adams introduced a resolution repealing the Twenty-first Rule of the House, and called for the previous question. The House seconded the demand, but refused to order the main question, and the subject was postponed from day to day for some time, when it was laid on the table by a bare majority. All parties saw that the gag-rule was doomed. An attempt was made at this session by the Southern members of the Committee on Claims to deprive Giddings of his chairmanship of that committee, on account of his action in the "Creole" case; but as the Speaker of the House was friendly to him, and as he also shared the warm friendship of Mr. Clay, the project was finally abandoned. Southern members, however, became more insolent and overbearing during this session than at any previous time, while the little group of men who defied them and dared to claim their souls as their own had grown no larger. And yet the spirit of liberty was gradually extending among the better class of men throughout the Northern States. The labors and sacrifices of Adams and Giddings had not been in vain. The constitutional doctrines of the "Pacificus" papers were spreading, while the growing madness of the slaveocracy was itself a sign of promise to its foes.

On the 14th of January, 1843, the question of property in human beings was brought before the House in a very offensive form. When General Jackson invaded West Florida in 1814, his camp-followers took with them, on leaving the Territory, more than a hundred slaves; and when he again invaded it, four years later, he took from the inhabitants a considerable amount of provisions. By the ninth article of our treaty with Spain, in 1820, it was stipulated "that the Spanish inhabitants shall receive compensation for any losses they may have sustained by reason of the operations of the late American army within that territory." Under this treaty all claims arising from the operations of the army in 1818 were adjusted; but those who had lost slaves during the invasion of 1814 now claimed indemnity. Mr. Crawford, at that time Secretary of the Treasury, rejected the claims. They were then sent to Congress, where they were also rejected. But the claimants presented them to the following Congress; and Mr. Everett, Chairman of the Committee on Foreign Affairs, to whom the claims were referred, reported in favor of payment. The House, however, did not sanction his report. Mr. Woodbury, who succeeded Mr. Crawford as Secretary of the Treasury, and to whom the claims were now referred, paid some thousands of dollars on their liquidation, but on learning the action of his predecessor, he refused further payment. The claimants again applied to Congress, and at the next session the case was referred to the Committee on Territories, of which the Hon. James Cooper of Pennsylvania was chairman, who reported a bill for the payment. As Mr. Slade was in declining health and Mr. Gates was unwilling to take the lead in debate, Adams and Giddings alone had to face the hungry and importunate demands of the slaveholders.

Mr. Adams spoke with great earnestness and effect. He carried the members with him as he progressed with his argument, and the fate of the bill was distinctly foreshadowed on the countenances of members. Giddings, like Adams, dwelt chiefly upon the moral character of slavery, and insisted that nothing which man could do could make one human being the property of another. Mr. Howard of Michigan said "a bill of sale from the Almighty" would do it; to which Giddings promptly replied that in such a case he would deny the handwriting. Holmes of South Carolina called him to order, but he was allowed to proceed with his argument. The delegate from Florida made a feeble speech in reply, after which the vote was taken on the bill, only thirty-six members giving it their support.

On the 14th of February another claim for the value of lost slaves came before the House. It related to the slave-ships "Comet" and "Encomium," which were wrecked near the British West India Islands, and the slaves made free by coming under the jurisdiction of British law, as stated in a previous chapter. The claim was first asserted under President Jackson, and on the false representation of Mr. Stevenson, our minister to England, that this Government had been in the habit of recognizing slaves as property, the British Ministry consented to pay some seventy-five thousand dollars for the benefit of slave-dealers. Without consulting Congress, the President paid out all but nine thousand dollars, for which no claimants appeared. When about to retire from office, President Van Buren paid over this balance to the Treasurer of the United States, who, however, refused to pay it to the claimants now asking it, without an Act of Congress authorizing him to do so. They therefore applied to Congress, and their petition was referred to the Committee on Ways and Means, which reported a bill authorizing the Treasurer to pay over the money to the claimants.

Giddings proposed to Stanly of North Carolina, who had the matter in charge as the representative of the claimants, who were his constituents, that the bill should simply authorize the Treasurer to replace the money in the hands of the Executive, which would answer every practical purpose, and relieve Congress of the odium of taxing the people for the support of the slave-trade. Stanly agreed to this, and at his request Giddings drew up a bill which Stanly accepted as a substitute for the original bill, and which was passed by the House. When it was taken up in the Senate, the original bill reported by the committee was substituted by the House bill, and came back in that form. Giddings was astonished at the apparent treachery of Stanly, who declined to make any explanation; and having charge of it, he was awarded the floor, and demanded the previous question. Giddings asked him to withdraw the demand; but he refused, and the question on concurring in the Senate's substitute was put and carried.

Giddings was of course indignant, and having voted in the affirmative for the purpose, he now moved to reconsider the vote, and entered into a thorough discussion of the policy of the Government respecting the traffic in slaves. He exposed the shameless falsehood of our minister to England, through which he prevailed on the British Ministry to allow these claims. He referred to our coastwise slave-trade, under the operation of which the slaves in this case became free by passing beyond the territorial jurisdiction of slavery, and to the readiness of the Government to aid the slave-dealer, while it gagged the men who would denounce his crimes. He reprobated the unauthorized action of Jackson and Van Buren in espousing the interests of these claimants without consulting Congress, thus making themselves the agents and solicitors of piratical slave-dealers. He pointed to the inconsistency of the Government in hanging men as pirates for trafficking in slaves on the African coast and keeping an expensive squadron there to guard it, while supporting a more execrable traffic at home. In conclusion, he said:

"Sir, place this subject in whatever attitude you please, throw around it whatever sophistry the human intellect is capable of calling into exercise, yet the disgusting *fact* will stand portrayed to the world in coming time that in the year 1843 this American Congress sat gravely legislating in aid of this traffic in human flesh. Let it go upon the record. Let the archives of this body bear to coming generations the proof that two hundred and forty-two American statesmen were on this day engaged in granting relief and encouragement to persons engaged in that execrable commerce which Mr. Jefferson declared had 'rendered us the scoff of infidel nations.' But let not my name be found among its advocates. Let not my descendants in future years be called to blush for their ancestor on reading the record of this day's proceeding. Sooner, far sooner, would I have it erased from the records of this House, — yea, sooner would I have it blotted from existence, — than see it placed on record in favor of the bill before us."

The motion of Giddings to reconsider the bill was laid on the table, after which he rose to a question of privilege touching an occurrence which had taken place during the proceedings. He said that while speaking he had noticed several persons standing in front of the clerk's desk, one of whom was Mr. Dawson of Louisiana; that the moment he closed his remarks he was violently pushed by what appeared to be the elbow of a man pressing against his side, while at the same instant Mr. Dawson passed him, on his way from the outside towards the clerk's desk; that he approached from behind, and was neither heard nor seen until this manifestation of his displeasure; that recognizing Dawson as he passed, he spoke in an undertone, but so loud as to be heard, saying, "Dawson!" when that member turned around and seized the handle of a bowie-knife, which partially protruded from his bosom, and immediately advanced towards Giddings until within striking distance, when, looking him in the eye, Giddings said, "Did you push me in that rude manner?" He answered, "Yes." "For the purpose of insulting me?" "Yes," said Dawson, as he partially removed the knife from the scabbard. Giddings rejoined: "No gentleman will wantonly insult another. I have no more to say to you, but turn you over to public contempt, as incapable of insulting an honorable man."

By this time Mr. Moore of Louisanna and other members, seized Dawson and took him from the hall. Giddings stated to the House that he felt it due to the members of the body to lay these facts before them, wishing it distinctly understood that he asked no protection from the House, but left that body to protect its own dignity. Mr. Calhoun of Massachusetts insisted on reading the manual relating to privileges of members, and Mr. Adams inquired whether Dawson threatened to cut Mr. Giddings' throat from ear to ear, as he had that of the gentleman from Tennessee a few days before, when Mr. Arnold said something unpleasant to Dawson. The matter of privilege was dropped at this point. Dawson had doubtless acted with the approbation of several members, who probably desired to try the experiment of threatening personal violence, to deter members from the expression of their views. It was generally believed that Dawson intended to provoke a blow from Giddings, which would have served as an excuse for assassination. The exhibition aroused in the public mind a feeling of disgust at the growing insolence of slaveholding members.

The question of annexing Texas to the Union was now coming to the front as a vital and overshadowing issue. The slaveocracy was secretly plotting for annexation, but the great body of the people of the Northern States were as yet ignorant of this conspiracy to bring them into political partnership with a new slaveholding State. It was Mr. Adams who sounded the alarm, and his character and sources of information were such that his words made a powerful impression on the public opinion of the country. On the 3d of March, twenty members of Congress united in an address to the people of the Free States, assuring them that the annexation of Texas had been resolved upon by the statesmen and politicians of the South; that the object was to extend and perpetuate the institution of slavery; that it must involve us in a war with Mexico for its support; that no act could be more dangerous than for the Government to enter upon the conquest of territory to enlarge its power; and that a dissolution of the Union would not only result from the policy, but the act itself would be an abandonment of the Union then enjoyed and the formation of a new one with foreign slaveholders. The address further declared that no act of the Executive, or of Congress, or of all the departments of the Government could impose upon the people of the Free States any constitutional obligation to submit to such a transfer, or to become subservient in any degree to the foreign slaveholders of Texas. This address was written by Seth M. Gates, and was signed by John Quincy Adams, Seth M. Gates, William Slade, Wm. B. Calhoun, Joshua R. Giddings, Sherlock J. Andrews, Nathaniel B. Borden, Thomas C. Chittenden, John Mattocks, Christopher Morgan, Jacob M. Howard, Victory Birdseye, Thomas Tomlinson, Staley N. Clarke, Charles Hudson, Archibald L. Linn, Thomas W. Williams, Truman Smith, David Bronson, and Geo. N. Briggs. It was published at the close of the session in the "National Intelligencer," and was generally copied by the Whig papers of the North.

The project was now fairly launched. This address called the attention of the Mexican Government to the conspiracy then on foot in the United States to dismember that Republic, and the Mexican Executive notified the President that Texas was a revolted province which the Government of Mexico was endeavoring to bring back to its allegiance, and that its annexation to the United States would necessarily involve a state of hostilities between the two countries. The President entered upon the work of negotiating a treaty of annexation, while the fact that Lord Brougham had declared in the House of Lords that "the abolition of slavery in Texas would cut off the market for slaves now sent from the slave-breeding States of the Union to Texas, and thereby tend to the abolition of slavery in the States," was referred to as an incident of an "alarming character."

When the Twenty-eighth Congress assembled, in December, 1843, two of the anti-slavery colleagues of Giddings, Messrs. Gates and Slade, had retired from public life, and their seats were filled by new and untried members. Mr. Adams alone, now seventy-six years of age, remained. His hand was unsteady and his voice feeble, but his mind was unimpaired, and although much discouraged, he was fully resolved to continue at his post of duty so long as his strength would permit. His age and historic position partially shielded him from the violence of his Southern assailants; but with Giddings the case was different. He was contemptuously denounced as an "Abolitionist" and an "agitator." It was the fashion of Democratic papers everywhere to assail him, while public meetings of the party singled him out for denunciation. The Press of his own party did not sustain him, and the common civilities usually extended to members of Congress were denied him. He exchanged cards with but few, and wholly abstained from making calls of ceremony. After having long served as Chairman of the Committee on Claims, he was now removed from that post, and assigned to the seventh position in the Committee on Revolutionary Pensions, which had no business and did not meet. Such were the circumstances under which he resumed his public duties. But he accepted the situation without flinching, and girded himself for the conflict.

At this session Mr. Adams succeeded in having a committee appointed, of which he was chairman, to report a code of rules for the government of the House. He made a report omitting the Twenty-first Rule, and the debate upon it during the morning hour was continued for several weeks, when it was laid on the table by a small majority. Giddings relates that during the progress of this debate, on entering the hall one morning, he found Mr. Adams greatly burdened in mind. His appearance indicated the loss of sleep. He declared that our government had become the most perfect despotism of the Christian world; that he was physically disqualified to contend longer for the floor; and that he must leave the vindication of his report to Giddings, as duty to himself forbade further attempt on his part. He said he had indulged the hope of living to see the gag-rule abrogated, but he now considered this doubtful. Giddings was touched by this appeal, and on obtaining the floor on the 2d of February following, he made a vigorous argument against the rule, which hastened its approaching overthrow.

On the 28th of December, a colored man named William Jones, who had been imprisoned in the Washington jail on suspicion that he was a fugitive, found means to send a petition to Giddings, stating that he was a free citizen of the United States, born in Virginia, and while residing in Washington, without any charge of crime or offence, he had been seized and imprisoned, and after considerable expense had been incurred, which he was unable to pay, he was advertised for sale to meet the costs of this proceeding. He asserted that he had no owner but God, and he prayed Congress to protect him in the enjoyment of his liberty. Giddings presented his petition, and moved its reference to a select committee. The presentation of this petition from one *presumed* by Southern laws to be a slave created some sensation, but there was no display of ruffianism, and no motion to censure the member presenting it. The petition was respectfully received, but the debate upon it was postponed until the following day, when Mr. Saunders of North Carolina declared that the law in all Slave States, and in the District of Columbia, presumed every colored person a slave who could not prove his freedom, and that respect for this law demanded the instant rejection of the petition. To this it was replied that no such presumption could be just or reasonable, or in accordance with the Constitution, and that it was neither more nor less than a mode of enslaving free persons, and was piratical in its character. The subject was debated at some length, after which the petition was referred to the Committee on the Judiciary, which never made any report.

In the course of the debate Mr. Adams referred to the fact that in the preceding Congress, when a citizen of Louisiana was shown to be illegally imprisoned in the Washington jail, the House promptly suspended the rules in order to pass a bill for his relief, and within a half hour from its introduction the bill reached the Senate. But the wronged man in this case was *white*.

On the same day the vigilance of Giddings found further employment in dealing with our home squadron. The subject was brought before the House by a resolution of Mr. Hale, of New Hampshire, calling for certain information respecting this establishment. Its ostensible purpose was the protection of American commerce; but Giddings joined Adams in warning the public that the interests of slavery were chiefly concerned in its operations. He referred to the fact that a lieutenant in command of one of our national vessels had prostituted the flag of his country to the base purpose of catching fugitive slaves on the coast of Florida. He declared that the coastwise slave-trade was no part of American commerce, as the Supreme Court had decided, and he was opposed to the use of the navy for the relief of slave-ships employed in transporting human cargoes around the peninsula of Florida to the New Orleans market. The agitation of this question seemed to be very distasteful to Southern members, and after a brief debate they managed to suppress it.

It was in the latter part of December that Mr. Adams introduced the memorial of the Massachusetts Legislature, praying an amendment of that feature of the Constitution which allowed three fifths of the slaves to be counted in the basis of representation. It gave rise to a memorable debate, and was referred to a select committee of nine members, consisting of Adams of Massachusetts, Rhett of South Carolina, J. R. Ingersoll of Pennsylvania, Gilmer of Virginia, Davis of Kentucky, Burke of New Hampshire, Morse of Maine, Sample of Indiana, and Giddings of Ohio. The question involved was seriously argued in committee, after which a resolution was unanimously adopted, declaring it inexpedient at that time for the House to recommend such an amendment of the Constitution, and the chairman, Mr. Adams, was directed to prepare a report to that effect. It was not ready till April, 1844, when every member was present to hear it read. It declared that the provision of the Constitution giving the enslavers of men superior power and influence in the government over non-slaveholders "is opposed to the vital principles of Republican representation; to the self-evident truths of the Declaration of Independence; to the letter and spirit of the Constitution itself; to the letter and spirit of the Constitutions of almost all the States of the Union; to the liberties of the whole people of the Free States, and to all that portion of the people of the Slave States other than the owners of slaves; that this is its essential and inextinguishable character in principle; and that its fruits, in its entire practical operation upon the government, correspond with that character." The report further declared that "the Declaration of Independence constituted a sacred pledge in the name of God, solemnly given by each State, to abolish slavery as soon as practicable, and to substitute freedom in its place;" and that "slavery is opposed to all the teachings of the gospel, is at war with God's attribute of justice, and should be eradicated from the earth."

While this report conceded that the time for recommending the proposed change of the Constitution had not yet arrived, the doctrines it enunciated were well calculated to arouse in the American people a spirit of liberty that would hasten the day of total emancipation. It was such an arraignment of the viciousness of slave representation as John Quincy Adams alone could make, and its influence upon public opinion was inestimable. Adams and Giddings alone signed this report, while the other members of the committee agreed upon three special reports, drawn to meet the views of the members who signed them. The memorial and resolves of the Legislature of Massachusetts were presented in the Senate, where they were denounced as "resolutions to dissolve the Union," and were laid on the table; but *the motion to print them was rejected*. A few days later, Mr. Berrien of Georgia presented resolutions from that State in opposition to the change of the Constitution prayed for by Massachusetts. These resolutions were respectfully laid on the table, and *ordered to be printed*. So craven was the Senate that this insult to Massachusetts and discrimination in favor of the barbarism of slavery was suffered to go unrebuked by any voice in that body.

On the 18th of April Giddings addressed the House on the claim of the Spanish pirates, Montez and Ruiz, for compensation for the loss of the negroes on board the "Amistad." This claim, as we have seen, had been declared void by the Supreme Court of the United States; but it was now brought before Congress in a bill from the Committee on Foreign Affairs, accompanied by an elaborate report from its chairman, Hon. Charles J. Ingersoll of Pennsylvania, who moved to print ten thousand extra copies.

The speech of Giddings has been referred to in a preceding chapter; but it does so much honor both to his head and his heart that some further mention of it is demanded. In his opening remarks he said, —

"The proposition goes one degree beyond any other ever made to this body. We have been called on to sustain our own coastwise slave-trade, but never were we asked to support the African slave-trade, until the presentation of the report under consideration. We have been called on, as the House is aware, to legislate for the encouragement of our own slave-merchants; but never, until this report came before us, were we asked to sustain the slave-dealers of Cuba. We have surely entered upon a new era in our national legislation. The people of the Free States should certainly understand the burdens we are about to place upon them.

"The advocates of oppression are desirous of preparing the public mind to receive the insult about to be tendered the people of the North. Hence the necessity of sending out this extraordinary number of the report, which is perhaps the ablest vindication of the foreign slave-trade that has emanated from any legislative body during the present century. And it is hoped that this argument will have the effect of reconciling our people of the North to the degradation of becoming involved in the guilt of sustaining this commerce.

"The author of the report is entitled to much credit for the boldness of his positions. To stand forth upon the records of our nation as the advocate of Spanish slave-merchants, to espouse the cause of foreign slave-dealers, and to denounce those who oppose that 'execrable commerce,' requires at this day no small portion of moral courage. The report in question, with great gravity, proposes to review and re-examine the solemn decision of the highest judicial tribunal known to our laws. It goes on to point out the supposed errors, and proposes that we shall correct them.

"This, I believe, is the first proposition of the kind ever brought before this body. A new precedent is sought to be established. We are to erect ourselves into a court for the correction of errors committed in the judicial branch of government. How far the precedent is to extend, I know not; nor am I able to say whether this supervisory power is also to extend over the executive department or not. We have generally found much more business than we have been able to transact while we confined ourselves to the legitimate subjects of legislation. But if, to these ordinary duties, we add that of a court for the correction of errors, it will become necessary to have another department formed, whose duty it shall be to *legislate* for the nation. And what, I ask, is the occasion which demands of us thus to assume new duties unknown to the Constitution? Why, sir, it is nothing less than to pay a sum of money from the public treasury to these slave-traders, in a case where the law will not give it; where respect for ourselves, for our own consistency, and for the character of the nation forbid it; where justice, humanity, and the Constitution forbid it.

"We appropriate a million of dollars annually to suppress the African slave-trade and to hang our own people who engage in it; and we are now asked to pay a large sum to the Spanish slave-dealers to encourage them to persevere in their accursed vocation. How many gentlemen who placed their names on record but a few days since in favor of so large an appropriation of money to suppress this African slave-trade, are now willing to record their names in favor of an appropriation of seventy thousand dollars to promote it? How many are prepared to vote for that trade to-day who voted against it yesterday?"

Giddings argued the case at length and with great thoroughness, presenting the legal and moral aspects of the question with much clearness and force. He concluded, —

"We have been called to legislate in favor of the slave-dealers of our own land. We have been asked to pay them for slaves lost and for slaves stolen; but never, until this report was made, has Congress been called on to pay foreigners for their losses while dealing in human flesh. I have felt it my duty to meet this proposition at the threshold, and to oppose it with what energy and influence I possess. I have done so, knowing the feeling arrayed against me; but the country, the people of this widespread Republic, now and hereafter, will pronounce judgment upon those attempts to prostitute our powers to the support of a commerce in our own species."

At the conclusion of his speech the motion to print was laid on the table, and neither the bill nor the report was ever called up for consideration afterwards. On the following day Giddings wrote, —

MY DEAR DAUGHTER, — ... You will see by the " Intelligencer " of this morning that yesterday brought me in contact with the famous C. J. Ingersoll, of Philadelphia. He had prepared a disgraceful report and bill to take seventy thousand dollars from the public treasury to pay to the Spanish slave-dealers on board the "Amistad." I felt indignant on reading the report. Ingersoll moved to print ten thousand copies for distribution. I broke forth and spoke as I felt. He felt my thrusts, for he constantly interrupted me, and each interruption placed him in a more unenviable situation than before. I used up my hour, and when I took my seat, my old and venerable friend Mr. Adams came to my seat and thanked me with great feeling, and added, "You have told us God's truth." Other friends assured me that I made a better speech than I ever made before. I expected that Ingersoll would be down upon me this morning with great power; but after examining my positions he submitted to have the motion laid on the table, and this is an end of it. You see by the "Intelligencer" a short sketch of my remarks; but it is meagre. The short passages at arms between us gave much amusement to members, who several times cheered me loudly, while the slave-holders sat around me in silent sadness. You must excuse me for not correcting what I have written; I have no time to do so. God bless you!

J. R. GIDDINGS.

On the 21st of May, Giddings addressed the House on the question of annexation. Many speeches had been made in favor of the project, but this was the first in opposition. Referring to the argument that the acquisition of Texas was necessary to the security of slavery, and that, therefore, the guarantees of the Constitution required it, he said, —

"Sir, this senseless jargon, this eternal repetition concerning the 'guarantees of slavery,' is daily sounding in our ears. It is put forth by men of character and those high in office. Sir, the idea that the Constitution contains a guarantee of slavery is an impeachment both of the sincerity and the judgment of the framers of that charter of American liberty; and I take this occasion to repeat my assertion that no such stipulation exists, or ever did exist, in that instrument. And standing here, in the presence of so many learned and able statesmen of the South, many of whom have repeated the unfounded assumption, I call upon any one or all of them to refer me to any such covenant or stipulation in the Constitution.

"Mr. BRENGLE of Maryland stated that at the formation of the Constitution slavery existed in most of the States, and that slaves were regarded as property, and, in that light, were the subject of protection as much as any other property.

"Mr. GIDDINGS. Will the gentleman point me to the section in which I may find this *guarantee?*

"Mr. BRENGLE. I don't refer to any section in particular, but to the whole instrument. [A laugh.]

"Mr. GIDDINGS. Well, Mr. Chairman, I have finally chased this notable guarantee into the region of Southern abstractions; but I declare I never came so near finding it before. [Laughter.] . . .

"But I ask, where is the power to annex territory to the Union for the purpose of sustaining slavery in a foreign state? To open up new slave-markets? To assume the war of a foreign state? To use the army and navy, and violate our treaties with other governments, for the purpose of perpetuating an institution which we detest? I denounce all these efforts to plunge us into a war, to pour out the treasure and the blood of a nation that slavery and the slave-trade may flourish, as violations of the Constitution and of the dearest rights of the people.

"I discard the idea of interfering with the institution in any of the States. I admit their power to hold slaves, independent of Congress or of the Federal Government. Sir, I admit your legal right, under the laws of Virginia, to hold your fellow-man in bondage. I cannot interfere with that privilege. But while I do this, I demand an equal respect for the rights and privileges of the people of my State. Ohio has an indisputable right to be free and exempt from the support of slavery."

Returning to the question of power, Giddings said:

"Sir, the President, in seeking to sustain slavery in Texas, proposes to annex that government to this Union. Those who oppose this policy deny the constitutional power to associate a foreign people with us in the administration of government. To this the gentleman from Alabama [Mr. Belser] replied rather sneeringly, as I thought, that there was a class of public men who deny the constitutional power of the Federal Government to annex Texas to this Union. He then went on to say that such were the views of the Abolitionists, and that their candidate for President [James G. Birney] had started this doctrine. Now, I beg leave to differ with that gentleman as to the authorship of this doctrine. It had been put forth long before Mr. Birney's letter was written. It was put forth by a greater abolitionist than Mr. Birney, by a man whom I have always regarded as a far greater man, and to whose opinions I have, from my youth up, been taught to pay the highest respect. [Cries, 'Who is it? Who is it?'] He was the author of the first abolition tract ever published in the United States, and, in my opinion, the best ever put forth. [Cries, 'Name him! Name him!'] I borrowed my own abolition sentiments from his writings, and have cherished them, and shall continue to do so, from respect to his memory, if from no other motive. His name was *Thomas Jefferson*. [A laugh.] And his abolition tract was called the *Declaration of Independence* [great laughter]."

The question of annexation now completely occupied the public mind in every section of the Union. In furtherance of the scheme, Mr. Webster had been retired from the State Department, and Mr. Upshur, a disciple of Calhoun, succeeded him. On Upshur's death Calhoun himself was made Secretary of State. Pending the negotiation of a treaty of annexation, the question found its way into our party politics and dictated the Presidential nomination. Mr. Clay was nominated by the Whigs, on the 1st of May, and his position on this question had been clearly defined in his letter to the "National Intelligencer" of the 17th of April, in which he declared that annexation and war with Mexico were identical, and placed himself squarely against it, except upon conditions named, which would make the project of immediate annexation impossible. On the slavery question he had not yet seriously offended the anti-slavery element in his own party, and was even trusted by some of the voting Abolitionists. In his speech at Raleigh, in April of this year, he declared it to be the duty of each State to sustain its own domestic institutions. He had publicly said that the General Government had nothing to do with slavery save in the matters of taxation, representation, and the return of fugitive slaves; and he had condemned the censure of Giddings, in 1842, as an outrage, and indorsed the principles laid down in his papers signed "Pacificus."

James K. Polk was nominated by the Democrats, on the 27th of May, solely on the ground that he was unequivocally committed to the policy of immediate annexation, and because Mr. Van Buren, in the face of a great temptation, had written his manly and statesmanlike letter in disapproval of the project. The Liberty party had nominated James G. Birney in August of the previous year, so that there were now three Presidential candidates, all chosen with special reference to the same great question.

The cordial friendship existing between Clay and Giddings at this time is shown in a letter to Mrs. Giddings, dated April 28, from which I quote:—

"Mr. Clay came to the city on Friday. I called to pay my respects and to introduce my colleagues. He is in fine health, and appeared glad to see me. Although many Southern men of high standing were present, he complimented me on the course I had taken in public life, and declared my views to be correct. By the way, while in North Carolina he avowed my principles, without, however, making any allusion to me. It is not unlikely that I felt flattered by the compliment he paid me; and I certainly felt a high gratification when I read his remarks at Raleigh, in which he set forth, in a short and lucid manner, the entire doctrines of 'Pacificus.'"

The confidence of Giddings in the anti-slavery character of Henry Clay is one of the remarkable facts of his public life. It may be partially accounted for by his admiration for the great leader, which he shared with all his fellow Whigs, and by the indescribable power of Clay's personal magnetism, which was even more potent in the social circle than in his public speeches. In the speech from which I have just quoted, he says,—

"I verily believe that Mr. Clay will administer the government, if elected, with a strict regard to the *constitutional rights of all the States*. This he stands pledged to do; and a long life of public service has given me and the public satisfactory evidence that he will wipe out the foul disgrace already brought upon our national character by attempting to make slavery and the slave-trade subjects of *national* support."

And yet in his famous speech in the Senate against the Abolitionists, in 1839, Clay had declared himself against the abolition of slavery and the slave-trade in the District of Columbia. He had justified the action of Congress in behalf of the coastwise slave-trade by referring it to the power of Congress to regulate commerce between the States. He had opposed the prohibition of slavery in the Territory of Florida. He had declared that "that is property which the law makes *to be* property," and that "two hundred years of legislation have sanctioned and *sanctified* negro slaves as property,"— doctrines which Giddings and all the Abolitionists on both sides of the Atlantic utterly repudiated. He had repeated the current accusation that the Abolitionists had tightened the chains of slavery and postponed indefinitely the work of emancipation, while he declared that as a citizen of any one of the planting States, he would oppose "any scheme of emancipation whatever, gradual or immediate." It should be remembered, too, that in the Senate, in 1840, he joined Calhoun in the effort to nationalize slavery and the traffic in slaves, by supporting the resolutions of the latter touching the slave-ship "Enterprise." Indeed, it was Clay's offensive record on the slavery question which armed the Liberty party with its power, and exposed Giddings to the hot shot of the followers of Birney on the one hand, and the equally galling fire of the annexationists on the other. It is quite evident, therefore, that when Clay declared it to be the duty of each State to sustain its own domestic institutions, and indorsed "the entire doctrines of 'Pacificus,'" he meant one thing, while Giddings meant a totally different thing.

But the issue in this canvass involved other considerations than the attitude of Mr. Clay on the slavery question. Giddings was a Whig, and thus far his Whig constituents had sustained him. In Congress the Whigs from the Northern States, as a rule, had stood by him in his fight over the "Creole" resolutions, his struggle for the right of petition, and his effort to denationalize slavery. Quite naturally he looked to the Whig party as the instrumentality through which he could best hope to give practical effect to his anti-slavery principles. In common with other Whigs, he believed that in this canvass the best elements of society, in a very large measure, stood behind Clay,— the men of intelligence, high character, public spirit, and uprightness in every walk of life; while Polk was backed by Southern fire-eaters, slavery extensionists, and nullifiers, who were ready to subordinate the Constitution itself to their zeal for their peculiar institution, and who were reinforced by nearly the solid foreign vote, and the vicious and criminal classes in all the great cities of the North and in New Orleans.

To Giddings the question of duty seemed perfectly clear. On the vital issue of annexation Clay had clearly defined his position in the papers already mentioned. Giddings firmly believed that his election would avert the calamities of war and the fatal ascendancy of slavery which would follow the acquisition of Texas. The slaveocracy agreed with him. Its champions believed the restriction of slavery foreshadowed its destruction, and their zeal for annexation proved the sincerity of this opinion. The issue could not be mistaken, nor could its magnitude be overstated. The duty of the hour was not to promulgate a creed and organize a new party, but to meet a fearful national emergency. An opportunity was now offered to strike at the life of slavery by strangling the only project through which it could hope to extend its dominion; and no member of the Liberty party could have labored more zealously and conscientiously for his candidate than did Giddings for the idolized leader of the Whigs.

The canvass, however, brought with it much anxiety to the Whigs, and this was chiefly caused by the action of Mr. Clay himself. On the 6th of July Giddings addressed to him the following confidential letter: —

DEAR SIR, — On my return from Washington I found our people as much engaged in the coming contest as I had expected. Our Fourth of July passed off in a manner highly flattering to our cause. Our people, of all political parties, regard the great questions to be, Whether the nation shall assume upon itself the support of slavery in the States? Whether the people of the Free States shall be involved in the expense of its maintenance? These questions, you are aware, are pressed upon our attention in the official correspondence accompanying the Texas treaty; and we regard them as important, and even vital, to our institutions. We are therefore rallying upon that issue. From your Texas letter, and the analysis of Whig doctrines given in your speech at Raleigh, we regarded you as opposed to these propositions. In the ninth article of the Whig faith, as given in your published remarks, you state "the maintenance *exclusively* by the several States of their own local and peculiar institutions" to be a fundamental doctrine of the Whig party. On the 4th instant the "National Intelligencer" arrived, with your Raleigh speech as written out by yourself. In it we find no allusion to the above doctrine. This has led many to apprehend that we have mistaken your views on this all-important point. Indeed, the absence of all allusion to it in your speech as written by yourself has created great apprehension in the minds of many of your friends. I regard it as important that we should be informed on the subject. Indeed, our people feel that they have the right to understand your sentiments in respect to this important question now pressed upon us by the opposition party.

I would, therefore most respectfully suggest that you cause your views on this point to be made public in such way as your judgment may dictate. The importance of such a step can only be appreciated by those who understand the deep feeling which now pervades the minds of a portion of the people of all the Free States against all participation in the support of the institution of slavery. If I have myself mistaken your views, I beg you will inform me at your earliest leisure.

With great respect,
Your ob't servant,
J. R. GIDDINGS.

To this letter Giddings received the following confidential reply: —

ASHLAND, July 19, 1844.

MY DEAR SIR, — I received, and thank you for, your friendly letter of the 6th instant, and I am extremely happy to receive the encouraging accounts which it communicates of the progress of the Whig cause. I had before received, from other sources, highly gratifying information of the zeal and ability with which you were sustaining it. The omission in my Raleigh speech, as published, of the principle of "the maintenance exclusively by the several States of their own local and peculiar institutions," was altogether accidental and without any design. I adhere faithfully to that principle, which I have on various occasions announced. The declaration of that principle by me once is as good as a thousand times; for I hope all men will do me the justice to suppose that I intend faithfully to execute, as far as I can, every public pledge or promise or assurance I may make. The Raleigh speech, as corrected by me, was written out by the aid of notes taken by a stenographer at the time it was delivered, and there are other omissions of what I said in the delivery of it unintentionally made. Your own experience in the preparation for the Press of speeches previously delivered, will have suggested to you how impracticable it is to write them out exactly as they were delivered. I have great repugnance to appearing before the public without an urgent necessity. You will understand and appreciate my motives. But if a suitable occasion shall occur I will take pleasure in complying with your request again to announce the principle, the omission of which in the Raleigh speech has occasioned your regret.

I offer you cordial congratulations upon our success in Louisiana. I consider that State as certain for us in November as any State in the Union; and I am happy to be able to add that the Whig cause will sustain no prejudice from the Texas question anywhere at the South or Southwest.

I am your friend and obedient servant,

H. CLAY.

To HON. JOSHUA R. GIDDINGS.

The omitted passage in the Raleigh speech was repeated in a letter from Clay published in the "Lexington Observer" of September 2; but his troubles were only fairly begun. His Southern supporters began to show signs of discontent respecting his attitude on the question of annexation, and in a moment of weakness he wrote his unfortunate "Alabama letters." In the letter of the 27th of July he said: "I do not think that the subject of slavery ought to affect the question one way or the other. Whether Texas be independent or incorporated into the United States, I do not believe it will prolong or shorten the duration of that institution." He also declared that he "would be glad to see it [the annexation of Texas] without dishonor, without war, with the common consent of the Union, and upon just and fair terms." These words were most chilling to Giddings and his anti-slavery supporters, who were utterly opposed to annexation on *any* terms, because the power of slavery would thus inevitably be extended and strengthened in the Union. The letter was a disastrous mistake, and grew out of Clay's besetting tendency to mediate between opposing policies, instead of planting his feet on the solid ground of principle and bravely accepting the consequences.

Giddings was sorely troubled, and he gave earnest expression to his feelings in a letter to Clay, which has not been preserved, but to which the latter replied as follows: —

[Confidential.]

ASHLAND, Sept. 11, 1844.

MY DEAR SIR, — Your friendly letter of the 4th instant, which I have just received, affords me a good opportunity of writing to you, which I very much desired. I am extremely sorry that my letters to Alabama should have produced any unfavorable impressions in your portion of Ohio. It was not my intention, in those letters, to vary the ground in the smallest degree which I had assumed in my Raleigh speech. It had been represented to me that in that speech I had displayed a determined opposition to the annexation of Texas to the United States, although the whole Union might be in favor of it, and it could be peacefully and honorably effected upon fair and just terms. It was my purpose, in those Alabama letters, to say that no personal or private motives prompted me to oppose annexation, but that my opinion in opposition to it was founded solely upon public and general considerations. I therefore said that if by common consent of the Union, without national dishonor, without war, and upon just conditions, the object of annexation could be accomplished, I did not wish to be considered as standing in opposition to the wishes of the whole confederacy, but on the supposition stated would be glad to see those wishes gratified.

Could I say less? Can it be expected that I should put myself in opposition to the concurrent will of the whole nation, if such should be its will? You appear to have rightly conceived me; and I think any one who will take a fair and candid view of all my letters together, must be satisfied with their import, and perfectly convinced of my entire consistency. But, my dear sir, as I had learned from Pittsburg that my last Alabama letter was operating mischievously there, I have addressed a letter to James Dunlap, Esq., and others, in which I reaffirmed all the sentiments and opinions which I expressed in my Raleigh speech, and go the length of saying that if three such States as Ohio, Massachusetts, and Vermont were to manifest a decided opposition to the annexation of Texas, it ought not to be annexed to the United States. That letter will be published, will probably reach you by the time that this does, and I confidently anticipate will be satisfactory.

My position is very singular. Whilst at the South I am represented as a Liberty man, at the North I am decried as an ultra supporter of slavery; when in fact I am neither one nor the other. This peculiarity of position exposes me to a cross-fire from opposite directions, and rendered it indispensably necessary that I should come out a few days ago with a note in relation to a letter of Cassius M. Clay, Esq., first published in the "Tribune." That letter, although I have no doubt it was written with the best intentions, was doing great mischief to the Whig cause even here in Kentucky, and there was much reason to apprehend that it would be much more extensively prejudicial in the States of Tennessee, Georgia, North Carolina, and Louisiana, upon whose vote we have strong reason for counting. You, I trust, will be satisfied with the position taken in my note, — that the existence, maintenance, and continuance of the institution of slavery depend exclusively upon State power and authority. As you had expressed regret that my Raleigh speech should have omitted that principle, I thought the occasion a suitable one for reasserting it. I shall be very sorry if Mr. Clay should be at all wounded by my note. Such was not my intention, and if he had been here, he would have felt the imperative necessity for it.

I am, with great respect,
Your friend and obedient servant,
H. CLAY.

The HON. MR. GIDDINGS.

These letters are given in full, because they clearly reveal the complications in which Mr. Clay needlessly involved himself by his anxiety to succeed.

He threw away his advantages when victory was within his grasp, and thus grievously disappointed and mortified his devoted friends in both sections of the Union. His mistake was irreparable; for although his partisans still kept up the fight, he had alienated thousands of anti-slavery voters, whose help would have carried him safely through the contest if he had possessed sufficient courage and coolness to rest his cause on his Raleigh speech. His foolish attempt to explain his position showed vacillation and weakness in dealing with a great question, and necessarily invited the result he had so anxiously sought to avert.

Giddings, however, did not slacken his labors for the Whig cause. Clay was unquestionably right in saying that annexation and war were identical; and although, on the slavery question he might be feared as a compromiser, there was no valid reason to doubt that if elected he would resist the annexation scheme, except upon conditions already stated, which could not fail to defeat it as a present danger, and avoid the calamities of a foreign war. The struggle, as it proceeded, became angry and bitter to the last degree. Nearly all the young Whigs of the District had joined the Liberty party, and hundreds of the most devoted friends of Giddings in previous years were now fighting him. Crimination and recrimination became the order of the day between the Whigs and the Liberty men; but the man who had withstood the power of slavery in Congress for so many years was not to be silenced by his new assailants, who found that blows were to be received as well as given. Some of the leaders of the Liberty party charged Giddings with having sold himself to Henry Clay. In their hearts they did not believe this, and were only grieved and vexed that he would not see with their eyes. They asserted that he was more in the way of the progress of the Liberty party than any other man; to which he replied that the Liberty party was more in the way of the anti-slavery cause than all its members would be if they were openly supporting the Democratic ticket. He and the followers of Birney were substantially agreed in principle, and differed only as to the method of serving a common cause; but controversies are never more bitter than when the difference between the disputants is very small. It has been aptly said that if you want to see the true white heat of controversial passion, you should look at controversialists who *do not differ at all*, but who have adopted different words to express the same opinion.

Party animosities increased till the State election in October, when the vote was found so close that it depended upon the Whig majority in Ashtabula County. The returns were slow in reaching the capital, those from Ashtabula being among the last, and for a time the Democrats felt so sure of the State that in several localities they began to celebrate their victory by the firing of cannon, and other demonstrations; but when the returns from Ashtabula were received, an unprecedented party majority was shown, which gave the State to the Whigs. Mr. Clay and his friends in Lexington felt so grateful to Giddings for his indefatigable labors in this canvass that they sent a delegation to present a beautiful silk banner to the Whigs of the county for their efforts in this remarkable struggle. All this was sufficiently exasperating to the zealous supporters of Mr. Birney.

But Clay was defeated. Polk's Kane letter on the

tariff was so marvellously utilized as to give him the State of Pennsylvania. Nativism, which had just broken out in the great cities, so alarmed our foreign-born citizens as to throw them almost unanimously against the Whigs. The Plaquemine frauds in Louisiana, which were engineered by John Slidell, and accomplished through the shipment of roughs and scoundrels from New Orleans to Plaquemine, undoubtedly gave that State to the Democrats, while New York was lost to Clay on account of his trimming on the question of annexation, which drove from him a sufficient number of anti-slavery men to accomplish his defeat. Such was the ill-fated result of this memorable struggle. Looking back to the strifes of that time, and judging them by the light of subsequent events, we see clearly that Giddings and those of his Whig friends who supported Clay as an anti-slavery man in any honest sense of the term were mistaken. They were not less mistaken in looking forward to the Whig party as a trustworthy agency in confronting the aggressions of the South, while it should be admitted with equal frankness that Texas would have been annexed at no distant time if Clay had been made President. The poison of slavery had so entered into the life of the people that the triumph of Polk and immediate annexation only quickened the march of events towards the final catastrophe of civil war, which the supineness of the people of the Northern States had already made unavoidable.

In previous chapters the mutual friendship of Adams and Giddings has been repeatedly referred to. It steadily grew stronger with time, and ripened into affection. In his later years Mr. Adams led a solitary life. His open hostility to slavery had greatly multiplied his enemies in both sections of the Union, and severely tried his faith in humanity. His intimate and trusted friends were few. While in age, acquirements, intellectual training, experience, and social advantages, he and Giddings were the opposites of each other, yet their relations were as kindly and dutiful as those of father and son. Each loved the other for the enemies he had made in battling for the rights of man. Their bond of union was the heroic service of a great cause, for which each was ready to suffer. Their friendship had in it the qualities of a religion. It was during this year, when Mr. Adams was nearly seventy-eight years old, that he gave expression to this warmth of his feelings towards his friend in the following lines, written in a trembling hand, in an autograph album kept by Giddings at that time : —

TO JOSHUA R. GIDDINGS,

OF JEFFERSON, ASHTABULA CO., OHIO.

When first together here we meet,
    Askance each other we behold,
The bitter mingling with the sweet,
    The warm attempered by the cold.

We seek with searching ken to find
    A soul congenial to our own ;
For mind, in sympathy with mind,
    Instinctive dreads to walk alone.

And here, from regions wide apart,
    We came, our purpose to pursue,
Each with a warm and honest heart,
    Each with a spirit firm and true.

Intent, with anxious aim to learn,
    Each other's character we scan,
And soon the difference discern
    Between the fair and faithless man.

And here, with scrutinizing eye,
  A kindred soul with mine to see,
And longing bosom to descry,
  I sought, and found at last — in thee.

Farewell, my friend! and if once more
  We meet within this hall again,
Be ours the blessing to restore
  Our country's and the *rights of men*.

              JOHN QUINCY ADAMS,
                    Of Quincy, Massachusetts.

H. R. U. S., WASHINGTON, 17 June, 1844,
  Anniversary of the Battle of Bunker Hill.

CHAPTER VII.

DECEMBER, 1844, TO MARCH, 1847.

Last Session of the Twenty-eighth Congress. — Repeal of the Gag-rule. — Insolence of Southern Members. — General Jessup as a Slave-trader. — Mr. Calhoun's New Argument for Annexation. — The Measure consummated. — First Session of the Twenty-ninth Congress. — The Oregon Question. — The War with Mexico. — Minor Questions. — Last Session of the Twenty-ninth Congress.

EARLY in this session, which convened on the 2d of December, 1844, Mr. Adams renewed his customary attack upon the gag-rule. Against all odds, and in the face of a furious opposition, he had kept up this fight for ten years, and at last his motion to strike the rule from the manual was carried by a vote of 108 to 80. The ranks of its supporters had been growing thinner year by year, until now only fourteen members from the Free States voted against rescinding it, while four members from the Slave States voted for its repeal. It was a great victory; but while the right of petition was restored to the people, it was practically nullified by the Speaker, who so formed the committees that petitions in regard to slavery were retained by them until the close of the session, when they found their final resting-place among the archives of the House.

The signal triumph of slavery in the recent election inspired Southern members with renewed courage and zeal, and rendered them less tolerant of opposition. This was illustrated on the 6th of February, 1845, when Giddings addressed the committee of the whole on the bill making appropriations to carry out our treaty stipulations with the Indian tribes. He discussed the subject in its relations to slavery, and among other things referred to the claim of certain Georgia slaveholders who, after receiving $109,000 as a compensation for their fugitive slaves, demanded of the Government, and were allowed, $141,000 more as a compensation for the slaves which the females *would have borne to their masters, had they remained in bondage.*

Mr. Black of Georgia obtained the floor to reply, and was immediately surrounded by Southern members. His abuse was too grossly personal and vulgar to be reported in full. He referred to the charge that Giddings was interested in the horses which one Torrey lost when attempting to aid slaves to escape in Maryland. He said that Torrey had died in the Penitentiary, and that Giddings ought to be there, and would be sent at once if the House could decide the question. He declared that Giddings had violated the law by franking through the post-office a calico dress to his wife; and he closed by advising him to return to his constituents and ascertain if he had a character, for Black asserted before Heaven he had none in that hall.

Giddings replied that as to the story about his connection with Torrey and his horses, which had been referred to a year before by the gentleman from Alabama (Mr. Payne) and denied, he knew nothing but what he had seen in the newspapers, and that he made this statement for the benefit of *gentlemen*,—of men who understood the decencies of life, and not for that of the member from Alabama, or his less worthy *confrère* from Georgia, to whom he owed no other respect than that which parliamentary law *constrained* him to observe. In regard to the charge of franking a calico dress, he knew nothing, and could only say that it was an unmitigated falsehood.[1] He said the member from Georgia was less responsible for his conduct than were the respectable members who stood around him while speaking, and prompted his coarseness and brutality; that in treating of the institution of slavery he had confined himself to matters of fact which were authenticated by official documents, and which the member from Georgia did not deny; and that he represented an intelligent constituency, who a few months before had indorsed his action in Congress by a fourth election, while Mr. Black had been discarded after one election as unworthy to hold a place among honorable men.

The scene which followed was described by the newspapers of the time and by Mr. Adams in his diary. While Mr. Giddings was speaking, Black passed through the lobby behind the Speaker's chair, and entered the small aisle on the right of Giddings, and raising a large cane which he held in his hand, said: "If you repeat those words, I will knock you down." Giddings, under the impulse of the moment, repeated the language he had used, in order to test the courage of Black, whose friends, seeing the position in which he had placed himself, now took charge of him. Mr. Adams says: "As he pressed on, with a face convulsed and the look of a coward fiend, Mr. Hammet threw his arms around

---

[1] A note addressed by Mr Giddings to Mr. Wickliffe, then Postmaster-General, led to the development of some interesting facts. The supposed calico dress was a shawl franked by a Democratic member of Congress from northern Ohio to his wife. Mr. Wickliffe and the member called on Giddings, and entreated him so urgently to take no further action in the matter that he reluctantly consented.

him and carried him away as he would a woman from a fire."

Giddings continued his remarks, when Mr. Dawson of Louisiana, who had assaulted him on a previous occasion, came across the hall within a few yards of him, and placing his hand in his pocket, said, "I'll shoot him, by G—d! I'll shoot him!" at the same time taking care to cock his pistol so as to have the click heard by those around him. Mr. Causin, a Whig from Maryland, instantly took his position in front of Giddings and directly between him and Dawson, folding his arms across his breast, with his right hand apparently resting upon the handle of his weapon, while Mr. Slidell of Louisiana, and Mr. Stiles of Georgia, with two other Democratic members, at the same moment took their positions near Dawson. At the same time Kenneth Raynor, a North Carolina Whig, fully armed, took his place on the left of Giddings, while Mr. Hudson of Massachusetts placed himself on his right, and Mr. Foot of Vermont at the entrance of the aisle through which Black had made his exit. With armed foes in front and friends on either hand, Giddings continued his remarks; but the slaveholders in front began to realize the awkwardness of their position, and quietly returned to their seats, except Dawson, who remained until Giddings closed his speech, with Causin firmly facing him. The business of legislation was then resumed. Giddings, in his "History of the Rebellion," says that this was the last effort made to silence a member of the House by threats of personal violence during his service in Congress.

The hostility of Southern members of Congress towards Giddings cannot be regarded as surprising. From the beginning of the government they had been accustomed to have their own way in its administration as well as on their plantations, and it maddened them to have their supremacy questioned. Giddings made it his mission to watch the encroachments of slavery upon the rights of the people of the Free States, and to hold the slave-masters strictly to their own avowed principle, that the existence and continuance of slavery depended solely on the authority of the States in which it existed. Wherever he saw this principle violated, he felt it to be his duty to lift up his voice in its defence; and, accordingly, only two days after the scene just described, he took occasion to expose the extraordinary character of a claim brought before Congress at its previous session, and now pending in the form of a bill providing for its payment.

Soon after General Jessup assumed command of our army in Florida, in 1836, he entered into a written contract with certain chiefs and warriors of the Creek tribe of Indians, by which they agreed to furnish two battalions, of not less than six hundred men each, to serve one year against the Seminoles; for which they were to receive ten thousand dollars, and such plunder as they might capture from the enemy. The law had provided the mode of enlisting troops, and determined the amount to be paid to each soldier; yet General Jessup did not appear to know that he was violating the law by entering into this contract. But the Executive and the War Department approved his action, and the Creek warriors entered upon the stipulated service. The Cherokees refused to furnish warriors for such a purpose, and their principal chief, John Ross, in an able letter to the Secretary of War, violently protested against the employment of Pagan warriors to fight the battles of a Christian nation.

The Creek warriors during the year captured more than one hundred negroes, who were claimed by the Indians as plunder under the contract, and were enslaved by their captors. General Jessup and the Secretary of War concurred in this action, and the practice of enslaving prisoners captured in war, which had long been abandoned by all Christian nations, was now revived by the American Government under the Administration of Jackson. But provisions being scarce, General Jessup published an order directing eight thousand dollars to be paid to the Indians as a compensation for these enslaved negroes, whom he ordered to be sent to Fort Pike, below New Orleans, as the *property* of the Government, which approved of these proceedings. The Commissioner of Indian Affairs, however, in an official communication, suggested that it was doubtful whether Congress would not hesitate in appropriating the money to carry out this arrangement. He did not appear to doubt the propriety of enslaving men in Florida, as well as on the African coast, but the novelty of these proceedings seems to have made an unfavorable impression upon his mind.

A solution of the difficulty was found. A rich slave-dealer from Georgia, James C. Watson, happened to be in Washington, and to him the whole subject was explained. A proposition was made for him to take these negroes, receive a bill of sale from the Creek Indians, to whom he should pay fifteen thousand dollars; and as the negroes were held by officers of the American army, the Secretary of War should issue an order to the officer having them in charge, directing their delivery to the slave-dealer.

But our military officers refused to respect the order of the Secretary of War. General Taylor positively declined to interfere in the matter, and General Gaines made vigorous efforts to save the negroes from Watson, who, after many disappointments and much expense, failed to obtain any of the negroes; and having paid his money for them at the request of our public officers, petitioned Congress for the refunding of the same, with interest and expenses. As already stated, Giddings had been removed from his place at the head of the Committee on Claims, and ex-Governor Vance, of Ohio, succeeded him. As he was without experience in his new duties, Howell Cobb of Georgia was added to the committee, with special reference to this claim, and he reported a bill to compensate Watson. Mr. Giddings tried in vain to get his Whig brethren interested in the case, and when it came before the House, he recited the facts already given, and gave his reasons for opposing the bill. He insisted that when General Jessup entered into a compact by which innocent women and children were to be captured and enslaved, he entered into a covenant for the commission of crime which we as a nation had declared piracy when committed on the African coast; that the place of committing such crimes could not alter their character; that both General Jessup and the Creek Indians deserved punishment for their conspiracy to deprive the Seminoles of the sacred rights which God had given them; that the Secretary of War, who sanctioned the contract, simply made himself a party to the crime, while the President was equally guilty; that the Constitution provides that "no person shall be deprived of life, liberty, or property without due process of law," — that is, without trial and conviction in a court of competent jurisdiction; and that Watson, who had attempted to make merchandise of human souls, certainly had no claim upon the people of the Northern States because he had failed to consummate the crime he had attempted.

Cobb and Stephens of Georgia, and Belser of Alabama, spoke in favor of the claim, after which Mr. Adams urged that all who participated in this attempt to enslave innocent people were criminals, and he moved to lay the bill on the table. Mr. Hammet of Mississippi, not being willing to risk a vote, moved an adjournment, and the bill was not again heard of during that Congress.

Mr. Calhoun's treaty for the annexation of Texas had been rejected on the 8th of June, 1844, and early in this session came before Congress for its action. Massachusetts and Connecticut had protested against the measure, and many remonstrances from the people of the Free States were submitted for the consideration of Congress. A new phase of the question was now presented by the instructions of Mr. Calhoun to our ministers at London and Paris, in which he argued that slavery is a humane institution, and advantageous to both master and slave. This new challenge of the slaveocracy was at once accepted by Giddings, and on the 22d of January, 1845, he addressed the House at length, and with much thoroughness and force, upon the economical and moral bearings of slavery upon the people of the South, both bond and free, and the constitutional powers of the Federal Government in dealing with it. He began by referring to the action of England, France, and Denmark against slavery, and said that —

"Even semi-barbarous nations are at this day lustrating themselves from its moral contagion. The Bey of Tripoli, in his decree prohibiting the slave-trade, which our honorable Secretary of State is so anxious to maintain, declared that he did it 'for the honor of man and the glory of God.' But while the Bey of

Tripoli and the Pasha of Egypt are extending the enjoyment of civil liberty, this government is openly engaged in endeavoring to extend the institution of slavery. While we ourselves are sending one fleet to suppress the slave-trade on the African coast, we are sending another to support the same traffic on the American coast. While we have entered into solemn treaty with England to exert our utmost effort to *suppress* this trade in human flesh, our Secretary of State is calling upon the king of France to assist us in extending and maintaining it. While we as a nation are professing to be lovers of liberty, our high officers of government are exerting our national influence to increase and extend slavery. . . . Of all the civilized nations of the earth, ours alone now stands as the advocate of negro slavery. The spectacle is humiliating; but so it is that the Executive of this nation is now remonstrating with European potentates against their efforts to promote human liberty, and using all the skill and intrigue of diplomacy to prevent the extension of human freedom."

Speaking of the economical bearings of slavery, as presented by Mr. Calhoun, Giddings said,—

"He urges upon Mr. King and the French Government that the abolition of slavery 'has diminished the exports of the British West India Islands,' and he infers that it would have the same effect in this country if our slaves were to follow their example in respect to emancipation. Now, sir, the argument is not legitimate. It places pecuniary profit in the scale against the natural rights of man, and gives preponderance to the former. Go to the thief, who lives and thrives by his midnight larcenies; remonstrate with him; tell him that the property of his neighbors of right belongs to them, and that he ought not feloniously to take it, — he may turn round, and, in the language of our honorable Secretary, say to you that were he to adopt your idea of justice, and cease his thefts, 'his exports would be diminished.' Go to the pirate, who robs the merchant-vessel of its rich lading, and, in order to destroy all evidence of his crimes, murders the crew and sinks the ship. Tell him that his practice is criminal, and that he ought to cease from further outrages; and he will reply, in the language of American diplomacy, that 'his exports would be diminished.' Still, we should regard him as a pirate, and hope that justice would overtake him. His excuse would not mitigate his crimes, — nay, it would aggravate his guilt. So with our Secretary's argument. If slavery be opposed to the natural rights of men, — if it be a self-evident truth that man is born free and has received from his God the right to enjoy his liberty, — then it is wrong; it is a crime for us to rob him of his God-given rights, although it may thereby increase our exports."

Giddings referred to slavery as an element of weakness.

"They [the slaves] are acquainted with the habits of their masters, — with their roads and streams, their arsenals and fortifications; in short, with all the circumstances with which they are surrounded. Now, sir, let an invading army of a hundred thousand men land in our Southern States, with the *material* for two hundred thousand, and let it proclaim freedom to such slaves as will unite with them, and as the slaves reach their encampment let them be armed and drilled, and sent out to liberate their wives and children and those who have been oppressed with them. Could more efficient troops be employed? Stimulated by a recollection of the wrongs which they had suffered, they would become desperate, and the consequences I will not attempt to describe! Sir, in case of invasion the master will not dare to send his servant abroad, or to the field, unless he is watched. If he does, the servant will not be likely to return. At night, too, they must be watched, and the family must be guarded against the domestics. Thus they detract from the ability of a nation to defend itself. In 1779 the authorities of South Carolina sent a special messenger to Congress to inform that body that their State could furnish no troops to repel the invasion then making upon them, as it required all their forces to remain at home in order to protect their families against their slaves. . . .

"I desire that Southern gentlemen will understand me as making these remarks strictly in answer to the doctrine advanced by Mr. Calhoun and others, and not with any desire to call up unpleasant feelings in the minds of any Southern man. General Jackson and others say that it is necessary that we should have Texas as a means of national defence. I reply, that every addition of slave territory renders us weaker, and places a heavier burden upon the Free States. This extension of slavery at the expense of our Free States is what the honorable Secretary regards as economy."

Mr. Giddings next referred to the economical bearings of slavery in connection with the Post-Office department, the navy, the public lands, and the cost of the Florida War; and then proceeded to contrast the condition of the leading Free and Slave

States. Turning next to Mr. Calhoun's position, that slavery is a moral institution, he said,—

"Gentlemen here become pathetic upon the sufferings to which the people of Texas have been subjected during their war with Mexico. They speak in melting terms of the predatory warfare heretofore carried on against Texas, and they ask the people of our Free States to relieve them from Mexican barbarity. Why, sir, there is more human suffering in this city every year, by reason of the slave-trade, than has been endured by the whole people of Texas during their entire revolution of eight years. The consumption of human life attendant and consequent upon the slave-trade in this district is greater every year than it has been in Texas during any period of their war with Mexico. It should be borne in mind that this slave-trade is authorized and maintained by *Act of Congress*, which the advocates of annexation refuse to repeal. The scenes which I have described and the sufferings I have mentioned are authorized by our laws, passed by this body, which we now keep in force. Gentlemen on this floor, who, by supporting the gag-rule, have for years voted to continue those laws and the scenes to which I have made reference, whose hearts are unmoved by all the sufferings of the slave population here, and by all the blood that is annually shed in this district, become eloquent upon the sufferings endured by the people of Texas. They are willing to spend the national treasure and pour out American blood to protect the Texans, while they authorize *by law* all those crimes and outrages and all the violence and bloodshed attendant upon the slave-trade in this district. Indeed, they are striving to extend and perpetuate those crimes in Texas, under the plea of *extending the area of freedom*."

Of the suffering and sacrifice of life among the slaves of the South, Giddings said,—

"Upon the cotton plantations they purchase none but full-grown slaves. The average life of the slaves thus purchased, after entering upon the plantations, is only *seven years*. I speak upon the authority of extensive cotton-growers, whose long experience and observation enable them to form correct opinions. It is regarded by cotton-growers as more profitable to drive their slaves so hard that the intensity of their labor shall produce death in seven years, and then to supply their places by fresh purchases, than it is to treat them more leniently; thus whole gangs of slaves, consisting of many hundreds on each cotton plantation, are consigned to their graves once in seven years.

The driver's lash impels them to excessive effort, and really causes their death as much as the knife or the pistol of the murderer causes the death of his victim. . . .

"The pirate thinks it more profitable for him to sacrifice the lives of his captives within an hour after he takes possession of them. The cotton planter regards it as more conducive to his interest to hold his slaves, under the torture of the overseer's whip, for seven years.

"Upon sugar plantations, however, the slaves are worked still harder, and the average life of slaves on sugar estates is computed at five years; that is, the planters on those estates regard it as more profitable to work their hands so severely as to cause their death in five years, and then to replace them by fresh purchases, than it would be to use them more leniently. The precise number of slaves thus sacrificed annually cannot be ascertained. . . . This tide of human gore is constantly flowing, and we are called upon to lend our official aid to increase and extend it. In order to effect this object, the honorable Secretary of State has urged upon us to consider the *humane and moral bearings of slavery.* It is therefore due to him that we examine them.

"Do we believe there is a Power above us who will visit national sins and crimes with national judgments? That He will visit upon this great people the just penalty due to us for the suffering we have inflicted, the blood we have shed, and the murders that have been committed under our laws? I am one of those who solemnly believe that transgression and punishment are inseparably connected by the inscrutable wisdom of God's providence. With this impression, I feel as confident that chastisement and retribution for the offences which we have committed against the down-trodden sons of Africa, await this people, as I do that *justice* controls the destinies of nations or guides the power of Omnipotence."

The project of annexation by treaty having failed, the question was brought before both houses of Congress early in December, in the form of various propositions for annexation by joint resolution. The proposition offered in the House by Milton Brown of Tennessee was adopted by that body on the 25th of February, 1845, by a vote of 120 to 98. This resolution was amended in the Senate on the motion of Mr. Walker of Mississippi, by giving the President power to conclude a treaty under certain conditions if he should deem it advisable. This amendment, and the positive promise of the incoming President that he would act upon it, secured for the measure the support of Mr. Benton and others who had opposed it as clearly unconstitutional. The resolution as amended passed the Senate on the 28th of February by a vote of 27 to 25, and on the same day the House concurred in it by a vote of 132 to 76. President Polk violated his promise and deceived the friends who had confided in him; but the success of the measure was thus secured, although the leading jurists of the country and a majority of both Houses of Congress denied the constitutional power of the Government to annex Texas by joint resolution.

Giddings thus records his impressions at the time:

"It was eight o'clock in the evening when the final vote was taken. No sooner had the Speaker announced the result, than cannon upon the terrace west of the Capitol sounded forth the triumph. Immediately bonfires lighted up the city, and the sound of revelry and drunkenness was heard in its various localities. Northern Democrats and Southern slaveholders rejoiced at a result which they believed would place them in undisputed control of the government. Members from the slaveholding States were rejoicing in the anticipated profits which they expected to reap from the increased price of human flesh. Pensively and alone, the writer walked to his lodgings. Never before had he viewed his country as he then saw it. The exultation of slave-breeders and slave-dealers at thus controlling the Congress of the United States constituted a spectacle that he had not expected to witness. The barbarous war, the bloodshed, the devastation, the corruption, the civil war which resulted from this triumph of the slave power, were at no subsequent period of his life more vividly before his mind than they were that evening while alone in his room, contemplating the results which would naturally follow the action of Congress on that sad day."

Early in this session Mr. Duncan of Ohio introduced a bill to organize a territorial government for Oregon, covering all that portion of country which was then in the joint occupation of Great Britain and the United States. An amendment excluding slavery from the Territory was adopted by a vote of 131 to 69. The bill also authorized the President to give notice to the British Government terminating the joint occupation of the Territory, and it passed the House by a vote of 140 to 59. About the same time a bill was introduced into the Senate authorizing the President to take possession of the whole of Oregon up to 54° 40': but no vote was taken upon it. On the 4th of March Mr. Polk was inaugurated as President, and in his inaugural address he assured the country that "our title to the *whole* of Oregon is clear and unquestionable." At this time the Democratic party seemed to be quite as ready to extend our national domain in this direction as it had been to acquire Texas, and quite as indifferent about the consequences.

Near the close of this session Florida and Iowa, which had been yoked together in their application for admission into the Union, were both admitted. The constitution of Florida prohibited free negroes from coming into the State, and prohibited the Legislature of the State from abolishing slavery. It was in the discussion of this question that Mr. Douglas of Illinois first asserted the doctrine of popular sovereignty, which he maintained so earnestly in later years. He argued that the people of a Territory have the right, in framing a constitution, to establish slavery if they choose, and that his own State could at any time do the same thing by changing its constitution. In thus denying the principles proclaimed by the fathers of the Constitution, that governments are instituted to secure men in the enjoyment of life and liberty, he remained steadfast and consistent to the end of his life.

President Polk, in his annual message to the Twenty-ninth Congress, in December, 1845, informed that body that all attempts to settle the Oregon question had failed, and called on Congress to make the necessary provision for maintaining our rights to the whole of the disputed territory. Early in the session General Cass offered resolutions instructing the Committees on Military and Naval Affairs to inquire into the condition of our fortifications on the sea-board, and our naval supplies. Joint resolutions were also introduced directing the President to give notice of the termination of the joint occupancy of the Territory of Oregon. These resolutions were adopted by the Senate and sent to the House, where they were referred to the Committee on Foreign Affairs, which reported them back with a recommendation of concurrence.

The danger of an immediate war with England was now regarded as imminent. The business interests of the country were seriously threatened, and there was a wide-spread feeling of alarm. Our title to the whole of Oregon was, to say the least, exceedingly debatable, but it was quite as "clear and unquestionable" as our title to the whole of Texas, as claimed by herself, for the assertion of which the Government was about to plunge the nation into a war with Mexico. England and the United States had each taken a definite and positive position, and there seemed to be no reason to suppose that either would yield. The President had the united support of his party, which seemed to be eager for the great conflict; and yet the Administration made no adequate preparations for the struggle. In the opinion of those who had most carefully studied the designs of the slaveocracy, he was playing a cowardly game of diplomacy.

Giddings, in a speech in the House on the 5th of January, 1846, reminded the slaveholders of some exceedingly disagreeable facts. He said, —

"It is the annexation of Texas that has rendered the whole of Oregon necessary to restore that balance of power. By the annexation of Texas the Slave States now have a majority in the Senate. They will continue to retain that majority unless we add territory to our northwestern border. By the annexation of Texas the protection of the free labor of the North has been surrendered to the control of the slave-power. Our constitutional rights and the honor of our Free States are delivered over to the keeping of slaveholders. . . . No, Mr. Speaker, it becomes us to act like men, to look our difficulties in the face, and to pursue the best mode of retrieving the advantages that have been thrown away. That can only be done by restoring the balance of power by adding new States at the West and Northwest. To admit new States on that border, we must have the territory out of which such States may be formed.

"But Southern gentlemen — whose voices at the last session were heard, loud and long, in favor of Texas and the *whole of Oregon* — now see a lion in the way. They were then chivalrous; now they are all for peace. Then they waxed valiant; now they 'roar you as gently as any sucking dove.' But a year ago their motto was '*now or never;*' at this time '*a masterly inactivity*' is their maxim. Last year they spoke in strains of fervid eloquence of the glory of extending the American sway over new territory, and of adding new States to our brilliant constellation; now they call upon their Northern friends to stop this mad career of extending the power of our Government, and to leave the political control of the nation in their hands for a few years, until Great Britain shall quietly give up her claims to that territory. They have suddenly called to mind the declaration of British statesmen that 'a war with the United States will be a war of emancipation.' They see in prospect the black regiments of the British West India islands landing among them, and their slaves flocking to the enemy's standard. Servile insurrections torment their imaginations. Rapine, blood, and murder dance before their affrighted vision. They are now seen in every part of the hall, calling on Whigs and Democrats to save them from the dreadful consequences of their own policy. Well, sir, I reply to them, this is *your* policy, not ours; *you* have forced us into it against our will and our utmost opposition; you have prepared the poisoned chalice, and we will press it to your lips until you swallow the very dregs."

After arguing that one of the consequences of a war with England would be the acquisition of Canada, Nova Scotia, and New Brunswick, he thus refers to the President: —

"It is most obvious to my judgment that he cannot be driven into a war with England. As I have already stated, a war with that nation must prove the total overthrow of slavery. Every reflecting statesman must see this as clearly as any event can be foretold by human perception. I do not think the slaveholding portion of the Democratic party were aware that the carrying out of their Baltimore resolutions would sacrifice that institution. They rather believed that by obtaining Texas, the price of human flesh would be enhanced, and slavery supported. The consequences of seizing upon '*the whole of Oregon*' were not considered. Mr. Polk, in his inaugural address and in his annual message, evidently overlooked the momentous effect which his twice-declared policy would produce upon the slave interest, to which he is indissolubly wedded. He and his cabinet and his party have made a fatal blunder. They will soon discover their error, and will recede from their position. With the same degree of confidence that I have in my own existence, I declare that they will, before the nation and the world, recede from their avowed policy, and will surrender up all that portion of Oregon north of the forty-ninth parallel of latitude, or let the subject remain as it now is. I wish to place this prediction on record for future reference."

These extracts sufficiently indicate the character of the speech. It was most timely and effective, whatever the real attitude of the slaveocracy might prove to be touching the question of war. If the President and his Southern brethren were indeed consumed by the desire for a war with England, the speech was an admirable counter-irritant, which could scarcely fail to bring relief. If, however, they were playing a game of duplicity and treachery, through which the interests of the people of the North and Northwest were to be sacrificed to the greed of slavery, then the chastisement administered by Giddings was exactly the thing called for by the situation.

No utterances could have been more opportune, and probably no congressional speech ever exerted a stronger or more decisive influence upon the settlement of a great question involving the preservation of the public peace. It struck the key-note of enlightened public opinion in every section of the Union, while it exposed the selfishness and rapacity of the slave interest to the gaze of the world.

But Giddings did not stand alone in the views expressed in his speech. A few days before its delivery, a veteran journalist and a master spirit in the arts of practical politics wrote him, —

DEAR SIR, — If the President in his message plays the game of war, why not out-trump him? Wars are sometimes national blessings, though generally the reverse. But are there not worse things than war? If war with England would give us a tariff, Canada, and freedom, shall we refuse it? But it has another aspect, — the duplicity of the Administration. Were you to take this ground in one of your strong, vigorous fifteen-minute-speeches, it would blow the war and the Administration sky-high. Very truly yours,

THURLOW WEED.

On the 16th of January J. A. Briggs, a prominent Whig politician of Cleveland, Ohio, wrote Giddings:

"I think you have settled the Oregon question, for, believe me, your speech will have more influence in the South than all that Calhoun can say, or President Polk can write. The fact is, you spoke the truth, the whole truth, and nothing but the truth; and spoke, too, as ninety-nine out of every one hundred Northern men feel, but will not all speak out so boldly as yourself. I am glad you made the speech, although you may expect to be abused like a pickpocket and thief for it. But abuse you are used to, and it will not hurt you. It takes well here. Even Allen said it was 'good talk,' and would frighten the South out of Oregon and settle the question."

On the 9th of February, Dr. Bowditch, of Boston, wrote : —

"Please to accept my hearty thanks for your manly, noble speech on the Oregon question. Thanks, as an Abolitionist, for the utterance of such sentiments. Would that Northern slaves and Southern lords more frequently heard such speeches. If anything will avail to wake up the so-called freemen of the North from their deadly apathy, speeches like this will do it. But what a farce it is to speak of freemen of the North! If to be freemen we must be bound hand and foot, if we must be so besotted as to hug our very chains as our greatest blessing, then indeed are we freemen; but not otherwise."

A few months later, when time had closed all controversy respecting the policy of the Administration, his old friend Governor Slade, of Vermont, wrote Giddings,—

"Great events have crowded so thick upon each other for the past few months as to hold me in almost breathless astonishment. Your prediction in regard to Polk's disposition to snatch at a peace notwithstanding all his blustering, has been verified. I think the Allens and Hannegans and Casses must feel cheap; but they should have expected nothing better from their coalition with slavery. It is false to everything but the instinct of its own preservation. When will the North learn this?"

Two days after the delivery of this speech Mr. Adams addressed the House on the same subject. In an elaborate argument he supported the claim of the Administration to the whole of Oregon, but did not admit that the assertion of our title would involve the country in a war with England. He, however, agreed with Giddings as to the disastrous effects such a war would have upon the institution of slavery, and joined him in the prediction that the Administration would surrender its belligerent position. In the mean time, Mr. Calhoun had re-entered the Senate on the 22d of December, and surprised his friends by throwing his whole weight against his party on this question. He saw as clearly as Adams and Giddings the effect of such a conflict upon the interests of the South, and vigorously urged the policy of concession. On the 16th of March he said,—

"Once settle the question of Oregon, and we may then settle the question of Mexico; but till then, Mexico will calculate the chances of a rupture between us and Great Britain; and if she sees any chance of a war against us, she will go over to the power which makes war upon us. Remove those chances, put an end to such a hope, and Mexico will speedily settle every pending question between her and the United States."

For weeks and months longer the debate upon the question continued in both Houses, while the President and his party followers still claimed the whole of Oregon, and the Democratic newspapers made "fifty-four forty or fight," the party shibboleth. When it was rumored that the President proposed to settle the question on the line of forty-nine degrees, Senator Hannegan of Indiana made his memorable speech, in which he declared that "so long as one human eye remains to linger on the page of history, the story of his abasement will be read, sending him and his name together to an infamy so profound, a damnation so deep, that the hand of resurrection will never drag him forth. . . . He who is a traitor to his country can never have forgiveness of God, and cannot ask mercy of man."

Meanwhile, the men who agreed with Adams and Giddings were rapidly multiplying, and the suspicion was steadily growing stronger that the difficulty would be adjusted without war. Finally, on the 10th of June, the President asked the advice of the Senate on the subject of a settlement which would surrender the whole of the vast territory lying north of forty-nine degrees. That body promptly advised him to accept such a settlement, and accordingly, on the 15th of June, a treaty to that effect was ratified; and thus ended the campaign of bluster which had so long been prosecuted under the leadership of Cass, Allen, Hannegan, and Douglas, with the treacherous connivance of Southern Democrats. Hannegan was forgiven by President Polk, who nominated him as minister to Russia, at the close of his senatorial term. Harmony in the Democratic party was restored. The power of slavery over the people of the Northern States had never before been so shamefully illustrated as in the obsequious and humiliating submission of the leaders, who for a year and a half had kept the nation in a ferment by their windy talk about war.

The Oregon trouble was now disposed of, but our relations with Mexico were yet unsettled.

Texas having accepted the conditions of annexation, Congress, by an Act which passed the Senate on December 22, 1845, by a vote of 31 to 14, and the House, on December 16, by 141 to 57, consummated the work. As early as August, 1845, General Taylor had been ordered by President Polk to Corpus Christi, situated at the mouth of the Nueces, on the boundary between Texas and Mexico. In March of the following year, in pursuance of further orders, his army took its position on the east bank of the Rio Grande, opposite Matamoras, at least one hundred miles beyond the boundary of Texas, and of course on the soil of Mexico. Hostilities followed, as predicted by the opponents of annexation, and after two battles the President, in his message to Congress of May 11, declared that "Mexico has invaded our territory and shed American blood upon the American soil." The message, with the accompanying papers, was referred to the Committee on Military Affairs, which reported a bill, the preamble of which declared that "by the act of the Republic of Mexico a state of war exists between that Government and the United States." The bill appropriated ten million dollars and provided for calling out fifty thousand men, and it passed the House of Representatives with only fourteen dissenting votes. The men who cast these votes, of whom it has been fitly said that they "looked rather to the day of judgment than to the day of election," were the following: John Quincy Adams, George Ashmun, Joseph Grinnell, Charles Hudson, and Daniel P. King of Massachusetts; Henry T. Cranston of Rhode Island; Erastus D. Culver of New York; Luther Severance of Maine; John Strahan of Pennsylvania; and Columbus Delano, Joseph M. Root, Daniel R. Tilden, Joseph Vance, and Joshua R. Giddings of Ohio. The bill passed the Senate the next day, with only two dissenting votes, those of Thomas Clayton of Delaware, and John Davis of Massachusetts.

On the passage of the bill no opportunity to debate it was granted. The documents accompanying the President's message were not allowed to be read. Not a word of explanation or argument was permitted, nor was any member even suffered to enter his protest against the bill or its preamble. At every stage of the proceeding the previous question silenced all opposition.

The champions of slavery now regarded their ascendency as complete and unquestionable. They compared those who voted against the war with the Federalists, who voted against that of 1812. They assumed that to oppose the war was to oppose the Government, and they spoke of all who condemned it as traitors to the honor of the nation. It was the cowardice of the Whigs which led the great body of them to vote for the War Bill, with its lying preamble. They feared they might be charged at the coming elections with betraying the cause of their country;

and to save themselves from this danger they voted to raise ten millions of money and fifty thousand men, to carry on a war which they denounced as a war of aggression and conquest. They tried to excuse themselves on the plea that General Taylor and his army were in danger of being destroyed or captured by the enemy; but the very despatch in which Taylor announced that hostilities had begun, demonstrated his perfect security. He was then making preparations for advancing into Mexico, and seven days after the fifty thousand men had been voted, Taylor, without waiting for the force he had asked for, entered the city of Matamoras in triumph. Moreover, the Whigs knew that if Taylor had been in danger, his fate would be decided long before any force raised under the Act could reach him, and that he had already been authorized by the President to call for and accept volunteers from no less than six of the nearest States. They also knew that the Democrats were strong enough to pass the War Bill without a single Whig vote.

But if any valid or even plausible excuse could be urged for voting for this declaration of war, there could be none for indorsing the glaring falsehood that Mexico was the aggressor. By voting against this falsehood, the Whigs knew that the country could not suffer, for the grant of money and troops was sure to be made, irrespective of their action. Their vote, therefore, was a perfectly gratuitous exhibition of moral cowardice, and placed them on the same level with the President and his supporters. It was utterly unworthy of the followers of Henry Clay, who said in a public speech in Kentucky, "No earthly consideration would ever have tempted *me* to vote for a bill with a palpable falsehood stamped on its face."

Yet these Whigs denounced the President for bringing on this war, as if they had not joined him in the act. Their inconsistency was only matched by their effrontery. Says Dr. Von Holst, —

"The Whigs always spoke of 'Polk's war.' It is true that Polk had purposely brought on the war; but both Houses of Congress had declared it superfluous to read even the documents that had been voluntarily sent them by the President, in order to form an independent judgment of the question how hostilities with Mexico had been brought on. Certainly, Polk had sinned deeply against the spirit of the Constitution when, behind the back of the assembled Congress, and under no necessity, he had deliberately worked to bring about an encounter on the Rio Grande, in order to win by a war California and New Mexico, which he had been unable to buy; but both Houses of Congress had sanctioned his conduct without any investigation. It was certain that Polk had done, by indirect and devious ways, what Congress alone could rightfully do; but both Houses of Congress had given their approval. Certainly, Polk's assertion that the United States and Mexico were at war was not true; but both Houses of Congress, by their confirmation, made the statement a fact. Certainly, Polk had treated Congress with an insulting want of respect, and certain it was that this criminal playing with the spirit of the Constitution would inevitably bear bitter fruit; but the two Houses of Congress had vied with each other in putting the gag into their own mouths, and in lowering themselves to mere tools of the President in a still greater degree than he had required of them. Certainly, Polk's message, with its disingenuousness, involved half-truths, and its intentional reservations, was an unworthy web of deceit; but both Houses of Congress, under no compulsion whatever, and with the exercise of a most disgraceful pressure on the minority, had set the seal of their approbation upon it. The war was, indeed, originally 'Polk's war,' but Congress was responsible for the fact that the Union had to carry on 'Polk's war;' and if the true and the official history of the origin of the war were so related to each other that, as Stephens maintained, Polk deserved the appellation of the 'mendacious,' then the same disgraceful word was branded on the forehead of the Congress, for it had voluntarily and deliberately pledged itself to the truth of the official history of the origin of the war, had repeated the lie, and formally made it its own."[1]

[1] Constitutional History of the United States, ii. 252-254.

The day following the passage of the War Bill in the House, Giddings, in Committee of the Whole, took occasion to express his views on the subject. His speech was a masterly examination of our relations with Mexico, growing out of the annexation of Texas. He exposed the false pretences of the President respecting the boundaries of Texas, and laid bare the mingled sophistry and knavery by which he attempted to defend his action and put Mexico in the wrong. He made the President himself a witness to the fact that the war was one of naked aggression and conquest, in which he was as completely the instrument of the slaveocracy as he had shown himself in his cowardly surrender of our claim to Oregon. I quote a single extract: —

"The rights of the several States and of the people now depend upon the arbitrary will of an irresponsible majority, who are themselves controlled by a weak but ambitious Executive. Am I asked for the evidence of this assertion? I point you to the invasion of Mexico by order of the Executive while Congress was in session; to the blockade of Matamoras; to those acts which have involved us in all the evils of actual war, without even deigning to consult Congress on the subject. When all this was effected, the majority of this House placed at his disposal the whole military and naval force of the nation, with ten millions of treasure, for the conquest of Mexico, and then indorsed his flagrant misrepresentation by declaring that '*war exists by the act of Mexico.*' Thus has Congress surrendered its honor, its independence, and become the mere instrument of the Executive, and been made to indorse this Presidential falsehood. This invasion of a sister republic, this usurpation of imperial powers, this most despotic act of making war, has been sanctioned by this body, and in a manner, too, which fully illustrates the disregard of Constitutional restraints entertained by this House.

"Sir, on this great and momentous subject of peace and war, involving the lives of thousands of our fellow-citizens and the welfare of two mighty nations, we were not permitted to speak, to deliberate, or to compare our views. No member was allowed to express his dissent, or state his objections to an act which is to tell upon the future destiny of civilized man. With indecent haste, with unbecoming levity, under the gag of the previous question, our nation is plunged into a bloody war for the purpose of conquest and the extension of slavery."

Giddings, however, did not allow the questions of Oregon and Texas to divert his mind from the tactics of slavery respecting matters of smaller moment. On the 18th of February, 1846, he addressed the House on the Indian Appropriation Bill, providing for the payment of forty thousand dollars, under our treaty with the Creek and Seminole Indians, concluded in 1845. He had explained the facts connected with this treaty in his speech of the 6th of February of the previous year, and he now made it clear that this appropriation was asked for in pursuance of the long-continued policy of the Government in making itself the agent of slaveholders in the recapture of fugitive slaves, or in compensating them for their loss. He showed that this treaty had never been published, and that Congress had been called on to vote appropriations under it without any knowledge of the facts and circumstances which led to it. "From the time of its approval to this hour," said he, "it has been entombed in the Executive archives, and kept from the view of gentlemen who are now called to act officially under it." He repeated the essential facts set forth in his speech on the Florida War in 1841, and called attention to the remarkable fact that under this treaty the President of the United States is to sit as arbitrator between slaveholders and savages in determining the pretended rights of property of the former to Seminole Indians who were, in fact and in law, free. He continued, —

"And now the question is distinctly before us. Shall we thrust our hands into the pockets of our constituents, and take this money, and pass it over to a slave-dealing President, to be expended in paying for the bodies of husbands and wives and children? Are the representatives from the Free States prepared to enter into the business of huckstering in human flesh? Shall we involve our constituents in this deep and damning crime of trading in the image of our God? Our votes must answer these questions."

Reverting to his favorite theory that the existence of slavery in the South depends exclusively upon the authority of the States in which it exists, he said:

"To appropriate the moneys proposed in this bill to pay for these slaves will be as clearly in violation of the Federal compact as it would be for us to abolish slavery in Georgia, or establish it in Massachusetts. If this Government possesses the power to deal in slaves, we may establish a slave-market in Boston or in New York, and set up business on Government account at any other point we please. If we possess the power to tax the people of the Free States to the amount of two hundred thousand dollars, to be expended in payment of slaves, as contemplated by this treaty, we may tax them two hundred *millions* for the same purpose. The question before us is one of *principle*, and not of amount. Had our Government entered into a treaty with those Indians, and agreed to pay them two hundred thousand dollars for assisting the slaves of Georgia to escape from bondage, we should all of us have pronounced such a treaty unconstitutional; and I do not believe that a member of this body would have voted to appropriate a single dollar in pursuance of it. Yet the unconstitutionality of such a treaty would have been no more obvious than is that of the treaty before us. It is a perfectly clear proposition that if the Government has power to restore slaves, it has the same power to entice them away; and if it has the power to pay out the money of the people for one purpose, it has equal power to pay it out for the other."

In affirming these propositions, Giddings challenged members to controvert them; but no one attempted to do so.

In the latter part of July, in compliance with the earnest wishes of Whig members of the House from New England, he addressed a series of public meetings in Maine. This was a novel experience to him, and he enjoyed it greatly. He gives this account of it in a letter written on his way back to Washington:

NEW YORK, July 26, 1846.

MY DEAR WIFE, — On reaching Boston, on my return from Maine, I found letters requesting my immediate return to Washington, thinking that the Tariff Bill may be returned to the House with amendments. I reached here this morning a little after daylight, and after spending the day intend to take the cars for Washington, so as to reach there tomorrow at 11 A. M.

I have had a most delightful trip, — one well calculated to please and to flatter my vanity. The respect and attention with which I was received everywhere was gratifying. All classes and all political parties appeared to extend to me a most cordial welcome. I was received with open arms and unlimited confidence by both Whigs and Liberty men, and I trust I have effected the object of my mission. The cordial respect bestowed upon me at some places rather overcame my feelings, and in some instances I found myself unable to respond to the grateful outpourings of gratitude with which I was received. I addressed large meetings at the cities of Bangor, Augusta, and Portland; and after spending six days in that State, I left it, much more to the regret of the people, I think, than I should have done if I had come away the day after I entered it. At Boston I was urged to stay and address the people, but could not. . . .   Affectionately,

J. R. GIDDINGS.

When the second session of this Congress assembled, the varying fortunes of the war entirely engrossed the attention of the House. The weakness and recklessness of the President's message were severely criticised, and his call for an additional military force in the work of subjugating Mexico aroused a formidable opposition, especially in the Senate, where Mr. Calhoun took the lead. Our army in Mexico was suffering from sickness, and the war had become so unpopular that several members who had voted for it made propositions looking to the restoration of peace without the acquisition of territory. The resolutions offered by Mr. Stephens of Georgia, to this effect, on the 22d of January, 1847, received an affirmative vote of 76, to 88 in the negative. The anti-war feeling of the country found a far more startling echo in Mr. Corwin's great speech in the Senate on the 11th of February. It electrified both Houses of Congress and the people of the Northern States. In a letter to Charles Sumner, written on the day of its delivery, Giddings said:

"I take pleasure in saying that Corwin has spoken, and retires this night in the proudest attitude of any man in the nation. I listened to most of his speech. In *substance* he has met my expectations. As to manner, he was evidently embarrassed. Strangers did not notice it, though it was most evident to all who had heard him before. Mr. Root informed me that before I entered the hall he made Mr. Webster look pale, by one of his inimitable appeals, which no man can appreciate who never heard him. His grounds are, that the war was commenced without cause; that we had long abused and insulted Mexico; that the President's message was a base fabrication; that the war will be fruitless of good; that the Mexicans will not yield, and that our army must be withdrawn; that it is right and proper to withhold supplies, etc. In short, I think he maintains every position the Young Whigs occupy. He declared that the people of the North will never yield; and that they will be burned at the stake, and their fingers shall blaze like candles, before they will permit further slave territory to be added to the United States. But you will see a better sketch than I can give you in the morning papers. His manner added much force to his speech; but the Young Whigs appeared to be in fine spirits, and some of them declared that it was the finest effort ever made by Mr. Corwin. They now regard him as their man for President."

On the 22d of February Charles Francis Adams wrote, —

HON. J. R. GIDDINGS, *Washington, D. C.*

MY DEAR SIR, — I find, by all the information I can gather, that Mr. Corwin by his late speech has given an impetus to opinion, the force of which he did not in all probability himself foresee. A very large part of the people is ready to rally round him at once. He must revise his speech with care for publication, as it will probably be a marking point in the country's history. People will look back to it and say here was the first glimmer and blaze of truth and right in the Senate chamber upon the Mexican war.

We are now all of us anxious that he should only go straight forward in the same path as it respects the other questions in the Senate chamber. Will he speak again upon the Wilmot Proviso and Mr. Calhoun's manifesto? If Mr. Webster should falter or equivocate, whom have we to look to but him. Can you do nothing with him? Tell him that there has not been in America since the Revolution such a chance for a man to make an everlasting reputation as is now before him. In comparison with that, all mere offices are contemptible objects to a true statesman.

I now half regret that I did not call to see Mr. Corwin when I was in Washington. But I have such an aversion to appearing to pump anybody for sentiments of a particular kind that I would rather forego any satisfaction to my own mind which I might get from a conversation, than to attempt it.

I think the country is becoming fairly roused to the issues before us. Firmness and moderation must be our policy. We believe the public is growing more and more sensible, — how much it owes to you! Yours very truly,

C. F. A.

This speech at once brought Corwin to the front as a Presidential candidate, while it awakened general alarm among the champions of slavery.

Giddings was not silent during this session. On the 15th of December he made an elaborate and unusually vigorous arraignment of the war policy of the Administration, as defined in the President's message. His exposure of his mendacity was unsparing and unanswerable, and in speaking of his demand for further supplies of men and money, Giddings reiterated his purpose to vote for neither. On this subject he greatly annoyed his Whig brethren who voted for the war, by vindicating the action of those members who had refused to join in that vote and to grant supplies for its prosecution. This he did by citing distinguished British precedents. When a war of aggression and conquest was waged against the American colonies by the British king, Giddings showed that Lord Chatham and Fox and Burke, and other distinguished friends of the colonies, refused to vote supplies for its prosecution, and demanded the withdrawal of the English armies from their work of conquest and rapine. They went farther, and even refused to vote thanks to General Clinton and others for their military services in America, because they regarded the war in which these services were rendered as unjust and indefensible.

On the 8th of January, Mr. Winthrop attempted a reply. He denied the applicability to the government of the United States of the English precedents cited by Giddings. He said: —

"I am not ready to admit that there is any close analogy between the struggle of the American colonies in 1776 and that of the Mexicans now. Still less analogy is there between a vote of the British House of Commons and a vote of the American House of Representatives. A refusal of supplies in the Parliament of Great Britain is, generally speaking, equivalent to a change of Administration. No British Ministry can hold their places in defiance of such a vote. A successful opposition to supplies in time of war is thus almost certain to result in bringing forthwith into power a Ministry opposed to its further prosecution; and the kingdom is not left to encounter the dangers which might result from a conflict upon such a subject between the executive and legislative powers. It is not so here. No vote of Congress can change our Administration. If it could, the present Administration would have expired on Saturday last, when a tax, which they had solemnly declared was essential to furnish them with the sinews of war, was so emphatically denied. If it could, the present Administration would have gone out on Tuesday last, when their demand for a Lieutenant-General was so unceremoniously laid on the table. No British Ministry, in these days, could have survived for an hour two such signal defeats.

"But our Executive is elected for a term of years, and his cabinet are quite independent of our votes. A refusal of all supplies might hamper and embarrass an Executive, and give an enemy the advantage of divided counsels, but could hardly enforce a change of policy, or secure a concerted action in favor of peace. Certainly it does not seem to be the mode contemplated by our Constitution for putting an end to a war when it has once been commenced. The people alone can apply the potent styptic, the magical *Brocchieri*, for stopping the effusion of blood, if it be the Executive will that it shall continue to flow. It is their prerogative to change the Administration; and the day is coming, though farther off than some of us might wish, when they will have the opportunity of exercising it."

Winthrop based a further reply to Giddings upon a letter quoted from John Jay to Timothy Pickering, dated November 1, 1814, in which, speaking of the War of 1812, he said: "We cannot be too perfectly united in a determination to defend our country."

The friends of Giddings, both in Congress and throughout the country, desired him to reply to these views and expose their fallacy, and he was anxious to do so; but he had already addressed the House at length, while many members who had not spoken were struggling for the floor. On the 15th of January, Mr. Sumner wrote:—

> MY DEAR SIR,—I am glad that you will reply to Winthrop. I hope you will unmask his perversion of John Jay. Invoke John Jay in a war of *offence*, or in an implied sanction of 'our country, right or wrong'! It seems to me that the contrast, the antagonism, the world-wide difference between *defence* and *offence* might be elaborated with effect. . . .
>
> The comment of Winthrop on the British statesmen seemed like an attempt to take advantage of the House. It is a juggle. The principle of duty which animated Fox and Chatham ought to animate the American Congress. Would to God that their spirit would descend upon the House! But because the minority went out on sustaining a defeat, and they do not go out here, does any conclusion follow? Clearly not. If any, it is one that should make us more vigilant in checking their course. They should be held to strict accountability at every step. . . .
>
> Yours faithfully,
>
> CHARLES SUMNER.

On the following day he made a further reference to the same subject:—

> MY DEAR SIR,—I cannot forbear writing a line to-day to say that President Adams expressed particular pleasure when I

told him that you proposed to reply to Winthrop's criticism on the English authorities. The President said that they were precisely in point; that the circumstance adduced by Winthrop did not affect their authority in our Congress. They denied the *justice* of the war in which their country was engaged, and therefore refused to sanction it, and called upon their country *to retreat*, — not from any enemy of human force, but from wrong-doing. . . .   Yours faithfully,

CHARLES SUMNER.

P. S. — I hope you will save John Jay from the imputation thrown upon him by Winthrop's speech. How puerile to discuss the phraseology of the message, or the conduct of the *Executive*, and spare the great crime of unjust, unnecessary, and murderous war!

On the 1st of February Giddings wrote to Sumner:

"I have some apprehension that I shall not be able to speak again at this session on the war. There are many who have not spoken, and who are yet desirous of speaking. Under these circumstances, I have imparted my views to my colleague, Mr. Delano, so far as regards my intended reply to Mr. Winthrop. I have also placed in his hands the extract from the Madison papers, giving Mr. Gorham's views in the convention that framed the Constitution, on the subject of controlling the Executive by withholding supplies in time of war."

Mr. Delano obtained the floor on the following day, and made it clear that the *object* in withholding supplies, whether in England or America, is to stop the Administration in a career of mischief and lawlessness; that in both countries the withholding of supplies compels the government to change its policy; that the resignation of the Ministry in England does not give the right to refuse supplies, but is simply a consequence of defeat; while in both England and America the end to be obtained is the same, and that the fact that our Executive is elected for a term of years does not make him independent of Congress during that time. On this point Mr. Delano said, —

"But if thus independent, may the President involve the country in a war, unconstitutional in its origin, expensive in its prosecution, wicked in its objects, and dangerous in its consequences? And is there 'no mode contemplated by our Constitution for putting an end to such a war when it has been commenced'? Is there no way in our government to stop the effusion of blood in such a war 'if it be the Executive will that it shall continue to flow,' except to let it flow on during the period for which the Executive was elected, and then let the people apply 'the potent styptic'?

"I am unwilling to sanction, even by silence, a doctrine which puts this country, for a period of four years, so entirely, absolutely, at the mercy of one man, — a doctrine which proposes, in time of war, when necessarily and inevitably the power and patronage of the President are increased, to make him and his cabinet 'independent' of Congress; which throws at once the reins of government upon the neck of executive power, and gives the steed full license to trample upon the liberties and lives of the people. The framers of the Constitution never looked for such an interpretation of it. They expressly reserved to Congress the right to *declare* war; they knew that money was necessary to wage war; and they supposed that as long as the power to grant and withhold supplies remained with Congress, the President, by a judicious exercise of this power, would be restrained from prosecuting any war longer than shall be necessary and proper."

In support of these views he cited the debates in the convention which framed the Constitution, and he disposed of Mr. Winthrop's quotation from John Jay by reminding the House that the War of 1812 was a war of *defence*, and that when Jay's letter was written, our Capitol at Washington had been burned, our frontiers were occupied by British troops, and our commerce was exposed to a British navy. The letter had no relevancy whatever to a war of conquest like that waged by the British Crown against the colonies in 1776, or our war with Mexico, which was wantonly and unconstitutionally begun by the President. Delano's reply to Winthrop was complete; and this radical difference of views between Giddings and Winthrop is here referred to, because of its bearing upon further matters of controversy between them which I shall hereafter have occasion to notice.

On the 2d of March, 1847, the Civil and Diplomatic Appropriation Bill was returned from the Senate to the House with an amendment granting to the claimants of slaves on board the "Amistad" fifty thousand dollars. In a letter to Sumner of that date, Giddings says, —

"You will recollect the story. I saw that our opponents intended to get out of committee without discussing that amendment, for the very purpose of stopping the debate. I obtained the floor, and called the attention of the House to this amendment, and stated the facts. After I was through, the chairman of the Committee of Ways and Means called for the reading of a letter from the Secretary of State urging Congress to make the appropriation, and declaring the claim to be *just* and *valid*. This was more than 'the old man eloquent' could withstand, and he broke out, notwithstanding the weakness of his voice and health. It would have done your heart good to see the members gather around him in a dense mass and listen to him in breathless attention. He spoke only to one point, and only about fifteen minutes; but it was regarded as probably his last speech in this hall, and was received with profound respect. There were only twenty-eight who voted for the appropriation in committee."

In the House it failed by a vote of 40 to 112.

CHAPTER VIII.

MARCH, 1847, TO DECEMBER, 1848.

Novel State of Parties. — Correspondence. — Meeting of the Thirtieth Congress.— Struggle for the Speakership. — Controversy with Winthrop. — Other Questions. — Death of Mr. Adams. — Speech on General Politics. — Escape of Slaves on the Schooner "Pearl." — Mob in Washington. — Speech. — Hope H. Slatter and Rev. Mr. Slicer. — The Claim of Hodges. — Campaign of 1848. — Letter to Truman Smith. — Effect of the Free-Soil Movement.

DURING the Congressional vacation the growth of anti-slavery opinion throughout the Northern States was unmistakable. The success of our armies in Mexico rendered the acquisition of territory certain, and made the prohibition of slavery therein a vital issue. On this question and that of voting supplies for the prosecution of the war the Whig party was threatened with disruption. In Massachusetts it was divided into "Conscience Whigs," who were earnest and outspoken anti-slavery men, and "Cotton Whigs," or conservatives, who subordinated the slavery issue to the unity of the party. The leaders of the former were Charles F. Adams, John G. Palfrey, Charles Sumner, Stephen C. Phillips, Henry Wilson, Charles Allen, Samuel and E. R. Hoar, and Richard H. Dana, Jr.; of the latter, Robert C. Winthrop, J. T. Stevenson, George Ashmun, and Levi Lincoln. Both parties were uncompromising and thoroughly in earnest. In the West a similar division revealed itself, with Mr. Giddings and Salmon P. Chase as the most conspicuous representatives of the liberal element.

The Democratic party was likewise threatened with serious division on the slavery question, particularly in New York, where the defeat of Van Buren, in 1844, for writing his anti-Texas letter, had paved the way for the formidable revolt which followed a little later. The political complications were still further aggravated by the victories of General Taylor, which brought him before the people as a prospective Whig candidate for the Presidency, while the anti-slavery men of the country, of different types and antecedents, began to talk about the formation of a new party on the issue of slavery, and to discuss the claims of Corwin, Webster, Judge McLean, and Martin Van Buren as Presidential candidates. The Liberty party was still in the field, with John P. Hale as its Presidential favorite; but it gave no promise of rallying to its support the mass of anti-slavery men who were ready to secede from the old parties. A considerable body of Whigs still looked to Clay as their great leader, and dwelt upon his opposition to the annexation of Texas, and his fulfilled prophecy that annexation would be followed by war.

At this season of political uncertainty and confusion which preceded the Free-Soil revolt of the following year and prepared the way for it, the correspondence of Mr. Giddings possesses a peculiar interest. His position at Washington gave him important advantages in surveying the field of politics. He was the active and uncompromising representative of the anti-slavery cause in Congress. His exceptional knowledge of the slavery issue in all its aspects was unquestioned, while his age and political experience also conspired to invest his opinions and counsel with authority. We can now read his correspondence in the light of accomplished facts, and are able to assign to his views their proper value.

Among his most intimate and trusted friends at this time were Charles F. Adams and Charles Sumner, with whom he was in frequent communication on political topics, and who often sought his opinions respecting public men and measures. But little of his correspondence with the former has been preserved, but Sumner carefully filed his letters from Giddings, nearly all of which were written from 1846 to 1851, when Sumner entered the Senate from Massachusetts. The friendship which ripened between him and Giddings was as perfect as that which had so long existed between the latter and ex-President Adams. On June 2, Giddings wrote to Sumner, —

" I was aware that Mr. Peters was partial to Judge McLean. I object to no man if his principles are right and his character suited to the place. On these points I fear Judge McLean. I think his political views nearly the same as they were when he left Jackson's cabinet. That he will call around him the 'Old Hunkers' of our party I entertain no doubt. Men of the 'old school' will be his advisers on the subject of slavery, and his administration will be a continuation of the practice of unconditional submission to the slave-power. He is doubtless in favor of granting men and money to carry on the war."

Giddings did not agree with the Whigs who desired the nomination of Mr. Clay, though still warmly attached to him. This will appear from the following letter, which also contains other matters of interest:

[Confidential.]

ASHLAND, Oct. 6, 1847.

I received, my dear sir, your friendly letter in all the spirit of kindness and amity in which it was dictated, and I answer it in the same spirit.

I am thankful for your friendship, which I cordially reciprocate. I hope that it will continue to be mutual between us, whatever may be the political events of the future.

You tell me that it is possible that I may be again a candidate for the Presidency by the nomination of the Whig convention, and, with honorable candor, add that you are not favorable to my nomination.

After the disastrous termination of the last contest, I never expected to be again a candidate. I do not now expect it, nor have I determined in my own mind that I would accept the nomination if it were offered me. It probably never will be necessary for me to decide that question; but if it should be, I should deliberately consider the circumstances which ought to influence my judgment.

I am not surprised at the progress of the anti-slavery feeling which you describe in the Free States. The annexation of Texas, this most unnecessary and horrible war with Mexico, and the overthrow of the tariff of 1842, were well calculated to produce that effect. But you, perhaps, ought to reflect that these measures could not have been carried without large Northern support; and perhaps justice would also require that it should not be forgotten that some of us were most decidedly adverse to them.

You kindly refer to the subject of the slaves I hold, and tell me what would be the good consequences of my emancipating them.

I regret as much as any one does the existence of slavery in our country, and wish to God there was not a single slave in the United States, or in the whole world. But here the unfortunate institution is, and a most delicate and difficult affair is it to deal with.

I have during my life emancipated some eight or ten, under circumstances which appeared to me to admit of their emancipation. The last was Charles, and I am not sure that he is benefited by his freedom. Of the remainder (some fifty odd), what I ought to do with them, and how, and when, is a matter of grave and serious consideration often with me. I am perfectly sure that to emancipate them forthwith would be an act of great inhumanity and extreme cruelty. I wish you would come and see me and them. Do come. You would behold among them aged and decrepit men and women and helpless children, utterly unable to gain a livelihood or support in the world. They would perish if I sent them forth in the world.

Alas, alas! my good friend, I fear you have a very inadequate idea of the duties, obligations, and relations which exist between my poor slaves and me.

But whatever I may or might do towards them must be wholly independent of all political motives or considerations; it must rest exclusively with my own sense of duty and propriety.

Nor do I believe that if it were possible for me to be influenced by the motive of my own political advancement in the emancipation of my slaves, at this time, it would tend in the smallest degree to the promotion of that end. My object and purpose would be alike assailed by the ultras on both sides, if not by others. I remain, very truly,

Your friend and obedient servant, H. CLAY.

The Hon. Mr. GIDDINGS.

In a letter to Mr. Giddings dated October 1, Mr. Sumner gave him an account of the Massachusetts State Whig convention, held at Springfield on the 29th of September, in which Mr. Webster was nominated for the Presidency, and declared himself in favor of the Wilmot Proviso. Giddings replied, October 8, —

"Your favor of the 1st instant is received. I am astonished that Mr. Webster should have made so bold a push for the nomination. I am, however, delighted with the expression of his views in regard to the withdrawal of our troops and in favor of the Wilmot Proviso. It must have given you and Messrs. Adams, Palfrey, and Phillips great pleasure to find him acting with you; but I regret that you had not learned the fact at an earlier day. Looking at the doings of your convention, so far as I am informed, I think the developments were, on the whole, favorable to the progress of correct principle. Even the nomination of Mr. Webster, under the circumstances, tells strongly in favor of the Young Whigs. I am gratified to see Mr. Palfrey standing forward as he did in your convention. He will enter Congress with no doubtful character, and I feel assured that he will not begin to 'play dark' after he gets before the nation. I assure you that I anticipate much pleasure at seeing him assume a portion of the responsibility that has so long rested upon a few of us.

"As to Corwin, I know not that I can give you any information. I have written him very fully, and when I get his answer will know more about his speech and his views. I have put to him such questions as I think will draw out his real sentiments. I had supposed that I knew his views upon the subject of slavery. In 1844 I was with him on the stump. At Cadiz, in the county of Harrison, at a very large convention, among whom were many slaveholders from Virginia, and some from Kentucky, among them Gen. Leslie Combs, I spoke my views freely and fully on the subject of slavery, the more so because there were also many Liberty men present who had asserted that I would say nothing in regard to slavery when slaveholders were present.

"Corwin followed me, and indorsed and confirmed my doctrines, and avowed them as his own. He also did the same on other occasions. Last winter we talked the subject over again, and he appeared to have no delicacy in the matter, but said he should not hesitate to declare his views at a proper time. I have cautioned him on this point since we returned from the last session. This is all I can say at present. It is certain that in his speech there was an intimation that I did not approve. Here the matter rests so far as I am concerned. If he shows the doughface, we shall cast him off without hesitation. Whatever Mr. Winthrop and others think in regard to voting for the best *slaveholder*, we of northern Ohio will sustain no doughface, were he a brother or a son. Corwin understands this now, and will understand it more fully when he shall have read the papers from the Reserve. He is and has long been the favorite of northern Ohio, much more than of the southern portion of the State; but we shall not again be Tylerized by any man."

The attitude of Corwin continued to engross the attention of anti-slavery Whigs both in New England and the West. On the 18th of October Giddings wrote to Sumner, —

"When Henry Clay's Alabama letter appeared in 1844, my former partner[1] swore he would favor a candidate at the next Presidential election who could neither read nor write. I doubt whether he should not include those who make speeches. I think, however, that the whole difficulty with Corwin has arisen from two causes, — first, he said more in regard to the *dangers* of the Wilmot Proviso than he should have said; second, what he did say was misrepresented. He is exceedingly vexed at the misrepresentations, and avows the same sentiments on the subject of extending slavery which you and I hold. In short, I think our friend Adams formed a very accurate opinion when he said Corwin had shown less boldness on the subject than became a man in his situation. I yet believe he will come up to that point as boldly as he did on the war. If he does not, however, we here shall feel under no obligation to support him."

On the 1st of November Sumner replied to Giddings. —

[1] B. F. Wade.

"Your favor of the 18th was duly received. Since then I have received a letter from Mr. Corwin, in which he shows some anxiety on account of the report of the Carthage speech. I regret that speech very much. The passage with Mr. Chase was unfortunate. It has undoubtedly disaffected the Abolitionists, who already inclined to Mr. Corwin. His shrinking from the Wilmot Proviso as a *dangerous question* was another mistake. That question, when rightly understood, is a source of safety. It is the beginning of a rally against the slave-power which will save the Union. I wish Mr. Corwin could see this as we do. I had begun to feel a personal attachment for him, and shall be unhappy if we cannot act under him. The courage which he showed against the war ought to inspire him to active demonstrations against slavery. Meanwhile, the Democrats in New York are in motion. I have assurances on which I rely that they are *in earnest*. Preston King says he does not care whether the Presidential candidate is a Whig or a Democrat, *but he must be a Wilmot Proviso man*. I may say, confidentially, that a letter has been received here from Albany inquiring if J. Q. Adams will join with Martin Van Buren and others in a call for an anti-slavery convention to nominate a Northern candidate. Mr. Adams was asked yesterday if he would do it. He expressed great pleasure in the plan, but pleaded that he was so old and infirm that he could not *do* what might be justly expected of him if he were to sign such a call.

"It seems that the continuance of the war will prevent such a call immediately; but when that ceases, nothing can prevent the coalition of the two anti-slavery sections. Let us try to prepare the way.

"I regret J. P. Hale's acceptance of the Liberty nomination. I urged him in vain to a contrary course.

"Your anticipation with regard to Palfrey will be fulfilled. He is true as steel. As a new member, of marked opinions, he will be exposed to trials. I know he may count upon your friendship and sympathy. I see that the Whigs will continue to vote supplies. Before going into caucus on the Speakership, should you not understand their proposed course?"

To this letter Giddings replied, November 8, —

"I rejoice at the proposition made to Mr. Adams. It shows advance on the part of the Van Burens more rapidly than I had expected, although I had strong assurances of their intentions to stand by the principles of the Wilmot Proviso; and from some I have the promise that they will go for a total and perfect separation of the Federal Government from all support of slavery. This

I think is the line which we should draw, and on which we should stand. Let us repeal all laws of Congress which now exist for the support of slavery, wash our hands entirely of it, and leave it altogether with the States in which it is situated. I am fully of the opinion that we shall affix the Wilmot Proviso to the first appropriation bill that passes; for although I have hopes that the army may be recalled, yet I make all calculations that Southern Whigs are to go for supplies. . . .

" Mr. Corwin can expect the anti-slavery Whigs to support him for President on no other ground than that of maintaining our doctrines and policy. He has during vacation been surrounded by timid doughfaces, who have felt that he was injuring himself and party. That influence has doubtless had an effect upon him. The papers speak much of Mr. Schenck's course in *opposing the war*, when in fact he voted for it, and, to the best of my recollection, has at all times either dodged the question, or voted for supplies, while it is true he has spoken against the war. Mr. Schenck has been much with Corwin, and I fear has had quite too much influence with him; yet I have confidence that he will come up to the work when he gets back to the Senate."

A little later, Charles Francis Adams wrote, —

BOSTON, Nov. 28, 1847.

MY DEAR SIR, — . . . I have concluded not to go to Washington at present. You have doubtless seen the base attack of the " Atlas " upon us, which was designed to curry favor for Winthrop with the Carolinians. The effort to manufacture public opinion is going on with great industry, and I suspect our Congressmen will be overawed. But I know nothing of them, not even of my father or Mr. Palfrey. If I were to go to Washington, the inference would immediately be that I was going in order to defeat *him* [Winthrop].

Mr. Clay's speech seems to be throwing the party into confusion. I suspect the Taylor movement will now begin in earnest, and that Winthrop will *secretly* favor it. He will not easily forgive Clay, whom he never loved overmuch.

What is to be done? I am very tired of the equivocations of the Whigs, and so far as I am concerned, am fully prepared for any movement which may be made *from any quarter*, resting upon the ground which you suggested in your last. But I will not start until I see my way not to embarrass you. What will the Democrats do? Are they going after the wild-goose project of trying Mr. Van Buren?

What we now want is union, and to understand each other. Cannot this be done at once?

Mr. Palfrey has been very unwell, and it is not certain that he can get on in season for Monday. He is true as steel.

After all, I have little confidence in anybody at Washington excepting in Palfrey and yourself. My father, of course, is not active. You *two* must sustain our cause. My own impression is that bold measures will be wisest, — union with other parties without scruple, wherever they act honestly in the support of the only principles now in question, and if possible a total defeat of any intrigue which shall attempt to stifle the slavery question in the delusion of no more territory.

What say you? Let me know early, so that I may bring the paper well out. I have been talking very gently of late.

Very truly yours,

C. F. ADAMS.

On December 1, Sumner wrote, —

"I find that the person who wrote to ascertain whether Mr. Adams would unite with the Van Burens and others in the call of an anti-slavery convention was not authorized to speak for the latter. He saw Mr. Van Buren, who said that he was in favor of the Wilmot Proviso, but that he must keep himself aloof from the agitation of that question. Old fox!"

Giddings, like Sumner and Adams, was reluctant to surrender his faith in Corwin. He clung to him as he had clung to Clay in 1844. Indeed, his hopefulness was one of the most perfectly defined traits in his character. He believed in humanity, and though often disappointed in his favorable estimate of men, he never lost his faith. To this quality of his mind he was doubtless largely indebted for the constancy and zeal which enabled him to prosecute his labors in the face of the most threatening forms of opposition and discouragement.

Respecting the course of Mr. Corwin, his anti-slavery friends were not long kept in suspense. They soon discovered that he had taken fright at the display of his own courage or at the plaudits of the Abolitionists, and that he lacked the moral nerve and steadfastness of purpose which would have fitted him for the leadership of a great movement.

He was witty, eloquent, versatile, sympathetic, and full of generous impulses. His oratory was as captivating as it was inimitable, and his geniality as abounding as his love of fun. These qualities made him the idol of the people, but they did not supply him with convictions. He had caught a glimpse of the truth which beckoned him forward as the prophet of the people, but having faltered in the supreme moment of his public life, he turned again to the beggarly work of party politics, took the stump for General Taylor, and by easy stages of descent reached the position of Secretary of the Treasury under Millard Fillmore, and defender of the Compromise measures of 1850. Henceforward till his death he was the despair of the men who had longed to fight the battle of freedom under his banner.

As the time drew near for the meeting of the Thirtieth Congress, the question of the Speakership of the House was discussed with increasing interest. The choice of a Speaker always involves grave considerations, but the condition of public affairs at that time made it pre-eminently momentous. We have seen that Sumner referred to it in his last letter; but Giddings had seriously pondered the question much earlier. In a letter to Horace Greeley, of September 7, he had stated, with great clearness and force, the attitude of the Whig party on the subject of annexation and war, the verified prophecies of the Whig leaders that war would follow annexation, and the undisguised hostility of the party to its further prosecution. I quote from this letter: —

"The Whig party has never ceased to condemn the war. Their disgust for it was never stronger than at present, and it is gaining strength every day. With these circumstances surrounding them, the Whig members of Congress will assemble. The first duty that will devolve upon them will be the election of a

Speaker. That officer exerts more influence over the destinies of the nation than any other member of the government except the President. He arranges the committees to suit his own views. If a Whig in favor of prosecuting the war be elected Speaker, he will so arrange the committees as to secure reports in favor of continuing our conquests in Mexico. If he be opposed to the war, he will so arrange them as to have reports in favor of withdrawing our troops. Which course will the Whig party in the House of Representatives pursue? A more momentous question was never presented to the Whig party. Should they elect an anti-war candidate, and the Committee of Ways and Means should be so constituted as to report against the further conquest of Mexico, it is quite possible that Whigs enough would vote with the Democrats to reverse the reports of committees, and to make the necessary appropriations to carry on hostilities. But such an act of a few individuals would not involve the party, and we may escape the odium and responsibility of such act. We should in such event remain upon the ground which we have long maintained, and the responsibility of the war will remain with those who brought it upon us. On the other hand, should they elect a Speaker in favor of carrying on the war, there will be a union between the parties in regard to it; and the distinctive principles on which the Whig party has hitherto stood will be surrendered. When we as a party shall thus desert our doctrines, and obliterate the lines that have hitherto separated the two parties, and make this a *Whig* war, and assume its crimes and disgrace, its final overthrow will not be far distant. Now, sir, I wish to avoid such a state of things. I am aware that our friends desire to see a Whig Speaker and a Whig clerk elected; but I submit whether it would not be a thousand times better for the Whig party to maintain its integrity and principles than to surrender them for the paltry advantages of electing a Speaker and clerk. If we are contending for great and holy principles, let us stand by our professions; but if we are fighting for office and power merely, why then the sooner we disband the better."

The significance of these views was soon to be practically illustrated. Their value was to be tested in the nomination and election of Robert C. Winthrop, of Massachusetts, as Speaker of the next House, while Mr. Giddings was to be brought face to face with one of the greatest trials of his public life. On December 4, he wrote to Sumner, —

"Mr. Palfrey has arrived in the same cars that brought me your favor of the 1st instant. His health is improving. I was most happy to see him. I thank God that I have one man on whom I can lean. Our party is now in caucus (10 o'clock at night) to nominate a Speaker. There are very few members absent. They entirely refused to state any principle on which our future action shall be based, and I refused to meet in caucus, as I might by some be considered as bound in honor to vote for the Whig nominee. I determined that no circumstances should induce me to vote for any man who is not pledged to arrange the committees so as to secure the withdrawal of the army, and reports upon Abolition petitions. I shall be set upon by the bloodhounds of the party, but that I am accustomed to. Winthrop has satisfied Hudson and others who felt somewhat on the subject of the war, and they will vote for him if nominated. Yet Mr. Palfrey and myself will probably hold his election in our hands. I therefore intend that our power shall be exerted and felt as far as we can make it tell upon humanity. Mr. Adams will vote for Mr. Winthrop, and I was compelled to take the stand at the dictation of my own judgment against the remonstrance of personal and political friends. But since Mr. Palfrey has arrived, I have stated the whole case to him, and he concurs with me in opinion, and approves my course. My only fears are that we may, by thus partially separating from our party, lose influence; but I hope not. I am sure that my absence from the meeting will cause inquiry, and think they will discover that I hold important cards in my hand.

"*Half-past eleven.* The meeting has adjourned; Winthrop is nominated for Speaker, and Campbell of Tennessee for clerk. Thus you see the subject has assumed a tangible shape. And now, my dear sir, though accustomed to meet responsibility in various ways, I frankly say that I feel some indecision as to the course I may hereafter adopt. I have no doubt that if King and Palfrey stand firm, we may yet defeat Winthrop and break up the present dynasty of our Whig party; while we may, I think, secure the committees in our favor by voting for him. Reflection is necessary. I would like to see you, and Mr. Adams, and Mr. Phillips for an hour or two on the subject; but we must decide for ourselves."

The dilemma in which Giddings was now placed was a painful one, but it was certainly not of his seeking. He had been actuated by no factious spirit in refusing to co-operate with his Whig brethren.

He was very reluctant to part company with his venerated friend Adams upon a question which he believed vitally concerned the national honor and peace. He was sorry to feel obliged to withstand the protests and entreaties of friends with whom he had been in accord for many years. He would gladly have avoided a step which threatened to separate him from the party with which he had acted since its organization. He had hitherto been loyal to all its reasonable demands, and had incurred the hostile criticism of many good men, and lost the support of many of his most devoted friends, by refusing to join the Liberty party in 1844.

But the political record of Winthrop left him but one alternative. Personally, he was unobjectionable. He belonged to one of the historic families of Massachusetts. He was a man of ability, and his patriotism was unquestioned. His parliamentary qualifications were conceded, and he was eloquent, scholarly, and accomplished. But by temperament he was conservative. He had an instinctive horror of what he called "ultraism," and boasted that he was no "agitator," and had no sympathy with "fanatics." He prided himself upon his political moderation. He belonged, naturally, to the school of conciliation and compromise, and was singularly wanting in the qualities which would have fitted him for leadership in wrestling with the thick-coming aggressions of the slave-power.

At a public meeting in Faneuil Hall, on July 4, 1845, before the annexation of Texas had been consummated, and when the leading statesmen of the country in both sections of the Union denied the constitutional power of annexation by joint resolution of Congress, he offered his famous toast, embodying the sentiment, "Our country, however bounded," which won him the favor of the South, rallied the conservatives and capitalists of New England to his standard as their leader, and brought sorrow and disappointment to thousands in the Northern States, who yet clung to the hope that the country might be saved from this concubinage with the slavery of a foreign territory. On the 25th of September, 1846, when an earnest and vigorous effort was made by the Whigs of Massachusetts in a State convention held at the same place to commit the party to a well-defined anti-slavery policy, Winthrop took the lead in opposing it, and was chiefly instrumental in balking the rising spirit of the people. On September 29, 1847, at another Whig convention in Massachusetts, when Mr. Palfrey moved a resolution pledging the party to support no men for President or Vice-President who were not committed by their acts or avowed opinions to the principle of the Wilmot Proviso, Mr. Winthrop opposed the resolution, for the obvious purpose of leaving the way clear for the nomination of General Taylor. On May 11, 1846, he voted for the war bill, with what Mr. Clay called "a palpable falsehood stamped on its face;" and this action was afterwards seconded by other votes in favor of men and money in aid of this scheme of slaveholding vandalism.

In the light of these facts, Giddings had no discretion. Events had so predestined his course of action that it had become logically and morally unavoidable, however painful it might prove. He had voted against the war, and against supplies to carry it on. His hostility to slavery in general, and particularly to its further extension, had long been well known. He could not belie his convictions and his record. He saw, however, one possible way of escape from his embarrassment, and that has been indicated in his letter to Sumner. If Winthrop himself would give satisfactory assurances respecting the formation of the various committees of the House, he might support him; and fortunately a way now opened to test this question through the intervention of John G. Palfrey, who had just taken his seat as a representative from Massachusetts.

Mr. Palfrey was not a politician by training, but a statesman in the best sense of the term. He was also honorably known as a Christian minister, a scholar, and a philanthropist. He had emancipated a large number of slaves who had descended to him on the death of his father, who resided in the South. His hostility to slavery was not a sentiment merely, but a profound moral conviction. He was no fanatic, but a trained thinker, who saw clearly that the warfare against the peculiar institution must be prosecuted by constitutional methods; and he firmly believed that such warfare, if courageously waged, would drive the curse from the Republic. No man ever more completely possessed the courage of his convictions, while he held a high rank in the literature of New England, and his ability and irreproachable life were unchallenged. Dr. Andrew P. Peabody, who knew him thoroughly, has recently described him as "a man who would have defied all the powers of earth and hell in pursuit of what he deemed right, and who never failed to have heaven on his side." When he made his first speech in the House in the following month, which fully justified the expectation of his friends, Mr. Adams exclaimed: "Thank God, the seal is broken! Massachusetts speaks!"

Giddings, as his letter to Sumner shows, welcomed his new ally, who agreed with him respecting Winthrop's record, and deemed it his duty to address an inquiry to his colleague touching his intentions in the formation of the committees of the House. Under the circumstances this certainly could not be regarded as unreasonable. Would he, if elected, so constitute the Committee of Ways and Means as to secure a report against granting further supplies for the prosecution of the war? Would he so constitute the Committee on Territories that it would urge the adoption of the Wilmot Proviso? Would he so form the Committee on the District of Columbia as to secure a vote of the House on the abolition of the slave-traffic, if not of slavery itself, in the District? Would he so form the Judiciary Committee that action would be taken on the question of granting a trial by jury to fugitive slaves, and of protecting the citizens of Massachusetts against outrages inflicted by South Carolina?

These were the questions propounded, not for the purpose of obtaining a public pledge, or a pledge of any sort, from Winthrop, but simply such indications of his intentions as would enable Palfrey and his friends to vote intelligently. Winthrop replied that if he should occupy the Speaker's chair, he must go to it without pledges of any sort, and that his policy in organizing the House must be sought for in his general conduct and character as a public man, stating that his votes were on record and his speeches in print. This, in substance, was an answer to all the questions in the negative; for his conduct as a public man and his votes and speeches had made these questions necessary. I do not see how Winthrop could honorably have answered otherwise in the light of his public record and his well-known conservative opinions. I cannot believe that Palfrey anticipated a different answer; but it became an authentic fact for his consideration in deciding the question of duty. Of course Giddings and Palfrey refused to give him their support. Winthrop, however, was elected by a majority of one, and was indebted for his success to P. W. Tompkins, a Democrat from Mississippi, and to Isaac E. Holmes, a disunion Democrat from South Carolina, who withheld their votes from the nominee of their own party for the avowed reason that Winthrop was an anti-Wilmot Proviso Whig; while Mr. Adams joined them in his support. Such a combination of political extremes has rarely been witnessed. The contest was peculiarly exciting, and in referring to it in a letter to Sumner, of December 26, Giddings said, —

"I have constantly felt that we should be more vulnerable on account of Mr. Adams' voting for Mr. Winthrop. I conversed with him about it beforehand, and knew how he would vote. Mr. Winthrop's father, I think, was an early and steadfast friend of Mr. Adams, and the recollection of former scenes constrained him to take that course. Perhaps you may not know that when we were about to take the third ballot, Mr. Adams sent a request to Mr. Palfrey that he would not vote. Mr. Palfrey, I thought, was somewhat embarrassed by the request. He told me of it. I assured him that by the aid of Southern Democrats Mr. Winthrop would be elected on that trial. He replied that if I were confident of that result, he would maintain his position as before. I was very desirous that he should, and went so far as to express my wish to that effect. He again voted, and as I then thought, exhibited as much firmness as any man I had ever seen under such circumstances."

Unmeasured abuse and denunciation were now lavished upon Giddings and Palfrey by the Whigs. In Massachusetts the latter had to face the party rancor and exasperation of Winthrop's friends, whose vituperation and venom had free course; but Giddings, who had been long in the public service, was singled out in every section of the country for special chastisement. The Whig Press and politicians branded him as an apostate and an ingrate whose past services to the party were completely cancelled by this single act of insubordination, and who was to be made an example and a warning to others. It is impossible now to realize the extent and bitterness of this warfare as we find it attested by the Whig newspapers of that time. Giddings, however, was not a non-resistant, and in self-defence he deemed it his duty to make some reply to his assailants. One of the most formidable of these was the "Cleveland Daily Herald," to which he addressed a public letter; and on account of the importance of the controversy which grew out of its publication, I think it due to Giddings to quote the essential part of it.

"You do not charge me with having violated any principle of Whig faith or any moral obligation, but you insist that I was bound to vote for certain individuals to office. You have not set forth any peculiar merit in them over the men for whom I voted. Were they better Whigs? You do not pretend that they were. Were they more capable? You make no such assertion. The only reason assigned by you is that they were selected as suitable candidates by other men, in my absence and against my wish. In other words, they were the 'caucus candidates.' Much has heretofore been said by our party of 'collar men' and of the 'servile submission to party dictation' which has controlled the members of the Loco-Foco party; but I had not expected to see a Whig, or a Whig Press, attempt to establish those doctrines on the Western Reserve.

"You insist that I was bound to vote for those men, although in my own judgment they were disqualified. This is substantially your charge, though not in words. I have not so understood the duty of a representative. Nor do I think you would have practised on such a principle had you been in my situation. I felt myself bound to act for the best good of my constituents and my country, and particularly to the extent of my power to preserve from further desecration the Constitution which I had sworn to support. For me to have voted for men who I verily believed would not sustain the Constitution, would have brought upon myself the guilt of moral perjury. To God and my conscience my first obligations were due. No man or set of men could relieve me from the moral responsibility under which I was placed by deciding upon the candidate for whom I should vote.

"At a meeting of the Whig members of the House of Representatives held on the morning on which our present war with Mexico was declared, Mr. Winthrop made a speech urging the whole party to vote for the war. While the bill was pending in the House, he went among his colleagues and personally urged them to sustain the bill, containing, as it did, one of the most flagrant falsehoods ever uttered by a deliberative body. He himself voted for it. He united with the opposite party, and voted with them to carry out the base designs of an arrant usurper. His vote and influence were lent to strike the most fatal blow ever aimed at American liberty. His name will descend to posterity as one who aided in plunging this nation into a war of conquest, rapine, and slaughter, — a war which has already deluged a sister republic in blood, and if not soon arrested, must bury in oblivion the last vestiges of our Constitution. This was not a mere hasty act of Mr. Winthrop, of which he repented upon mature reflection. On the contrary, he subsequently, in his public speeches, attempted an elaborate justification of these acts, and continued his official support of the war up to the day on which I was called to vote for him for the responsible office of Speaker.

"With these facts before me, had I voted for him should I not thereby have sanctioned his course on this subject? Destructive of the Constitution as I considered his acts, could I with any regard to the oath I had taken, vote for him? Let a candid and unbiassed people judge. Should I not by supporting him have approved of his course on this subject of the war? Should I not by voting for him tacitly have said to the world that his policy was right and his course meritorious? I may be in error, but I feel that I should have lent my sanction to a continuance of this war while I was conscious that his official influence would be lent in favor of continuing the work of bloodshed in Mexico. That I *could not do*. The blood of those who shall hereafter perish in this unholy crusade against the rights of man shall never stain my garments. No part of the moral guilt of this war shall rest upon my constituents by any act of their present representative. Those were my feelings at the time, and I frankly expressed them to my friends.

"But I was told that Mr. Winthrop had changed his views in relation to supporting this war. After mature reflection and consultation with others who entertained views similar to my own, and for the purpose, if possible, of gaining such information as would in good faith enable us to vote for Mr. Winthrop, my honorable friend from Massachusetts (Mr. Palfrey) addressed to him most respectful inquiries on this subject as well as some others. He distinctly asked Mr. Winthrop whether it was his intention, if elected Speaker, so to arrange the Committee of Ways and Means and that on the Judiciary as to insure reports in favor of arresting the existing war. To this Mr. Winthrop gave no direct answer, but referred us to his votes for an indication of the course he should pursue. This reference was saying in direct language that he should so arrange said committees as to have reports in favor of continuing the war; for such had been the votes to which he referred. Mr. Palfrey further inquired whether it was Mr. Winthrop's intention so to arrange the Committee on the District of Columbia as to have reports in favor of repealing the laws of Congress which involve the people of the Free States in supporting the slave-trade now carried on in this district. On this point he gave no direct answer, but referred to his former votes and acts.

"Having thus exhausted every means of convincing myself that the influence of Mr. Winthrop, if elected, would be in favor of arresting the effusion of human blood now going on in Mexico, and to restore to the people of Ohio and of the Free States their constitutional rights of being exempt from the support of that traffic in human flesh which now disgraces the nation, and believing before Heaven that if elected he would so arrange those committees as to continue the war and the slave-trade, I had no alternative left but to surrender the dictates of my conscience and judgment, my independence as a representative, and, indeed, my own self-respect, to the dictates of my party friends, and vote for Mr. Winthrop, or I must oppose his election.

"The duty was painful. I saw before me the attacks which were then threatened, and which have since followed. I was perfectly aware that the bloodhounds of party would be let loose upon me; but had I faltered in my course on that account, I should have forfeited your confidence and the respect of all good men. Nothing short of stern necessity could have induced me on that occasion to separate from so many personal and political friends. They, however, felt confident that Mr. Winthrop would so constitute the committees I have mentioned as to insure reports in favor of arresting the war; otherwise they would not have supported him, nor could he have been elected. On this point we separated. Upon those worthy friends I cast no imputation. They are as sincere and as patriotic as I profess to be. I could not interfere in the discharge of their duties, nor could I permit them to control my action; and it is but an act of justice that I should say they manifested no desire to do so. To our own masters we must each stand or fall. We honestly differed on a matter of evidence. Time will soon disclose which of us was correct, and which in error. I pray Heaven that the error may be found to rest on me, and that my friends may show themselves to have formed correct expectations of Mr. Winthrop's course. I would not be understood as saying anything in derogation of his personal character. He is a gentleman of the first order of talents and of highly cultivated mind. To me, and so far as I know to all others, he has ever shown himself kind and courteous. My objections were only to his political views and official acts, nor would I have spoken of them had not duty to myself compelled me to it."

The tone of this defence of himself is singularly unimpassioned and kindly, considering the many provocations to harshness of speech which he had received. He decidedly condemns the political course of Winthrop, but speaks of him personally in terms of respect and friendship. He does not call in question his motives, nor those of his Whig supporters, but simply vindicates himself by a plain statement of facts; and yet the publication of this statement instantly kindled the ire of Winthrop's friends, and opened the way for a controversy between him and Giddings which lasted for years, and was only terminated by the final retirement of Winthrop from public life. He did not himself take the lead in this contest, but his special organ and representative, the "Boston Atlas," espoused his quarrel with an animosity which completely surprised Giddings and his friends. The passage in the letter of Giddings which gave deadly offence to the "Atlas" was the following: —

"At a meeting of the Whig members of the House of Representatives, held on the morning on which our present war with Mexico was declared, Mr. Winthrop made a speech urging the whole party to vote for the war. While the bill was pending in the House he went among his colleagues and personally urged them to sustain the bill, containing as it did one of the most flagrant falsehoods ever uttered by a deliberative body."

The "Atlas," on January 27, denied these statements in the following words: —

"We state, and we do it without fear of contradiction from any quarter, that Mr. Winthrop never attended such a meeting as is here spoken of; he never made a speech such as is here spoken of, or anything having any resemblance to it anywhere. And we further state that no such meeting was ever held."

The surprise of Giddings at these denials is shown by a letter to Sumner of January 28.

"I can scarcely credit the report that he denies being at the meeting of the Whigs. Yet I am assured here that he says he has no recollection of it. I felt it due to myself to make some inquiry, and was not a little astonished to find that the scenes of that morning, which I regarded as the most important of my political life, had made such slight impression upon the recollection of gentlemen whom I knew to have been present. Some have forgotten the meeting altogether; some have a slight recollection of it, but can't tell who spoke at it. *Others have a knowledge of facts, and know that Mr. Winthrop was there and spoke, and can give other particulars.* In the mean time it is due to Mr. Winthrop that I should say, after conversing with others who were present, and finding them so entirely incapable of stating the facts, that I must suppose him to have forgotten what transpired at that meeting. When I penned my letter I could not have believed that an individual who was there could have failed to recollect all that passed. If, however, he denies the accuracy of my statement, I shall have but one course left to pursue."

Winthrop, however, had made no denial, and Giddings of course could not engage in any newspaper controversy to which Winthrop was a party if he chose to stand aloof in dignified disdain and apparent indifference. Giddings therefore addressed a letter to him, dated February 7, asking whether he had authorized the editor of the "Atlas" to make the denial which purported to be by his authority. Winthrop replied on the same day, charging Giddings with having made unwarrantable statements respecting his course in Congress, and particularly in relation to the Mexican War, and declining to be drawn into any controversy on the subject. This placed Giddings in a somewhat embarrassing situation, and he felt obliged to confer freely with his friends and to avoid hasty action. Among the letters he received pending the consideration of the matter was the following from Charles Francis Adams: —

BOSTON, Feb. 17, 1848.

MY DEAR SIR, — My judgment remains unchanged that you had better keep back your proof until you have all in your hands that you can reasonably expect to procure, and then to deal if possible only with Winthrop himself.

Every day makes it more necessary that this gentleman should act. We have driven up the "Atlas" so hard that it has ceased for a day or two to answer.

But a new and more responsible champion has appeared in the person of Mr. George T. Curtis, who writes an article for the "Daily Advertiser," which you will get from Mr. Palfrey. This Mr. Curtis is the same man who made the only defence of Mr. Winthrop during the canvass that was made; and *this justified his vote*. This calls out our reply this morning, which will move Winthrop to the point of answering in some shape or other, if anything can. But even if it do not, you will gain something in transferring your notice to a more responsible and respectable man and paper.

I deeply regret all this business, because it will make permanent enmities here, to last us all through life. But there is no help for it. Winthrop's ambition has pushed him into it, and the folly of his friends has done the rest. They chose to irritate and to defy us; and the accidental success resulting from the voluntary secession of the Democrats from the polls, in order to help him at his election, elated them to the point of extravagance, of arrogant denunciation. Had they treated us with ordinary civility, and conceded to us the right of exercising our judgment in perfect freedom, the painful part of the inevitable difference would have been saved. As it is, I feel more encouraged in the belief that we shall ultimately save Massachusetts, than I have been at any time. Things are rapidly coming to an issue, and the feeling on our side in the Legislature grows firmer.

There is one thing to be considered, and that is that all minor questions will be merged in the great one of the Presidential question. The more I think of it, the more am I convinced that the Whigs, when once convinced that General Taylor never surrenders, will surrender to him, — first haggling about conditions, perhaps, but giving up at last, if they shall be refused.

But I have no time to write more. I see the "Atlas" to-day replies to the "True Democrat" in regular blackguard style, determined to brazen out a falsehood

I think we have this morning placed you in the right position to come forward whenever you please. The "Advertiser" is a responsible paper, and *if it do not now withdraw*, may be regarded as speaking for Mr. Winthrop. Wait and see what will come of it. Very truly, C. F. A.

The "Atlas," on the 3d of February, had declared that it spoke by Winthrop's authority in its denial of the statements of Giddings; and as this authority had not been disclaimed by Winthrop, Giddings deemed it his duty to prepare his proofs and make his defence, which appeared in the "Boston Whig" on March 18, and in the "Atlas" on the 19th. These proofs, besides the clear and vivid recollection of Giddings himself, consisted of statements made by Luther Severance of Maine, A. R. McIlvaine of Pennsylvania, Columbus Delano and Robert C. Schenck of Ohio, and E. D. Culver of New York, fellow-members of the House of Representatives. Applying this proof to the statement of Giddings that a meeting of Whig members was held on May 11 to take action on the subject of the Mexican War, Mr. Severance said, —

"You know we had caucuses frequently, and I have always had the impression that we had one that morning. I recollect most distinctly that I was notified to attend the caucus. That a caucus was called I have no manner of doubt."

Mr. McIlvaine said, —

"I have to say there was such a meeting in the Capitol on that morning; I was at it."

Mr. Delano said, —

"I was at the meeting of a part of the Whig members of Congress on the morning of the day that the House passed the bill that has brought the country into its present calamitous position."

Mr. Schenck said, —

"I remember that there was such a meeting of the Whig members of the House of Representatives in one of the committee-rooms on the morning of that day. My colleague, Governor Vance, I think, was chairman of the meeting. I was present."

Mr. Culver said, —

"I would state that I was at the Whig caucus in the northeast corner of the Capitol on the morning of the 11th May, 1846."

The positive denial of the "Atlas" that such a meeting was ever held, made "without fear of contradiction," is thus completely overthrown, and it naturally awakens distrust as to the truth of other denials made with the same positiveness.

On the question whether Mr. Winthrop attended this caucus and made the remarks attributed to him, Mr. McIlvaine said, —

"My impression is that Mr. Winthrop was there."

Mr. Delano said, —

"I cannot say that I saw Mr. Winthrop at the meeting. I have an impression that he was there."

Mr. Schenck said, —

"My impression is that Mr. Winthrop was there. I cannot clearly remember whether he spoke, or who did."

Mr. Culver said, —

"I think Mr. Winthrop, Mr. Vinton, Mr. Hunt, and yourself [Mr. Giddings] and others were present and spoke. The precise sentiments advanced by Mr. Winthrop I cannot call to mind; but the *purport*, the *general scope*, of his remarks was that we (the Whigs) must not oppose the measure; that policy would require us to support it."

This evidence is corroborated by the positive statement of Giddings himself, made from his distinct recollection that Winthrop was present, and made a speech urging the whole party to vote for the war. The weight of this evidence is not materially affected by the fact that others who were present did not see Winthrop, or hear him speak, since positive statements, where the witnesses are equally trustworthy, must prevail over negative ones.

Concerning the statement that Mr. Winthrop went among his colleagues and urged them to vote for the bill, Mr. Severance said, —

"You are unquestionably correct in saying that Mr. Winthrop advised his Whig friends to vote for the bill."

Mr. McIlvaine said, —

"I sat beside Mr. Abbott, and while the bill was pending, Mr. Winthrop came to him and held conversation with him at his seat. He then went to Mr. Grinnell, who sat near me, and conversed with him. Mr. Abbott did not vote when his name was first called, but afterwards voted for the bill. He was much embarrassed by his position, and on the same day gave me distinctly to understand that he had been influenced by his colleague, Mr. Winthrop. He also spoke of it on subsequent occasions during the session."

Mr. Culver said, —

"After we entered the hall, and while the Ayes and Noes were being called, I think some of the Massachusetts delegation remarked to me that Mr. Winthrop was going for the bill, and was endeavoring to persuade others of the delegation to do the same."

Mr. Delano said, —

"Just before the bill above alluded to was put upon its passage, I saw Mr. Winthrop go to the seats of several of the Massachusetts members. Mr. Hudson sat by me, and Mr. Marsh, of Vermont, before us. Mr. Winthrop stopped in the aisle opposite our seat, and a conversation ensued, in which Mr. Winthrop urged the necessity of voting for the bill. I did not participate in the conversation, because I felt that my opinion could not, and ought not, to have influence with either of the distinguished gentlemen who were holding the conversation. I very well remember, however, that Mr. Winthrop used arguments in favor of voting for the bill, and I am quite certain he alluded to the fate of those who opposed the War of 1812 as a reason for his then opinions."

It will be seen that this third statement of Mr. Giddings is fully sustained by the evidence he produced, and, in fact, it was never denied by Mr. Winthrop or his friends. The two other statements, so positively denied by the "Atlas," are supported by evidence which in any court of justice would fairly warrant the favorable verdict of a jury.

The "Atlas" reviewed this evidence, and affected to treat it with contempt. In the mean time, other parties had become involved in the controversy. The "Boston Whig," then edited by Charles Francis Adams, espoused the side of Giddings, while Sumner occasionally lent a hand in the same service. This exasperated the "Atlas," and it became as envenomed against them as it had shown itself in dealing with Giddings. The feelings of Winthrop towards them were forcibly expressed in a speech relative to this controversy delivered in the House of Representatives two years later, in which he said: "There is a little *nest of vipers*, sir, in my own immediate district and vicinity [Sumner, Adams, and Palfrey], who have been *biting a file* for some three or four years past, and who, having fairly used up their own teeth, have evidently enlisted in their service the fresher fangs of some honorable members of this House" (Giddings and others).

The most remarkable fact about this warfare of Winthrop and the "Atlas" was that it raged around purely incidental and perfectly immaterial points. The facts stated by Giddings, which provoked it, were side issues, which might be affirmed or denied without touching the real question, which was *Winthrop's support of the war.* As already stated, he had voted for the War Bill — preamble and all — on the 11th of May, 1846, providing for ten millions of money and fifty thousand men for the invasion of Mexico. On the following day he voted to raise "a company of sappers, miners, and pontoniers," in addition to the fifty thousand men already provided for. On the 19th of May he voted for the Army Bill, making large appropriations for military operations in Mexico. On the 15th of June he voted for the bill making appropriations for the naval service for the year ending June 30, 1847, embracing large sums in aid of the war. On the bill passed by the House on the 16th of July "for the support of volunteers and troops authorized to be employed in the prosecution of the war with Mexico," he did not vote either way; but as a member of the Committee of Ways and Means he had voted to commend it to the House. On the 8th of January, 1847, he voted against the appointment of a Lieutenant-General to supersede General Scott; but this was purely a political movement, having no bearing whatever on the prosecution of the war, and was opposed by many Democrats. He voted against the Ten Regiment Bill on January 11, 1847; but less than half the fifty thousand volunteers already provided for had been called into service, and the only question involved was the policy of employing regulars instead of volunteers, and thus increasing the patronage of the President. It did not in any way involve the question of continuing the war, but merely the manner of doing it. The sole war measure he ever opposed was the Army Bill, which passed the House on the 23d of February; but he had given it his sanction as a member of the Committee of Ways and Means, which reported it, and he only voted against it after it had been amended in the House. That his action in this case did not prove his opposition to the war is shown by his vote four days later to increase the pay of the army, which was strictly a war measure.

Such is the record; and in thus supporting the President in the prosecution of a war of conquest wantonly begun by himself, it must be said that Mr. Winthrop was consistent. He held, as we have seen in the last chapter, that the British Parliament may rightfully withhold supplies in the case of an unjust war, because it works a change of Administration and thus affords a prompt correction of executive usurpation; but that in the United States, where the President holds his office for a fixed term of years, executive lawlessness must be endured until the people themselves can find a remedy by electing a new President.

The facts I have cited are shown by the Congressional Records, and they constitute Winthrop's "official support of the war," and the declared reason why Giddings could not favor him for Speaker without some assurance that he would change his course. Winthrop did not deny these facts, nor authorize the "Atlas" to do so, but rushed into an embittered controversy about the question whether he had attended a Whig caucus on the day the War Bill passed the House, and spoken in its favor, and whether he had urged his colleagues to join him. If he was right in supporting the war, he was right in making speeches in its favor and in urging his colleagues to vote for it. If he could not deny the fact that he voted for it, an angry controversy about the question whether he had been an accessory to it before the fact was simply a waste of temper and of words.

It is difficult to account for all this except upon the supposition that Winthrop secretly regretted his course and became morbidly sensitive to criticism. The "Atlas," it is true, insisted that there was "a question of veracity" between Giddings and Winthrop; but there was no such question. It was a question of fact as to occurrences more than a year and a half before, and which rested upon the recollections of men who were supposed to have information on the subject. It was a question of memory; and when Winthrop, in his speech of February 21, 1850, produced sundry letters from members showing that certain persons were not present at the Whig caucus who were mentioned by Mr. Culver as having attended it, he simply showed the difference of recollection among persons equally trustworthy, and the fallibility of human memory. There is no question of veracity involved between them, or between Winthrop and Giddings. No one can read the letter of the latter to Sumner, already quoted, and doubt for a moment his perfect good faith in the statements he made concerning Winthrop, who should have been as ready to acquit him of any intentional misstatement as the latter was to account for Winthrop's positive denial on the score of his having forgotten the fact which Giddings distinctly remembered.

In dealing with this controversy it has not been my purpose to treat Mr. Winthrop with the slightest unfairness. My sole object has been to do justice to Giddings as an honest man and a brave and faithful public servant. He was not only completely justified in refusing to vote for Winthrop on account of his support of the Mexican War, but his action was vindicated by time. His predictions respecting Winthrop's formation of the committees were verified. If there was any anti-war and anti-slavery committee in the House in the Thirtieth Congress, it was the Committee on Territories; and that committee only reported a Wilmot-Proviso Bill after it had been instructed to do so by the House. I think Giddings was right in saying, in one of his letters to Sumner, that the Committees on the District of Columbia and the Judiciary were so arranged that no favorable reports on the petitions to repeal the laws of Congress establishing slavery and the slave-trade there were allowed to be made, and that they were as manifestly slaveholding in their character as they had been under slaveholding Speakers. This was equally true of the Committee on Ways and Means, which reported bills appropriating all the money demanded by the President to enable the army and navy to prosecute the war against Mexico; while the Committee on Foreign Relations did nothing to indicate its sympathy with the anti-war and anti-slavery feeling of the country.

It is true that a gentleman no less distinguished than Horace Mann did not believe that Winthrop had shown himself faithless to freedom in the formation of these committees; but the character of the committees, as established by the authentic record of what they actually did and failed to do, settles the question against him. Indeed, he would not have been Winthrop if he had constituted them otherwise. His action was prompted by his strong conservative instincts. In placing Giddings on the Committee on Indian Affairs, and Palfrey on the Committee on Agriculture, he was true to himself and faithful to duty as he saw it; for he did not believe in the leadership of men whom he regarded as mischievous agitators and fanatics. No other explanation of his course is reconcilable with the facts which define it.

To all this it may properly be added that Winthrop still further vindicated the course of Giddings by the acts of his later life. His intense hostility to the Free-Soil movement has already been shown. He was among the early and zealous champions of General Taylor for the Presidency. Under the pressure of his Administration he declined to vote for the Wilmot Proviso on the 4th day of February, 1850, and a few weeks later openly espoused the President's policy of Congressional "non-action" with slavery in the Territories, which the Whig party had combated as a Democratic heresy in 1848, under the name of "non-intervention." In his speech in the House of Representatives of May 8, 1850, he argued that the extension of slavery over our Territories would not increase the number of slaves nor strengthen the institution. When the Republican party was organized, in 1856, he opposed it in public speeches, and voted for Fillmore against Frémont. He opposed the election of Lincoln in 1860, giving his vote for John Bell, and in 1864 he spoke and voted for General McClellan. I do not refer to these facts as matters of reproach, but merely to indicate how well Giddings divined his character and political tendencies when he refused to support him for Speaker in December, 1847.

It will not suffice to argue, as Winthrop did in his speech of Feb. 21, 1850, that extreme men in both sections of the Union condemned him on directly opposite grounds, and thus defended his action. If this fact proved anything, it proved his neutrality; and neutrality is not statesmanship. Nor will it do to say that he was chosen by the entire Whig party, consisting of Southern as well as Northern members, and that he could not be expected to discriminate, but to hold the balance fairly between these conflicting forces. "No man can serve two masters;" and it is equally true that in struggling for a great principle "he that is not for us is against us." When Winthrop was a candidate for Speaker, a fearful crisis was at hand, which the Mexican War and the greed for more slave territory had precipitated. The hour had struck for the people of the Free States to take their stand. In refusing to stand with them and represent their earnest wishes, he necessarily espoused the cause of slavery. No middle ground was morally possible. Neutrality at such a time was treachery to liberty; and although his patriotism is not questioned, the refusal of Giddings and Palfrey, in the face of caucus dictation, to support him, was as righteous as it was manly.

During this session Giddings continued to oppose every movement tending to make slavery a national concern. On Jan. 17, 1848, he offered a resolution for the appointment of a select committee to inquire into the facts of a recent outrage in Washington by slave-traders, and the propriety of repealing all laws for the support of the slave-trade in the District. After debate the resolution was laid on the table by a vote of 94 yeas to 88 nays. On January 31 he offered a similar resolution, which gave rise to debate, and was laid over under the rule. On February 7 he voted, alone, against thanking Generals Scott and Taylor for their victories in Mexico. John P. Hale stood alone in giving the same vote on this question in the Senate.

This action called for the highest courage. It was sure to be misunderstood and misrepresented; but no other honest and consistent course was possible for those who had condemned the war in all its stages. And they could plead the high authority of Chatham, Burke, and Fox, who refused to vote thanks to the commanders of the British army for their services in America in our revolutionary struggle, because the war against the colonies was unprovoked and unjust. These great men and exalted patriots made an obvious distinction between thanks and praise. They were ready to admire and applaud valor and military genius, but they saw clearly that gratitude for the display of these qualities in an unholy war is both unnatural and undeserved. The world honors their heroism, as it will honor that of the brave men who dared to follow in their footsteps on a question involving precisely the same principle.

On February 21, the country was startled by the news that Mr. Adams had been stricken down by an attack of apoplexy. On the morning of that day he was in his seat at the usual hour, and when Giddings made his customary inquiry about his health, Mr. Adams shook hands with his usual cordiality, while a faint smile lighted up his face. When the House proceeded to business he took up his pen, and had commenced an apostrophe to the genius of history, which was represented by the recording angel sitting on the clock of time, at the front entrance of the hall, when he suddenly fell from his seat, and was carried to the rotunda in an apparently unconscious state, and laid upon a sofa. He was soon afterwards removed to the Speaker's room, where he remained till death came to his relief on the evening of the 23d. Both Houses of Congress, speaking through their representative men from every section of the Union, honored his memory by glowing eulogies, while the entire Press of the country, of all parties and shades of opinion, joined in unmeasured praise of the great patriot. A committee of one member from each State was appointed to accompany his body to its final resting-place.

Giddings was at that time the oldest member in the Ohio delegation, both in years and service. He had long been associated with Mr. Adams in the great work of redeeming the government from slaveholding domination, while they were bound to each other by the strong ties of friendship and affection. Giddings naturally desired to accompany the remains to the tomb, and his selection as a member of the committee was anticipated; but the Speaker appointed another member from Ohio, who, however, declined to serve. The chairman of the committee then called on Giddings to inquire if he would serve on the committee if appointed. Giddings told him that under the circumstances he could not refuse, as such refusal might subject him to the charge of subordinating his respect for Mr. Adams to the expression of his feelings towards Winthrop for not appointing him in the first instance. Giddings, however, was not appointed, and did not then expect to be; but he was inexpressibly pained. A reference to the matter is found among his private papers, in which he says he longed to accompany the remains of his venerated friend to the tomb, and "drop a friendly tear at parting from them forever," and speaks of the action of Speaker Winthrop as "one thing I would forget if I could." He, however, attended the funeral at Quincy.

On February 28, Giddings addressed the House in

a speech in which he reviewed the state of political parties, and reiterated his views on the questions of slavery and the Mexican War. He predicted the disbandment of the Whig party, and said: "I now hazard the declaration that on this principle of opposing all attempts of the Federal Government to extend and uphold slavery beyond that which is provided for in the Constitution is now based a party, *or the germ of a party, that will at no distant day become dominant in this nation.*" He justified his opposition to the war and his vote against thanking its generals for their achievements, while he referred to the formation of the committees of the House in vindication of his vote against Winthrop for Speaker. He ridiculed the claims of General Taylor as a Whig, while refusing to make known his opinions on any of the doctrines of the party, and declared that "both Whigs and Democrats are in favor of General Taylor, not because they know his political sentiments to be right, but because they don't know whether they are right or wrong. They support him, not because they *know* his views, but because they *don't* know them." His speech clearly foreshadowed the disintegration of parties which followed.

On April 13, some eighty slaves attempted to escape from the District of Columbia on the schooner "Pearl," lying at the wharf south of Washington, under the command of Captain Drayton and his mate, Sayres. They were pursued and captured, and brought back to the city, where they were confined in the District jail. A mob gathered about the wharf when they landed, and followed them to the prison, threatening vengeance against Drayton and Sayres, who were afraid of being lynched, while Giddings received several notes warning him of personal danger. When the House met, on the following day, he asked leave to present a preamble and resolution, setting forth the imprisonment of the persons who had been captured on board the schooner, and thrown into the United States jail for the District, without being charged with any crime other than an attempt to secure their liberty, and asking that a select committee of five members be appointed to inquire and report by what authority said prison was used for the confinement of such persons. Mr. Holmes of South Carolina proposed an inquiry whether "the scoundrels who induced the slaves to escape ought not to be hanged." Leave to introduce the resolution was not granted, and such was the timidity of members that Giddings could not obtain the yeas and nays on the question.

In the evening the mob gathered around the office of the "National Era," and entered upon acts of violence; but the editor behaved with great firmness, and by his coolness prevented bloodshed. Mr. Giddings determined to visit the jail and relieve the distress of Drayton and Sayres by assuring them that the mob would not be allowed to harm them, and that they should have a fair trial. Hon. Lawrence Brainerd, one of the Senators from Vermont, and Hon. E. S. Hamlin, of Ohio, formerly a member of the House, accompanied him. They found their way through the mob into the hall into which the cells of Drayton and Sayres opened, and spoke to them through the grated doors. At this time the mob obtained the key to the lower gate, ascended the stairway, and called on Giddings to retire immediately, at the peril of his life. He told them he would soon be through with his business, and would then accompany them downstairs. The jailer induced the mob to return to the vestibule below, but hesitated in permitting Mr. Giddings and his friends to pass through the gate into the presence and power of the mob. He was requested, however, to do so, and they passed safely out through the enraged masses, who saluted them with threats and imprecations.

On his return to the House, he related the incidents of his visit to the prison, and Mr. Palfrey offered a preamble and resolution, referring to the mob which had assembled on the two preceding nights, and set at defiance the authorities of the United States, and asking the appointment of a select committee of five members to inquire into the facts referred to and report their opinion whether further legislation was necessary in the premises. The resolution involved a question of privilege, and an exciting debate followed. Southern members appeared to be sincere in the opinion that the fugitive slaves had committed a grievous wrong in leaving their masters, and that those who had aided them in their attempt to escape were guilty of a high crime. They thought that Giddings in visiting the prison was guilty of a violation of law, and Mr. Haskell of Tennessee inquired whether he believed it morally right for a slave to leave the service of his master.

Giddings replied that he believed, with Jefferson, that all men hold from the Creator equal rights to life and liberty; that whenever an individual steps between God and his fellow-men to deprive them of those rights, he does it at his peril; that it was not only the right of the oppressed to obtain their liberty if they could do so, even by slaying their oppressors, but it was their unquestioned duty, even to the taking of the life of every man who opposed them. Haskell replied that Giddings "ought to be hanged as high as Haman, but that his effrontery was so much beyond his own conception that he would interrogate him no further." Giddings closed the debate. The presence of a pro-slavery mob in the city, and the personal assaults of members, had armed him with perfect courage and qualified him for his task. His speech was at once timely and incisive. It was inspired by righteous indignation, and breathed the spirit of absolute defiance. He did not deal in innuendoes, or mince the honest truth. Never before had the slave-masters been treated to such an entertainment. It was a brave and manly speech, and gave the country a new definition of the freedom of debate.

In the Senate Mr. Hale asked leave to introduce a bill to prevent riots and unlawful assemblages in the city of Washington, which gave rise to a debate there not less exciting than that in the House. Mr. Davis of Mississippi spoke of Hale's bill as "a bill to protect incendiaries and kidnappers;" and Mr. Foote uttered his famous saying that if Hale would visit Mississippi, "he should be hanged by a mob to the first convenient tree."

While this debate was progressing, one Hope H. Slatter, a Baltimore slave-dealer, having purchased some fifty of the slaves who had attempted to escape, marched them from the jail to Pennsylvania Avenue, and thence to the railroad depot. The scene was described by those who saw it as heart-rending. Giddings relates that the Rev. Henry Slicer, then chaplain of the House, entered the car which contained the slaves, and walking between the agonized victims, greeted Slatter cordially, and then turned aside to reprove one of the men sitting near him, and a member of his church, for having attempted to regain his liberty. On the following day, when the

House was called to order, and the chaplain ascended the desk and spread his hands in the attitude of prayer, one of the members,[1] putting on his hat preparatory to retiring from the hall, began to swear as Slicer began to pray; and while the latter invoked the blessing of God upon members, the former called on the same Almighty Being to damn such preachers; and a goodly number of those present appeared to feel that the prayer of the one and the curses of the other were about equally efficacious.

In the latter part of June, the particular friends of Giddings in Massachusetts urged him to address a series of public meetings in that State. This seemed to him a questionable venture. He had not been accustomed to speak to the cultivated audiences of New England, who were privileged to hear such orators as Charles Sumner and Wendell Phillips, and he feared his efforts would fail to satisfy the people. Mr. Sumner, however, insisted on his coming. On the 23d of June he wrote, —

"There is an intense desire to see and welcome you in Massachusetts. Let me exhort you to renounce all those compunctions to which you refer, and to speak to us from your heart. Give us your views on slavery and the duty of the North. Say what you would say in Ohio."

Giddings finally consented, and the following letter to his wife will show how gratified and delighted he was by his welcome among the anti-slavery people who had so long watched his course in Congress as the champion of their cause in the West, and the faithful ally of John Quincy Adams: —

SPRINGFIELD, July 2, 1848.

MY DEAR WIFE, — Here I am, in the old Bay State! I have been to hear the venerable Dr. Osgood to-day, as he came to hear me yesterday. Last night I thought they had

[1] Hon. J. M. Root of Ohio.

pretty much used me up, but after a night's rest I begin to feel like myself again. Well, I have seen these Yankees as they are. I have met their hearty greetings, their loud shouts of praise. I have stood before the assembled thousands while their deafening plaudits seemed to rend the very heavens as they shouted in praise of *Giddings;* I have listened to their songs composed in honor of my name; I have seen the big tears roll down their manly cheeks as they have grasped me by the hand, tendering their thanks for my labors in behalf of humanity. Their hospitality has been showered upon me in unstinted profusion; their State and County conventions have passed resolutions of thanks for my efforts in behalf of our country; I have seen the foundations of the great deep of public sentiment broken up, and party names discarded, and thousands of good and virtuous citizens, throwing aside party prejudices, declare for freedom and humanity. When I have witnessed these things for the last four days, I have shed many a tear of gratitude and joy. I could not restrain my emotions. I have at times surrendered to the impulse of feeling, and suffered myself to be carried along in sympathy with the vast crowds around me. . . . I have lived very fast during the past week. I have been amply compensated for all the toil and anxiety which I have suffered during my public life.

I spoke at Worcester on Wednesday, at Lowell on Thursday, at Lynn in the afternoon of Friday, at the Tremont Temple in Boston in the evening of that day, and at this place last evening. At Worcester and Lowell I spoke in the open air; no building would contain the audience. At Lynn and Boston and this place it rained, and we were obliged to meet under cover. Tremont Temple was the finest place I ever spoke in, and the audience there the finest I ever addressed; three thousand persons were said to have been assembled there. Every aisle was crowded, and every step and seat in the spacious galleries was filled. I don't know what the audience thought of me. I was pleased with them, however, and my friends assured me that I sustained myself. I believe a spirit of liberty is aroused in the old Bay State which will not be allayed until we shall be relieved from the dominion of the slave-power.

It has been a hard labor; on each night when I retired my clothing has been about as wet as it would have been had I been swimming with it on.

I leave this place in the morning, but may stop at Hartford. I want to set the ball rolling there as it is now going forward here. I shall then go to Washington. Give my love to all the family.   Affectionately,   J. R. GIDDINGS.

Of these meetings Mr. Sumner wrote to a friend in the West, —

"I cannot forbear letting you know the good work that has been done by Mr. Giddings in Massachusetts. He attended the Free Soil Convention held at Worcester on the 28th June. The greatest interest was felt in seeing and hearing this champion of Freedom. When he rose to address the Convention, which was assembled in a beautiful grove, the air rang with shouts; cheer followed upon cheer. The vast audience — numbering, it is supposed, seven thousand — were profoundly moved with gratitude to one who had rendered such signal service to our great cause; and as he proceeded in his clear and careful development of his views, they hung with constant interest upon his lips. The papers will inform you of the labors of the Convention. They have responded to the call of the Columbus Convention, and have put forth an address and resolutions pledging themselves against any candidate who is not known by his acts or declared opinions to be opposed to the extension of slavery.

"Mr. Giddings has spoken to large audiences in Lowell, the city of factories; in Lynn, famous for its Quakers and shoe-makers; and in Boston. In all these places he produced a marked impression. I was present when he spoke in Boston. The Tremont Temple, which is our largest hall, was crowded to suffocation; and yet this immense audience was held in breathless attention. The Taylorism of Boston received a strong blow on that evening.

"This new movement touches the hearts of the people. It is popular in its character. It takes hold of all who have souls and sympathies. I cannot doubt now that it will extend throughout all the Free States. It must be triumphant.

"We are all awaiting the action of the Buffalo Convention, which is to assemble August 9. Its nominee we shall support. I think Massachusetts may be counted as certain for him."

Giddings was evidently gaining in popular favor, and he had now become a recognized authority on all matters pertaining to slavery. This is illustrated in the following letters: —

BEDFORD, WEST CHESTER CO., N. Y.,
March 25, 1848.

DEAR SIR, — I am preparing for the press a review of the causes and consequences of the Mexican War. There are three points on which I want information; and knowing both your habits of investigation, and the facilities afforded by your present position, I venture to solicit your friendly assistance. I wish to ascertain, — (1) The whole number of troops of every kind that have entered Mexico since the commencement of the war. I had estimated them at eighty thousand, but have been assured the estimate was *too small*. (2) The whole amount of appropriations made by Congress for prosecuting the war. (3) The quantity of land given by law to soldiers serving in Mexico.

Could you, without too much trouble to yourself, enlighten me on these points, you will enhance the obligations I already feel to you for your Christian, patriotic, and CONSISTENT opposition to this accursed war, waged for plunder and human bondage.

I am, my dear sir, with most sincere respect,

Yours faithfully, WILLIAM JAY.

J. R. GIDDINGS, Esq.

BOSTON, April 12, 1848.

DEAR SIR, — I hope you will excuse one who is a stranger to your person for troubling you with this note. I say to your *person*: to *yourself* I do not feel a stranger. I wish to ask some questions about your late friend, Mr. J. Q. Adams, which your long acquaintance with him will enable you readily to answer.

1. Had he many *personal* friends, — men who loved him, not for his *learning*, or his *fame*, or because he could *help* them, but for himself, and because they could not help loving him? It has seemed to me that he had none such, or an exceedingly small number.

2. Was he animated by any hostility towards the South other than that which came *incidentally*, on account of their attachment to slavery? That has been often alleged, but I have found *no proof* of it, and not many *signs* thereof.

3. When he was Secretary of State, I have seen it stated that he wrote the Mexican Government on occasion of the abolition of slavery by the Mexicans, and considered that abolition an act unfriendly to the United States. Is that a *fact*? If so, where are the papers published? Again, it is said that he tried to induce the Mexican and Spanish Governments to consent to restore our *fugitive slaves*. But I have found no *proof* of this, though I have not seen *all* the papers which passed between the several Governments on the occasions referred to.

When he was President, I know the course he pursued in the matter of Hayti, Cuba, and the congress of Panama. In negotiating the Treaty of Ghent, he contended that the British should pay for the fugitive slaves that took refuge on their fleet.

I suppose he had *orders* from home to do so. Am I right? for I cannot suppose that he took that step on his own authority.

I venture to write this note, and ask the favor of an answer, because I intend to write a little paper on Mr. Adams, and I wish to do *justice* all round. If you will favor me with a reply, you will do me a substantial service, and oblige,

Very respectfully and truly yours, THEO. PARKER.

Hon. MR. GIDDINGS.

P. S. — One thing I have forgotten above; namely, what were Mr. Adams's *motives* in claiming the whole of Oregon? Did he think we had a *right* to it, or only wish to force men into certain measures?

WEST ROXBURY, near BOSTON, June 17, 1848.

HONORED AND DEAR SIR, — A writer in the "Boston Post" of June 14 (I send the paper) denies a statement I have made on page 40 of my "Letter to the People of the United States touching the Matter of Slavery," namely, "that General Jackson was a dealer in slaves, and so late as 1811 bought a coffle and drove them to Louisiana for sale." I want to know, — 1. *If General Jackson ever sold a slave or slaves?* 2. *If he was ever engaged in the internal slave-trade?* 3. *If he conducted a "coffle" to Louisiana in* 1811, *for sale*. I am not at all anxious to prove myself in the right, but only to ascertain the truth. If you can aid me, you will do me a real service, and I shall be grateful to you for a *special* reason, as I have long been for your general services to the nation and the cause of mankind.

Very respectfully and truly yours, THEO. PARKER.

Hon. J. R. GIDDINGS.

The replies to these letters are not in my possession, but the information asked for was doubtless made available, and found its way into the anti-slavery literature of the time, to which William Jay and Theodore Parker made large and valuable contributions.

Near the close of this session another question engaged the attention of Mr. Giddings. In the protracted controversy between the United States and England concerning deported slaves under the treaty of Ghent, a list of slaves claimed to have been lost was made out and presented to the British Ministry. Although this list was afterwards found to be fraudulent, containing the names of imaginary slaves, it was made the basis of negotiations, and our Government was thus used as the instrument of slavery. A Mr. Hodges, of Maryland, now petitioned Congress for indemnity for a slave who left the country on board a British ship in 1814. The petitioner had not filed his claim under the treaty, but he called on Congress to pay him the value of his lost chattel. The petition was referred to the Committee on Foreign Affairs, which had been appointed by a Whig Speaker, and consisted of six members from the Free States and three from the Slave States, with Truman Smith, of Connecticut, as its chairman. This committee, apparently without a dissenting voice, reported a bill to pay for this slave.

Giddings made an exhaustive speech upon the question, referring to the several stipulations of the treaty, which he quoted, and overhauling from the beginning the congressional precedents on the question of paying for slaves by the Federal Government. He showed that the petitioner in this case had not brought himself within the provisions of the treaty, and had no claim whatever upon the Government; that the treaty-making power could impose no obligation upon Congress to interfere with slavery either to support or abolish it; that slaves are not recognized as property by the Constitution, and that Congress had no power to pay for them or to assess their value as such; and that all such legislation was dishonorable and disgraceful to the United States. In the course of this speech he said,—

"I wish to address some inquiries to the honorable chairman of the committee who reported this bill [Mr. Smith]. He appears to have united in this extraordinary report, which estimates the value of this man at precisely two hundred and eighty dollars.

That gentleman is from Connecticut,—from the very county in which my parents long resided. I should like to inquire of him the price current of humanity in that land of steady habits. By what rule does he arrive at the value of men? Is he governed by the brilliancy of their virtue, by their intellectual endowments? Does he estimate men by their religious devotion, or by their learning? Is he guided by their complexion? If so, which is the more valuable, black or white? Or is a mixture of blood to be preferred? What price in gold and silver does he place upon his constituents? How would he sell them? Sir, I feel humbled when I see Northern representatives consent to enter upon this slave-dealing legislation, and become the instruments of the slave-power to strike down the honor, the dignity and independence of the Northern States."

The bill, however, was sanctioned by the committee of the whole, and when it was reported to the House its opponents could not muster votes enough to secure the ayes and nays, and it passed without leaving any record showing who voted for or against it.

While both Houses of Congress, during this session, were absorbed in the slavery question as they never had been before, the state of political parties throughout the country was equally novel and unprecedented. The sacrifice of Van Buren in 1844 because of his manly letter on the annexation of Texas, led to a division of the Democratic party in New York, and threatened revolt in other States. The favorite candidate of the party was General Cass, who was nominated by the Baltimore National Convention on May 22, 1848. His "Nicholson letters," in favor of the policy of non-intervention with slavery in the Territories, did not satisfy the South; but with General Cass as its expounder, it was cheerfully accepted; for among all the leading Democrats of the Northern States he was perhaps the most obsequious and crouching to the slave-power. New York had two sets of delegates in this convention, both of which were admitted as a compromise;

but the Van Buren, or Free-Soil, wing refused to take their seats, holding themselves in reserve for such independent action as might afterwards seem advisable.

The Whig National Convention met in Philadelphia on June 7. The party was in search of "an available candidate," and inspired by the miserable policy of expediency which had been so barren of results in 1840. General Taylor had been growing into favor with the party for more than a year, and was now a formidable candidate. But he had never identified himself in any way with the Whig party. He had spent his life on the frontier as a soldier, and had never voted. He said frankly that he had not made up his mind on the questions which divided the parties. He was a very large slave-owner, and his active supporters were chiefly from the slaveholding States and those Free States which had generally given Democratic majorities; but he could not be induced to define his position on the Wilmot Proviso, while the Whigs from the Free States vouched for his soundness on the slavery issue. The spectacle was a melancholy one, since it demonstrated the readiness of this once respectable old party to make complete shipwreck of everything wearing the semblance of principle, for the sake of success. His nomination, moreover, was accomplished by the treachery of the Whig managers to Mr. Clay, which exceeded that which had sacrificed him at the Harrisburg Convention of 1839. No platform of principles was adopted, and Horace Greeley branded the convention as "the slaughter-house of Whig principles." Charles Allen, Henry Wilson, and other prominent Whigs of Massachusetts left the convention in disgust.

A new party was now inevitable. The followers of Mr. Van Buren, in New York and other States, longed for the opportunity to make themselves felt in avenging the wrong done to their chief, and were quite ready to strike hands with the members of the Liberty party. The latter were generally ready to withdraw their candidate for President and unite with the anti-slavery Whigs and Democrats of the Northern States, if an honorable basis of action could be agreed upon. The Conscience Whigs of Massachusetts, and thousands of Whigs in other States, who regarded the freedom of our Territories as a vital issue, were equally ready to fuse with the other elements of political discontent and make their voices heard in a new and independent organization. In response to these indications a call was issued for a national Free-Soil Convention at Buffalo on August 9.

The convention was one of the largest political gatherings ever assembled in the country, and animated by unbounded earnestness and enthusiasm. Its leading spirits were among the foremost men in New York, Ohio, and other States, representing the Barnburners, the Conscience Whigs, the Liberty party, the Land Reformers, and many of the admirers of Henry Clay, who now declared themselves for "liberty and revenge." The platform was a most admirable and timely declaration of principles, affirming, among other things, that "Congress has no more power to make a slave than to make a king," and that "it is the duty of the Federal Government to relieve itself from all responsibility for the existence or continuance of slavery wherever that Government possesses authority to legislate and is thus responsible for its existence." The Whigs in this convention, and many members of the Liberty party, in the beginning could not endure the thought of nominating Van Buren; but on mingling freely with men of different opinions, and catching the spirit of the movement, they yielded up their prejudices and cordially acquiesced. Mr. Van Buren had certainly gone considerable lengths as the servant of the slave-power; but there was *one* great and vital issue to freedom on which he had taken the right side, and maintained it without flinching, in the presence of a great temptation; and for this he had been anathematized by the South, and driven into retirement. It has been aptly said of him that he was the only one of the living statesmen of that period who was man enough to turn from the error of his way and assume the thankless and thorny championship of the right. Moreover, the whole country had been so demoralized by slavery that it was not easy to find any public man of eminence whose record had been spotless. Van Buren's nomination undoubtedly meant the freedom of our Territories and the denationalization of slavery. There was no element of compromise in the movement which he represented, and it was wholly unhampered by a Southern wing.

The most remarkable feature of this campaign was the bitterness of the Whigs towards the Free-Soilers, and especially those who had deserted from the Whig ranks. Mr. Webster claimed Free Soil as a distinctive Whig doctrine, and lost his temper because the new movement, as he declared, had stolen his "thunder." The Whigs were not content with claiming the complete monopoly of anti-slavery virtue and parading it before the country. Their spiteful gabble about "renegades" and "apostates" was as abounding as it was ceaseless. The hostility of the Whig leaders was relentless. They seemed to believe that all opposition to their party was sacrilege. The worst passions of humanity were set on fire among them by this provoking insurrection against their party as the mere tool of slavery, while animosities were engendered that still survive, and which many men have carried to their graves.

Giddings entered into this canvass with his whole heart. It was in large measure the outcome of his long and patient labors, and directly connected with the strife about the Speakership at the beginning of the session. Indeed, his refusal to support Winthrop was the first act in a succession of events which destroyed the Whig party and organized the forces of freedom for their final victory. I first met him in the Buffalo Convention, where he addressed an immense audience in the great tent in which the people assembled; and I well remember the indescribable earnestness which was depicted in his face while he spoke of "carrying the war into Africa," if the slaveholders should persist in scoffing at the reasonable demands of the Free States. From that time till the election he was on the stump, smiting his assailants right and left, who seemed bent upon crushing him utterly for deserting the Whig party. In Ohio he encountered his old friends, Corwin and Ewing, who were denouncing Van Buren for his servility to slavery; and he replied to them effectively by exposing their own more vulnerable political records. So rampant was party feeling that his old preceptor, Elisha Whittlesey, entered the lists against him in a printed circular charging him with taking illegal mileage. This circular was scattered in every school district in the four counties represented by Giddings; and it was put on duty for years afterwards, and only finally silenced by his speech in Congress in 1853, completely vindicating his action. Even his old partner, Benjamin F. Wade, still clinging to the Whig party, joined in this warfare. Near the close of the canvass Truman Smith, of Connecticut, joined these Whig assailants in a public letter in the "National Intelligencer," abounding in gross personal abuse of Giddings, and malicious accusations. Smith was understood to be seeking a cabinet position in General Taylor's Administration, and had openly repudiated the policy of the Wilmot Proviso; and he was now smarting under the uncomplimentary allusion to him by Giddings in discussing the claim, already referred to, of Hodges for compensation for a slave. He also complained in this letter that Giddings had "reviled" him in a public speech. On November 16, Giddings replied to Smith in a public letter, from which I quote:—

"You say that I *reviled* you for the opinions which you entertained of General Taylor. It is very extraordinary that you should allege that I reviled you, without letting your readers know what I said. You must have been wrongly informed. I stated very distinctly, and with feelings of sincere regret, that your views in regard to the constitutional rights of the people of the Free States were radically different from mine. I held that Congress had no constitutional power to involve the people of Ohio in the expense, the disgrace, or the turpitude of sustaining the slave-trade or slavery; while you held that we were bound to contribute to their support, to share in their disgrace, and to participate in their guilt. As evidence of these facts I stated to the audience that in the last Congress you were a member of the Committee on Foreign Affairs which reported a bill to pay from the Treasury seventy thousand dollars to Spanish slave-merchants who pretended to own the people on board the 'Amistad;' that the records thus show you to be in favor of supporting the Spanish slave-trade at the expense of the people of Connecticut and Ohio. I thus referred to the official documents of the nation showing your public acts; and this you seem to regard as a *reproach* upon your character.

"I also stated to the audience that in the present Congress you were chairman of the same committee, which, during the late session, reported bills to pay over certain moneys to slaveholders in Maryland, as a compensation for slaves who, during the late war with England, escaped from their masters in that State on board the British fleet; that you held it to be your constitutional duty, as a representative in Congress, to legislate upon the price of human flesh and blood and bones and sinews; while I regarded such legislation as subversive of the rights of the people of the Free States, and disgraceful to the representatives of free men. You voted for those bills. There stand your official acts upon the records of the country. If they constitute a *reproach*, the fault is yours, not mine. I spoke and voted against those bills. There you and myself were placed in direct opposition to each other. It was therefore quite natural that you should support a candidate for President who would be willing thus to involve the people of Ohio in the disgrace and turpitude of slavery, while I, with my views of the Constitution and of our rights under it, could sustain no man who held such doctrine."

The effect of the Free-Soil movement, though it did not carry the electoral vote of a single State, was most remarkable. It placed Chase in the United States Senate from Ohio, and sent to the lower branch of Congress a sufficient number of anti-slavery men to hold the balance of power in that body. Its influence was savingly felt in Congress in July of this year on the vote by which Oregon, with a territory nearly equal to that of the thirteen original States, was saved from the curse of slavery; it launched the policy of cheap postage for the people, and the freedom of the public lands for actual settlers, and speeded the final triumph of these measures; its power was felt in creating the public opinion which compelled the admission of California as a Free State; and it was the prophecy and parent of the larger movement which rallied under Frémont in 1856, elected Lincoln in 1860, and played its grand part in saving the nation from destruction by the armed insurgents whom it had vanquished at the ballot-box.

CHAPTER IX.

DECEMBER, 1848, TO MARCH, 1851.

Second Session of the Thirtieth Congress. — Slavery and the Slave-trade in the District of Columbia. — The Pacheco Case. — The Ohio Senatorship. — Address of Southern Members. — The Effort to establish Slavery in California. — Meeting of the Thirty-first Congress. — The Speakership. — Defence of the Free Soilers. — Speeches. — Work of this Congress.

THE courage and uniform hopefulness of Giddings were put to the test on the meeting of the second session of the Thirtieth Congress. Mr. Adams was no longer with him, and he was cut off from the friendly companionship of the Whigs, who were exulting in the triumph of General Taylor. After long and faithful service in the party, he was now dealt with as a renegade, and obliged to face a new experience in social outlawry at the hands of his old friends. Of all the members of the House he alone was not invited to Speaker Winthrop's parties. But recruits were soon to be added to the ranks of freedom. A little later Mr. Sumner wrote, —

"I cannot forbear writing to express my joy in the triumph of Judge Allen, so peculiar and marked, against a most powerful personal opposition. It will have important influences. He will join your *holy alliance* at Washington. His courage, nerve, tact, and determination will give him great influence over some of our weak brethren. Then there is Preston King. Verily, next year you will be strong. If you can prevent mischief during the present session, I do not fear the next. I observe that the signal has been given to attack you and other friends at Washington. The Whigs are now in full cry upon you. No matter; they cannot harm you."

On the 13th of December Mr. Palfrey asked leave to introduce a bill to repeal all Acts of Congress and parts of Acts authorizing the existence or support of slavery or the slave-trade in the District of Columbia. Leave was refused by a vote of yeas 69 against nays 82. On the 18th, Giddings asked leave to introduce a bill authorizing the people of the District to express by ballot their desire as to the abolition of slavery therein. Leave was granted, and the bill passed its first and second reading; but on the question of engrossment Mr. Thompson of Mississippi moved to lay it on the table, and the motion prevailed by a vote of 106 yeas to 79 nays. The object of these movements was to place before the country the fact that both the Whig and Democratic parties were committed to the support of slavery and the slave-trade in the District. To this end Mr. Gott of New York, on December 21, introduced the following preamble and resolution: —

"*Whereas*, The traffic now prosecuted in the metropolis of this Republic, in human beings as chattels, is contrary to justice and the fundamental principles of our political system, and a serious hindrance to the progress of republican liberty among the nations of the earth; therefore,

"*Resolved*, That the Committee on the Judiciary be instructed to report a bill as soon as practicable, prohibiting the slave-trade in said District."

Gott demanded the previous question. Haralson of Georgia moved to lay the resolution on the table; but Venable of North Carolina declared that he wished to see Northern Whigs and Northern Democrats constrained to show their hands, to let the country see how they voted. The motion to lay the resolution on the table was negatived, and the demand for the previous question sustained. This brought the House to a direct vote, and produced consternation among Northern conservatives, while it was exceedingly gratifying to Giddings and his associates. Ninety-four votes for the abolition of the slave-traffic were cast by the Free States, and but fifteen in favor of continuing it. The vote stood 94 in the affirmative, and 88 in the negative, while nearly fifty members declined to vote, including Truman Smith of Connecticut and Caleb B. Smith of Indiana, who were in their seats. The result alarmed the politicians, and Stuart of Michigan moved a reconsideration, and this motion finally prevailed by 119 yeas to 81 nays. This was accomplished by slaveholding influence, which led many members who had failed to vote on adopting the resolution, and sundry others who had voted for it, to unite in voting to reconsider. The resolution was never heard from afterwards.

On the following day, Giddings wrote to Sumner:

"Permit me to call your attention to the conduct of Messrs. Abbott, Ashmun, Hale, and Grinnell yesterday. When Mr. Gott's resolution was presented, the first question was on a motion to lay it on the table. If this had been carried, it would have saved all responsibility of the party and of individuals. To vote for it would have been regarded as a direct support of the slave-trade. This, few Northern men were willing to do. They therefore dodged the vote, as you see they were present at the next call of the yeas and nays. The vote was in effect a censure upon the Speaker. There is the committee which he appointed. Thousands of petitions are before them, yet they refuse to speak on the subject. This was the first time we have ever been able to get a vote directly on this subject of the slave-trade in this District. Indeed, eleven years since, when in debate I referred to that traffic, it caused such commotion and excitement in the House that many Northern men actually turned pale. Now the sense of the House is clearly in favor of the entire abolition of this disgrace of our nation. Our Taylor friends are thrown into the most perfect consternation. C. B. Smith, so strong in his abolition last year, did not vote, although he was in the House during the whole day. He is a candidate for Postmaster-General, it is said. My particular friend Truman Smith voted against the previous question, — which was equivalent to a vote to give the subject the go-by. Such, too, was the case with Vinton of Ohio; but when the trial came, he was constrained to vote for the resolution. It was a curious spectacle to look at the members and witness their various emotions. Some were cursing, some looked daggers, some left the hall in disgust, and some were laughing. Holmes of South Carolina moved that all Southern men leave the hall, and then he gravely walked out."

The action of the House on this resolution was a surprise to all parties. The Free-Soil members were greatly encouraged, because they saw that their labors were bearing fruit ; the Northern champions of General Taylor were sorely tried, being anxious to make fair weather with the incoming Administration without offending their anti-slavery constituents; and Southern members were exasperated at the evident growth of anti-slavery opinion in the Free States. Among the other surprises revealed by this vote, as it will appear to this generation, is the fact that Abraham Lincoln, then a member of the House, voted to lay the resolution on the table, voted against its adoption, and then voted for the successful motion to reconsider the vote on its passage, which finally disposed of the question. Unlike several of his Northern brethren, he showed no disposition to dodge the question, but placed himself squarely on the side of the South. He was a moderate Wilmot Proviso man, but his anti-slavery education had scarcely begun; and this was true of the great body of the Whigs of the Free States at that time.

The refusal of some Northern members to vote for this resolution because its preamble was offensive to the South was a despicable subterfuge. The preamble told the simple truth, and the slaveholders, who had united with the North in branding the foreign traffic as piracy, had no right to be offended when our home piracy, which was still more un-Christian and inhuman, was fitly characterized.

A few days later, another and more vital question came before the House. It grew out of the action of the Government in the conduct of the Florida War. In 1835 one Antonio Pacheco, then residing in Florida, claimed a negro man named Louis as his slave. Louis was very intelligent, speaking four languages with facility, and the master hired him to an officer of the United States as a guide to the troops under the command of Major Dade, for which he was to receive twenty-five dollars per month. After the surprise and massacre of Dade and his troops by the Seminole Indians on the 28th of December, 1835, Louis deserted to them or was captured by them, remaining with them in their depredations against the whites until 1837, when General Jessup says he was captured by a detachment of troops under his command; that he [Jessup] regarded him as a dangerous man; that he was supposed to have kept up a correspondence with the enemy from the time he joined Major Dade until his defeat; and that to insure the public safety, Jessup ordered him sent West with the Indians, which was done. Pacheco presented his petition to Congress, asking for one thousand dollars as the value of his slave.

The case was referred to the Committee on Military Affairs, and Mr. Burt of South Carolina, the chairman of the committee, reported a bill for the payment of the claim. He frankly stated that the only question involved was whether slaves are to be regarded as property under the Constitution of the United States. It was not a new question. Similar claims had been presented at different times and uniformly rejected; but Southern members persisted in urging them. Giddings was determined to meet them. He saw that if slaves are property under the Constitution, the slaveocracy could not be resisted. The Wilmot Proviso would be unconstitutional, and the demand for a slave code for the Territories would be justified. Slavery in the District of Columbia and the coastwise slave-trade could not be rightfully assailed. Toombs of Georgia would be right in declaring that the Constitution protects slavery "wherever our flag floats." It was the dispute about this pregnant question which led the slaveholding States to secede from the Union; and it was because Giddings fully grasped its significance that his tireless vigilance never permitted it to escape him. So deeply was he interested in this case that he prevailed on the minority of the Military Committee to make an elaborate adverse report, which by request was prepared and drawn by himself, and submitted by Mr. Dickey of Pennsylvania.

After debate in committee of the whole, the bill was favorably reported to the House by a vote of 70 against 40, and a motion to lay it on the table failed then by a vote of 85 against 66. This was a surprise to Giddings; and having made himself thoroughly familiar with the subject, he now voted in the affirmative on the question of engrossment, so that he might be heard on a motion to reconsider. At this stage of the case I prefer to let him speak for himself. In his long-neglected diary, which he resumed during this session of Congress, he makes the following record on the 3d day of January, 1849:

"The ordinary business of legislation was resumed to-day. Several members called on me to assure me that the bill for the relief of Pacheco will pass, and that I am wrong in entertaining the doctrine that there is no property in man. Among those who appeared thus determined to adhere to cherished errors was Horace Greeley, of the 'New York Tribune.'

"*January* 4. — My motion to reconsider the report upon the engrossment of the bill to pay Antonio Pacheco for a slave, came up to-day in order, but I postponed it to give opportunity to pass the bill to establish a board of private claims. From different parts of the country the papers teem with abuse of myself, and it is quite evident that the doughfaces here are trying to prepare themselves and others to sustain the bill of Pacheco against my opposition. The subject rests with so much weight on my mind that I cannot sleep at night, and it is visibly affecting my health. I have prepared the argument with much labor, and never entered upon a case with better preparation. My friend Horace Mann of Massachusetts advises me to pass over the Constitutional arguments, and make a strictly legal effort. Mr. Palfrey advises me to go into a Constitutional investigation. I feel that I am to speak to the country, and I shall therefore address the reader of my speech rather than the hearer, — posterity rather than the House of Representatives.

"*January* 6. — The first business in order this day was my motion to reconsider the vote on the Pacheco bill. I went to the House trembling with fear of failure. My health was poor. Mr. Rockwell of Connecticut appealed to me to postpone the matter. I could not do so without endangering my health, and hence I proceeded with my speech. I soon saw that I had the ear of the House. Certain slaveholders and some doughfaces attempted to keep up conversation and laughter for a while, but I soon saw the deep-seated feeling that worked in their breasts. I had no lack of words or of thoughts, and the appearance of the House indicated that my argument told. When I sat down, I felt that I had never made a more effective speech. . . . Some friends came to me and said that I had surpassed all expectation, and had undoubtedly killed the bill. Some members who had not spoken to me for weeks, came to my seat and congratulated me on my effort. The slaveholders looked solemn and perplexed. In order to save time and test the full effect of my remarks, I withdrew my motion to reconsider, and took the vote on the passage of the bill. The scene that followed I will not attempt to describe, but leave it to the newspapers; but when I saw the Speaker constrained to give a vote on the bill, — the House being divided, eighty-nine to ninety, — I rejoiced greatly, and really now think those among the happiest moments of my life. . . . At evening I met our Free-Soil friends at Dr. Palfrey's. They all congratulated me upon the manner in which I had acquitted myself, and were united in the opinion that it had been a great day for freedom."

These confidences of Giddings, which were intended for his own family, are quoted because they best reveal his real personality. With unreserved frankness and the simplicity of a child, he tells the story of his struggle against this latest attempt to nationalize slavery; and while it is charmingly flavored with his native diffidence and his growing self-appreciation, every sentence bears witness to his supreme devotion to the great cause which he believed himself commissioned to serve. He was proud of his speech, and he had good reason to be; for it was one of the best and most effective of all his public efforts. He proved by citations from Madison, Sherman, and Gerry that the idea of property in man was studiously and by common consent excluded from the Constitution by its framers. He cited the authority of the Supreme Court of the United States to the same effect. He reviewed all the cases that had been brought before Congress from the beginning of the government in which the claim of property in man was asserted, and showed that they had been uniformly rejected. Assuming for the sake of the argument that the slave Louis in this case was property under the Federal Constitution, he showed that the Government could not be required to pay for him, because his master hired him out at the rate of twenty-five dollars per month, and the bailment ended with his capture by the enemy. He showed that when General Jessup afterwards took him as a prisoner of war and sent him west for the public safety, the liability of the Government, if any existed, ceased, and that it made no difference whether the act of General Jessup was authorized or not. He pointed out the mockery of justice as well as law involved in the claim of Pacheco for the value of a slave who for years had been a public enemy, and was sent out of the country for the protection of the claimant himself, in common with other citizens, against his outrages. Finally, he showed that there was nothing to hinder Pacheco from pursuing and retaking Louis, if so disposed, and that that was his only remedy.

At the close of the speech of Giddings the vote was taken on the passage of the bill, and it was defeated by yeas 89, nays 91. The slaveholding members and their allies were disappointed and mortified by this result, and the friends of freedom greatly rejoiced. A motion was made, however, to reconsider the vote, and after searching the city, one hundred and five members were found who were persuaded to vote for the bill, while only ninety-five opposed it. But the opposition to the measure was now found so formidable that its friends never brought it before the Senate for action, and the claim was abandoned.

During this winter a Senator from Ohio was to be chosen, and Giddings and Chase were brought forward by their particular friends as candidates. Two Free-Soil members of the Legislature held the balance of power between the old parties. These were Townsend, a representative from Lorain County, who had been a Democrat, and Morse, from Lake County, who had been a Whig. It was thus possible to elect either of the candidates by a coalition with one or the other of the old parties. The contest was a protracted and exciting one, and the result depended upon skilful leadership, in which Chase had the advantage, being on the ground. The relations of the candidates, however, continued most friendly, as their correspondence during the struggle shows; but Chase had a further advantage. He had not been identified with the strifes of the old parties, while Giddings had to face the furious hostility of the Whigs, which he had incurred by deserting them. It required the vote of the Free-Soil members and all the Whigs to elect him, as the Democrats were united on Chase. In his journal of January 24, Giddings writes,—

"By the mail of this evening I received several letters from Columbus which speak cheerfully of my prospects for the Senate. One from Dr. Townsend gives me some little hope of election, for which, however, I do not feel anxious, as I think I can do more good in the House, where I have established an influence, than I can in the Senate, where I should meet with intellects of a higher order,— men of nerve, experience, and of far greater intelligence. But the moral effect of my election would be great, and on that account I feel a desire to succeed to that office."

The Whig members of the Legislature from Cuyahoga County could not be induced to vote for Giddings under any circumstances, and Chase was finally elected by a coalition with the Democrats. On the 3d of February, Giddings wrote in his journal,—

"In the 'Intelligencer' of this morning I found the news of Mr. Chase's election to the Senate. I was so far from being mortified at this result that I may truly say it gave me pleasure. I felt that it would probably promote the cause more than my own elevation to that office. Mr. Palfrey seemed to feel some degree of mortification, and expressed regrets at my failure. This gave me more pain than I felt at the defeat of my election."

The triumph of Chase was very distasteful to the Whigs and to a portion of the Free Soilers, on account of his known Democratic sympathies, and efforts were made to persuade Giddings that Townsend and Morse, whose votes elected Chase, were governed by corrupt influences. Giddings would not listen to this. He wrote to Mr. Sumner,—

"From the bitter attacks made on Messrs. Morse and Townsend for their support of Mr. Chase, you may suppose I am dissatisfied with them. Such is not the case. They both acted by my advice in that election. The reasons which you mention had from the first been strongly on my mind in favor of Mr. Chase. I felt neither mortification nor disappointment at his success over me. On the contrary, I regarded his election as a great victory. Not that I was by any means insensible to the honor of holding a seat in the Senate; nor did I lightly esteem the gratification which I might have derived from a vindication of my course; but I felt forcibly the reasons which you suggest, and I could not disguise the fact that his election would carry conviction to the doubting portion of the community that our cause was rapidly advancing, and that in the end he might do more in that body than I could."

During this session twenty Southern members of Congress united in an address to the people of the South, which appeared on the 28th of January. It was prepared by Mr. Calhoun, and it complained that the people of the Free States refused to assist in the re-capture of fugitive slaves, that they regarded the institution of slavery and the slave-trade as sinful, and that they were endeavoring to abolish both in the District of Columbia, and to prohibit the latter as carried on upon our Southern coast. Giddings thought that this address should be answered by a counter address from an equal number of Northern members; but this idea was not favored, nor could he persuade any Northern member that any reply was called for. He therefore sought the floor himself, and on the 17th of February proceeded to discuss the several complaints mentioned, and to re-state in different forms his well-known views on the relations of the Federal Government to slavery. He believed in "line upon line," and "precept upon precept." He had no fear of superfluity of speech on the great question which formed the burden of his public life; and while he proposed only constitutional methods in dealing with the unconstitutional pretensions of slavery, he felt it to be his duty to meet those pretensions just as often as they were asserted by representative men of the South.

One more subject demanded the attention of Giddings near the close of this session, and that was the question of admitting California and New Mexico as Slave States. Charles Francis Adams, in a letter to Mr. Palfrey, had warned the Free-Soil members that an effort would probably be made, at the close of the session, to secure the territorial extension of slavery. When this attempt was made, on the 2d of March, in the form of a clause of the Civil and Diplomatic Bill, Giddings and his little band of heroic associates were prepared for it, and resolved, at all hazards, to defeat it.

In his journal of this date he wrote,—

"This has been a day of intense anxiety. At the assembling of the House this morning I was told that the President-elect had been electioneering with the members to sustain the amendment of the Civil and Diplomatic Bill, which in effect extends slavery into California. Soon after the House was called to order, the Committee on Ways and Means reported an amendment to the Senate amendment. This I much regretted, as it admitted the correctness of placing this important measure in an appropriation bill. When the vote was taken in committee of the whole, on a question of order, I obtained a decision which strikes out the Senate amendment entirely. This brought down upon me the censure of the whole Whig party, who raised the cry that I had defeated the whole object of the committee; but the vote of the House showed my correctness. We rejected the amendment by 114 to 100. It was a trying time, and but one man appeared unmoved amid the general excitement, and that was my colleague, Mr. Root. . . . The House adjourned at twelve o'clock, having appointed a committee of conference on the subject of a government for California."

On the 3d of March Giddings continues,—

"When we met this morning, we learned that the committee of conference had failed to agree. The doubt which hung over the subject became painful. Men became excited, and forgot other business. The House proceeded in the ordinary course of legislation. The committee of conference reported their disagreement at about three o'clock P. M. At this point great excitement was manifested in all parts of the House. The galleries were filled to suffocation, and every part of the hall was crowded, while a contest ensued for the purpose of obtaining a parliamentary advantage. The House receded from its former amendment, and then proceeded to amend the Senate's amendment, by providing for the continuance in force of the Mexican laws. At this point the excitement became intense. Several gentlemen had abandoned their former position and voted with the South. Southern men were boisterous; many Northern men were so excited that they appeared to know little what was going on. My friend Mr. —— of Illinois came over to the Whig side of the House, where I was sitting, and told me that if violence occurred on their side of the House, I must not forget them, nor leave my friends there to suffer. . . .

"The vote was finally taken, and an amendment to the Senate amendment was adopted. By it the laws of Mexico were to continue in force until July 4, 1850. Under this state of things the bill was returned to the Senate. The Southern men appeared in exceedingly ill humor, and about two o'clock an affray between Mr. Johnson of Arkansas and Mr. Ficklin of Illinois occurred, in which many blows were exchanged and some blood was shed.

"I then visited the Senate Chamber. Several members of that body were greatly intoxicated, — too much to appear in public. A long discussion on the amendment took place, which lasted until five o'clock on Sunday, March 4, when they receded from their amendment, and the bill was sent to the President for his signature."

The plot to make California a Slave State was thus defeated, while the exasperation of Southern members showed how perfectly they realized the consequences of their failure.

The prohibition of slavery in our national Territories was the overshadowing question which confronted the Thirty-first Congress when it assembled on the 3d day of December. That question had already disorganized and defeated the Democratic party. The Whig party, although it had elected

General Taylor, was also seriously divided and demoralized. The last hopes of Mr. Clay and his worshippers had perished forever in the nomination of the hero of the Mexican War and the owner of two hundred slaves; while the devotees of Mr. Van Buren had found their coveted revenge in the defeat of General Cass. Party insubordination quite naturally led to formidable party coalitions, which still further complicated the situation. One of these, as already stated, made Salmon P. Chase a Senator of the United States from Ohio, as John P. Hale had been chosen from New Hampshire some time before, and Charles Sumner came in a little later from Massachusetts; while the House of Representatives now contained nine distinctively anti-slavery men, chosen from different States by kindred combinations, who had renounced their allegiance to the old parties, and held the balance of power in that body. These were David Wilmot and John W. Howe of Pennsylvania, Preston King of New York, Joseph M. Root and Joshua R. Giddings of Ohio, Charles Allen of Massachusetts, Charles Durkee of Wisconsin, George W. Julian of Indiana, and Amos Tuck of New Hampshire.

The little party of three in the preceding Congress had thus grown to nine; and as neither of the old parties was strong enough to organize the House without their votes, the slavery question had to be met at once, and in a new and peculiarly aggravating form. It was involved in the election of a Speaker; and no question could more completely have presented the entire controversy between the Free and Slave States, which had so stirred the country during the previous eighteen months. In view of the well-nigh autocratic power of the Speaker over legislative measures, these Free Soilers could not vote for a candidate who was not known to be trustworthy on the great issue. The Democratic candidate was Howell Cobb of Georgia, and of course they could not vote for him. The nominee of the Whigs was Robert C. Winthrop, and they could not vote for him, because Giddings, Palfrey, and others had shown that he was wholly unreliable in facing the rugged issue of slavery. They therefore united in the determination to vote for neither of these candidates.

The struggle was prolonged till the 22d of December, when Cobb was chosen on the sixty-third ballot. The result was effected by adopting, at the instigation of the Whigs, what was called the "plurality rule," the operation of which enabled a minority to choose the Speaker. The Whigs, when they entered upon this proceeding, well knew that the Free Soilers were willing and anxious to vote for Thaddeus Stevens or any other reliable member of the party, and that they would not vote for Winthrop under any circumstances, for excellent reasons, which they announced. They also well knew that without Free-Soil votes Cobb would certainly be chosen under their plurality rule; and yet the cry was raised by the Whigs in Congress and throughout the Northern States that the Free Soilers had elected a slaveholder Speaker of the House. For a time the ridiculous charge made some impression upon the country; but the masterly refutation of it by Giddings, and the subsequent career of Winthrop himself, finally and entirely vindicated the action of the men whose resolute opposition had stood in his way.

But the abuse of these Free Soilers by the Whigs

was not confined to their opposition to Winthrop.
The thirty-eighth ballot showed that William J.
Brown, a Democrat from Indiana, had received 109
votes out of 226, being a larger vote than any candidate had received. Winthrop thereupon withdrew
from the contest; and during the evening the Free-
Soil members learned that Mr. Brown was ready to
pledge himself so to arrange the committees as to
secure reports upon petitions concerning slavery.
They had constantly assured the other parties that
whenever either of them would select a candidate
pledged to arrange the committees of the House so
as to secure the right of petition they would vote for
him. I was not then in the House, being detained
at home by sickness; but if I had been present I
would not have supported him, because I knew him
to be as inflexibly true to slavery as any man in Congress, and that no pledge with such a man behind
it could have the least value. The other Free-Soil
members, however, with the exception of Mr. Root,
were in favor of giving him their votes if he would
make the required pledge, and Messrs. Wilmot and
King were appointed a committee to wait on him
and obtain such pledge in writing. Mr. Brown
replied as follows: —

WASHINGTON CITY, Dec. 15, 1849.

DEAR SIR, — In answer to yours of this date I will state that should I be elected Speaker of the House of Representatives I will constitute the committees on the District of Columbia, on the Territories, and on the Judiciary in such manner as shall be satisfactory to yourself and your friends. I am a representative of a Free State, and have always been opposed to the extension of slavery, and believe that the Federal Government should be relieved from the responsibility for slavery where they have the constitutional power to abolish it.

W. J. BROWN.

Hon. DAVID WILMOT.

When the House met the next morning there was an evident uneasiness among the Whigs, and as the balloting for Speaker was resumed and the name of Charles Allen was called, who answered "William J. Brown," a sensation was caused, which was renewed when Charles Durkee made the same response; but when the letter "G" was reached, and Joshua R. Giddings responded in the same way, the interest in the contest was intensified, and the Whigs seemed to be greatly astonished. Southern Democrats were not less astonished, and several of them changed their votes when they found the Free Soilers supporting Brown, in consequence of which he lacked two votes of an election. The novelty of the situation gave birth to the suspicion that some secret arrangement had been made between Brown and the Free-Soil members; and after the balloting, while Mr. Bayly of Virginia was on the floor, Mr. Ashmun of Massachusetts asked him whether a secret correspondence had not taken place between some member of the Free-Soil party and Mr. Brown, by which the latter had agreed to constitute the committees on the Judiciary, on Territories, and on the District of Columbia in a manner satisfactory to that party. Mr. Bayly scouted the idea, and asked Mr. Ashmun what authority he had for the statement. Ashmun replied, "Common rumor;" to which Mr. Bayly rejoined, "Does not the gentleman know that common rumor is a common liar?" Turning to Brown, he said, "Has any such correspondence taken place?" Brown shook his head, and Mr. Bayly became more emphatic than ever in his denial.

But the fever was now up, and Southern members scented treason. Brown found himself in a very trying dilemma with his Southern friends, while the

Free Soilers who had supported him were also placed in a peculiar predicament. In the course of a long and exciting debate the fact of the correspondence between Wilmot and Brown was finally revealed, when the disappointment and rage of Southern members compelled Brown to withdraw from the contest; and the catastrophe of his secret manœuvre was so unspeakably humiliating that even his enemies pitied him. I regretted this affair most sincerely; but the action of the Free Soilers was generally approved by anti-slavery men. On the 22d of December, the Rev. Joshua Leavitt, of New York, wrote to Giddings, —

"I must snatch a minute to tell you that, for an old dog, you hold on well. Congress screams at the top of its voice in the ears of the nation in a monotone such as I have heard when the whole population of our streets joins in the cry of 'Fire!' But the cry is 'Slavery! Slavery! Slavery!' No chance now to cry 'Loco-foco!' or 'Tariff!' or 'Bank!' or 'Harbors!' That one word fills the ear of the nation, and there is no power to change the key, or stop the cry, or alter the word, or deceive the people.

"I rejoice that you voted for Brown. Not that he is a favorite of mine, as you know. But he had put himself plainly and handsomely in the position which we demanded, and you were right in meeting him. He answered your questions in a handsome manner; and you voted for him, as the papers say, with a full and distinct voice, so as to leave no mistake; and I dare say you did just so. Now, I want you to help the poor fellow a little; heap some coals on his head, to make him think of his past sins. He made a bad blunder, but it was owing to his bringing up. His mistake consisted in supposing that it was just as innocent and lawful and honorable to play a game of double-dealing with the interests of slavery as has *always* been played by himself and others with those of freedom. He has found the difference to his cost. Slavery is too sacred to be thus trifled with. Will the grindstone ever cut away to the quick, so that our Northern Taylor and Cass men will see how degradingly they are treated by their slaveholding confederates? Turn away at the crank; I see by the speeches that there is some sensibility."

The defeat of Mr. Winthrop was a great disappointment to the Whigs, and they charged it entirely to the Free-Soil members, and dealt with it as an unpardonable sin. They had evidently hoped to drive them back to their party allegiance by forcing upon them the alternative of choosing between a slaveholder and the Whig candidate; and when this hope failed, the abuse of these "disorganizers" by the Whig Press of the Northern States was rancorous and unmeasured. Giddings felt it to be his duty to defend himself and his associates, and to this end he obtained the floor on the 27th of December. He reminded the Whigs that they were in a minority in the House, and that without the aid of Free-Soil votes they could not have elected Winthrop; that if the Free Soilers had disbanded and voted according to their former party affiliations, Cobb would still have been chosen; that as the parties were divided, however, he could not have been elected without Whig votes; that the plurality rule, fathered by the Whigs, providing that after three ineffectual ballotings the candidate having the highest vote on the following ballot would be declared Speaker, opened the way for the election of Cobb, which was accomplished by the passage of a resolution to that effect, in which the great body of Whigs and Democrats united; and that to *prevent* the choice of a Speaker who would fairly represent the sentiment of the Free States, both the old parties thus joined hands as the servants of the slave-interest. In the course of his speech he was interrupted by Schenck and Vinton of Ohio, by Rockwell, Winthrop, and Ashmun of Massachusetts, and others, and a running debate followed which compelled him to re-open his old controversy with Winthrop, and justify his action respecting the

Speakership in the preceding Congress. In speaking of the influence of General Taylor's Administration over the Whigs of the Free States as shown in the formation of the committees of the House in the last Congress, and the action of members on Mr. Gott's resolution against the slave-trade in the District of Columbia, Giddings said, —

"I will not say that the gentlemen voted to uphold that traffic under the promise or expectation of reward; I have not the record evidence on which to base the assertion. Yet one of those gentlemen who voted thus to protect the slave-trade [Mr. Smith of Connecticut], received the offer of a seat in the Cabinet, but for some reason did not accept it; another [Mr. Preston of Virginia] is now a cabinet officer; another [Mr. Collamer of Vermont], who did not vote at that time either for or against the slave-trade, also holds a seat in the Executive Cabinet; another [Mr. Barringer of North Carolina] represents this nation at the court of Madrid; another [Mr. Marsh of Vermont] is our Minister to the Grand Sultan of Turkey; another [Mr. Caleb Smith of Indiana] is Commissioner of Mexican Claims; another [Mr. Alexander Irvin] is Marshal of the Western District of Pennsylvania; another [Mr. Edwards of Ohio] is a General Superintendent or Examiner of Hospitals in the United States ; and the son-in-law of another [Mr. Vinton of Ohio] is Chief Clerk in the Department of the Interior. I repeat that I cannot say these offices were conferred as rewards for the votes given on the occasion referred to; but it is a remarkable coincidence that not one of those gentlemen who opposed the slave-trade on that important vote has, so far as my information extends, received any favor whatever from the Executive."

This speech was very timely and telling. There was a sting in it, but it was called for by the relentless and savage attacks of his Whig assailants throughout the Northern States, who were made to feel the weight of his sturdy and well-directed blows. Respecting this effort, Mr. Sumner wrote him,—

"I ought sooner to have thanked you for the satisfaction I have derived from your speech. Like everything from you, it is solid in matter, and in style also. It is a contribution of real value to our cause. Your vote against Winthrop is completely vindicated. Your explanation with regard to the Territorial Committee shows the lukewarmness of that committee. The conduct on Gott's resolution is admirably exposed, and Winthrop's management of the District of Columbia Committee also. . . .

"I cannot close this letter without expressing my indignation at the manner in which you have been pursued by the Whig Press. I cannot disguise the expression of the deep regard and reverence with which your unselfish devotion to high principles has filled me."

Charles F. Adams, in a letter dated Jan. 27, 1850, wrote,—

"I have to acknowledge the reception of a copy of your speech, which I had already read in the 'Republican' with great satisfaction. If your vote for Speaker needed any justification from the history of the *past*, I think you have supplied it. What they may have wanted from the *futurity* of the Whig party has already come, in part, from the message of General Taylor. To my mind it is clear as demonstration that nobody is entitled to the name of leader of that party so fully as General Cass, inasmuch as he supplies all of the position on the most difficult public questions which it pretends to take. If non-intervention be indeed the right doctrine, surely he can prove the fact of prior discovery.

"Of course we look to you as one of the veterans who teach the youthful soldiers how to stand fire. Much may be done by you in the course of the present session to mark the backward course of those from whom we ought to expect better things. Nowhere is a worse influence at work than here. We shall do what we can to counteract it, but we shall need all the aid that an exposure of facts at the seat of government can give us. Pray let us have it whenever you can."

The indignation of Mr. Sumner at the course of the Whig Press did him honor. Its tide of personal abuse and political defamation had now reached its flood. Two years before, when Giddings refused to support Winthrop for Speaker, the party lash was applied unsparingly as a means of discipline; he, however, was now no longer a Whig, but branded as a deserter, and the party Press pursued him with the ferocity of a sleuth-hound. No one can ever know what it cost him to withstand his foes in this crisis. He was a good fighter. There was not a drop of the coward's blood in his veins. When the interests of freedom were involved, he would allow nothing to stand in his way. But it would be a great mistake to suppose that he enjoyed the fierce turmoil of his public life. His disposition was not combative. His nature was sensitive, and he felt keenly the cruel assaults of his old friends. He loved the approbation of his fellow-men, and deeply deplored the course of events which made his life a continuing battle. This will be seen in the following private letter to his friend Henry Fassett, dated Jan. 5, 1850:—

"I do not think there has ever been such an extensive plan concerted and put in action to crush a poor individual in this government as that brought to operate upon your humble servant. You may think this rather blowing myself into importance, but I speak it to a friend, — to one who I am sure sympathizes with me. I would not say it to the public, nor am I permitted in any way to complain or ask for sympathy. No, I have but one course; and that is, to stand up, to face my enemies, to meet them in open combat, to trust to truth and the power of our cause to bear me through the calumnies, the vituperation and detraction with which I am assailed. No human being here seems to suspect that I feel these attacks. They coolly compliment me on my tact, my boldness, my independence, etc., and laugh about the assaults making upon me through the entire Whig Press, from the 'National Intelligencer' and 'Republic' down to the 'Telegraph' and 'Reporter.'

"But, sir, I sigh and long for peaceful retirement, for the quiet of domestic life, — to step aside and leave the stage for younger and more able managers. Twelve years of turmoil, strife, and bitter persecution have prepared my mind for rest and repose; but the difficulty is, and long has been, for me to retreat under the hot fire of my enemies."

It was during this session that the charge was made against him — undoubtedly inspired by party animosity — that he had purloined papers from the General Post-Office. It was published simultaneously in the leading Whig papers of Cleveland, Philadelphia, New York, and Boston, and was first brought to the notice of Giddings in this way. He promptly demanded an investigation; but such was the feeling of the House that a committee to inquire into the case was refused. One of the Assistant Postmasters-General, being a Whig, sent to the House a reiteration of the charge, to which Giddings promptly responded that that officer was guilty of falsehood and a violation of official duty, and that he pledged himself to show those facts if the House would grant a committee. The Speaker, a slaveholder, thereupon appointed a committee, composed of members neither personally nor politically friendly to Giddings. The first witness examined was the Assistant Postmaster-General, who had reiterated the charges; but after a cross-examination he asked the committee to place on their journal the fact that he then withdrew all imputation against the accused. To this Giddings responded that the charge had been made, and could not be recalled, and that he therefore desired to disprove every *circumstance* alleged. The committee consented to this, sent to Ohio and Boston for witnesses, and having taken the testimony, reported the charges to have been made without any foundation in truth; and this attempt to destroy his reputation recoiled with effect upon the party it was intended to serve.

Probably no member of either branch of this Congress displayed more activity and zeal in the public service than did Giddings. Respecting the great question which had so long and so completely engrossed his public life he was never idle, and his vigilance was never intermitted. On the 21st of February, Winthrop addressed the House at length in an elaborate defence of himself against the attacks of Giddings, Palfrey, Root, and their political associates. It was an eloquent outpouring of the hoarded animosity of years, but not a vindication of his course; for vituperation is not argument, however embellished by the graces of rhetoric. He devoted a liberal portion of this speech to the subject of his controversy with Giddings, and was exceedingly personal. On the 18th of March the latter replied; and although his speech was brief, it was a sufficient response to the attack. He reiterated his former charges, and reproduced his proofs; and he again fortified them by referring to the actual character and performances of the committees appointed by Winthrop, and his open abandonment of the policy of the Wilmot Proviso.

On the same day Giddings addressed the House on the President's message transmitting the Constitution of California. His speech was in reply to Mr. Toombs of Georgia, who on the 27th of February had argued that under the compromises of the Constitution "we are bound to maintain the dominion of the slaveholder over his slave with our blood, and to carry slavery wherever our flag floats." The speech of Giddings was a careful review of the positions of Toombs, and clearly exposed their fallacy.

On the 12th of August Mr. Giddings spoke on the Texas Boundary Bill, and the change of policy which followed the death of General Taylor and the appointment of Mr. Webster as Secretary of State. He showed that the passage of this bill was accomplished by trampling under foot the well-settled principles of parliamentary law; that the payment by the Government of ten million dollars to Texas for territory which she never owned was a naked and monstrous robbery of the national treasury; and that the measure was carried by the bluster of Texas slaveholders and the bribery of Northern members of Congress. It was in this speech that he took occasion to define his position respecting the right of secession. "I would not," said he, "compel them [the Slave States] to remain with us by force of arms. I do not believe in a government of bayonets and of gunpowder, in this age of the world. The people of each State must govern themselves; or if they see fit to leave the Union, I would say, 'Go in peace, and may the blessing of God rest upon you.'" He was not alone in this opinion, and ten years later, when the slaveholding States seceded from the Union, and asserted their right to do so by arms, men no less famous than Winfield Scott and Horace Greeley were in favor of letting the "wayward sisters" go in peace. It is perhaps needless to add that Giddings then changed his opinion, and assisted one of his own sons in organizing a regiment which rendered distinguished service in the war for the Union.

During the summer of this year, Giddings was urged by leading philanthropists and reformers on both sides of the Atlantic to attend the Peace Congress which was to assemble at Frankfort-on-the-Main in the following autumn. They offered to pay the expense of his journey, in order to secure the presence of so distinguished a representative of his country in this World's Parliament of Peace. Mr. Sumner was particularly desirous that he should go, while Elihu Burritt, in a letter from Germany, begged him to come, and to accept the office of Vice-President of the Congress. Although Giddings was a well-known advocate of peace and of the policy of international arbitration, and was most anxious to attend this gathering, yet in view of the great questions then pending in Congress which demanded his presence, he reluctantly abandoned the project.

Giddings again addressed the House, on the 9th of December, on the President's annual message, exposing the apostasy of Mr. Fillmore from his antislavery faith, and denouncing and defying the new Fugitive Slave Law.

On the 26th of February, 1851, Giddings spoke at length on "the agitation of the slavery question." He exposed the systematic efforts of Whigs and Democrats to make the compromise measures a "finality," by suppressing all discussion of this question. He replied sharply to the speech of Mr. Clay in the Senate, in which he denounced the mob of colored men in Boston who had defeated the execution of the Fugitive Slave Law in the case of the slave Shadrach. He defended the action of Charles Allen of Massachusetts in charging Mr. Webster with having accepted office under the promise of pecuniary assistance from financial men in New York and Boston, while he defended his Free-Soil friends against the assaults of Mr. Ashmun of Massachusetts and Mr. Levin of Pennsylvania; and he opposed the increase of our army for what he declared to be the manifest purpose of enforcing the Fugitive Slave Law, which he again denounced as unconstitutional and disgraceful to the nation.

The Thirty-first Congress was remarkable for the eminent men who shared in its labors. In the Senate the great triumvirate of Calhoun, Clay, and Webster appeared for the last time. Associated with them were Benton, Cass, Douglas, Seward, Chase, Bell,

Hale, Ewing, Corwin, and Jefferson Davis. In the House were Thaddeus Stevens, Winthrop, McDowell, Alexander H. Stephens, Ashmun, Giddings, Schenck, and others equally well known.

But this Congress was still more remarkable for its work. It abandoned the early policy of the government, which protected our Territories from slavery by positive prohibition, and provided that new States might be admitted from our Mexican acquisitions either with or without slavery, as their people might determine. This implied condemnation of the Missouri Compromise line as a violation of the principle of "popular sovereignty" was sure to breed the mischief which followed four years later. The Texas Boundary Bill, in recognizing the right of Texas to a vast territory which did not belong to her, and paying her millions of dollars therefor, was a fit companion-piece to the surrender of the Wilmot Proviso. But the new Fugitive Slave Law was still more atrocious; for it made the *ex-parte*, interested oath of the slave-hunter final and conclusive evidence of the fact of escape and of the identity of the party pursued, while the simplest duties of humanity were punishable as felonies.

These several enactments were called a "compromise" and "final settlement" of the slavery question, and they constitute one of the great land-marks in the history of slaveholding aggression. The parties which joined hands in this shameless surrender to slavery were not content with their triumph. They did their best to silence the further agitation of the question; and in this mad attempt to gag the people they were aided by the Press and by powerful ecclesiastical backing. Giddings and his associates were anathematized as pestilent fanatics and disturbers of the peace. They were placed under the ban of social excommunication, and dealt with as "outside of any healthy political organization." Their position was offensive, because it rebuked the recreancy of famous men in Church and State, and menaced their ascendancy. But they had the courage of their opinions, and the satisfaction which accompanies manliness of character. Nor were they entirely exiled from society; for they were solaced by delightful gatherings, which met weekly at the residence of Dr. Bailey, where they met reformers, philanthropists, and literary notables. Of the Free Soil leaders of 1848 one only remains. Their names, so familiar to the public in their day, are now seldom mentioned; but what they wrought endures. The question which so stirred their blood and kindled the wrath of their opponents is now lifted out of the tangle and jargon of debate into the clear light of accomplished facts. History will take care of their memory; while the political graves of recreant statesmen are eloquent with warnings against their mistakes.

CHAPTER X.

MARCH, 1851, TO MARCH, 1855.

Effect of the Compromise Measures. — Meeting of the Thirty-second Congress. — Agitation to prevent Agitation. — Encounter with Stanley. — The Welcome of Louis Kossuth. — Death of Mr. Clay. — Slave Claim of Watson. — Speech on the Compromise Measures. — Presidential Nominations of 1852. — The Second Session of the Thirty-second Congress. — Claim of William Hazzard Wigg. — Meeting of the Thirty-third Congress. — The " Amistad " Case. — Repeal of the Missouri Compromise. — The Case of the " Black Warrior." — Second Session of the Thirty-third Congress.

THE passage of the compromise measures of 1850 was followed by vigorous efforts of both Whigs and Democrats to suppress the further discussion of the slavery question. Great meetings were held in Philadelphia, New York, Boston, and other cities, which pledged themselves to discountenance anti-slavery agitation; and these efforts were seconded by leading clergymen and doctors of divinity, whose sermons were plentifully scattered over the land. The power of the Press was put forth in the same service, while the Executive and Judicial departments of the government insisted that resistance to the Fugitive Slave Law was a " levying of war against the United States." It was a wonderful reaction against the anti-slavery tide of 1848, and seemed to promise the complete re-establishment of the time-honored rule of the slaveocracy.

But these appearances were misleading. The growth of anti-slavery opinion was promoted by the extraordinary schemes employed to suppress it, and anti-slavery men were therefore encouraged. The election of Sumner as a Senator from Massachusetts inspired the friends of freedom everywhere with fresh courage. This was accompanied by important Free-Soil accessions in the House of Representatives. Another sign of promise was the election of Benjamin F. Wade to the United States Senate from Ohio. He was a new and formidable accession from the Whig party, and a fellow-townsman of Giddings, who on the 17th of March, 1852, wrote Sumner, —

"Our Free Soilers took up Mr. Wade as their candidate for Senator, believing him to be perfectly reliable. I think I know the man. He read law with me, was a partner in business eight years, residing in my family most of that time, and has since lived in our little village. He is a man of talents, a very powerful declaimer, and a hater of slavery. He was among the earliest Abolitionists of our State, and took bold ground in our Senate in 1838. He was defeated in 1839 on account of his abolitionism, but succeeded in 1850.

"He was ambitious. I stood in his way, and in 1848 he went for Taylor and opposed the Free Soilers. When, in March of last year, Mr. Webster made his servile speech, Mr. Wade denounced both him and the speech; and when he was appointed Secretary of State, Mr. Wade denounced the Administration in the most scathing language, and has continued to do so up to this time. It was this bold position which he has thus maintained for the last six months that induced our Free Soilers to go for him. I take this early opportunity of giving you his character."

The opening of the Thirty-second Congress, in December, 1851, was signalized by the rivalry of Whigs and Democrats in their zeal for the compromise measures. A regular system of agitation to prevent agitation was inaugurated, and the awkwardness of this performance by the men who triumphantly claimed to have made a "final settlement" of the slavery question was effectively exposed and ridiculed by Mr. Hale in the Senate. Senator Jones of Iowa presented resolutions of the Legislature of that State laudatory of the Fugitive Slave Law, and referred to it as wise, just, and in all respects proper. Mr. Jackson of Georgia offered resolutions declaring the compromise measures of the Thirty-first Congress, including the Fugitive Slave Act, to be just, constitutional, and obligatory upon all the States and upon the citizens of each State. Senator Miller of New Jersey presented resolutions of the Legislature of his State, similar to those presented from the State of Iowa; and Senator Foote of Mississippi presented resolutions of the same character from his State. In the mean time the business of the House had been so ordered that the customary discussion of public questions in committee of the whole on the President's message was suppressed. This was done to prevent anti-slavery speeches, while the champions of the compromise measures were heard in the way of these laudatory resolutions of State Legislatures. Giddings complained of this. If the agitation of the slavery question was to be continued, he desired to share in it. Accordingly, when the resolutions from New Jersey were reported, on the 11th of February, 1852, having obtained the floor on the motion to print, he expressed his opinions with his customary frankness and force. After referring to the slave-trade and slave-prisons of the District of Columbia, which were sustained by the laws of Congress, and the coastwise slave-trade carried on under the flag of the United States, he addressed himself to the Fugitive Slave Law. He said, —

"The State of New Jersey, by her Legislature, may proclaim that it is our duty to take upon ourselves the appointment of officers to run after and seize your slaves for you, but I deny that position altogether. We have no constitutional authority thus to degrade Northern men. Let me say to Southern men: It is your privilege to catch your own slaves, if any one catches them. It is not our duty to play the bloodhound for you; it is your duty to meet the expense of it, and not ours. We tax our constituents, our laboring-men, to defray the expense of chasing down and securing your fugitives. Catch them yourselves, — you have a constitutional right to do it; but we will not turn out and play the bloodhound for you. When you ask us to pay the expense of arresting your slaves, or to give the President authority to appoint officers to do that dirty work, give them power to compel our people to give chase to the panting bondman, you overstep the bounds of the Constitution; and there we meet you, and there we stand, and there we shall remain. We shall protest against such indignity; we shall proclaim our abhorrence of such a law. Nor can you seal or silence our voices."

This open defiance of the attempt of the slaveocracy and its Northern allies to suppress anti-slavery agitation provoked a reply which had no precedent in the debates of Congress. The slaveholders were quite willing to talk about their "final settlement" of the slavery question, and the duty of good citizens to abide by it; but this display of the freedom of speech was intolerable. The reply to Giddings came from Mr. Stanly of North Carolina, and it was a surprise both to Congress and the country. As a Southern Whig he had won quite a reputation for ability, fair-mindedness, and moderation of opinion. He was regarded as liberal, manly, and chivalric, and had never been understood as belonging to the type of men who had been put forward on previous occasions to assail anti-slavery members; but he now appeared in a new *rôle*. He tried his hand in the arts of ribaldry and billingsgate, and was eminently successful. What he said is unfit to be quoted or printed; but whoever will read it in the "Congressional Globe" must be convinced that he was chosen for this particular service by the leaders of the slaveocracy. He was their mouthpiece; for Giddings had not assailed him, nor even alluded to him in any way. He poured forth his tirade without any personal provocation. The sole offence of Giddings was the expression of his opposition to the compromise measures; but it so stung the champions of these measures that they determined upon this method of chastisement.

The pro-slavery Press and politicians of the Northern States were delighted with Stanly's exhibition of himself. The " New York Tribune," strangely enough, condemned both Stanly and Giddings as equally culpable, although the latter gave no provocation, and simply attempted to defend himself against the brutal assaults of the former. The "New York Express" said, —

"The severe scorching and lashing Mr. Stanly of North Carolina gave that arch-demagogue, Mr. Giddings of Ohio, *delighted the House and men of all parties.* It was terribly severe, and its terrible truth made it seem unmerciful, as Stanly laid on the blows; and as Giddings winced, pity was mingled with the sense of justice that Giddings deserved it all."

To this Henry J. Raymond, of the "New York Times," replied, —

"Of course such billingsgate as that by which Mr. Stanly disgraced himself 'delighted the House.' The taste of that dignified body has been for a long time established, and when Mr. Stanly went on to call Mr. Giddings a *dead dog*, and to talk about his having eaten oysters with *negroes*, and to boast of having cut him up in a *dissecting-room*, etc., he knew perfectly well how to hit the sense of the House and 'delight men of all parties.' If he had used such language in a respectable bar-room, he would have been set down as a voluble blackguard. If he had used it in a gentleman's parlor, he would have been kicked out. But as he was only talking *in Congress*, as a matter of course he 'delighted the House.'"

This rebuke of Stanly's speech and of the House which tolerated it was accepted as just by all decent men throughout the Northern States. Even the champions of slavery must have felt that the suppression of anti-slavery agitation by such methods would be accomplished at too great a cost, while Stanly never regained the honorable position he had lost by this prostitution of his manhood and self-respect.

Early in this session, Senator Foote of Mississippi introduced a joint resolution in honor of Louis Kossuth, who had fled from Austrian despotism and been invited by the President to visit the United States. Other Senators from the South seemed equally willing to join in honoring this great defender of liberty; but they faltered a little when Charles Sumner eloquently espoused his cause. They scented danger, and so did their Northern allies. When the resolution came before the House, Mr. Brooks of New York took occasion to say what he meant by voting for it, taking particular pains to declare that he had no sympathy with the views of Giddings and his associates. The speech is interesting as a revelation of the vigilance of slaveholders and their readiness to find in the most innocent facts the proof of some deadly plot of abolitionism in disguise.

Mr. Brooks said, —

"I stand, as a Northern man, upon one ground, upon one political principle, — that is, non-interference with other people's affairs; and upon that breakwater alone can I defend myself from the surges which rise up around me, and which seek to deluge portions of this country, as well as other Governments over the sea. If once this Washington principle of non-intervention or non-interference with other Governments can be broken down, I see no land ahead, — nay, nothing but a dark and stormy sea before me. If interference with other states or other people is ever to become the rule, or a leading principle, in this government, has it never occurred to gentlemen that it will not stop in Europe, but begin on this continent, and perhaps first in this country, in intermeddling with and revolutionizing the peculiar organization and institutions of a portion of our complex society? I am quite sure the thought has occurred at least to one gentleman I see before me, — the shrewd, keen-eyed gentleman from Ohio, whose zeal and whose energy to-day, though a member of the Peace Society, in the general cause of war, can only be accounted for by his determination to break down the barrier of non-intervention and non-interference that stands between him and the society and governments of large portions of this country. While preaching peace, bringing peace propositions within this hall, denouncing all of us who will not vote against armies, and clamoring against all of us who are ever for war, — even for just war, — I see him anxious to-day, with others of his class, to sally forth upon the general principle of intervention and war — *bella, horrida bella*, — with universal creation.

"I protect myself from the surges of social and domestic intervention which that gentleman and those who act with him would raise about me when they are clamoring for the principle of universal liberty, — liberty for all races, all colors, and all breeds, — by saying that it is my duty, as a peaceful citizen, living within my own government, to attend to my own business and concerns, and let other people attend to theirs. I am no Peter the Hermit. I have no chivalrous mission to go forth and enlighten the whole earth. I will not take my little candle and walk among the powder-magazines of all mankind and set those magazines on fire, and then rejoice at the general and glorious explosion. I defend myself from that gentleman and his associates when they assail our own State governments, and clamor for universal liberty, by the general declaration that it is none of my business what is done in other State governments than my own, that I am opposed to intervention of all sorts. Attend to your own concerns, mind your own business, take care of your own household affairs, is the primary duty of a nation as well as a family or individual.

"This, I am sure, is the duty of a good citizen and a good legislator. If we once lay down and establish the principle that this Government has a right to interfere and intervene and take up arms against slavery in Hungary, or any other portion of the continent of Europe, there stand in my own State more than a million who cry, 'There is no slavery on God's earth so horrible as the chattel slavery of the Southern States, and that our first duty, before we arm ourselves against European despots, is to seize the cannon, the musket, the torch, and the firebrand, go across the Potomac, and set fire to the whole Southern country at once.' I do not stop to discuss this question with such people theologically or economically; but, constitutionally, I say Southern slavery is none of your business, you have no authority over or right to interfere with it. If ever, then, this principle of non-intervention in the affairs of other people is broken down, it is in vain for me and those who act with me to attempt to resist the universal crusade which will sweep us, not towards Europe, but across the Potomac, into the whole Southern country."

Giddings replied, —

"I am astonished at the excitability of gentlemen on this floor. It would appear that no subject whatever can be introduced here but some minds will seize upon it and give it a connection with matters which are not legitimately connected with it. Most heartily do I concur with the gentleman from New York [Mr. Brooks] in paying the tribute of my respect to this distinguished foreigner. I shall do it most cheerfully. The act is one simple in its character and obvious in its tendency. But, sir, what right has the gentleman upon the present occasion to drag my name in and attempt to arraign me before this House and before the nation? Why attempt to charge me with a design of involving the nation in war? I have not uttered a word upon that question. I sat here in silence, without the remotest idea of mingling in this debate; and had I taken upon myself to address the committee, it would never have entered into my mind to connect this resolution with the question of slavery, as the gentleman has done, or connect it with war, as the gentleman has wantonly accused me of doing. Far, far from my thoughts would have been such an idea, and I deny the right of that gentleman, or any other, before I have spoken, to anticipate the positions which I should take, and arraign me before the House and before the country for those positions. Have I ever at any time hesitated to express my views openly, with perfect frankness, on any and on every question that has been presented to this body since I have had the honor of a seat in this hall? I appeal with confidence to those who have served with me, to the country who have read my remarks and votes on every subject brought before us, against this unfounded, this ungenerous, charge of the gentleman. My whole political life bears testimony in contradiction of it. Whenever a proper occasion shall present itself, I shall not hesitate to express my opinion on the subject of peace with other nations, and among *all* nations, in favor of *universal* peace.

"But I cannot be dragged into discussion of those principles on a subject so unsuitable as that now before us. What authority had the gentleman from New York to charge me with *inconsistency* in relation to my avowed principles of peace? Certainly from nothing which I have *said*, nor from any vote which I have ever given. There is something most wanton in his charges. I surely had not provoked it at his hands. To him I would say: Your charge is unfounded and false; you have travelled out of your way to assail me; on those charges I will meet you most cheerfully at the proper time, or whenever the proper occasion shall arrive. The gentleman has spoken of popular sentiment, of which he appears to stand in great dread. I have no such fears. The popular mind is lighted by the intelligence of the people, and it will mete out justice, and no more than justice, to the gentleman and to myself. However much he may shrink from it, he must meet it. The gentleman appears now to tremble in view of the penalty of that higher law 'written upon the hearts of men by the finger of God.' This law he has contemned and ridiculed. For the subversion of this law he has sent so many thousands of '*lower law sermons*' broadcast throughout the Free States. He must, however, meet the penalties of the popular will; he may fear and tremble and turn pale at its approach. It must come; he cannot avoid this *supreme* law, before which we must all bow. It is already inflicting its penalties upon him, and ere long will consign him to the charnel-house of political apostates."

A few days after this, Mr. Stanly of North Carolina followed Mr. Brooks in the same vein, referring to the presence of Giddings at a recent meeting of the Pennsylvania Anti-slavery Society which adopted a resolution expressive of sympathy with Kossuth, and of hope that his labors would conduce to the overthrow of oppression, not in Hungary alone, but in the United States. Giddings made a brief and dignified reply to these references to himself, but declined to be drawn into the discussion of his anti-slavery opinions in debating the foreign policy of the Government. He thus refers to this debate and to his speeches in Pennsylvania in a letter to his son: —

"You ask why I don't write about my journey to Pennsylvania among the Quakers. Why, I wish you could see the piles of letters before me. My absence brought me behind, and I have not yet got up with my business. I had to attend to attacks in the House, as you see. But I had a fine time at Philadelphia. It was a fine gathering, and I think I made one of my happiest hits. The broad-brims and straight-coats stamped and clapped their hands and shouted in great style. Lucretia Mott said it was the noisiest meeting she ever saw among that class of people.

"At West Chester, the next week, I met a tremendous gathering. Francis James, formerly a member of Congress, lives there, but the Quakers said he was too timid to attend; but I knew he would be there, although I had not seen him for eight years.

"He was the first man on hand, and I greeted him warmly, and in the course of ten minutes he asked the privilege to introduce me to the meeting. He did so, and while I was at breakfast next morning he called to see me, and did not leave me until I left the city. He entered warmly into the subject, and I understand there is now quite an awakening there.

"As to my course here, you of course see the attacks of Brooks and Stanly and Taylor. The latter I have not yet answered, as I could not get the floor; shall do so soon. Brooks has left us, and has not been here since the day following his attack. I had the feelings of the whole House with me."

On the 28th of January he addressed the House at length on Kossuth's doctrine of foreign intervention, and he showed that that doctrine is by no means new to the Government of the United States; that that Government intervened in behalf of the South American Republics when they proclaimed their independence and assumed their position in the brotherhood of nations; that in the year 1823 President Monroe declared in his annual message that "we could not view any interposition for the purpose of oppressing them, or controlling in any other manner their destiny by an European power, in any other light than as a manifestation of an unfriendly disposition towards the United States;" that the same policy was asserted by Mr. Clay when Secretary of State in his instructions to our commissioners to the Congress of Panama; and that the same principle was asserted by him in 1826 in a letter to our minister at St. Petersburg, directing him to solicit the intervention of Russia to put an end to the war between Spain and her colonies on this continent. Coming down to later precedents, Giddings referred to the case of some Texans who in 1842 had gone to Santa Fé for the purpose of conquest, and were captured by the troops of Mexico and cruelly treated by the Mexican authorities. Mr. Webster, then Secretary of State, said :

"It is therefore that the Government of the United States protests against the hardships and cruelties to which the Santa Fé prisoners have been subjected. It protests against this treatment in the name of humanity and the laws of nations, in the name of all Christian States, in the name of civilization and the spirit of the age, in the name of all republics, in the name of Liberty herself, enfeebled and dishonored by all cruelty and all excess."

Giddings insisted that the same protest should be made "in the name of humanity and the laws of nations" against Russian outrages in Hungary, and he complained that the Government, speaking through Mr. Webster, declined to follow its own precedents. Referring to the recent public utterances of the latter, Giddings said, —

" He was willing to see popular meetings and resolutions and public dinners and speeches in favor of Hungarian freedom and Hungarian independence. He avowed his willingness to let these demonstrations go forth to the world, — to let them be borne on the winds of heaven to the uttermost parts of the earth; but he carefully avoided all reference to the duties of this Government to speak officially on the subject, to enter its solemn protest against the intervention of Russia to crush the spirit of liberty in Hungary, to subject twelve millions of people to the despotism of Austria."

But Giddings cited another precedent which still more glaringly exposed the inconsistencies of the

Government in dealing with the question of foreign intervention, and the recreancy of the Administration to its own avowed principles. The champions of slavery, North and South, who were snuffing disaster in the mission of Kossuth to the United States, must have felt the force of this capital home-thrust:

"But no Government on earth, perhaps, has gone farther in practical intervention than ours. When Texas was struggling for independence, and Mexico continued the war, we sent our army and assumed the responsibility of intervention, — forcible and armed intervention. I well recollect the time when the question came up in this hall; and of the whole number of votes then present, only fourteen were cast against that kind of intervention. I opposed it for the reason that Texas had constituted one of the Mexican States; that she and Mexico constituted but one people, and that we ought not to interfere in their domestic strife. But I was overruled, and the people of the United States expended two hundred millions of dollars to carry out the practice of intervention by force of arms, and that, too, between parties in a domestic strife. The case was beyond that now presented, dissimilar, and can have no other bearing upon the present question than to show the inconsistency of those who supported that kind of intervention, and oppose all efforts at this time to maintain the law of nations, urging that it has been our established policy not to interfere in controversies between other Governments."

It should be remembered that the principle so eloquently pleaded for by Kossuth was not intervention against the wrong-doing of one nation by the physical power of other nations, but only the exercise of their moral power in the form of a solemn official protest in the name of humanity and the law of nations. It was moral intervention for the rights of man; and when Giddings found the Administration opposing it, after having openly espoused the principle of forcible intervention in Mexico for the extension of slavery, he impaled it as a spectacle before the nation. Probably Brooks and Stanly did not relish the entertainment, but they had now succeeded in getting Giddings to define his position, and they had no right to complain if in doing so he took occasion also to define their own.

Giddings was equally happy in dealing with the subject of "entangling alliances" with other nations, which gave him still further opportunity to refer to the painful attitude of the slaveocracy and its allies. He said, —

> "I know that a gentleman standing high in the nation, a candidate for the Presidency [Mr. Douglas], on a late public occasion said he would not unite with England in a protest while she withheld justice from O'Brien and his Irish associates. If England will unite her influence with ours in maintaining the law of nations, surely we ought not to refuse protection to the people of Hungary because we cannot give protection at the same time to those individuals of Ireland. Why, sir, suppose when we solicit Great Britain to unite with us in this national duty she should turn around and say to us, 'No, let the people of Hungary suffer, *let despotic oppression weigh them down, until your Government shall relieve your American serfs, until justice be done to the Africans of your own land.*' Would not such language be offensive to that gentleman? Why, sir, it would be our duty to unite with all the civilized nations of the earth, whether Mohammedan or Christian, in this work of maintaining the law of nations and the rights of humanity.
>
> "I am aware that objections are constantly made to any alliance with Great Britain for the purpose of maintaining the law of nations. But this is a novel objection. We now are in alliance with that nation, and have been for many years. The object of that alliance is the protection of the people of Africa. By that alliance we are bound to keep up constantly a naval force on the African coast, at an expense of about two million dollars annually, to maintain the law of nations there. Yet no gentleman objects to this alliance on account of the injustice of England towards Ireland, nor does any one quote Washington's Farewell Address against 'entangling alliances,' for that purpose. And are the people of Hungary less entitled to the protection of the law of nations than are those of Africa? I am constrained to say that it is difficult for me to discover the consistency of gentlemen who are so sensitive in regard to our uniting with Great Britain in a protest against the intervention of Russia, while we are in strict alliance with that nation for the protection of Africa."

After a lingering illness Mr. Clay died at the National Hotel in Washington on the 27th of January, 1852. Giddings visited him a short time before his death, and found him sitting in an easy-chair, and able to converse in a low tone of voice. Mr. Clay alluded at once to the friendship that had existed between them, the fidelity with which Giddings had supported him for the Presidency in 1844, and the coldness which had subsequently grown out of the question of slavery. He said he had no doubt that his own feelings had been too strong; and Giddings responded in the same tone, assuring him that he could retain no feelings but those of kindness under the circumstances in which they had met. Mr. Clay said he had no unkind feelings towards any one, and the conversation turned upon the future, on which his thoughts appeared to dwell.

In a previous chapter I have given an account of a claim brought before Congress by J. C. Watson for the loss of one hundred slaves whom he had purchased of certain chiefs of the Creek Indians in 1837. They were captured under the orders of General Jessup, as plunder, but without any warrant of law, and Watson bought them as property of the United States. The negroes, however, were sent west by order of General Gaines, and Watson filed his claim in the Twenty-eighth Congress for compensation for his loss. The matter was debated at length, but opposed so vigorously that Watson's friends did not feel safe in pressing it to a vote. In view of the prevalent feeling in the two pro-slavery parties since the passage of the compromise measures, Watson now renewed the claim. Of course every Southern member voted for it, and twenty-five members from the Free States joined them, the vote standing 75 yeas to 53 nays; and thus, after years of effort, Watson obtained indemnity for his loss, though in flagrant disregard of law.

On the 16th of March Giddings addressed the House at length on the compromise measures. Up to this time no Free-Soil member of the House had taken any part in the general debate on these measures, which had been continued by their advocates almost constantly from the beginning of the session. Mr. Hillyer of Georgia, in a speech expressing his horror of anti-slavery agitation, had referred to Giddings, assuring him that notwithstanding all the efforts of anti-slavery men, negroes brought as high a price at the South as they had done at any previous time. Giddings reminded him that his language "would have been better fitted to the quarter-deck of an African slaver, or to the barracoons of the African coast." He ridiculed the notion that any final settlement of the slavery question had been made, or that its agitation could be suppressed. He said, —

"I am aware that men in high official stations have announced to the country that the slave-questions are settled, that all agitation has ceased; but what are the facts? We see and know that discussion has increased and extended more rapidly since the enactment of those laws than at any former period. Our elections are very generally made to depend on the slave-question. It has placed new and able members in the Senate, and it has driven others into retirement. It has occasioned great changes in this body. Where now are the Northern members who advocated these compromise measures? Gone, sir, most of them, to the land of political forgetfulness, from which they will never return. And while on this point, I would ask what has blasted and withered the last political hope of the present Secretary of State? Every man knows that it is this very question of slavery. While he has been writing letters and making speeches to demonstrate that the slave agitation has ceased, it was operating in the popular mind, was silently stealing his political breath, and has now pronounced the sentence of death to his political hopes."

The burden of this speech was the diabolism of the compromise measures and the guilt of the Whig and Democratic parties in upholding them as a finality. He declared that —

"When a man, either here or elsewhere, avows himself in favor of the compromise measures, he in substance and fact avows himself in favor of breeding men and women for market in this District and in our Territories, and of prostituting our flag in the protection of a commerce in human flesh. I would be as willing to traffic in God's image as I would to sustain the owner of yonder slave-prison in his accursed vocation, by upholding the law which authorizes him to pursue it. I would as soon vote for Williams, the slave-dealer and owner of yonder barracoon, for the office of President, as I would for any man who sustains him in his execrable commerce."

Referring to the Fugitive Slave Act, he said, —

"This law, which takes from the laboring-men of the North a portion of their earnings to pay for catching and returning fugitive slaves, is a thousand times more repugnant to their feelings than was the Stamp Act or the tax on tea. Under this law they are involved in the support of an institution which they detest, compelled to contribute to the commission of crimes abhorrent to humanity. This oppression, this violation of conscience and of their constitutional rights, this tyranny they feel and deprecate. It is impossible that an intelligent, a patriotic people, can long be subjected to such violations of their rights and the rights of humanity."

Giddings next addressed the House on the 23d of June. The old parties had then selected their Presidential candidates and adopted their platforms. The Whig National Convention met on the 16th of June, and nominated Gen. Winfield Scott as its candidate. The platform of the convention proclaimed the acquiescence of the party in the Compromise Acts of 1850 "as a final settlement, in principle and substance, of the subjects to which they relate;" and it deprecated "all further agitation of the questions thus settled, as dangerous to our peace," and pledged the party "to discountenance all efforts to continue or renew such agitation, whenever, wherever, or however made."[1] This action was the natural outcome of the submission of the party to the nomination of General Taylor, and the still further demoralization which followed the accession of Fillmore to the Presidency. Indeed, the old party had gone astray too far to return, and now determined to seek its fortunes in the desperate effort to outdo the Democrats in cringing servility to the South. It had completely surrendered its integrity, and verified all that had been said by Free Soilers as to its treachery to freedom.

The Democratic National Convention assembled on the 1st of June, and nominated Franklin Pierce as its candidate. The platform adopted pronounced the Fugitive Slave Act equally sacred with the Constitution, and pledged the party to "resist all attempts at renewing, in Congress or out of it, the agitation of the slavery question, under whatever shape or color the attempt may be made." It thus became a recognized and authoritative principle of American democracy to muzzle the Press and crush out the freedom of speech as the means of upholding and perpetuating its power. The only issue of the canvass was thus declared by both parties to be slavery, and on this they were perfectly agreed; while in their common struggle for the spoils of office each sought to surpass the other in the damning proof of its treason to humanity and its contempt for the fundamental truths of republican government.

Giddings in the following speech addressed himself to the platforms of these parties. He said, —

"We, sir, the Free Democracy, will agitate the subject of slavery and its correlative, — freedom. Here, sir, is an issue

[1] Henry L. Dawes of Massachusetts, and Justin S. Morrill of Vermont, now members of the United States Senate, voted for these resolutions.

formed between us. I, sir, am about to agitate this question. I intend to speak plainly of slavery, of its most revolting features. I will endeavor to use no offensive language, but I will talk of the practice followed by men in this District, of purchasing slave-women, and then selling their own children into bondage. Now, when I do this, the Democrats are bound to *resist*, and the Whigs to *discountenance*, my efforts. In order that we may start with a perfect understanding of this conflict, I desire to learn the manner in which the Democrats will manifest their resistance. I am now agitating this subject, and what will you do about it? Now, I hope gentlemen will not feel any particular delicacy in showing their resistance. Do not be alarmed; just stand up here and now before the country. Show your resistance. Be not afraid, gentlemen; I am less than the stripling of Israel who went forth to meet Goliath. You stand pledged to *resist* God's truth, — to silence the tongues of freemen. I meet you, and hurl defiance at your infamous attempts to stifle the freedom of speech. And now, who speaks for the carrying out of this resolution?

"Mr. Chairman, we may 'call spirits from the vasty deep,' but they will not come. I repeat to the Democrats: I want to know what you are going to do. You are pledged to resist. The Whigs, in their convention, also resolved that they 'will discountenance all efforts to continue or renew such agitation, *whenever*, *wherever*, and *however* the attempt may be made.' The language of this resolution differs from that of the Democracy, but its spirit and object are the same. They intend to suppress the freedom of speech here and among the people. On this point the two great parties of the nation have cordially united. A coalition for a more odious purpose could not have been formed. Duty to myself, to this body, and the country, demands an exposure of this conspiracy against the Constitution, against the rights of members here, against the people. . . .

"Agitation is not only to be put down here, but among the people; they are to have no more anti-slavery meetings; no more Free-Soil conventions; no more sermons in favor of God's law; no more prayers to Heaven for the oppressed of our land. The Declaration of Independence is to be burned, our printing establishments broken up, and our social circles are to speak no more of the rights of all men to enjoy life and liberty. A new political police is to be established, and the American people placed under slaveholding surveillance. But I am paying undeserved attention to these base, these puerile attempts to stifle discussion on the subject of humanity. I hold these resolutions in unutterable contempt; I trample them under my feet."

Referring to the proposition of a leading Whig editor to pay for fugitive slaves with the funds of the nation, he said, —

"When the barbarians of Algiers seized and enslaved our people we sent an armed force there and slew them, holding them unworthy of a place upon God's footstool. No, sir, by all the hallowed associations which cluster around the memory of English and American patriots, I avow that I would sooner see every slaveholder of the nation hanged than to witness the subjugation of Northern freemen to such a humiliating condition. Sir, when it comes to that, I, for one, shall be prepared for the *dernier ressort*, — an appeal to the God of battles. I am a man of peace, but am no non-resistant; and I would sooner have the ashes of my own hearth slaked in my own blood and the blood of my children than submit to such degradation. And here I will take occasion to say that if this law continues to be enforced, civil war is inevitable. The people will not submit to it. Why, sir, civil war already exists. At Christiana, civil war, — with all the circumstances of force under color of law, resistance in defence of natural right, — bloodshed, and death took place. In my own State a similar transaction occurred, and I assure gentlemen that other instances will occur, if attempts be made to enforce that law. In my own district are many fugitives who have informed their masters where they may be found. These men have become desperate. They desire to see the slave-catchers. They pant for an opportunity to make their oppressors 'bite the dust.'"

His arraignment of the old party with which he had so long acted was perfectly justified by the facts. He said, —

"The doctrines of the Whig party, as I have shown, pledge them and their candidate to maintain slavery; the breeding of slaves for market; the sale of women in this District and in the Territories; to uphold the Fugitive Slave Law in all coming time; to admit as many Slave States as shall apply, from New Mexico and Utah; and to silence discussion on all these subjects. This is as far, I think, as human depravity can go. If the Democratic party has dived deeper into moral and political putridity, some archangel fallen must have penned their confession of faith."

I quote the concluding paragraph of this remarkable speech, which struck the key-note of a rapidly growing anti-slavery opinion, and was extensively published and applauded throughout the North: —

"Sir, we are in the midst of a revolution. The two great parties are striving to convert this free government into a slaveholding, a slave-breeding republic. Those powers which were delegated to liberty, are now exerted to overthrow freedom and the Constitution. It becomes every patriot, every lover of freedom, ever Christian, every man, to stand forth in defence of popular rights, in defence of the rights of the Free States, of the institutions under which we live, in defence of our national character. Sir, I am growing old; the infirmities of age are coming upon me; I must soon leave the scenes with which I am surrounded; it is uncertain whether I shall again address this body. But one thing I ask, — that friends and foes, here and elsewhere, in this and in coming time, shall understand that whether in public or in private, by the wayside or the fireside, in life or in death, I oppose, denounce, and repudiate the efforts now put forth to involve the people of the Free States in the support of slavery, of the slave-trade, and their attendant crimes." [1]

The result of the Presidential election of this year was a surprise to men of all parties. The triumph of the Democrats was far more signal than the most sanguine men among them anticipated. Pierce received 254 electoral votes, and Scott only 42, — representing only four States of the Union. The defeat of the Whigs was overwhelming, and the party was

[1] The speech called forth the following sonnet from a young poet of the West: —

THE MORAL HERO.

> The thirst of fame inspires the soul-lit page,
>   And bids the canvas glow, the marble breathe;
>   O Immortality! thy burning wreath
> Hath lured the human soul through every age.
> Nor vain the hope, even in this earthly stage;
>   Nor aught, even here, save virtue, gives the crown!
>   'T was twined for Phocion, Cato, 'neath the frown
> Of fortune, and the fickle people's rage,
> And brighter blooms while sculpture falls to dust.
>   Even thus, O GIDDINGS! shall it deck thy brow,
> While all earth's marble piles betray their trust;
>   Yon "Modern Capitol" to time must bow,
> But bravely, sternly, "obstinately just,"
>   A victor of the immortal heights art thou!

buried forever in the grave it had dug for itself. John P. Hale, the Free-Soil candidate, received only a little more than 156,000 votes,— being about one twentieth of the entire popular vote cast at this election. Senator Dix, the Van Burens, David Dudley Field, Samuel J. Tilden, and a host of others, including even Robert Rantoul and Preston King, had given their support to Pierce, while the "New York Evening Post" and the "New York Tribune" cravenly joined in this anti-slavery retreat. These were very discouraging facts, and were naturally interpreted by the victorious party everywhere as foreshadowing the complete triumph of the final settlement made by Congress in 1850.

But the Free Soilers were undismayed. They took courage from the very fact that the Whig party had been annihilated. They saw clearly that what slavery needed was two pretty evenly divided parties pitted against each other upon economic issues, so that under cover of their strife it could be allowed to have its way. A new movement was now practicable, basing its action upon moral grounds, and gathering into its ranks the unshackled conscience and intelligence of the Northern States. The small vote for Hale was by no means discouraging, for it represented the *bona fide* strength of the Free Soil movement after the elimination of the Van Buren element, which had been inspired largely by personal devotion to Mr. Van Buren and hatred of General Cass.

An extraordinary effort was made to defeat the re-election of Giddings in the canvass of this year. Through the management of men in the Legislature of Ohio who were hostile to his anti-slavery principles, the State was re-districted during the preceding year with an eye single to this result. He was thrown into the Twentieth District, composed of the counties of Ashtabula, Trumbull, and Mahoning, and his enemies were confident of his defeat. The counties of Cuyahoga, Geauga, and Lake were now known as the Sixteenth District; and one of the results of the gerrymander was the election of Edward Wade, a brother of B. F. Wade and a thorough anti-slavery man, to represent this district, while Giddings was triumphantly chosen in the new and hostile district, receiving 5,752 votes as the Free-Soil candidate, against 4,428 for Woods, the Democratic candidate, and 4,169 for Newton, the Whig candidate. A great dinner was given at Painesville in celebration of this triumph, to which many famous men were invited, while the friends of Giddings in every section of the country rejoiced in his victory and the humiliation of his foes.

Giddings was a member of the Committee on Territories which reported a bill for the organization of a government for Nebraska, early in February, 1853. Hon. John W. Howe of Pennsylvania publicly inquired of him why there was no prohibition of slavery in it. Giddings replied that by the eighth section of the Act admitting Missouri, slavery had been prohibited in all the territory ceded by France to the United States in what was called the Louisiana purchase, north of 36° 30'. Mr. Howe was satisfied with this explanation; and the incident shows that at that time no one thought of disturbing the Missouri Compromise. The bill passed the House without debate, and was transmitted to the Senate, where it was retained without action upon it during the session. Mr. Douglas made an earnest effort to secure its passage near the close of the session, and declared that he had been pressing it for eight years; and even Mr. Atchison then favored it, though deprecating the prohibition of slavery by the Missouri Compromise, which had settled that question. The motion to take up the bill, however, was laid on the table, and the slaveocracy thus gained time to incubate the great conspiracy which the passage of the House bill would have made impossible.

On the last night of this session a motion was made to suspend the rules of the House in order to take up a bill from the Senate providing for the adjustment of the claim of William Hazzard Wigg, who had been a prominent and zealous South Carolina patriot in the Revolutionary War, and had sustained heavy losses, chiefly in slaves, by the depredations of the British. Such claims had uniformly been rejected. It was simply impossible for Congress to give relief to the thousands of citizens, North and South, who had been ruined by the wanton acts of the enemy in this struggle. But it was insisted that this claim was an exception to the general rule, and that Wigg had been held as a hostage while the depredations upon his property were committed, and was thus entitled to indemnity as such under the law of nations. The truth, however, was that he had been merely a prisoner of war, and not a hostage in any other sense than are all such prisoners.

The real facts of the case seem to have eluded the vigilance of the anti-slavery members of the Senate, and when it reached the House Giddings, who had watched its progress and understood its character, went among Northern members and warned them of the action of the Senate, and that an effort would be made during the last hours of the session to pass the bill without any opportunity to debate it. As predicted, the measure was called up at eleven o'clock. Mr. Skelton of New Jersey said, "I object; the bill ought not to be passed; it introduces—" Cries of "Order, order," were heard from slaveholding members. Mr. Duncan of Massachusetts said, "I object, and I wish to state the reasons for my objections." Cries of "Order, order," were again made. Mr. Colcock of North Carolina then moved to suspend the rules, and Mr. Walsh of New York said, "I hope the bill will be taken up and passed." The vote was taken, and the rules were suspended by a vote of yeas 122 to nays 46. Mr. Colcock then demanded the previous question on the passage of the bill, which was seconded, and the bill became a law. On the motion to suspend the rules in order to pass the bill, fifty-one members from the Free States voted in the affirmative, and the South thus secured another victory for the compromise measures.

When the Thirty-third Congress convened in December, 1853, the Democratic party controlled the majority in each House and the Legislatures of nearly all the States of the Union. President Pierce in his annual messages lauded the compromise measures, and declared that the repose which they had brought to the country should receive no shock during his term of office if he could avert it.

In his message he recommended the prompt adjustment of the old Spanish claim for compensation for the negroes who had asserted their right to freedom on board the ship "Amistad." This claim has been noticed in previous chapters, and its rejection by Congress and condemnation by the Supreme Court of the United States will be remembered; but the slave-power was now in the ascendant, and the claimants deemed it a favorable time to renew it. The part of the President's message recommending it was referred to the Committee on Foreign Affairs, of which Mr. Bayly of Virginia was chairman, who avowed his purpose to demand action upon it. Giddings believed that a systematic and vigorous effort would be made to carry the measure, and he therefore determined upon a thorough exposure of the character of the claim. He was the only member of the House whose public life had been contemporaneous with it, and on the 21st of December, on the usual motion to refer the message to the appropriate committees, he addressed the House on the subject, going fully into the history of the claim, and demonstrating its monstrous injustice and inhumanity by referring to the law and the facts of the case. Mr. Bayly attempted no reply, but promised to do so at the first opportunity, and afterwards repeated the promise when challenged by Giddings to face the country in the attempt to vindicate the justice of the measure. But he never made the attempt, and the claim was tacitly abandoned, while the Democratic Press and politicians denounced Giddings for agitating the slavery question.

But a question of far greater moment now demanded attention. The immense region north and west of Missouri was ready for organized territorial governments, and it had been secured to freedom by the Missouri Compromise of 1820. California had been made free, and the slaveholders recoiled from the prospect of additional Free States in the northwest. To avert this was no easy task; but after some hesitation and a good deal of legislative diplomacy the repeal of the Missouri Compromise was resolved upon, and Mr. Douglas of Illinois chosen as the champion of the measure. This movement belonged to the logic of slavery, which made every concession to its demands the occasion for further exactions. It required no gift of prophecy to foresee that if freedom and slavery were to have equal rights in New Mexico and Utah, the same principle of non-intervention by Congress would be asserted for the Territories north of 36° 30', and this line regarded as a rock of offence to be removed. This idea was illustrated by the famous bill of Mr. Douglas, which declared the Missouri restriction to be inoperative and void, because "inconsistent with the principle of non-intervention by Congress with slavery in the States and Territories as recognized by the compromise measures of 1850." It is true that those measures had not abrogated that line, and related only to our Mexican acquisitions; but they affirmed a principle, and if that principle was sound, the Missouri Compromise should never have been made. The Abolitionists were therefore right in declaring the measure of Mr. Douglas to be a sprout from the grave of the Wilmot Proviso.

On the 19th of January, 1854, the Free-Soil members of this Congress sent forth a paper touching the proposition of Mr. Douglas entitled an "Appeal of the Independent Democrats in Congress to the People of the United States." It was signed by S. P. Chase, Charles Sumner, J. R. Giddings, Edward Wade, Gerrit Smith, and Alexander DeWitt. Giddings made the first draft of this address, which was revised and rewritten by Mr. Chase. It was then submitted to Mr. Smith, who made some verbal changes, and referred it to Mr. Sumner, who made a further revision, after which it went to the Press. The appeal says, —

"We arraign this bill as a gross violation of a sacred pledge, as a criminal betrayal of precious rights, as part and parcel of an atrocious plot to exclude from a vast unoccupied region immigrants from the Old World and free laborers from our own States, and convert it into a dreary region of despotism inhabited by masters and slaves."

The style of this address was admirable, and no paper called forth by the crisis analyzed with more clearness and vigor this atrocious conspiracy for the spread of slavery over the continent. It implored the people of the Free States and Christians and Christian ministers not to "submit to become agents in extending legalized oppression and systematized injustice over a vast territory yet exempt from those terrible evils;" and it concluded, —

"For ourselves, we shall resist it by speech and vote, and with all the abilities which God has given us. Even if overcome in the impending struggle, we shall not submit. We shall go home to our constituents, erect anew the standard of freedom, and call on the people to come to the rescue of the country from the domination of slavery. We will not despair, for the cause of human freedom is the cause of God."

This address was widely published in the Whig and Free-Soil papers of the Northern States, and it played no inconsiderable part in creating a sound public opinion. Mr. Douglas felt it keenly, and a few days later made a personal attack upon its signers, to which Mr. Chase replied with decided force and effect. Mr. Douglas reiterated his personalities instead of defending the doctrines and policy of his bill, and Mr. Sumner answered with deserved severity, referring to his bill as "a soulless, eyeless monster, horrid, unshapely, and vast." After a debate of four months the bill became law, receiving forty votes from the Free States in the House, and twelve in the Senate; thus opening the way for the organized border-ruffianism through which the slaveocracy sought to establish its ascendancy in Kansas and Nebraska, and the organized resistance of these outrages by the people of the Free States.

On the 17th of May Giddings addressed the House in a vigorous speech on the bill organizing territorial governments in Kansas and Nebraska. He referred to the character of slavery as defined in the slave codes of the South, and argued against its extension on both economic and humanitarian grounds. He gave particular attention to the theory of popular sovereignty in the Territories, and ridiculed the notion that any such theory can be reconciled with the rights of a portion of the people to enslave another portion, or with the sovereignty of Congress over them, and the appointment by the President of their chief officers.

In speaking of the asserted right of slaveholders to take their slaves into the Territories as property, and of the Northern members of Congress who adopted that idea, he said, —

"But perhaps the views of gentlemen ought not to be commented on with too much severity; for if reports be true, some of these members have 'sold themselves' at prices perhaps below that often paid for Southern negroes. I could tell of some rare conversions to the support of this measure; some quite as sudden, if not as miraculous, as that of Saint Paul. But I prefer to withhold names until the vote shall be given and the Executive appointments made; these names will then be published. I speak of it at this time, that Northern members who voted for this bill may understand that the eye of the public is upon them. It is time that this slave-trade now carried on in the bodies of members of Congress should be prohibited. Why, sir, for the first time in the history of our government, the President has come out, through the columns of his organ, the 'Union,' of this city, and advertised for the purchase of members of Congress. I refer to an article in that paper some weeks since, stating, in substance, that if Northern members, by sustaining this bill, incurred the displeasure of their constitutents, the President would sustain them by Executive favors. This was the substance of a long article, in which Executive appointments were unblushingly tendered, through the public Press, to buy up Northern doughfaces, to purchase the very men who now designate their fellow-men as 'property.' I do not wonder that they entertain low opinions of mankind, and term their brethren 'property.' But they should remember that no colored man ever degraded his race by *selling himself.*"

Giddings never lost an opportunity to strike a blow for freedom or to resent a wrong to the colored race. In a debate on the Homestead Bill on the 28th of February, Mr. Wright of Pennsylvania offered an amendment confining its benefits to "free white" persons. Giddings, for the purpose of making the amendment ridiculous, moved to amend it by inserting before the word "white" the words "more than one half." He reminded the gentleman from Pennsylvania that in his State negroes had been voters only a few years before; that they had served their country upon the battle-fields of the Revolution, as they had also under General Jackson at New Orleans; that some of the best citizens of Ohio had colored blood in their veins; and that it would be a monstrous injustice to deny them the right to settle on our public lands and establish homes for themselves and their children.

In watching the drift of public affairs under this Administration the attention of Giddings was invited to a significant event. In the month of February a steamer called the "Black Warrior" cleared from Mobile for New York by way of Havana, and on arriving at that place was reported by the captain as "in ballast," while she really had four or five hundred bales of cotton on board that were not mentioned in her manifest. When these facts became known to the proper officers the steamer was of course seized and held for trial. It was generally understood at this time that the Administration was anxious to acquire Cuba, and that the leaders of the Democratic party would welcome a war with Spain for the purpose of obtaining that island. On the 10th of March Mr. Phillips of Alabama presented resolutions calling upon the President to communicate to the House such information as he might deem proper relative to the seizure of the "Black Warrior" and the confiscation of her cargo. The resolution was adopted, and a few days later the President sent to the House full information on the subject. In doing this he performed his whole duty, for there was nothing unusual in the seizure of the ship under the circumstances. It was an ordinary transaction in the commerce between nations, and afforded no provocation whatever to the United States. But the President took advantage of this opportunity to say, —

"There have been in the course of a few years past many other instances of aggression upon our commerce — violations of the rights of American citizens, and insults to the national flag — by the Spanish authorities in Cuba; and all attempts to obtain redress have been protracted by fruitless negotiations. The documents in these cases have been voluminous, and when prepared will be sent to Congress."

The House had not called for these statements, and the President went out of his way and transcended his authority in thrusting them upon that body. But he still further revealed his burning desire to stir up strife with Spain and play into the hands of his Southern masters:—

"In view of the position of Cuba, its proximity to our coast, the relations which it must ever bear to our commercial *and other interests*, it is in vain to expect that a series of unfriendly acts infringing our commercial rights, and *the adoption of a policy threatening the honor and security of these States*, can long consist with peaceful relations."

The message was lauded by Mr. Bayly of Virginia, the chairman of the Committee on Foreign Affairs, who had moved its reference to that committee. The motion prevailed, and the slaveocracy was pleased; but the next morning, March 16, Giddings moved to reconsider this reference, and made the extracts quoted the text of an hour's speech. It was in his best style, and the cry of danger was never sounded more opportunely. He did not wait for a convenient season to talk about the designs of the Administration upon Cuba, but seized the very moment when those designs were officially foreshadowed, and laid them bare before the eyes of the nation. He began by rebuking the President's assumption and audacity.

"Neither the Constitution nor usage justifies this attempt to excite in us unfriendly feeling towards a neighboring Government. We come from the people; we hold our commissions from them; they are our masters; and when they speak we are bound to listen with respect. We are not dependent on the Executive; he is our servant, bound to execute our laws, to obey our directions, and not to read lectures to tell us that we have silently borne insults from her Christian Majesty of Spain. Does he attempt to excite our indignation, and through this body to stir up the people to war? That is the obvious tendency of these charges. Why, sir, the Government of Spain is at this moment as unconscious of these complaints as it is of matters now transpiring in this body. No complaint has been made by the Executive to her Majesty, nor to her ministers. The President is unable to say whether that Government will or will not do us perfect and complete justice. . . . Why then does the President send these complaints to us before he presents them to Spain? Why charge her with *insulting our flag* before he demands the proper apology from her Majesty? It would hardly be courteous to say that the President wishes to make this House the forum from which to harangue the people who are his political creators. No; we will suppose he intended his message for ourselves. Still, however supine and neglectful he may regard us, we are unwilling to admit ourselves so oblivious to the public interest as to need lectures from a co-ordinate branch of government. We possess powers of thought as well as the President, though perhaps not to the same extent. Still, when we want information from him relative to the past history of our government, we will call on him for it; or if we desire an essay on Spanish encroachments, we surely will invite it."

The reference of Giddings to the question of a war with Spain was equally timely, and it recalls his speech on the Oregon question in 1846, which so mollified the rampant spirit of the slavocracy respecting a war with England. He said, —

"Nor will a war for the conquest of Cuba prove any child's play. The combined navies of England and France will present to us a force not to be despised. They will surround Cuba with a wall of iron and a sheet of flame. They will prove themselves worthy of our steel. Once relieved from their European employment, they will have an army which may be easily thrown upon our Southern coast wherever they may deem it most assailable. They will doubtless strike at our weakest points. They may bring the war into this American Africa, and rear the standard of freedom on our own soil, while our army shall be fighting for slavery in Cuba. It is right that Southern gentlemen should look at this subject in all its aspects. If they go to war under the black flag of oppression, they should count the cost. If they should find an army of twenty thousand British and French troops in South Carolina or Georgia, rearing the standard of liberty, and the slaves flocking to it, they must understand that our Northern militia will comprehend the cause of such war. They may not hasten as rapidly to mingle in the fight with slaves armed with foreign muskets and commanded by foreign officers, as men would who feel a deep interest in the prosperity of the peculiar institution."

In referring to the war power of the Government, he said, —

"It is acknowledged on all sides that when such war shall exist, this Government may interpose terms of peace, even at the price of liberating every slave in the nation. I announce these facts to Northern men to inspirit them to deeds of manly bearing, that no one may despond, though war shall actually come. . . . Thus, sir, I can easily imagine that this war which the President invokes may prove the overthrow of slavery in Cuba as well as in our own land. Such results would best accord with the feelings, the desires, of the Free States and of the whole Christian world."

Giddings concluded this speech by reminding Southern members of the war with Mexico, waged for the extension of slavery at the cost of two hundred millions of dollars and eighty thousand human lives, which had given us a Free State on the Pacific and extended free institutions on the continent; and he warned them that similar results would follow a war with Spain.

During the Congressional vacation he devoted himself to his regular biennial canvass for re-election. The political situation was new. Within the preceding year the old Whig party had been routed and dispersed, and a new movement, called the Know-Nothing party, had appeared. It was a secret, oath-bound political order, and the basis of its policy was the proscription of Catholics and a probation of twenty-one years for foreigners as a qualification for the suffrage. It was composed of bolters from all the other parties, but the Whig element predominated. The growth of this movement was marvellous, but its control by demagogues, whose animating spirit was greed for office, soon revealed itself. Like the Whig and Democratic parties, it was soon found ready to subordinate the slavery issue to the propagation of its narrow and bigoted dogmas and to political success. Of course Giddings had no sympathy with this movement; and he had quite as little with the popular rallying cry of "the restoration of the Missouri Compromise." He opposed slavery upon principle, and irrespective of any bargain or compact concerning geographical lines. He believed that to restore this compromise would be to propitiate the *spirit* of compromise. It would re-affirm the binding obligation of a compact which should never have been made, and from which we now had the opportunity of deliverance. It was openly urged by many of its advocates as a retreat to the compromise measures of 1850, and the finality platform of 1852. The repeal of this compromise was only a single link in a chain of measures aiming at the absolute supremacy of slavery in the government, and thus inviting a resistance commensurate with that policy. Giddings demanded the dedication of all our national Territories to freedom, and the total denationalization of slavery.

During the second session of the Thirty-third Congress the question of slavery was not much debated, and only incidentally. On the 19th of December, 1854, when a bill was before the House granting additional powers to the corporation of Washington, Giddings proposed an amendment that no person shall be imprisoned unless charged with crime. This was aimed at the law authorizing the arrest, imprisonment, and sale into slavery of colored men found in the District who were unable to prove their freedom, and providing that even after such proof they might be sold unless they were able to pay the costs and expenses of their imprisonment. The amendment was rejected. On the 4th of January, 1855, in committee of the whole on the bill graduating the price of public lands, he discussed the slavery question in its relations to the Know-Nothing party. On February 6, in the general debate on the bill providing for the payment of Texas creditors, he spoke at length on the action of the Government in dealing with Texas, and its duties pertaining thereto. These are a few only of the matters which enlisted his attention during this session; and at no previous session of Congress had his vigilance in the matter of slavery been more constant and remarkable.

CHAPTER XI.

MARCH, 1855, TO MARCH, 1859.

The Congressional Vacation. — Meeting of the Thirty-fourth Congress. — State of Political Parties. — The Speakership. — Election of Banks. — Birth of the Republican Party. — Letters from John Brown. — Speech on the Deficiency Bill; on the Assault on Sumner. — The Philadelphia Convention and its Platform. — Last Session of this Congress. — Speeches. — Letters from John P. Hale. — The Dred Scott Decision. — Work in Vacation. — First Session of the Thirty-fifth Congress. — The Lecompton Constitution and the Crittenden-Montgomery Amendment. — Diary of Giddings. — The English Bill. — Speech on "American Infidelity;" on the African Slave-trade. — Nomination of his Successor. — Letters from Friends. — Voice of the Press. — Second Session of the Thirty-fifth Congress. — Farewell Speech. — Testimonials.

THE effort to plant slavery in Kansas by organized vandalism was unremitted during the Congressional vacation. This naturally fired the hearts of the people of the Free States and rapidly multiplied anti-slavery men; but there was no organization of their forces against the common enemy. The members of the Free-Soil party were so cheered by the tokens of formidable accessions to their cause that they did not deem it wise to press the claims of their organization. The Whig party was disbanded, but its scattered members had too long worn the collar of slavery and denounced its outspoken enemies to be ready to join them. They generally favored the restoration of the Missouri Compromise and the freedom of Kansas and Nebraska; but beyond this they declined to commit themselves. The position of the bolters from the Democratic party was substantially the same. The Know-Nothing party divided on the slavery issue in 1855; but even the members of the Northern division declined to take any higher ground than that occupied by their Whig and Democratic allies. As early as the summer of 1854 these forces had met in State convention in Michigan, and organized themselves into a Republican party. This action was followed by kindred movements in Wisconsin and Vermont, but in New York the Whigs refused to disband, and the attempt to form a new party failed. The same was true of Massachusetts and Ohio, in which conservative Whiggery and Know-Nothingism blocked the way of progress. The outlook as to the formation of a triumphant anti-slavery party was by no means assuring, while all could see how much easier it was to break up old party organizations than to organize their fragments into a new party on a just basis.

Under these circumstances the Thirty-fourth Congress assembled in December, 1855. The Democrats were in a minority in the House, and this was due in part to the Know-Nothing movement, which had surprised the whole country by its phenomenal success, and now desired to subordinate the slavery issue to the personal and party interests of its members. The situation was painfully complicated, while the great question of the Speakership completely engrossed the thoughts of men of all parties, and involved far more momentous interests than ever before. Giddings had not forgotten the position which he and his friend Palfrey had taken nine years before, and which time and events had fully vindicated. On the Friday preceding the meeting of the House a conference of Republicans and Free Soilers was held for the purpose of taking into consideration the choice of a Speaker. About forty members were present, with a number of Know-Nothings. Giddings submitted the following resolution: —

"*Resolved*, That we will support no man for Speaker who is not pledged to carry out the parliamentary law, by giving to each proposed measure ordered by the House to be committed, a majority of such special committee; and to organize the standing committees of the House by placing on each a majority of the friends of freedom who are favorable to making reports on all petitions committed to them."

The resolution was unanimously adopted, being supported by seventy members; and when the House met on the following Monday, the balloting for Speaker began. William A. Richardson was the Democratic candidate, Lewis D. Campbell the Know-Nothing candidate, Humphrey Marshall the Southern Know-Nothing candidate, and Nathaniel P. Banks the Republican candidate. On the twenty-third ballot Mr. Campbell withdrew his name; but the struggle continued, with every indication that it would be indefinitely prolonged. The work of the House, however, alternated between balloting for Speaker and a lively running debate, which sometimes extended through successive days. One of these occurred on the 18th of December, in the course of which Mr. Letcher of Virginia referred to the resolution just quoted, and asked Giddings if he wrote it, and whether it was adopted by the meeting to which it was submitted. Giddings answered the question in the affirmative, explaining that among men who had heretofore belonged to different parties it was necessary to find some common ground on which they could stand, and that the resolution was necessary in order to restore to the people of the

Free States the right of petition, which for twenty-three years had been trampled under foot by the Speaker. He added, —

"Let me say to gentlemen, we are each of us now writing our biography with more rapidity than we generally imagine. Coming generations, looking back upon this time, and seeing these principles adopted by the American people, will rejoice, and their hearts swell with thankfulness, that there were men at this day who stood forth so proudly and firmly in favor of these principles of justice, liberty, and the Constitution. And now, gentlemen, I will come to a more minute part of my subject, if my friend from Virginia [Mr. Letcher] has got through asking questions.

"MR. LETCHER. I have got all I want to go to my section of the country with.

"MR. GIDDINGS. Oh, my friend, with what emotions I hear that word 'section'! Instead of looking to the good and for the approval of coming generations, men are always looking over their shoulders to see if the devil is not coming after them. [Laughter.] When will men learn that we are not sent here to cavil on mere sectional issues? Gentlemen of the Democratic party, I say again, in your attempt to extend this sectional institution you have called down the vengeance of the American people upon your heads. The handwriting upon the wall has been seen and read of all men. Your history is written, and your doom is sealed; the sentence pronounced against you, 'Depart, ye cursed.' [Laughter.] You need not trouble yourselves about our petty difficulties. We will take care of them; you cannot help us. We can do without you. We have a working majority in this House against you. When organized, we shall raise the standard of united opposition to your party. Indeed, whether we elect a Speaker or not, we shall unite in opposition to your Kansas-Nebraska bill and to its principles."

This reminder must have been as surprising to the slavcocracy as it was unwelcome. Giddings had long been a member of a small and despised minority, and had been treated by Southern members as a fanatic and a castaway. But he now gave notice that he was an active working force in the movement which controlled the House and was soon to dominate the government. He evidently felt that the country had entered upon a new political dispensation, and he did not disguise his pleasant emotions in referring to the fact. Continuing his remarks, and alluding to the question of disunion, he said, —

"We at the North will stand by the Union. And let me say to timid gentlemen from the North, be not anxious about the Union. We do not intend to dissolve the Union, and we do not intend to let you do it. [Laughter.] Understand that. We mean what we say; we will not only maintain the Union, but we will tell Southern traitors who threaten it that they shall not dissolve it. It has been cemented by the blood of our fathers, who fought for its establishment. We are bound to maintain it by all the obligations which bind men, and we mean to do it. Threaten its dissolution, reiterate the threat as often as you please, and we meet you with a stern front and unwavering resolution that such a traitorous object shall not be reached. I speak in all kindness. We have already got this House. Next year, with God's blessing, we shall have the President; and in two years we shall have the Senate. Then the Executive and Legislative branches of the government will be in our power. Then those who threaten disunion had better look out."

This speech produced quite a sensation among Southern members. It was not now the speech of a hated fanatic, but of a recognized leader of a powerful movement which he had done more than any living public man in the nation to create. Mr. McMullen of Virginia replied with great bitterness, declaring that should the party with which Mr. Giddings acted obtain the control of the government and restore the Missouri Compromise or repeal the Fugitive Slave Law, the South would dissolve the Union.

During this tedious struggle over the Speakership no member of the House was more alert and active than Giddings. On the 31st of December he joined in the general debate on the question of receiving the President's message before the House had been organized. On the 11th of January, 1856, he spoke on

Mr. Zollicoffer's resolution, declaring it to be the duty of all candidates for political position frankly and fully to avow their opinions upon important political questions. On the 18th of January he spoke at length on the plurality rule, under which the Speaker was finally chosen, as he had been in December, 1849, after a similar struggle. He was equally active in the debates on minor questions, and especially where the issue of slavery was in any degree involved. The struggle for Speaker finally closed with the election of Mr. Banks, on the one hundred and thirty-third ballot, on the 2d of February, having continued through nine weeks. This was the first victory of the Free States over the power of the South, and it was largely due to the repeal of the Missouri Compromise and the border-ruffian outrages in Kansas which followed.

After the Speaker had been conducted to the chair, and had delivered an appropriate address, the clerk of the House called on Giddings, as its oldest member, to administer the oath of office. As the Father of the House, with his large physical frame and silvery white hair, walked forward into the area in front of the Speaker's chair, the galleries at once recognized him, and recalling his long and faithful labors in the cause which had finally triumphed, a hearty cheer was given in his honor. The oath was administered according to the form used in New England from the time of the Pilgrims, and the words were pronounced in a loud voice and in tones full of earnestness and emotion. Soon after this victory Giddings wrote to his friends at home, —

"The 2d of February, 1856, will mark an important era in the history of Congress. On that day a man who dared declare that he held, with the early fathers of our Republic, 'that all men are endowed by their Creator with the inalienable right to life and liberty,' was elected Speaker of the House of Representatives. He stood firmly on this rock of truth. The shafts of slaveholding calumny and vituperation were hurled at him; but he looked his opponents in the face, bade defiance to their impotent assaults, and triumphed. He was elected upon the identical doctrine for the utterance of which I was driven from this body fourteen years since. . . . I have labored for the reestablishment of those principles for which our Revolutionary fathers contended. I have lived to see them recognized by a majority of the popular branch of Congress. I regard myself among the most fortunate of public men. I have attained the highest point of my ambition. *I am satisfied.*"

Pending these proceedings in Congress and the progress of slaveholding violence and outrage in Kansas, measures were taken by representative men in Ohio, Massachusetts, Pennsylvania, Vermont, and Wisconsin for calling a National Republican Convention at Pittsburg, on the 22d of February, for the purpose of organizing a national Republican party. This convention was largely attended and full of enthusiasm, and it provided for the holding of a convention at Philadelphia, on the 17th of June, to nominate candidates for President and Vice-President. In the Pittsburg convention the two most attractive personalities were Horace Greeley and Mr. Giddings. The moment the former was seen in the audience, he was vociferously called for, and responded briefly, saying that he had been in Washington several weeks, and that friends there "counselled extreme caution in our movements." This was the burden of his exhortation. At the close of his speech Giddings was tumultuously called for, and replied to Greeley that Washington was the last place in the world to look for counsel or redress. He illustrated his meaning by an amusing anecdote, and then introduced Owen Lovejoy of Illinois. There was an element of conservatism and Know-Nothingism in this convention, but the hearts of the masses in attendance were with Giddings. The men who were profoundly in earnest in their opposition to slavery everywhere looked to him for counsel. This was illustrated in the following letter from the city of Weston, Missouri, dated Jan. 27, 1856.

HON. J. R. GIDDINGS, *Washington City:*

DEAR SIR, — I presume an apology is unnecessary in addressing a letter to one so warmly interested as yourself in the great question of the day, — namely, the freeing of this great country from the curse of slavery. Sir, six months ago I left my native State, York, for a home in Kansas. I settled, on my arrival in the Territory, about four miles from Lawrence, and built me a good house, where I resided until the border ruffians invaded the Territory. They, knowing my adherence to the cause of freedom, and my being a Northern man, took me a prisoner and kept me as such for four days, treating me worse than one of their slaves. After my release, they told me I must leave the country. I did not do it, but went to Eaton, and remained there quietly till last Friday week, the day of the election. They then sent their minions out to disturb our election, which they did. They killed two men for us. How long are we to be treated like dogs? General Pomeroy promised us men and means to carry on the war. Sir, are we to have them, or are we to be driven from the Territory after all the sacrifices of time and money we have made? Will you, sir, inform me if we are to have the means to drive the last B. R. from the country? I, for one, am ready to stay if we are. If we do not have them soon, we shall be driven from the land. Answer requested immediately. I must close for fear of interruption.

Respectfully yours,

JOHN BROWN.

The following letter is still more impassioned.

OSAWATOMIE, KANSAS TERRITORY, Feb. 20, 1856.

HON. JOSHUA R. GIDDINGS, *Washington, D. C.:*

DEAR SIR, — I write to say that a number of United States soldiers are quartered in this vicinity, for the ostensible purpose of removing intruders from certain Indian lands. It is, however, believed that the Administration has no thought of removing the Missourians from the Indian lands, but that the real object is to have the men in readiness to act in enforcement of the hellish enactments of the [so-called] Kansas Legislature, — absolutely abominated by a great majority of the inhabitants of the Territory, and spurned by them up to this time. I confidently believe that the next movement on the part of the Administration and its pro-slavery masters will be either to drive the people here to submit to those infernal enactments, or to assume what will be termed treasonable grounds, by shooting down the poor soldiers of the country, with whom they have no quarrel whatever. I ask in the name of Almighty God, I ask in the name of our venerated forefathers, I ask in the name of all that good or true men ever held dear, will Congress suffer us to be driven to such "dire extremities"? Will anything be done? Please send me a few lines at this place. Long acquaintance with your public life, and a slight personal acquaintance, incline and embolden me to make this appeal to yourself. Everything is still on the surface just now. Circumstances are, however, of a most suspicious character.   Very respectfully yours,

JOHN BROWN.

One of the most manly speeches delivered in this Congress was that of Giddings on the Senate amendments to the Deficiency Bill, on the 8th of May. These amendments had been repeatedly rejected by the House, but the Senate still urged them; and Giddings now stated the reasons why the House should adhere to its position. He first opposed the item in the deficiency appropriations for the Judiciary which covered the amount of twenty-seven thousand dollars expended by the marshal of the southern district of Ohio in arresting and returning to Kentucky the slaves of Mr. Gaines, including the mother, who took the life of her own child to prevent its being sent into slavery. This was the famous "Margaret Garner case," which so stirred the country at the time. Between four and five hundred deputy marshals were appointed for this service, and "if we agree to this appropriation," said Giddings, "we shall be told by our constituents that we have made appropriations to assist the Administration to corrupt the very fountains of political action, and by fraud to induce beings who bear the *forms* of men to assume the nature of bloodhounds, to hunt down fugitive slaves."

Giddings next opposed the Senate amendment appropriating three hundred thousand dollars for suppressing Indian hostilities in Oregon. In this speech, as in several earlier ones, he showed himself as true a friend of the Indian as he was of the negro. "For many years," said he, "I have felt a deep interest in the policy which guides our intercourse with these sons of the forest. We have driven them from the Atlantic coast, from their hunting-grounds, from the graves of their fathers, step by step, until they are now confined to the far West." Referring to the Oregon Indians in 1808, when Lewis and Clark visited that region, and the friendly treatment those pioneer explorers received from these savages, he said, —

"Since that day we have become a mighty nation, with twenty-five millions of people and boundless resources; we have pushed our settlements to the Pacific, and the doom of the savage tribes now stands plainly written in the book of fate, and is as clearly understood by them as it is by us. We are a Christian people; they, like the Athenians, worship the unknown God. Yet here in this hall, and in the western region, efforts are put forth to hasten the extermination of these comparatively defenceless tribes; and this appropriation is intended to hasten the consummation of that policy."

The humanity of the following passage recalls the opinions repeatedly expressed by General Harney many years ago, and the recent utterances of General Miles respecting our latest Indian war: —

"Mr. Speaker, every man acquainted with the Indian character is aware that two, and only two, incentives operate upon the Indian mind to excite him to war. These are *revenge* and *want*. Treat them kindly, and there will be no cause for revenge; feed them, and there will be no inducement for them to commit depredations upon our people. Why, sir, if the money expended in Oregon within the past three years had been expended in provisions, and those provisions distributed to the Indians, it would have secured our frontiers, from the Mexican line to the British possessions, against all savage depredations for twenty years. But I grieve to say that the conduct of our friends in Oregon does not commend this appropriation to my judgment. I can only notice a paragraph from the letter of General Wool read to us yesterday. In that we are informed that one of the most powerful chiefs met the volunteers of that Territory with a flag of truce, suing for peace. Our troops refused to treat for peace on any terms, but advised him to return to his people and fight. Sir, what a spectacle! A savage asking peace, and Christians denying it! But, what was far worse, they sent him and his four companions to the rear of the army, safely guarded, and then commenced the work of death upon his people. The Indians resisted, and the next day our civilized troops, in cold blood, slew this chief and his companions. The white flag, which for centuries has been regarded by all civilized and semi-barbarous nations as consecrated to friendship, — the emblem of peace, — was spattered and stained by the blood of those who bore it."

The last Senate amendment which Giddings opposed was that appropriating fifteen hundred thousand dollars for the support of the army. He charged that this item was intended to cover the expense of compelling the people of Kansas to submit to the laws enacted for their subjugation by the border ruffians of Missouri. The fact of this invasion of Kansas by the ruffians of that State, and their government of the Territory by laws in the enactment of which her people had no voice, was perfectly notorious and unquestionable. In referring to this subject, Giddings said, —

"This embodied force, with arms in their hands, moving upon Kansas for the very purpose of violating the laws just quoted, and the actual invasion of that Territory and usurpation of the government, was attended by every circumstance necessary in law to constitute *treason*. It was 'a levying war against the

United States;' and every man concerned in the movement consummated that crime, and is now guilty; and long ere this should have been suspended from the gallows if not made the subject of Executive pardon. No sophistry, no pretence that they went there to prevent voters from giving illegal votes, can evade or modify this important, this prominent fact. Gentlemen on this floor, and the Executive of the United States, may uphold and encourage this treason. This House may encourage it by voting the appropriations before us; but I will repudiate it by my vote and by my voice."

Giddings referred to the slave code of Kansas, making it a felony punishable at hard labor for not less than two years for any person by speech or writing to deny the right to hold slaves in the Territory, and to the further provision making it a felony, to be punished by imprisonment at hard labor for not less than five years, for any person to print or circulate any opinions or doctrines "*calculated* to promote disorderly, dangerous, or rebellious disaffection among the slaves of this Territory." He denounced this conspiracy to force slavery upon the people of Kansas and compel the people of the Northern States to pay the expense of the proceeding. He said, —

"The people, through their representatives, may withhold all appropriations, may effectually block the wheels of government, — ay, sir, and roll them back upon the desecrated bodies of unfaithful rulers. It is a great primal truth, lying at the very foundation of our institutions, that whenever this government becomes destructive of the rights of the people, it will be their right and their duty to *alter* or *abolish* it. And, sir, I would far rather see this government dissolved than see the humblest citizen of Kansas murdered for refusing obedience to the infamous enactments alluded to, and such murder effected by means of appropriations made in this body. . . . At this moment the army of the United States — like the Swiss guards in Paris — are encamped in Lawrence, ready to shoot down the first man who raises his voice for freedom. American citizens are held in subjection by military force. The voice of liberty is hushed into silence by the display of swords and bayonets. For any man in Kansas to assert that 'governments are constituted to secure liberty to all men under our exclusive dominion,' would render him a felon under the laws now in force there by military rule; and this sad, this humiliating fact is to go down to posterity as existing in this age, while you and I hold seats in this hall. Our names are to be associated with those who submit to such tyranny, or with those who stand firmly in the cause of freedom."

The cruel and cowardly assault upon Senator Sumner by Preston S. Brooks of South Carolina awakened a thrill of horror throughout the Northern States. It was the natural counterpart of slaveholding ruffianism in Kansas; but as an attempt to strengthen the power of slavery and silence the freedom of speech it was utterly disastrous to those who made it. Giddings took part in the debate on the resolution for the expulsion of Brooks, and his speech on the 11th of July was singularly dispassionate; it was marked by earnestness, moderation, and strong common-sense. In reply to the argument of Southern members that the House had no power to punish Brooks without an enactment defining his offence and prescribing its penalty, Giddings reminded them of the trial of John Quincy Adams, in 1842, for presenting a petition praying for the dissolution of the Union, which he asked to have referred to a select committee, with instructions to report adversely, with the reasons therefor. He had violated no statute, but simply performed his constitutional duty as a representative of his State. Giddings said, —

"The friends of Mr. Adams often inquired wherein that gentlemen had offended. Why, sir, he had offended the slavepower; and the representatives of the slave-interest felt that they had an excuse, — a fact on which they could found an effort to strike down his influence, to destroy his fair fame, to deprive freedom of its sternest advocate. They sought for no rules or law defining the offence, or declaring the penalty attached to it: but they assailed him in every way which hatred could invent or malice express. He was charged with treason to our government, with moral perjury, and with almost every crime found in the catalogue of offences. There he sat, in the seat now occupied by his successor, — a man venerable for his age, for his great learning, for his exalted patriotism; venerable for his services to his country; around his brow clustered all the honors which a faithful, upright, and wise administration of the highest office known to mortals could confer. Yet, sir, for thirteen days he was subjected to these assaults. During that time the waves of slaveholding invective, detraction, and calumny rolled and dashed around him in wild confusion, until the raging elements had spent their force; while, from the first introduction of the resolution to its final disposition, not one word was uttered by a Southern Democrat indicating the want of full constitutional powers to act on the subject, *without any rule or law prescribing the penalty.* Then, sir, *Massachusetts* was on trial, and *slaveholders* were the prosecutors. Now, sir, a son of *South Carolina* is on trial for a wrong, a crime, perpetrated against the sovereign right of Massachusetts. This change of position by slaveholders is very remarkable."

Giddings also referred to the case in which he himself had been censured and driven from his seat in the House for offering resolutions denying the power of Congress under the Constitution to involve the people of the Free States in the support of slavery and the slave-trade on the high seas. No one attempted to controvert the principles affirmed by these resolutions, but they were offensive to slaveholders, and therefore could not be tolerated. He said, —

"Gentlemen from the Slave States did not wait to inquire for the *prescribed rule or statute* declaring the penalty attached to the crime of presenting resolutions. So far from that, they voted at once to seal my own lips and those of my friends; and without permitting me or any friend of free speech to say a word in my defence, the resolution was adopted by a vote of *one hundred and twenty-three to sixty-nine.* I was condemned unheard, and driven from my seat. Sir, I spurned the tyranny and appealed to the people. They hurled contempt at the efforts of the slave-power to strike down the freedom of speech, to extinguish the lamp of liberty, which was then flickering in its socket, casting but a dim light upon the legislation of Congress. They ordered me back to my post, and directed me to maintain the freedom of debate; AND AS THE LORD LIVETH, AND AS MY SOUL LIVETH, I WILL NEVER SURRENDER IT."

Giddings argued with clearness and force the points involved in the pretended defence of Brooks, and concluded by contrasting the manners and habits of the people of the Free States with those of the South, as illustrated by this latest and desperate attempt of the slave-power to stamp out the freedom of debate.

On the 24th of July Giddings wrote from Washington the following letter to Sumner, who was then at Cape May, —

MY DEAR FRIEND, — When the attack on you was made, I was on my way home. I reached this city on Monday following. I found our friends here in a state of great excitement. Much was said about *fighting*, and I was told that Wade and Wilson were disposed to fight. I went to those gentlemen and told them plainly that our cause was one of high moral character, appealing to the conscience, the judgment, and Christianity of the age, and not to the violence and bloodshed of a barbarous and darker period. I insisted that if either of those gentlemen should go out and slay his man, the political death of the victor would be as certain as the physical death of the other; and this view I endeavored to inculcate with all our friends.

With Mr. Burlingame I had a long conversation, in which I stated these views. It is, however, due to him that I should say, while he approved my plan, he intimated that he had made up his mind to a different course. When, on Monday morning, I read his card, I was aware that a hostile meeting must ordinarily occur. I was not ignorant of the practice of the British Parliament, and that it has in one instance been followed by our House; but in others it has been rejected. I felt perfectly conscious that no effectual measure could be adopted by our House as it is now constituted.

Some gentlemen consulted with me as to the measures for preventing the meeting by an application to the police. That was, however, too late to arrest Mr. Burlingame, who had put out that evening. Brooks was arrested in the morning, but Burlingame had started for Canada.

That our cause has gained nothing by Mr. B.'s coming down to Brooks's level is very evident. The customs of South Carolina ought not to be copied by Massachusetts men.

I endeavored to express my views of the different state of

civilization in the Free States from that of the Slave States in my House speech on Brooks's trial, a copy of which I herewith mail to your address.

I greatly sorrow at the length of your indisposition, and could not avoid an expression of my own views in reply to taunts thrown out by Brooks's friends, which I trust you will pardon under the circumstances.

Most truly, J. R. GIDDINGS.

Giddings was a delegate to the first nominating convention of the Republican party, which assembled in Philadelphia on the 17th of June and nominated John C. Frémont for President. He was also a member of the Committee on Resolutions which prepared the platform afterwards unanimously adopted by the convention. He took an active part in the proceedings, and was especially prompt and decisive in opposing any alliance or negotiation with Know-Nothingism, which had now become a vanishing side issue. By far the most important part of the platform was written by Giddings in his library at Jefferson, and is here copied: —

"*Resolved*, That, with our republican fathers, we hold it to be a self-evident truth that all men are endowed with the unalienable rights to life, liberty, and the pursuit of happiness, and that the primary object and ulterior design of our Federal Government was to secure these rights to all persons within its exclusive jurisdiction; that as our republican fathers, when they had abolished slavery in all our national territory, ordained *that no person should be deprived of life, liberty, or property without due process of law*, it becomes our duty to maintain this provision of the Constitution against all attempts to violate it for the purpose of establishing slavery in any Territory of the United States, by positive legislation, prohibiting its existence or extension therein. That we deny the authority of Congress, of a Territorial legislature, of any individual or association of individuals, to give legal existence to slavery in any Territory of the United States, while the present Constitution shall be maintained."

Nothing could have been more opportune than the adoption of this resolution as the basis of the new party. It had become the fashion of Southern politicians and a growing number of Northern ones to treat the self-evident truths of the Declaration of Independence with ridicule and contempt. They were branded as "self-evident lies," as "glittering generalities," or declared to be applicable only to superior races of men. The logic of slavery made this necessary, and it became equally necessary to re-affirm these truths in laying the foundations of a great national party. The action of the convention in dealing with the territorial question was not less admirable. The Northern wing of the Democratic party, with Douglas as its leader, affirmed the right of the people of a Territory to establish slavery therein if they so desired, while the Democracy of the South maintained that slaves are recognized as property by the Federal Constitution, and demanded a slave code for the protection of such property in all our national Territories. These issues were accepted by positively denying "the constitutional authority of Congress, of a territorial legislature, or of any individual or association of individuals, to give legal existence to slavery in any Territory of the United States."

Giddings rejoiced at the approval of these principles, which he had unflinchingly advocated during his public life. He rejoiced especially at the indorsement of the self-evident truths of the great Declaration. He had made them the burden of his public speeches for more than twenty years. They constituted his religious, not less than his political, faith. They had never before been incorporated into the creed of any political party, and he was now quite as jubilant as he had been at the election of Banks as Speaker.

The first session of the Thirty-fourth Congress

adjourned on the 18th of August; but an extra session was immediately called in order to provide for the support of the army, which had become necessary in consequence of the failure of the regular session to make provision therefor. On the 30th of August the special session adjourned, and Giddings entered upon the canvass of his district for re-election, devoting a portion of his time to the general canvass outside of his district and State. Buchanan had been unanimously nominated for President by the Democrats on the 2d of June. The platform adopted was satisfactory to the South, and the issues were now joined with the Republican party. Fillmore had been nominated for the Presidency by the Know-Nothings; but the contest was between Buchanan and Frémont, and it was pre-eminently a conflict of principles. It was a struggle between two civilizations, between reason and brute force, between the principles of Democracy and the creed of absolutism. Giddings entered into it with his whole heart, and never intermitted his labors till its close. The triumph of Buchanan was largely due to the baleful intervention of Know-Nothingism; but the country was not yet fully ripe for a victory over the slave-power. The canvass for Frémont did a great work in the education of the people. He received a popular vote of 1,341,264, carrying 11 States and 114 electoral votes. This was an immense gain on the vote of John P. Hale, four years before, and was confidently interpreted as the prophecy of success in 1860.

The President's message and the troubles in Kansas constituted the chief topics of discussion in the third session of this Congress. On the 10th of December Giddings spoke at length on the Kansas policy of the President, the principles of the Republican party, and the position of the Democrats. Of this speech Joseph Medill, editor of the "Chicago Tribune," wrote him, —

"We are much delighted with your bold, cogent talk to the doughfaces, Pierce, and the Oligarchy. That is the only course to pursue. Pitch the rocks right into them. Every man that voted for Frémont sustains you, and thousands who supported Fillmore and Buchanan admire your candor and manhood. The *people* are ready for stronger meat than the politicians suppose."

In this speech Giddings also referred to the argument of Mr. Stephens of Georgia that slavery is sanctioned by the Almighty, and that Abraham was a slaveholder and a slave-dealer. He said, —

"At the same time another distinguished individual is proclaiming in the far West, among the mountains of Deseret, that polygamy was also an institution of God. Brigham Young, with his retinue of threescore wives, vindicated his doctrines by precisely the same arguments; he referred to Abraham also. Both he and the gentleman from Georgia, with great gusto, appealed to the civilized world, saying, 'Have we not Abraham to our father?' [Laughter.] If Abraham be good authority in one case, he ought to be in the other."

On the 17th of January, 1857, while earnestly discussing a private claim, Giddings was suddenly prostrated by a serious heart-trouble to which he was liable under excitement or overwork, and for a time life appeared to be extinct. But he slowly rallied, and was able soon afterwards to return to his home. This circumstance called forth the following letter, which fairly indicated the feelings of his many devoted friends: —

WASHINGTON, Jan. 25, 1857.

MY DEAR FRIEND, — I cannot permit you to leave this place for your home under the existing circumstances, without expressing to you, in this emphatic manner, the very great satisfaction I have enjoyed in your acquaintance and friendship for so many years, and the admiration and respect I entertain for the patience, courage, fidelity, and ability with which you have, through your

Congressional life, maintained a just but an unpopular cause. There are very painful considerations connected with the necessity, which at this time compels a suspension, if not a final termination, of your very valuable labors in the House, but they are not all so. There is a pleasant and cheerful aspect which it presents; you or myself do not believe that accidents, strictly speaking, ever occur, but that the minutest incidents in the physical world are parts of that chain of events by which the natural and spiritual worlds are connected, and that what men blindly call accidents are the results of laws fixed and unerring as those by which the universe moves in its course through the illimitable regions of space.

In the light of such a faith the highest wisdom is to learn the teachings of every event. And what, my dear sir, is the palpable instruction of the severe teaching you have just had? Is it not manifestly this, that God has just now no more work for you to do in the particular field in which you have so long labored, but that you are to be transferred to another and less exciting, but not less profitable, sphere of action? And if there has ever lived, since Paul, a man who, without arrogance, might appropriate to himself the words of the apostle when he declares, "I have fought a good fight, I have kept the faith," I believe you are the one. I hope and trust that many years of physical and mental vigor may be added to your life; but whether your future years be few or many, whether they be years of feebleness or strength, I have no doubt that you will ever enjoy the affection of many friends, the respect of your opponents, and the prayers and blessings of the unfortunate and oppressed, in whose behalf you have done so much. But whatever the future may have in store for you, your success in life is no longer a problem. You have succeeded; for

"They never fail who die
In a good cause; the block may lick their gore,
Their heads may sodden in the sun, their limbs
Be strung to city gates and castle walls, —
But still their spirits walk abroad, though years
Elapse, and others share as dark a doom;
They but augment the deep and sweeping thoughts
Which overpower all others, and conduct
The world at last to freedom."

Very sincerely, your friend,
JOHN P. HALE.

On the second day after the inauguration of President Buchanan the Dred Scott decision opened a new chapter in the struggle of the slave-power for absolute supremacy. This decision affirmed that Congress had no power to prohibit slavery in the Territories, and that inferentially, at least, the Constitution carried with it the right to hold slaves there, even against the will of their people. It fully indorsed, in substance, the principles of the Democratic platform, and utterly repudiated both the letter and spirit of the self-evident truths of the Declaration of Independence as a guide in the administration of the government. The political significance of this decision was clearly indicated by the fact that a committee of the Senate at once printed large editions of it for circulation, which were scattered by thousands throughout the Northern States under the frank of Democratic members. All the departments of the government had now openly joined hands in the conspiracy to stay the rising tide of freedom and nationalize the curse of slavery.

Giddings was not idle during this Congressional vacation. He prepared and published a series of vigorous and well-written letters to Chief-Justice Taney, in which he exposed the legal sophistry as well as the inhumanity of this decision. These letters are largely historical, and embody much valuable information touching the rights of free persons of color under English and Colonial law, and the legislation of the States after the adoption of the Constitution. He wrote articles on the Church and its relations to freedom. He delivered occasional speeches on current anti-slavery topics, and wrote various communications for the Press in exposition of his views. In the mean time, the struggle to plant slavery in Kansas went forward as the practical counterpart of the Dred Scott decision. The Legislature of the Territory, which had been chosen by the ruffians of Missouri, provided for holding a convention at Lecompton for the formation of a constitution, with a view to the admission of Kansas as a State; and the constitution framed by this convention provided that "the right of property is before and higher than any constitutional sanction, and the right of the owner of a slave to such slave and his increase is the same and as inviolable as the right to any other property." No provision was made for the submission of the constitution to the people, who would thus be obliged to accept it if approved by Congress. It was forwarded on the 7th of November to the President, who transmitted it to Congress on the 20th of January, 1858. On the 2d of February he sent a message to Congress fully committing himself to the Lecompton project, and declaring that Kansas was as much a Slave State as South Carolina or Georgia.

The bill for the admission of Kansas into the Union, with this constitution, was called up for action in the Senate on the 23d of March, when Mr. Crittenden offered a substitute, providing for the submission of the constitution to the people of the Territory, and that if adopted, the President was immediately to announce the admission of Kansas by proclamation; but that if rejected, they might choose delegates to a new constitutional convention. The amendment was rejected by yeas 24 to nays 34, every Republican in the Senate voting for it, save Durkee of Wisconsin. The bill was then passed by yeas 33 to nays 25.

In the House, on the 1st of April, Giddings moved to reject the bill; but the motion was negatived by a majority of 42. A crisis had now been reached in this momentous struggle. A very exciting debate upon the question had been carried on for four months, during which the feeling on both sides had steadily increased in intensity. The danger of admitting Kansas with her Lecompton constitution was now regarded by Republicans as imminent. Douglas and his friends, however, had rebelled against the attempt of the Administration to force Kansas into the Union against the will of her people, and there were now twenty-three of his followers in the House, and six slaveholding members who belonged to the Southern Know-Nothing party, who were willing to oppose the Lecompton Bill, unless the people of Kansas were allowed to pass upon it. Under these circumstances Mr. Montgomery of Pennsylvania proposed a substitute for the Lecompton Bill, which afterwards became known as the Crittenden-Montgomery Amendment, and was substantially identical with the substitute offered by Mr. Crittenden in the Senate. This opened the way for the possible defeat of the Lecompton Bill, inasmuch as the Senate had already rejected the Crittenden Amendment, and a coalition of the Republicans, Douglas Democrats, and Southern Know-Nothings would be strong enough to carry it. The last, however, demanded of the Republicans a pledge to support the bill on its final passage. This was exceedingly objectionable, and seriously complicated the question.

The situation was a novel one, and to the Republicans exceedingly perplexing. They were quite ready for any manœuvre which promised the defeat of the Lecompton Bill without compromising their well-known principles; but many of them hesitated about becoming the followers of Southern Know-Nothings and Douglas Democrats, and surrendering their hostility to the principle of popular sovereignty in the Territories. The Senate might concur in the action of the House on this question, and then the same system of fraud and outrage which had thwarted the will of the people of Kansas before might be repeated. Could Republicans afford to assume such a responsibility? Moreover, the strife about Kansas was only a single fact in the grand struggle between slavery and freedom. Mr. Lincoln declared that "If the earth had swallowed up all Kansas, and with it all remembrance of the contest over it, the struggle would still have to go on without interruption, because the slavery question could disappear only with slavery." The defeat of the Lecompton Bill would simply be the repulse of the enemy at a single point, while the fight all along the line would have to be maintained; and to many Republicans it seemed a fatal mistake so to magnify a local and incidental struggle as to confound it with the great cause whose principles they had no right to betray. They had a still further danger to encounter in entering into the proposed coalition, and that was that some of its members might be swerved from their integrity by the power of Federal patronage.

The Republicans of the House, however, finally made the required pledge, and the Douglas Democrats also solemnly bound themselves to stand by the Crittenden-Montgomery Bill to the end. The history of this struggle constitutes one of the most curious and interesting chapters in the anti-slavery legislation of Congress. Giddings was sorely tried in facing the tangled question of duty which now confronted him; and in a diary which he kept during the latter part of March a graphic account is given of his own experience and of the situation in the House at this time. The importance of the subject will justify me in quoting his entries: —

"*March* 28. An accurate history of current events is due to the people. We have reached an important period in the progress of our cause. Just at this particular juncture, when the contending hosts of slavery and freedom are brought face to face upon the battle-field, we find various opinions prevailing among the Republicans. These different views of policy, of principle, and of duty have been developed within the past week.

"The Republicans at Philadelphia demanded the immediate admission of Kansas as a Free State, and arraigned 'the President, his advisers, agents, supporters, apologists, and accessories, either *before* or *after* the facts,' for the crimes committed in Kansas for the purpose of establishing slavery therein; and they avowed their 'fixed purpose to bring the perpetrators to a sure and condign punishment.'

"This solemn and all-important issue Mr. Crittenden proposed to compromise and settle by sending this heathenish constitution, which declares the right of property in human flesh to be superior to human legislation, back to Kansas; and if the people there should vote for it, or indeed if the border ruffians of Missouri, aided by the votes of the United States army, shall by fraud, intimidation, and violence, obtain a reaffirmance of it, the President shall declare it a member of the sisterhood of States.

"All our Republican Senators but one voted for this compromise *as an amendment* to the original bill; but the amendment failed, and Messrs. Bell and Crittenden voted with the Republicans against the passage of the bill.

"After Messrs. Bell and Crittenden had so voted, we were told that six slaveholders in the House, called 'South Americans,' would now vote with us to lay the bill on the table. This cheered the Republicans, and for the first time many of us entertained the expectation of defeating this Lecompton swindle.

"I think it was Tuesday, the 23d of March, we were asked if Republican members of the House would vote for substituting Crittenden's amendment for the original bill. Some at first said they would not; but on consultation they gave up their objections, as the proposed amendment was less objectionable than the original bill, and it was stated and understood that all the Republicans would vote for the amendment and compel the Democrats to pass the bill thus amended, or kill their own measure. Thus far everything promised success to our cause.

"On Wednesday, however, we were told that the South Americans would only vote for placing Crittenden's amendment upon the bill on condition that the Republicans would pledge themselves to vote for the bill *thus amended, upon its final passage.*

"Many Republicans at once in the most emphatic language spurned the proposition. Others treated it with more respect, and urged upon their friends a calm and dispassionate consideration, expressing the opinion that we should exercise the utmost forbearance and kindness towards each other.

"At this point the arguments *pro* and *con* commenced. Some urged the necessity of forming a *national party*, declaring that we never should succeed until we could get a party in the Slave States. Others insisted that we must unite the American party with the Republicans in order to obtain success. Others insisted that we ought to regard no platform, no avowal of principles heretofore put forth, if we could by the proposed union make a Free State of Kansas and defeat the Administration. Others argued that no general principle could or ought to guide our votes, but we ought to meet each question as it shall be presented; while others insisted that the Republican party had been founded upon great and undying principles, always to be kept in view, and never to be departed from; that these principles were fixed and eternal, embracing all men, in all countries, under all forms of government; that the real work of the Republican party was to educate the popular mind and bring it up to the maintenance of these doctrines; that the question of slavery in Kansas constituted a mere incident in the progress of our cause; that the mere political squabbles which constitute the highest thoughts of the Democratic party are as far below the great moral enterprise of converting our nation and the world to the support of truth and justice, as pandemonium is below heaven.

"I do not mention individuals. All of these subdivisions of the Republican party appeared equally honest, equally sincere. Those who sought an alliance with the South Americans were sincere, and appeared to regard such alliance as a most important object. Others surely regarded the repudiation of platforms as important. In short, I must say all were kind and conciliatory.

"On Friday, 26th, there was much excitement among Republican members. Probably three fourths of the entire party were now willing to vote for the bill on its passage, and the minority were urged and pressed to accept the proposition of the South Americans. The 'Tribune' of Thursday had spoken of those who refused the compromise as 'impracticables,' and it was said that in some instances they were threatened with expulsion from the party; but I heard nothing of that character. If such threats were made, they were uncalled for, as all with whom I conversed disapproved it. Outsiders and Senators, with the kindest feelings and purest motives, as I believe, urged us to vote for the Crittenden amendment.

"Saturday, the 27th, I thought the excitement increased rather than diminished. In my whole life I had seen nothing so unaccountable as the feeling which now pervaded most of the Republican party in regard to this matter.

"One man of distinction, not a member, called me aside, told me that our friends were exceedingly anxious to have me vote for Crittenden's bill, and had desired him to urge me to vote for it, but said that the feeling was so strong that he was unwilling to have it known that he agreed with me.

"On Saturday evening I attended a social party at Dr. Bailey's. I had scarcely got seated when the subject of adopting Crittenden's amendment was introduced, and the conversation was kept up during the entire evening. I met Governor Robinson of Kansas at this party, and he made a most solemn appeal to me in behalf of the people of that Territory to permit them to repudiate this constitution by vote, and save them from bloodshed.

"On Monday I reached the hall at ten o'clock. Hon. Francis P. Blair met me there. He had come from home for the purpose of seeing me, in order to persuade me to consent to Crittenden's amendment. We came to my room. We had long acted together, and fully sympathized in support of the great cause. He insisted that we had by our discussions made up a collateral issue with the slave-power upon the fact that the Lecompton constitution was not the voice of the people of Kansas, while the Administration had insisted that it was, and the President had staked the existence of his party upon it; that we knew the people had repudiated it by at least thirteen thousand votes, while not more than twenty-five hundred could be found in favor of it. He insisted that we ought to refer it to the people of the Territory, who would act as the jury to convict the President and his party of falsehood and tyranny, and of maintaining a military despotism in that territory since its invasion by border ruffians; that on such conviction the people of the United States would pass sentence upon the President and his party. We should then be safe from Cuban annexation and from other outrages.

"I again went to the House. Mr. Morris of Illinois came to my seat, said that the Douglas Democrats were to hold a caucus within the approaching hour, and were fearful that a number of their men would leave them and go back to the Democratic party unless we agreed to vote for Crittenden's amendment; that the whole issue depended on my decision; and closed by assuring me that it was important that they should know my opinion before going into caucus.

"I at once went to the Senate and consulted with some old friends of experience who sympathized with me in the cause, but who were evidently unwilling to decide for me, or advise me what course to pursue, but left me to rely altogether upon my own judgment.

"As I reached the Hall of Representatives I met Senator Crittenden of Kentucky, and Mr. Davis of Maryland. They both appeared to think, with me, that if our friends had at first consented to go no farther than to vote for amending the bill, the South Americans would have demanded nothing more; but that, as it now appeared, both the Douglas men and South Americans were united in the course which ought to be pursued, and most of the Republicans were with them, and that it was too late to think of changing the programme. Mr. Davis spoke of his own sacrifice in voting for us. Mr. Crittenden did the same thing. He also referred with great feeling to old times and old associations; spoke of the time when he and Mr. Clay came from the Senate Chamber to witness my departure from the House of Representatives when censured in 1842. He thought an opportunity now offered to act together for the purpose of paralyzing the Administration, and rendering it harmless to the country in future; that in this we all felt a mutual interest and a mutual desire; and if we failed to do it, we should be responsible to the country.

"It was under these circumstances that I yielded to the judgment of friends and consented to the arrangement, but reserving to myself the privilege of consulting some personal and political associates with whom I had long acted, and abiding by their judgment if I thought best. But without delay some gentlemen informed the Douglas Democrats of my new position, as they felt it important to do so before that wing of the Democratic party should retire for their appointed caucus. Many warm friends came to my seat and heartily thanked me for taking the position which I had assumed, as it relieved them from embarrassment.

"Under the excitement attending these movements, and the responsibility under which I was placed, my nervous system became affected. I found myself unable to sleep, and soon became conscious of those pains in the head and in the region of the heart which indicated danger of death at any moment. Friends to whom I made known these facts urged me to leave the city, and by their anxiety contributed to increase the difficulties surrounding me.

"On Tuesday, the 30th, some eight or ten warm personal friends who had viewed the subject at first as I had done, invited me to a conference. We retired to a committee-room, expressed our opinions freely, and all but one or two united in consenting to support the bill if necessary to pass it.

"I was also told that my new position had served to strengthen the Douglas men. Some warm anti-slavery men expressed the fear that associating with slaveholders, South Americans, and Douglas men would cause the Republican party to modify its position. To this I replied that the people constituted the Republican party. Their platform was written, known, and read of all men, and we members of Congress could have little effect upon it.

"Near evening a distinguished Senator — with whom I had acted in former times while he was a member of our body, on some trying occasions — came to the House, thanked me for having consented to support the bill, and said he thought nearly every Republican Senator concurred in my determination.

"On Wednesday evening we were informed that the Democrats had totally failed to unite, or to agree upon any plan of union.

"All appeared to promise a united vote. At half-past eleven a distinguished statesman from Pennsylvania came to my seat. He had for many years sympathized with me on the subject of slavery, and while a member of Congress had voted with me. I had not met him for some years, and being both old men, we were pleased at meeting once more. I soon discovered that he was laboring under excitement in consequence of the Republicans indicating a disposition to vote for the amendment of Mr. Crittenden.

"The House continued in session until near one o'clock of Thursday, for the purpose of closing the debate on the Kansas bill. At eight o'clock I received my evening mail, which brought me two remonstrances against our voting for Crittenden's amendment; one was signed by the Republican members of the Senate, and the other by those of the House of Representatives of our State Legislature.

"Most of the delegation from our State had left the hall when these papers reached me. I at once appointed a meeting for the Ohio delegation, to be held at my room at 10 o'clock A. M. the next morning, and took measures for giving each absent member notice, those present being notified at the time by myself in person.

"At the time appointed, Senator Wade and all the Republican members of the House met, according to appointment. Mr. Campbell, not professing to be a Republican, did not meet with us, and E. Wade and Mr. Horton had not been notified, through mistake. On comparing views it was easily discovered that argument rendered each more firm and unyielding in his opinion. The views of our members of the Legislature were treated with great respect, but appeared to have changed the opinion of no one. I endeavored to soothe the feelings of all, and urged that it was not so important which course was pursued as it was that the Republican party should act together.

"With these feelings we all repaired to the Capitol, and the scenes which transpired there on the 1st of April will soon become the subject of general history.

"Our triumph was hailed with rejoicing in all parts of the Free States. I was congratulated by friends upon our success, but I constantly replied that difficulties remained for us to encounter; and as I saw in one of the papers of my district some reflections upon me for my unwillingness to go with my Republican friends in voting for the amendment, I stated in a letter for publication the fact that I had from the first opposed the proposition, and only yielded for the purpose of voting with my friends and keeping the party together.

"The Senate, having disagreed to our amendment, returned to the House a message announcing that fact. Now commenced the anxiety and fears of those who had advocated the adoption of the amendment. They feared that some of our men might yield to the influence and patronage of the Executive, and that all might yet be lost."

This ends the diary. It closed with the 1st of April, when the House voted on the Crittenden-Montgomery Amendment, which was adopted by a vote of yeas 120 to nays 112. With much reluctance and many misgivings, Giddings supported it. His true attitude would have been to stand alone, as he had done on some notable occasions; but he yielded his own judgment to the persuasions and entreaties of his friends. Every Republican member of the House voted for the measure, as every Republican in the Senate, with a single exception, had done. But they were all wrong. In playing their game of party tactics they abandoned their fundamental principles touching the question of slavery in the Territories and the admission of more Slave States, and accepted the position of the Douglas Democrats. They unitedly pledged themselves to the admission of Kansas with the Lecompton constitution, if the people of the Territory should favor it; and this betrayal of their cause proved utterly fruitless of good.

On the next day after the vote in the House the Senate rejected the Crittenden-Montgomery Amendment by a vote of 32 yeas to 23 nays, and asked for a Committee of Conference; thus forcing the two Houses again to face the necessity for some plan of compromise by which the freedom of Kansas might be sacrificed. English of Indiana, who had all along opposed the Lecompton Bill, was placed at the head of the House Committee, and the final result of the conference was a bill denying to the people of Kansas the right to be heard on the question of slavery as completely as did the Lecompton Bill, and containing other provisions still more atrocious. This bill was passed by the House on the 30th of April by a vote of yeas 112 to nays 103; and on the same day the Senate adopted it by a vote of 31 against 22. Such was the deplorable outcome of the coalition formed by the Republicans with Douglas Democrats and Southern Know-Nothings for the purpose of saving Kansas from slavery. The twenty-three Douglas Democrats who had solemnly pledged themselves to stand by the Crittenden-Montgomery Amendment dwindled to twelve, and thus justified the apprehension expressed by Giddings in the closing sentence of his diary that "the influence and patronage of the Executive" might prove fatal to the freedom of Kansas. In spite of the recreancy of Congress, however, and solely through the heroism of her people, the English Bill was repudiated, and the way thus left open for her final admission as a Free State.

The action of the Republicans in dealing with Kansas undoubtedly exerted a demoralizing influence upon their party. It was followed by a very formidable effort to stampede its members from the principles broadly affirmed in the national platform of 1856. The "New York Tribune" took the lead in beating this retreat, openly favoring the disbandment of the Republican party and the formation of a combination against the Democrats, composed of Republicans, Douglas Democrats, Know-Nothings, and Whigs. The abandonment of Republicanism was likewise favored by such papers as the "Cincinnati Gazette," which pronounced the policy of Congressional prohibition worthless, and openly committed itself to the admission of more Slave States when demanded by a popular majority in any Territory. The "Indianapolis Journal" and other leading Republican organs spoke of Congressional prohibition as "murdered by Dred Scott." According to many Republican leaders, Republicanism simply meant opposition to the latest outrage of slavery, and acquiescence in all preceding ones. Fortunately, this downward tendency was arrested by the Republicans of Illinois, who refused to follow Douglas, and thus opened the way for the memorable debate between him and Lincoln, and the successful struggle of 1860, which followed.

The Kansas struggle did not divert the attention of Giddings from other topics. On the 26th of February he addressed the House on "The Conflict between Religious Truths and American Infidelity." He said, —

"The Philadelphia Convention will be remembered in coming time as first in the history of the political parties of our nation to make religious truths the basis of political action, and first to proclaim the rights of mankind as universal, to be enjoyed equally, by princes and people, by rulers and the most humble. It was the first to proclaim the fatherhood of God and the brotherhood of man. The result of the Presidential election of 1856 showed the advocates of oppression that there was but one alternative for them. They were constrained to take distinct issue with the advocates of liberty by denying these religious truths, or disband their party in every Free State."

This was the key-note of his speech, and he proceeded to arraign as "American Infidels" the men who sought the repeal of the Missouri Compromise, who justified the raid into Kansas for the purpose of making it a Slave State, who defended and lauded the Dred Scott decision, which denied the right of all men to life, liberty, and the pursuit of happiness, and who even contended that slavery was sanctioned by the Almighty. The speech was widely circulated and warmly welcomed in the Northern States, and called forth from his old friend Arnold Buffum a letter, from which I quote : —

" On reading thy speech delivered in Congress, exposing the infidelity of enslaving our fellow-creatures, I exclaimed to my daughter, 'I should like to go into the future or spirit world in Joshua R. Giddings's carpet-bag.' I felt an undoubting assurance that I should be safe. Oh, my dear friend, I rejoice to see thee growing stronger and stronger as thee draws nearer to the termination of thy earthly career. I do from the bottom of my heart approve every word uttered in that speech."

On the 7th of June Giddings addressed the House upon the joint resolutions proposing hostilities with England on account of her exercising the right of visitation. He reviewed in detail the action of the Government in favoring or conniving at the African slave-trade, and referred to the fact that slaves, direct from Africa, were landed upon our Southern coast, and that Southern conventions had for years been publicly discussing the propriety of restoring this traffic, while slave-ships were being built in our own ports, under the very eye of the Administration. He also frequently took part in incidental discussions, and it was while responding to a question by Marshall of Kentucky, touching the Lecompton Bill, on the 29th of April, that he was suddenly prostrated by heart trouble, as he had been in the preceding Congress.

When Giddings returned to his constituents after the adjournment of this session, he found them discussing the question of his renomination. His friends insisted on his making the race, not on personal grounds, but solely because his long service in Congress eminently fitted him to represent the principles of his constituents. They had no doubt of his nomination, nor had Giddings; for he had been unanimously nominated two years before, and had done nothing whatever to forfeit his standing in the district. The question, however, was embarrassing. He felt admonished by advancing years and failing health that he could not much longer bear the burden of his public duties; and yet he had been so long in Congress and had become so habituated to his work that he hesitated as to his decision. He was finally persuaded to stand as a candidate and leave his constituents to decide the question of his final retirement. A great surprise awaited him and his friends. The Congressional convention which met on the 25th of August gave the nomination to his competitor, John Hutchins, of Warren, by one majority. Giddings, who was present, seemed to find relief in this solution of his dilemma, and cheerfully and cordially indorsed the action of the convention in an admirable speech; but his friends were inexpressibly disappointed and vexed. They were the victims of their own over-confidence and inactivity; they had taken his nomination for granted.

Giddings himself made no personal efforts, and would not, for the reason that he was thoroughly known to his constituents, who had stood by him faithfully for twenty years, and were abundantly able to decide the question. In his own county six delegates were lost to him because they considered his nomination assured without their help, while seven other delegates who were well understood to be his friends had been induced by the secret tactics of the opposition to oppose him. All of his old enemies, including Know-Nothings and old Whigs who had through many long years labored in vain for his defeat, worked with all their might for Mr. Hutchins. They saw that their opportunity had come, and they used it. In the disguise of friendship for Giddings they could plausibly urge his retirement on the score of his age and precarious health. The unquestioning confidence of his friends in his success put them to sleep, and left the field clear for the unscrupulous and unhindered tactics of his foes.

Mr. Hutchins was a man of character, who had been a member of the old Liberty party, and was as thoroughly committed to radical anti-slavery principles as Giddings; but the enemies of the latter knew that in no other way than through the support of Hutchins was there any hope of their success. Their fight was personal. Giddings had been steadfastly and bravely in the right, and they now hated him because they had wronged him, and were not willing to confess it by abandoning their opposition. These men were reinforced by others whom Giddings had unavoidably displeased in his disposition of Federal patronage in the course of his long public service, and by still others whose ambition for his place had been or might be thwarted by his continuance in office. One of his most indefatigable opponents was Jacob D. Cox, since well known to the country by his civil and military services, and then the law partner of Mr. Hutchins. Another was Hon. Milton Sutliff. Both these gentlemen had always been supporters of Giddings, and were supposed to be his friends till the morning of the nominating convention. These various forces operated against him very actively and quietly. Their campaign was a "still hunt," while his friends rested in the serene faith that his nomination was a matter of course. Had they understood the situation, there would not have been the slightest doubt about his triumph, while their disappointment was now aggravated by self-reproach.

Giddings, however, maintained his customary equanimity and cheerfulness. He did not manifest the slightest ill-will towards those who had accomplished his defeat. He showed no coldness towards old friends who had deserted him, and no unwillingness to surrender the position he had so long honored. He did not agree with those of his friends who felt that he had received a slight at the hands of his constituents, and was as ready as ever to continue his warfare against slavery. In a letter to an old friend, speaking of his early service with John Quincy Adams, he said, —

"Many years since that day have come and gone. The storms which gathered around him while living, subsequently beat upon my own political pathway. I have met them as best I could, until their violence appears to have been spent, the clouds are breaking, and the sunlight of truth is arousing the nation to action."

This was his sufficient consolation. The consciousness of having been faithful to duty, and that the great cause he had served was advancing, made him satisfied, and left no room for personal resentments.

The slaveocracy and its Northern allies were of course delighted, and manifested their joy by characteristic demonstrations, while the disappointment of the friends of Giddings was by no means confined to his own district or State. William H. Seward wrote him from Auburn, —

"I shall have some curiosity to see the bold man who is to come into your place at Washington. He will come there under prodigious responsibilities. I sincerely hoped that your term of service, protracted as it has been, might not end before my own. But you have nothing to regret. You have overcome resistance the most prejudiced and violent, and have established for yourself a name that the friends of humanity will never suffer to perish."

Senator Wilson of Massachusetts wrote, —

"I have just returned from the battle-field of Maine, and I now write to say to you that wherever I have been, the people express their surprise and deep regret at your failure to be renominated. Here in New England you are dear to the hearts of the people; and we indulged the hope that your district, which has honored itself so long, would continue you in Congress as long as you could stand up there on the field of your glory and uphold the great cause. I have tried to get reconciled to your failure to be renominated, but I cannot. I do not see how any one can be a candidate in your district against the veteran friend of our cause who more than any one has the love and respect of our true and tried friends all over the country. This cannot be right, and our friends feel that it is wrong, — that it is a wrong to you, and above all to the cause by whose infancy you stood in the halls of Congress."

His old and devoted friend, Dr. Palfrey, of Cambridge, Massachusetts, wrote, —

"Permit me to say in a word how greatly I am grieved to learn that your public career — for the present, at least — is brought to a close. Your services to the public have been so important through so many years that when they are withdrawn it seems as if the whole mechanism of freedom was dislocated.

"I will not allow that I am so much vexed as grieved. But I am afraid I am too much vexed for equanimity. Your successor is an historical character, without fail; whatever he may do or forbear hereafter, the future historian is sure to erect a pillory for him, as for the man who intrigued — or, if he did not intrigue, who consented — to supplant the twenty years' champion of freedom. If he wanted $3,000 a year, he has got it. If he wants a place in the memory of man, he has got that too, to a certainty, such as it is; but Heaven forbid that such a place should be mine!

"I trust and pray, my dear sir, that the public loss may be your gain; that in retirement from public cares your strength may be invigorated and sustained; that you may have many happy years before you in which to enjoy the gratitude of good men and the testimony of an approving conscience for your duties wisely and bravely discharged; and that 'serus in coelum redeas.' God bless you!"

Giddings received many messages of sympathy and friendship, of which none was more gratifying than the following: —

MONTPELLIER, FRANCE, Feb. 1, 1859.

MY DEAR GIDDINGS, — The very earnest counsel of my physicians, and the requirements of the medical treatment which I am still pursuing, make it more than doubtful if I shall be in my seat during the present session of Congress. Reluctantly I yield to my fate, in the full conviction that, by the blessing of God, the next session will see my long catalogue of pains, aches, and smarts brought to an end. But I shall feel another then of a different kind, the anticipation of which adds to my present troubles, in missing you from that seat of eminent duty which you have so long honored.

I write with great sincerity, and simply because I cannot help it, to express the emotions which your retirement is calculated to produce in the breast of those who have at heart the welfare of their country and the improvement of the great family of man.

Among the reminiscences of John Quincy Adams, which I have ever guarded with profound respect, is one which concerns yourself. Pardon me if I mention it now. I sat by the bedside of this veteran soldier of our cause not long before that death which took him so suddenly from among us. While I listened, he dwelt at length and with especial satisfaction upon your public life, and concluded by declaring, with an emphasis that at the time penetrated my soul and still reverberates there, "Mr. Giddings is the most useful man in Congress." He who uttered these words knew well how to measure the different kinds of usefulness in a public man; he knew full well how to recognize that *best usefulness* which is found in the unflinching support of those sacred principles which constitute the soul of society, which for their sake is not ashamed to bear reproach and contumely, which is deterred by no menace or danger, and which, in an assembly ruled by vulgar slave-drivers and packed by their cowering accomplices, proclaims the rights of freedom and humanity.

I am no prophet, but I see clearly in the future that your public career will be enrolled in history for the admiration and gratitude of mankind.

I pray that, though withdrawn from active service, you may be long spared in health to cheer by a hearty God-speed those of us who are left to continue the battle. Though your voice may not be heard, your example will speak, saying constantly, as in times past: "Be firm, and yield not; have faith in the justice and dignity of your cause, and know for certain that you cannot fail!"

Good by! From my distant exile across the sea I send you all best wishes. Believe me ever sincerely yours,

CHARLES SUMNER.

The Anti-slavery and Republican Press joined in voicing the wide-spread and heartfelt regret which the unexpected news of this event awakened among the people. Even conservative journals, which had occasionally criticised the course of Giddings as extreme and impracticable, now deplored the displacement of the veteran leader of the cause of freedom in Congress. As an example, I quote the following from the "New York Evening Post": —

"The people of a congressional district of course have the right to manage their own affairs in their own way, but people elsewhere have an equal right to comment on their doings. We are not surprised, therefore, at the general disapproval which is manifested by the Northern Press at the recent action of the Republican Convention in the Ashtabula district of Ohio in discharging their long-tried and faithful representative, Joshua R. Giddings; for we presume the nomination of a successor terminates his public career. Notwithstanding the impaired condition of his health, which unfits him for active labor, and the many subjects on which we differ from him, we cannot help concurring with the universal feeling expressed at the prospect of his retirement.

"Mr. Giddings is now the oldest member of the House. For twenty-two years his venerable head and stalwart frame have rendered him conspicuous among his associates, from whom he was not less distinguished by the peculiarity of his principles and his bold, uncompromising style of enforcing them. Embodying, as he did, in an extreme degree, the opinions of a small and exceedingly unpopular party, he was for a long time a mark for the fiercest assaults of the influential leaders of both the great political organizations; but the courage with which he has confronted them always won a renewed tribute of confidence from his constituents.

"When John Quincy Adams entered on that career of agitation for the right of petition which a friendly biographer declares to have been the most illustrious and honorable period of his life, Mr. Giddings was at his side, fighting the same battle, and sharing, without flinching, in its obloquy. The vote of censure in 1842 passed upon him by the House for his temerity in offering resolutions commending the conduct of the insurgent slaves of the 'Creole,' was the most noted attempt to single him out as a subject of intimidation. He resigned his seat, and threw himself upon his constituency only to be immediately returned by a largely increased majority. Since then his right to free speech has seldom been successfully questioned; and it must be confessed he has exercised it, to use a pertinent colloquialism, 'with a vengeance.' Whenever the occasion arises, he is on his feet to protest against some new attempt of the enemy to press forward, openly or covertly, or to give legislative sanction to the projects of that institution which he so abhors. Just as regularly as a new Congress opens, he is up at the first opportunity to deliver one of his 'incendiary' reassertions of principles, reviewing, somewhat on the plan of Lord Lyndhurst's famous tirades in Parliament, the shortcomings of the Government and the progress of the cause of which he was a representative; and yet such has been his courtesy and regard for the rules of order, and such his obvious sincerity, as to command ultimately the respect, if not the approval, of his bitterest foes.

"There is something, too, in the boldness and independence of Mr. Giddings, something in that sympathy which he always shows for the weak and oppressed, whether it be the negro or the fugitive Indians whose wrongs he has so faithfully presented in his 'Exiles of Florida,' that commands an instinctive respect, even from those whose convictions are adverse to his own. His mania is not a restless itching for notoriety, it is a certain noble rage, the overplus of an honest and genuine humanity. He has not succeeded in popular estimation as a politician, but he has at last obtained a foremost place on the good angel's book 'as one who loved his fellow-men;' and we are not displeased to find that he is even now receiving something of the respect and admiration with which posterity will repay his unfaltering and unselfish zeal for a great and noble cause."

In speaking of the retirement of Giddings the "Atlantic Monthly" said, —

"A winter such as rounds his days is fuller of life and promise than a century of vulgar summers. He has won for himself an honorable and enduring place in the hearts and memories of men by the fidelity to principle and the unfaltering courage of his public course. Among the ignoble hundreds who have flitted through the Capitol since he first took his place there, —

'Heads without name, no more remembered,'

his is one of the two or three that are household words on the lips of the nation. And it will so remain and be familiar in the mouths of posterity, with a fame as pure as it is noble. The ear that hath *not* heard him shall bless him, and the eye that hath *not* seen him shall give witness to him."

But the retirement of Giddings at the close of this Congress was for the best. As an anti-slavery pioneer and leader his mission was accomplished. He was no longer a lone knight in battling with the armies of slavery. Others were now ready to take his place, as he had been ready to take up the work of John Quincy Adams, when the latter laid it down. The great party which was soon to take possession of the government had openly espoused the principles for which he had so long toiled, while it was abundantly supplied with leaders, many of them in the prime of their manhood, who were able to marshal its forces and direct their operations; and Giddings certainly had no desire to "lag superfluous on the stage."

Besides, with his constitutional heart trouble, his life might be cut short at any moment; it hung upon a thread. The Thirty-sixth Congress was to bring with it the excitement and turbulence of civil war, while his personal safety demanded tranquillity and rest. If his constituents had required the sacrifice, he would have remained in Congress while he lived, and have fallen at last at his post of public duty. This would have seemed to his old and devoted friends the fit ending of his long and honorable career; but it was ordered otherwise, and he was finally restored to the endearing claims of home and kindred, which had been so long and so painfully interrupted by the pressure of his public duties.

The second session of the Thirty-fifth Congress was more orderly and less exciting than the first. The discussions related mainly to the foreign affairs of the government, although the question of slavery was involved. On the 15th of January, in a debate on the codification of the revenue laws, Giddings reiterated his views on the coastwise slave-trade and the obligations imposed upon the United States under the treaty of Ghent to suppress that trade as well as the foreign traffic. On the 21st of the month he joined in the debate on the bill to provide for the examination and payment of certain claims of citizens of Georgia and Alabama on account of losses sustained by depredations of the Creek Indians. The question of slavery was not involved, and it was strictly a legal argument. On the 12th of this month he delivered his last anti-slavery speech. It was a brief historical review of the anti-slavery conflict in Congress. In speaking of the campaign of 1856 and the principles avowed by the two parties at that time, he said, —

"To effect this object I had toiled for many years. I had, in this body, asserted the doctrine of man's inalienable rights, and called on gentlemen of the Democratic party to admit or deny it; but I had called in vain. I had travelled and spoken in thirteen States; I had written essays and newspaper articles; I had compiled a volume of romantic incidents, showing the secret workings of the slave-power. These had been gathered with great labor from more than two hundred documents reposing in our library under the accumulated dust of many years. To expose this moral and political infidelity I had encountered Southern opposition and Northern distrust; and I greatly rejoiced to see that party compelled to avow its doctrines, for I well knew that the avowal of its principles would show that its days were numbered."

He concluded his farewell speech as follows: —

"Mr. Chairman, from childhood I have mingled with the people. I know their love of justice, their devotion to liberty. The great American heart beats in sympathy for the oppressed, for justice to ourselves and to mankind. The popular voice demands the exercise of our constitutional powers to drive oppression from our Territories, from our ships while sailing upon the high seas, from this District; to exclude it from all support by Congress, by the Executive, by our courts; to condemn it as an outlaw; and that the legitimate powers of government shall be exerted for freedom. Give the people an opportunity, and they will elect a President and Vice-President, a Senate and House of Representatives, pledged not merely to these purposes, but to put forth the moral influence of our nation to drive oppression from the earth.

"To the attainment of this object my official labors have long been directed. Those labors are now drawing to a close, and I shall soon surrender the cause, so far as I am officially concerned, to other and abler hands. My political pathway has been rugged, beset with difficulties. I have been constrained to meet many of my fellow-members in intellectual conflict, and at times those conflicts have been severe; but I am not conscious of having assailed any man except in self-defence, and I separate from my opponents without a feeling of unkindness. Indeed, if my desire, my earnest prayer, could avail, they should all be just and wise and pure and happy. Here for many long years I have counselled with friends and combated opponents. The scenes through which I have passed rush upon the recollection as I am about to bid adieu to this arena of my political life. I shall leave it with emotions, but not with regret. I shall bear with me to private life many interesting recollections of the great contest which gives character to the age in which we live. And I beg to assure you, Mr. Chairman and gentlemen, that whether in public or in private life, in prosperity or in adversity, whether living or dying, my heart's desire and prayer to God shall be that every human soul may enjoy that liberty which is necessary to protect and cherish life, attain knowledge, and prepare for heaven. And when I shall have passed away, let my epitaph announce that *I hated oppression and wrong*, — that *I loved liberty and justice.*"

Near the close of this session Giddings was made the recipient of a beautiful testimonial from his fellow-members. It consisted of a solid silver tea-set of six pieces, and a highly ornamented tray, on each of which are engraved representations of the tea-plant, water-lilies, etc. The handles and spouts are beautifully wrought in scroll and leaf work, and on each piece is an ornamented shield bearing the following inscription: —

> PRESENTED BY 104 MEMBERS OF THE 35TH CONGRESS
> TO JOSHUA R. GIDDINGS,
> AS A TOKEN OF RESPECT FOR HIS MORAL WORTH
> AND PERSONAL INTEGRITY.

Accompanying the service of silver was a walking-stick of rare and beautiful wood, mounted with a massive gold head, which bears a similar inscription to that on the tea-set.

Soon after the adjournment of Congress Giddings received another handsome present. It was a gold watch, presented by the colored people of New York and Brooklyn as a token of their regard for him as the champion and defender of the rights of their race in the United States, and of the cause of universal freedom. The gold of this watch had been dug by free hands from the mines of California, and the works were manufactured in Waltham, Massachusetts. The inscription on the watch was as follows: —

PRESENTED TO THE HONORABLE JOSHUA R. GIDDINGS,
THE CHAMPION OF AMERICAN FREEDOM,
BY THE COLORED PEOPLE OF NEW YORK AND BROOKLYN,
MARCH 28, 1859.

The presentation was made by Rev. Hiram Garnet, and was accompanied by a large Family Bible, handsomely bound and beautifully inscribed, — a gift from the ladies of the Giddings and Joliffe Association.

CHAPTER XII.

MARCH, 1859, TO MAY, 1864.

The "Exiles of Florida."— The John Brown Raid. — The Lecture Field. — Scene in the Chicago Convention. — Campaign of 1860. — Letter to Hon. Thomas Ewing. — Another Literary Venture. — Appointed Consul-General to Canada. — Correspondence with Sumner. — Life in Montreal. — The Reciprocity Treaty. — Further Correspondence. — Declining Health. — " History of the Rebellion." — Death.

BEFORE we follow Mr. Giddings into his retirement it will be proper to refer to a topic which had engaged his serious attention. Notwithstanding his busy life during the first session of the Thirty-fifth Congress, he found time to complete and publish an interesting and valuable contribution to the history of slavery in the United States. It is entitled "The Exiles of Florida; or, The Crimes committed by our Government against the Maroons who fled from South Carolina and other Slave States, seeking Protection under Spanish Laws." It opened a new and unexplored field of historic research bearing upon the question of slavery, and was a surprise to men of all parties and sections. Few subjects have been so little understood by the great body of the people as the genesis and character of our Florida wars. The public has been made to believe that they were caused by the depredations of the savages of Florida upon the contiguous States, and the further excuse has been urged that these savages had made this province a refuge for fugitive slaves.

The general impression has also prevailed that these slaves were recent fugitives, whose real masters were seeking their recovery. But the truth is that long before the War of the Revolution, slaves fled to Florida, and that at least three quarters of a century prior to the purchase of Florida by the United States, a colony of negroes had been established there, who gradually mingled and became identified with the Seminole or Southern Creek Indians, who had also made it their refuge from Carolina slavery. These negroes and Indians intermarried, lived happily together, planted and hunted as friendly allies, and enjoyed the fruits of their toil in peace. They were in all respects free citizens of the Spanish Crown, and were permitted to occupy lands upon the same terms as other subjects of Spain. When they passed away, their children took their places, and were in turn followed by their grandchildren and their descendants; and although the founders of the colony had fled from slavery, they and their descendants were as free in this province of Spain as the thousands of slaves who from time to time found an asylum in Canada.

But the slaveholders of Georgia did not relish this spectacle of a free and independent community of Indians and negroes in an adjoining province. They dreaded its influence on their cherished institution, and determined to break it up by a vigorous slave-hunt. They claimed these exiles as their property, and the Federal Government espoused their cause. The exiles determined to fight for their liberty, and the army of the United States was employed for their subjugation. Native citizens of the province and subjects of the king of Spain who had been free for generations were reduced to hopeless bondage in furtherance of the claims of imaginary owners. More than five hundred persons, some of them recent fugitives, but generally natives of the province, and all of them free on Spanish soil, were made slaves, at a cost to the United States of forty million dollars, or eighty thousand dollars for each pretended fugitive reclaimed.

The Government at last became weary of its barbarous and unprofitable work, and determined upon the removal of the Seminoles to the Cherokee lands west of Arkansas. Under the solemn pledge of the nation that they should be settled in villages separate from the Creeks, and protected by the Government, they removed to their new home. Relying on its good faith, they built their huts, planted their ground, and entered upon the work of providing for their wants, when two hundred armed Creek warriors, stimulated by the offer of a slave-dealer of one hundred dollars for each exile captured and delivered, pounced upon them; and although they were repulsed, they seized a portion of the exiles, carried them to their employer, and received the price stipulated for their services. The prisoners were taken before an Arkansas judge, who, in violation of express treaty stipulation, and in utter defiance of law, ordered them to be delivered to the slave-dealer, who sold them in the Southern market. The exiles now clearly saw that no reliance could be placed upon the plighted faith of the Government, and those of them who had successfully resisted the crusade of hireling Creeks, resolved to seek an asylum in Mexico, where slavery did not exist. They took up their march by night, holding themselves in readiness for an attack. They were pursued by the Creeks, who were repulsed, leaving their dead upon the field; and these hunted victims at last found a home on foreign soil.

Such, in the fewest words, is the story of these exiles. Giddings tells it at length, and in all its horrid details. It is the story of a war waged by a great nation against unoffending negroes and Indians, whose heroism in defending their liberty must forever challenge the admiration of the world. It was a war instigated by Carolina and Georgia slaveholders, — not, in fact, for the recapture of fugitive slaves, but for the enslavement of men and women who were free, and whose example menaced the security of slave property; and nearly every Administration of the government, from Washington's to Polk's, both inclusive, was an accessory, either before or after the fact, to this national crime against a brave and helpless people. Giddings found the facts which support his statements buried in the archives of the government, and often disguised or perverted by the officials who played their part in the shameful business; but through great labor and patience in ransacking the musty records, he compelled them to yield up their secrets, which he exposed to the gaze of the world in this book. No such indictment of the slaveocracy had ever been framed, nor had the nation ever been so solemnly arraigned before the judgment-seat of history for its cold-blooded treachery to freedom and humanity.

In a notice of this work soon after its publication, the "Atlantic Monthly" (then edited by James Russell Lowell) said, —

"It is full of pathetic and tragic interest, and melts and stirs the heart at once with pity for the sufferers, and with anger, that sins not, at their mean and ruthless oppressors. Every American citizen should read it; for it is an indictment which recites crimes which have been committed in his name, perpetrated by troops and officials in his service, and all done at his expense. The whole nation is responsible at the bar of the world and before the tribunal of posterity for these atrocities, devised by members of its Cabinets and its Congress, directed by its Presidents, and executed by its armies and its courts."

In a letter to the publishers the venerable Josiah Quincy said of this work, —

"It opens new and painful views of the sufferings of these exiles, and casts a glorious light on their principles and perseverance. It is a sad and humiliating fact that Americans — men boasting of their freedom, with the flag of our Union waving over them, with liberty, law, and religion in their mouths — were their oppressors and persecutors. The work illustrates with great power and unquestionable truth the inherent spirit of the slaveholder, — his pride, his cupidity, his disregard of the rights of nature, of the feelings of humanity, and the extinction of the moral sense in every bosom in which the spirit of masterdom predominates. It ought to enkindle in the Free States a feeling, a will, and a resolve to relieve the Union of this incubus, which depresses our hopes of the preservation of our free institutions, disgraces our character, and while it brutalizes one portion of our population, demoralizes and makes callous another."

The style of the book is admirable. The story is told as simply and naturally as if the facts narrated had been every-day occurrences; and yet they are so thrilling and tragic as to give the work the charm of a romance. Giddings indulges in no exaggeration or distortion, and uses none of the indignant rhetoric which we find in his Congressional speeches. He writes with elegant simplicity and perfect coolness, and the reader is thus left to form his own opinions and find expression for his own emotions. This enhances the effect of his statements. It was a new and startling revelation of the cruelty and rapacity of slavery and its lordship over the National Government, while it created one of the great moral currents which finally united in sweeping the curse from the land; and it earned for the writer the thanks and praise of coming generations.

We have seen that Giddings was in correspondence with John Brown in 1856 respecting the troubles in Kansas. Brown afterwards visited Jefferson, where he addressed the people on the same subject, and was assisted by Giddings in raising funds for his relief, having lost all his property in Kansas by border-ruffian outrages, and being now poor. After the famous raid into Virginia the champions of slavery and their allies at once attempted to involve the Republican party in the transaction. An election was pending in New York and New Jersey, and members of the Democratic party, believing that great odium would attach to those who sympathized with Brown, charged Giddings with having stimulated him to invade Virginia and give freedom to her slaves. While wounded and a prisoner, Brown was visited by Senator Mason of Virginia and Hon. C. L. Vallandigham of Ohio, who endeavored to draw from him facts that would implicate Republicans. Their conversations with him were published, and purported to involve Giddings. He at once replied in a card published in Philadelphia, where he happened to be on business, declaring that the murder of Brown's son in Kansas, and the barbarities exercised there under Democratic influence, had impelled Brown to make his raid into Virginia. He also addressed an immense audience in that city, frankly stating his acquaintance and relations with Brown, and disavowing any knowledge of his movement in Virginia till he heard of it through the newspapers. In response to these statements an advertisement appeared in the papers published at Richmond, Virginia, offering a bounty of ten thousand dollars to any one who would bring Giddings to that city alive, or five thousand dollars for his head. A committee of Democrats, who had been appointed in New York to ascertain and report the facts concerning Brown's invasion, made a report asserting in substance that John P. Hale, Gerrit Smith, and Joshua R. Giddings were involved; but on receiving official notice that they would be called to account in an action for libel, they acknowledged their error, paid the costs and counsel fees, and legal proceedings against them were discontinued.

Mr. Giddings left Congress a poor man. The congressional salary during his long term of service was much less than it is at present, and having a large family, it was only by the strictest economy that he was able to save anything from his earnings. The methods by which members of Congress have grown rich in later years were wholly unknown to him; and as he was now too old to resume his professional labors, he determined to enter the lecture field. He prepared an address on the trial of John Quincy Adams, and delivered it at various points during the winter of 1859–1860. This brought him face to face with multitudes of his friends and admirers, while it gratified the long-established bent of his mind towards politics, and pleasantly occupied his thoughts with the old familiar question.

As the time for another Presidential election approached, Giddings critically watched the political signs of the times. He saw and deplored the disposition of a portion of the Republican leaders to abandon the broad ground on which the party had planted itself at Philadelphia in 1856. He was anxious, if possible, to check this evil tendency; and to this end his friends made him a delegate to the Chicago Convention, which met on May 15, and nominated Lincoln and Hamlin. He did not attend the convention as the champion of any particular candidate, but as the representative of the *principles* of the party; and he so declared to his friends on reaching Chicago. In the hope that he could do something to prevent the threatened retreat from these principles, he asked the delegates from his State for a place on the Committee on Resolutions; but the old conservative Whigs in the delegation were strong enough to prevent this. These men belonged to a faction described by Giddings as still believing in the principles and policy of the Whig party, but who joined the Republicans to avoid isolation from political life; and they now wished to change the Republican creed rather than admit that they had been wrong in their past action.

When the platform was reported, Giddings listened to its reading with anxiety and apprehension. In the main it was an admirable declaration of principles, clearly setting forth the practical issues of the canvass which the course of events had produced; but it failed to re-affirm the self-evident truths of the Declaration of Independence, as embodied in the platform of 1856. Giddings obtained the floor and moved to amend the first resolution by adding the omitted words, making an earnest speech in support of his motion. Hon. David K. Cartter of Ohio opposed the amendment, declaring that it was "all gas" that had been expended by his colleague on the amendment, and that "we might as well insert the Golden Rule as the Declaration of Independence." Mr. Eli Thayer, delegated from Oregon, said that "many great truths have been left out of the Declaration of Independence. For one, I believe in the Ten Commandments, but I do not desire to see them embodied in the platform." Mr. Oyler of Indiana said "it would be as proper to put in the Bible, from the first chapter to the last." No member of the convention came to the support of Giddings, and in the general eagerness for a vote, and the prevailing opinion that the platform was substantially sufficient, the amendment was voted down. Giddings was sorely disappointed, and left the convention for his lodgings, followed by sympathizing friends, who deplored this break in the harmony of the proceedings, and urged him to return. On his way out, George William Curtis, one of the delegates from New York, and then a young man, asked him where he was going, and he replied: "I see that I am out of place here." In giving an account of this affair afterwards, Mr. Curtis says: "It seemed to me that the original impulse of the party was leaving the convention in his person, and I begged him to remain, saying that I would try the amendment again." While the friends of Giddings were persuading him to remain in the convention, Curtis mounted upon his seat, and having caught the eye of the president, moved to amend the *second* resolution by adding thereto the prelude to the Declaration of Independence, — being substantially the amendment which the convention had rejected. Mingled applause and disapprobation followed, and Mr. Cartter made the point of order that the convention had already voted down the amendment, which was therefore out of order. The president, George Ashmun of Massachusetts, a conservative old Whig who defended Webster's 7th of March speech, was evidently displeased with this motion, and promptly sustained the point of order. Frank Blair of Missouri instantly rose to his feet, and so energetically addressed the president that he was obliged to see him. Blair urged the point that the amendment offered by Mr. Curtis was to the second resolution of the platform, and therefore in order. The president reluctantly acknowledged this; and Mr. Curtis was awarded the floor. He said, —

> "I have to ask the convention whether they are prepared to go upon the record before the country as voting down the Declaration of Independence? I rise simply to ask gentlemen to think well before, upon the free prairies of the West, in the summer of 1860, they dare to wince and quail before the assertions of the men in Philadelphia in 1776, — before they dare to shrink from repeating the words that these great men enunciated."

This speech took the convention by storm, and a scene of the wildest excitement followed. The amendment was unanimously adopted, and Giddings returned to his seat, while ten thousand voices swelled into a roar so deafening that for several minutes every effort to restore order was in vain. It was a magnificent victory for the gifted young orator and his venerable friend. In a recent letter, Mr. Murat Halsted, who was present, says, —

> "It was a great scene, and as I think of it every feature of it comes vividly before me. I had very often seen Mr. Giddings in Congress, but never saw him when his figure appeared so stately and his snowy head so lofty as on this occasion; and the play of emotions in his face, visible to the whole convention, was as frank as a child's."

This was not merely a great personal triumph for Giddings, and as gratifying to his hosts of friends as to himself, but it was a triumph of courage over timidity, of principle over policy. The cowardly fear of abolitionism was rebuked. The trimmers and time-servers in the party, who had for years labored so energetically and yet so stealthily to lower the Republican standard, could not fail to see that their rank in the grand army of freedom was henceforward to be that of subordination, and not of leadership.

The defeat of the Giddings amendment would have been a deplorable blunder, and he was bravely right in turning his back upon the convention. It would have been a scheme of salvation by suicide. Giddings understood the timely significance of the principles of the Declaration of Independence. In his earlier years he had sat at the feet of John Quincy Adams, and caught the spirit of his solemn appeal to the people at the Jubilee of the Constitution, in 1839. Said he, —

"Lay up these principles in your hearts and in your souls. Bind them for signs upon your hands, that they may be as frontlets between your eyes. Teach them to your children, speaking of them when sitting in your homes, when walking by the way, when lying down, and when rising up. Write them upon the doorplates of your houses and upon your gates. Cling to them as to the issues of life; adhere to them as to the cords of your eternal salvation."

Mr. Lincoln was as religiously devoted to these principles as were Adams and Giddings. In speaking of those who cavil at them as "glittering generalities," he had declared in a published letter a few months before that "they are the vanguards, the sappers and miners, of returning despotism." "All honor to Jefferson," said he, "to the man who, in the concrete struggle for national independence by a single people, had the coolness, forecast, and capacity to introduce into a merely revolutionary document an abstract truth applicable to all men and all times, and so to embalm it there that to-day and in all coming days it shall be a rebuke and a stumbling-block to the harbingers of reappearing tyranny and despotism." Mr. Giddings was verily right in declaring himself "out of place" in the convention when it refused to voice the words of Jefferson and the fathers in its declaration of fundamental principles; and posterity will honor him for the heroism and unflinching fidelity which averted a deadly peril.

Immediately after Mr. Lincoln's nomination Giddings addressed to him a friendly note congratulating him on his success, confidently predicting his triumph in November, and expressing himself with much warmth as an old friend. To this Lincoln made a brief and characteristic reply: —

SPRINGFIELD, ILL., May 21, 1860.

Hon. J. R. GIDDINGS:

MY GOOD FRIEND, — Your very kind and acceptable letter of the 19th was duly handed me by Mr. Tuck. It is, indeed, most grateful to my feelings that the responsible position assigned me comes without conditions, save only such honorable ones as are fairly implied. I am not wanting in the purpose, though I may fail in the strength, to maintain my freedom from bad influences. Your letter comes to my aid in this point most opportunely. May the Almighty grant that the cause of truth, justice, and humanity shall in no wise suffer at my hands! Mrs. L. joins me in sincere wishes for your health, happiness, and long life.

A. LINCOLN.

In this memorable canvass it was simply impossible for Mr. Giddings to be idle or indifferent. Notwithstanding the precarious condition of his health, he felt impelled to take the stump, and his labors extended into different States. He was everywhere greeted by large and enthusiastic audiences, and in every direction he saw unmistakable signs of victory. To him the campaign was a sort of jubilee, and he probably enjoyed it more than any in which he had ever participated. All the cherished principles for which he had so long labored were now embodied in the creed of a great party, which he had done as much as any man in the Union to create and inspire; and no man had a clearer title to its leadership and its honors than himself.

Towards the close of this canvass Hon. Thomas Ewing made a remarkable speech at Chillicothe, Ohio, which invited the particular attention of Mr. Giddings. Ewing was an old Whig, who had thus far opposed the Republican party, and whose choice for the Presidency was John Bell of Tennessee; but as there was no hope of his election, and as Ewing had satisfied himself that Lincoln would succeed, he determined to support him, with the evident purpose of influencing his Administration. At the Chillicothe meeting he clearly defined his position as a conservative and an inveterate hater of Republican principles. He argued that the Republican party arose out of the repeal of the Missouri Compromise, and that when that compromise should be restored, the mission of the party would be ended; that in the present or early part of the coming year its destiny would be fulfilled, unless it placed itself on a basis of substantial national policy, while it could not possibly sustain itself as a general anti-slavery party; that it had fallen under the control of "men of extreme opinions, Abolitionists, higher-law and irrepressible-conflict men, all shades and degrees," and could not hope to succeed without the inspiration and guidance of the conservative Whig masses; that the eighth resolution of the platform, declaring that "the normal condition of all the territory of the United States is that of freedom," is not true in fact, and should not have been incorporated; that the adoption of that portion of the Declaration of Independence which embodies its self-evident truths was not in "good taste," and that it is only "true in the vague and general sense in which it was used by the framers of the Declaration, who were, three fourths of them, slaveholders," and that Mr. Lincoln, with his political training as an old Whig, "from the first to the last, in his inaugural address, in which words will be things, and in his final message, will show himself the President of the nation, and not of a section or a party." Ewing also arraigned the Republican Legislature of Ohio for its refusal to enact a law to prohibit the fitting out of marauding expeditions against sister States, and Governor Dennison for refusing to surrender fugitives from justice charged with offences not made criminal by the laws of Ohio.

Mr. Ewing was a man of great ability, and had been a power in the politics of Ohio in the days of the Whig party. He was elected to a seat in the United States Senate in 1830. He held the office of Secretary of the Treasury in the Cabinet of General Harrison, and that of Secretary of the Interior under General Taylor. In his prime he was everywhere recognized as one of the great party leaders of his day. When such a man attempted to persuade the Republican party to belie its principles and record and commit the fortunes of the people to the leadership of old Whigs, it was not to be expected that Giddings would remain silent. It was for the relegation of such men as Ewing to private life, and for the inauguration of a new dispensation in the interest of the people, that the Republican party had been formed; and there was something strikingly akin to effrontery in this effort of an incorrigible political Bourbon to restore a dead party to life and to persuade a live one to commit suicide. Although Giddings could not fail to see that this speech was aimed at just such men as himself, he did not find time to notice it till early in November, when he addressed Mr. Ewing a public letter in reply. This letter is

not without a certain historic value as an exposition
of the Republican creed and a sign of Republican
progress, while it shows the skill of the writer in the
way of argument and retort. It also illustrates the
amazing diversity of opinion which prevailed among
those who united in the election of the first Republican President. It is as follows: —

SIR, — I have read your speech delivered at Chillicothe with
interest. That interest was excited from the circumstance that it
was made after you became satisfied that Mr. Lincoln would be
elected; the whole speech also showing it was not made to promote his election, but to guide his action and the action of his
Administration after he should come into power. I was also
aware that other gentlemen who have united with us, probably
for similar reasons, are endeavoring to bring influences to bear
upon the President-elect that would lead him to disregard the
doctrine on which he has been elected, in order to re-establish the
old Whig party, and be guided by the counsels of men who have
long since been weighed in the balance and found wanting. For
this purpose we are informed by the public Press that a member
of one of the past Executive Cabinets visited Mr. Lincoln before
he was elected, and then assured his friends at Washington that
the incoming Executive would enforce the Fugitive Slave Law,
which the people of the Free States hold in contempt. Republicans who have labored for ten, fifteen, or twenty years, — spent
their fortunes to establish the principles of that party, have given
existence, power, and energy to the organization that has elected
Mr. Lincoln, — quietly confide in the pledge he has given the
country to support the platform on which all have agreed to
stand. Those doctrines are clearly expressed and well understood, and it were an insult to ask him to violate them; no
honorable man will do it.

There is but one real issue between the Republican party and
those factions who stand opposed to it. That is the question of
slavery. There is really no other issue formed. The Republicans are pledged to exert the constitutional powers of government in favor of liberty against oppression and slavery *wherever
it holds exclusive jurisdiction;* and if they exert those powers to
sustain slavery or the slave-trade, at any time or in any place,
they will bring upon themselves the same displeasure of the
people that the Whig, the Democratic, and the Bell-Everett
parties have brought upon their organizations.

Now, sir, I do not doubt your patriotic intentions when you advise the incoming Administration to adopt the policy and follow the example of the Whig party; but I cannot forget the fact that you have assisted to inaugurate two Whig Administrations, you being a member of the Cabinet in each instance; that these Cabinets dissolved, and the party substantially disbanded, before the close of the first session of Congress that assembled under them. I cannot suppose these signal failures will very strongly commend your policy to Mr. Lincoln or to any Republican. Indeed, every intelligent man must be aware that subserviency to the slave-power, which you recommend, has destroyed all former factions; while manly resistance to that power, and steady adherence to the doctrines of the Declaration of Independence and of the Constitution, has given the Republicans influence, and control of the national government. If we fail to profit by example, if we disregard the lessons of history, if we remain stupid in spite of experience, our Republican organization must also fail at no distant day.

But, sir, I desire to correct you in regard to historical facts. You say, "The Republican party arose out of the repeal of the Missouri Compromise." If this assertion pass into history as true, it will place on Mr. Douglas responsibilities which you ought to share with him. The repeal of the Missouri Compromise was but an incident in the progress of the slave-power, which by a series of despotic acts extending through many years, gave rise to the Republican party, and doomed the other parties to premature graves. You and I certainly ought to understand the circumstances out of which the Republican party arose.

The winter of 1841 found Mr. Adams and myself struggling in the House of Representatives against gag-rules and in favor of the right of petition and the freedom of debate. We had labored for the election of Mr. Harrison, were zealous Whigs, expecting that the President-elect and his Cabinet, of which you were one, would lend their influence to maintain the constitutional right of petition and free debate. After due consultation, I prepared a speech upon the Florida War, by which I intended to expose the despotism of slavery and of the gag-rules. It was delivered on the 9th of February, A. D. 1841, about the time of the President's arrival, as well as yours, in the city of Washington. In that speech I shadowed forth the doctrine that Congress possessed no constitutional power to involve the people of the Free States in a war for the recovery of fugitive slaves; that our Federal Government had no authority to maintain or abolish slavery in the States. It excited much indignation with slaveholding members, one of whom publicly insulted me at the time.

He was soon appointed to a foreign mission, and at the end of four years retired with a fortune, although he had not even voted for General Harrison; while I, having labored zealously for that object, received from the Executive unmistakable evidence of his displeasure. And as you intimate what you think Mr. Lincoln's inaugural address will contain, you may perhaps recollect that General Harrison's inaugural, as it was originally prepared, contained a paragraph severely condemning those who in Congress were agitating the subject of slavery, and that this offensive paragraph was stricken out at the suggestion of Mr. Clay, to whom the address was submitted. I do not know that you were conversant with this fact; though I then supposed you were, and still presume you must have been consulted in regard to it. I speak upon the authority of one whose name shall be given you if desired. To Mr. Adams, more than to any other man, are we indebted for the reiteration of our Republican doctrines; but you and the country are aware that the practical application of those doctrines as the basis of political organization was put forth by the humble individual who now addresses you. It was the surrender of the Whig party to the slave-power during the Twenty-seventh Congress, and the efforts of a Whig President to involve our nation in the crime and disgrace of supporting an execrable commerce in human flesh, that induced me to present to the consideration of the House of Representatives a series of resolutions denying the authority of the Federal Government to involve our nation in a war to support the coastwise slave-trade. These resolutions embodied the essential doctrines on which the Republican party is now based. For thus expressing my own convictions, for this assertion of the rights of the Free States, I was arraigned, censured, and driven from my seat in the House of Representatives by a vote of 125 to 69, — that body having a Whig majority of twenty members, and acting under an Administration which you had assisted to inaugurate, and which you now hold up as an example worthy to be followed by Republicans. I believe the country will award to both you and myself the merit or demerit of adhering to our doctrines and policy. I continue to maintain the duty and policy of separating the Federal Government from the support of slavery, and leaving that institution entirely with the several States. On this point I stood entirely alone in that body for some years, Mr. Adams refusing to admit that the Federal Government might not, under some circumstances, abolish slavery in the States.

When you were again selected as a Cabinet officer for the purpose of inaugurating a second and last Whig Administration, you found me still in the House of Representatives, associated with seven as good and true men as ever served the cause of freedom. We were united upon the doctrines which now constitute the basis of the Republican party. You continued to maintain the Whig policy, under which that party disbanded and forever disappeared from the theatre of political power. I and my friends continued to maintain these doctrines; you retired to private life. The advocates of liberty increased in number and influence until, at Philadelphia in 1856, a convention of as high moral character as any that ever convened on this continent assembled. I penned the second resolution of that platform, which asserts the rights of all men to life, liberty, and happiness; that the primal object and ulterior design of our Federal Government was to protect all persons under its exclusive jurisdiction in the enjoyment of their rights. These fundamental principles were reasserted by the Chicago Convention. You say such insertion was in "bad taste." I deny your criticism. You say these doctrines are true "in a vague and general sense." I do not understand "vague" truths. Our fathers called those "self-evident" which you term "vague." You fear to admit, but dare not deny them. This timidity is not consistent with that indelicacy which prompts you, uninvited, to thrust your opinions upon a party to which you have ever been, and still are, opposed.

When you hold up to the Republicans the humbug of "dissolution," you detract from the dignity of your own manhood; none but cowards, none but unvirile minions of the slave-power, will be alarmed at it.

In assailing the Legislature and people of our State, you assume a self-importance, you evince an arrogance, seldom united with great moral worth. You censure Governor Dennison for adhering to a practice that has been followed by Executives of both Slave and Free States for more than thirty years; and in a note contained in a pamphlet edition of your speech you half apologize, saying the *heresy* had its origin *ten* years since, when *you* were engaged in official duties, and did not notice it. You next read a lecture to the people of our State for not electing a judge whose opinions *they* disliked, while *you* always approved them; and then condemn the Legislature of our State for not passing a law to protect slavery, by prohibiting the organizing of a military force in Ohio for the purpose of invading other States. No such organization has ever occurred in our State, nor have our people ever invaded any other State. But while our State has been often invaded by armed forces from other States, while innocent men have been barbarously shot down upon our soil, our citizens driven by armed force from other States, and free men, born under our laws, have been kidnapped and carried to slavery, you do not ask protection for them. But the electors of our State have responded to your attacks in language more emphatic than I can use.

You speak sneeringly of "irrepressible-conflict men," of "extreme opinions," of "Abolitionists," of "higher-law men." Epithets are not arguments. They are adapted to minds that revolve in a certain sphere of thought, but are seldom uttered by statesmen or philosophers. You, however, are understood as referring to men *who are your peers*, — to men whose statesmanship, whose integrity, will not suffer by a comparison with yours; to men who will not shrink from the judgment of the present or coming generation. I, sir, believe in that "higher law" of the Creator which holds the sun in mid-heavens, guides the planets in their courses, gives action to your throbbing heart and heaving lungs, which inspires you with a love of life, a thirst for happiness, a consciousness that *liberty is yours*, impresses you to acquire knowledge, and removes you to another sphere at the close of this life. You sneer at these doctrines; a cold atheism pervades your speech. In it there is no recognition of right, of enduring principle, of God, his attributes or laws. You evidently hold that human governments possess the same power to legislate for the murder of innocent men and women which they have to protect human life, — the same power to enslave men which they have to protect liberty. Republicans hold with the fathers that governments are instituted to secure the enjoyment of life and liberty; that the murder or enslavement of the humblest of the human family is not merely unjust, but *criminal;* that all enactments by Congress, authorizing or proposing to authorize one man to hold another in bondage, to flog him, rob him of his labor, his wife, his children, his intelligence, his manhood, are not only despotic, but barbarous, and in direct violation of that clause in our Federal Constitution which declares that "no person shall be deprived of life, liberty, or property without due process of law," — that is, without trial before a court of competent jurisdiction, by a jury of his peers.

For the establishment and maintenance of these views I have labored long and steadily. You have labored long and just as steadily to oppose them. We have lived to see an overwhelming expression of the American people in their favor. They have elected a President pledged to their support. *Will he redeem that pledge?* I believe he will. Time will solve the problem.

Very respectfully,
J. R. GIDDINGS.

JEFFERSON, O., Nov. 7, 1860.

Giddings now ventured upon a new task. Soon after his retirement, Senator Wilson of Massachusetts advised him to write a history of the anti-slavery conflict in Congress. He urged him to do this, as did other influential friends, on account of his peculiar qualifications for the work, and the demand for it as an important contribution to the history of the country. Giddings had thought of undertaking it before; and notwithstanding his age and declining health, he now entered upon the task, devoting such time to it as he could spare during the winter of 1860–1861. During this period, however, he closely watched the course of events in Washington, and strongly condemned the compromising policy of the Republican leaders near the close of the Thirty-sixth Congress.

In the spring Mr. Lincoln tendered him the position of Consul-General to Canada, which he accepted. This was not a laborious position, and it afforded him the leisure he desired for the prosecution of his History. He was now in a foreign country, but he did not forget his own, nor the great question which had so long occupied his thoughts. This will appear in the following letter, dated Montreal, April 2:

DEAR SUMNER, — I write for advice. Some two years since I wrote D. Appleton & Co. that Benton had grossly perverted facts touching the slave question in the "Abridgment of Congressional Debates," which they were publishing. In reply they assured me that the error should be avoided in their further volumes. I have just examined the four last volumes published, and never was there more gross injustice perpetrated in any standard work than has been done in this towards Mr. Adams and all those statesmen who from 1840 to 1850 maintained the doctrines of the Republican party.

Now, sir, what becomes your duty and mine in this matter? Are we bound to expose facts, to make them known to the world? I have written Messrs. Appleton, complaining of this garbling of the historic record, and giving examples. But what say you? Pray advise me.... Very sincerely, J. R. GIDDINGS.

To this Mr. Sumner replied on the 28th of April:

MY DEAR CONSUL-GENERAL, — On my return to Boston after a long detention in Washington, I found your favor of April 2d.

I have not examined the "Abridgment of Debates," but am not surprised at what you say. You will remember it was made in great haste, and I suppose it may be said with truth that Colonel Benton, with all his great merits, had no real sympathy with the anti-slavery cause, — certainly in those early struggles where you and Mr. Adams bore a conspicuous part.

But surely you are right in making your protest against the injustice done. To render this effective, there should be a proper statement, drawn up by yourself, the living witness of the truth, which the publishers ought to print and bind with the volumes in question.

From your distant retreat I doubt not that you watch the great events of to-day with intense interest. Only a short time ago it seemed as if there must be a separation; but this generous and mighty uprising of the North seems to menace defeat to the rebels, and the extinction of slavery in blood. How does it look to you?

I hope you are enjoying your new position; but I cannot reconcile myself to your not being at Washington. Good-by.
    Ever sincerely yours,
        CHARLES SUMNER.

Giddings answered thus on the 30th: —

DEAR SUMNER, — Thanks for your kind advice. I wrote a communication to the Appletons, stating the general injustice done to those who were early engaged in the anti-slavery cause, and then gave two of the most striking instances as examples, and was about to mail it when I began to entertain doubts, and concluded to write you for advice.

I have an intense anxiety now to be at Washington. Never was my desire to be there so strong as at this time. But you know I am always hopeful, and never were the political heavens more bright or auspicious. The first gun fired at Fort Sumter rang out the death-knell of slavery. But the promptness, the unity and zeal of the people of our Free States must excite the admiration of all nations; and should we come out of the contest without stain upon our honor, our government will in future be regarded as more permanent and efficient than ever before.

All honor to Massachusetts! She has borne herself worthy of her ancient fame. The 19th of April should be remembered and observed by her people as the day of her proudest achievement. . . .   With great respect,
        J. R. GIDDINGS.

These letters show that while Giddings was abroad, his heart was constantly at home. We read between the lines how intense must have been his longing to be among his fellow-citizens in the struggle that was then stirring the nation to its depths, and which was the outcome of the great conflict to which he had devoted his public life. There were probably moments when his life in Montreal seemed to him a cruel exile; but his prevailing hopefulness and philosophic temper reconciled him to the situation. The work of his office occupied a portion of his time, and during the remainder he continued his labors upon his History. The question of reciprocity with Canada was then an exciting one, and it naturally led to a correspondence with Mr. Sumner, then Chairman of the Committee on Foreign Relations in the Senate. On the 7th of April, 1862, Giddings wrote, —

DEAR SUMNER, — I notice there appears to be much hostility to our reciprocity treaty in the House of Representatives. I think it unfounded. Our former treaties with England admitted us to the British markets "upon the same terms as the most favored nations." The reciprocity gave to us and to the people of Canada mutual extension of our fishing privileges. It gave us the privilege of navigating the canals of Canada, the British of Lake Michigan, and then exempted certain articles named in the schedule from duty when taken from Canada to the United States, or from the States to Canada.

There was no attempt to change the duty on any goods; those made free were the only subjects of negotiation. But it is objected that the Canadian Government raised three or four times as much revenue from dutiable goods imported from the United States the year after this treaty went into operation, as they had previously done in the same length of time, — that is, we exported to Canada more goods on which duties were paid than ever before. But how the increase of our exports of dutiable goods should operate against the treaty is not so obvious. The treaty, however, could have had no other effect than that which naturally arose from more unrestricted commercial relations of the two Governments, and that must be certainly *favorable* to the treaty.

But an objection still more extraordinary, if possible, is raised against the treaty. It is said that by a proper construction the articles enumerated in this schedule are not only admitted to the States free of duty, but after they are in the United States cannot be subjected to direct taxation, tolls, or assessments, to which the same articles of American growth are subjected. How such a forced construction can be given to the treaty is incomprehensible to me. I have made inquiry of the members of the Board of Trade, of the president of that association, and of commercial men here, all of whom say they never heard nor thought of such a construction. The anthracite coal of Pennsylvania and the bituminous coal of Ohio are now used to some extent in Quebec, to a much greater extent here, and perhaps I may say, extensively in Canada West; but I cannot find that any man ever supposed that this coal was not subject to all local assessments, taxes, and license that Canadian productions are subjected to.

But, as we are informed, coal has been exempted from direct taxation in the States for the reason that the article imported from Halifax and New Brunswick cannot be taxed under the treaty; and if our own coal were taxed it would give foreign coal a preference in the market. This exemption of the coal from Pennsylvania and Ohio is not only wrong, but is most important. In my opinion a proper tax on that article would increase the revenue $50,000,000 annually. Flour, furs, and some other articles are said to be exempt from duty on the same grounds. I am sure you will look to the matter and see that no errors of the kind are committed by the Senate.

Thanks, a thousand thanks, for the abolition of slavery in the District of Columbia! Thanks also for sending the President's views in regard to emancipation in the States.

Very faithfully,

J. R. GIDDINGS.

Among his correspondence a characteristic letter was found from Horace Greeley, dated June 29, 1862, relating to the speech of Lord Palmerston in the British Parliament on General Butler's famous military order concerning the rebel women of New Orleans. This was one of the darkest periods of the war, and Mr. Greeley, as will be seen, shared with many others the most gloomy apprehensions: —

MY DEAR MR. GIDDINGS, — I wrote an *exposé* of Palmerston's malignity the very night we received the news of it, and published it next morning. The old scoundrel knows better, and it would be folly to waste explanation on him. But it is idle to hope for justice from the British governing classes. They are bent on our destruction, and imbecility and lack of earnestness here will enable them to attain their end. We are going to ruin. McClellan is certainly a fool, probably a traitor, and Halleck is no better. We are doomed.

Yours, sadly, HORACE GREELEY.

During this year the utterances of Mr. Seward touching the management of our foreign affairs were much criticised by the more radical members of the Republican party. On December 1, Giddings wrote to Sumner, —

"I am dissatisfied with Seward's view of the French mediation. Is it possible that he intends saving the institution of slavery? Pray let me know. The British Government and Press and people are rapidly coming round to our position, and our example in this important crisis is to have an immense influence on the nations of the earth.

"What does the political horoscope indicate to you?"

On July 26, 1863, Mr. Sumner wrote, —

MY DEAR GIDDINGS, — I am anxious about your health. Pray, how are you? Let me know by a word from yourself that you are well. You must live to see slavery die, — as die it will very soon. God bless you, who have done so much good work to prepare and guide our country!

Ever sincerely yours,
CHARLES SUMNER.

To this, Giddings replied on the 30th, —

MY DEAR SUMNER, — Thanks for your kind wishes! Be assured I am not unhappy. My regrets are that I am unable to do more in the cause on which the labors of my life have been bestowed.

My constitution is giving way under these repeated attacks of atrophy, two of which came upon me before leaving Congress. The fifth was on the 1st of June, at Montreal. It was the most severe. From it I shall not probably recover. For a while, both mental and physical powers were suspended. Slowly but gradually have I improved. My memory is yet imperfect, and you would think the decrepitude of age had suddenly befallen me, were you to see me. My physicians say the next will probably be final. I am sure it must disqualify me for usefulness, and am therefore not unwilling that the prophecy may prove true. Judging from the best data that I have, I think it probable that I may remain some months, possibly a year. But while I continue, my hopes, my anxious prayer, will be for the destruction of oppression and crime from our country and the world.

I flatter myself that the extensive enlistment of soldiers from the colored population is the *beginning of the end*. It will elevate the negro, teach him the value of freedom and the only mode of defending it; and my readings of the book of future events assure me that, as soon as the death of slavery shall take place, the nation's life will commence.

From the British Government we have nothing to hope, except a fear of war, which must prove disastrous to them. The feeling of hostility which existed among the aristocracy at the close of the Revolution has long been suppressed and silent, but to-day is the same, only more intensified. The anti-slavery and laboring portion of the British people are very decidedly with us; and if our diplomatic relations be properly managed, Great Britain will never again be involved in a war with the United States.

On looking over the whole field I am to-day as confident and hopeful as at any former time. I fully believe our nation will come out of this conflict the freest and purest government of earth. In life and in death,

Your friend, JOSHUA R. GIDDINGS.

Although Giddings was now fully conscious of his failing faculties, and though his physician told him that the next attack of atrophy would be the last, he maintained his usual cheerfulness, as is shown in the following extract from a letter to his wife of the 31st of May: —

"You and the family and friends should prepare your minds for the separation which must come, and you should not be surprised to hear that I have taken my departure at any time. It is a matter of gratitude that I have lived so long, that I have enjoyed life so much, that the future looks so pleasant, that my hopes are so buoyant. Let me say that so far as I am myself concerned, I would not even ask delay. I live not for myself, conscious that the sooner I depart, the sooner shall I leave the infirmities which now beset me, the sooner shall I be free from the evils which surround me, the sooner shall I meet with dear friends from whom I have long been separated."

On the 15th of September he wrote from Jefferson:

DEAR SUMNER, — I have just received your lecture at Cooper Institute. That production excites in my heart the deepest gratitude and the highest pleasure. When John Quincy Adams, our venerated friend, lay upon what he supposed his death-bed, — or, to use his own expressive language, when he was "on the verge of eternity," — I was sitting by him. His mind was absorbed in the subject of reforming the government, when, looking me full in the face, he said, " I have more hope from you than from any other man."

Feeling myself unworthy of the high compliment, I have never repeated the language till now, for the *first* and the *last* time. I say, " I have more hope from you than from any other man." With the highest respect,

Your friend,   JOSHUA R. GIDDINGS.

On October 9 following he wrote, —

MY DEAR SUMNER, — I am anxious to see whether Earl Russell has attempted to *answer* your argument, or merely to avoid an answer by declamation. I judge that he has taken the same line of defence that his supporters have done, — that they did all they could under their " Foreign Enlistment Act," — a matter of which we know nothing and care less. But I have never been able to make a real Englishman understand that we were not bound by their enlistment law. They cannot comprehend that we are only authorized to judge the nation and Government by its acts, or that a ship leaving an English port must be regarded as an English ship until registered under some other Government; that the " Alabama," having sailed from an English port, where she was built, is regarded as English until she enters some port of some other Government, and by sale is transferred and registered under such Government, thereby becoming identified with such other nation. But I am anxious to see the correspondence between Mr. Adams and Lord John.

I am glad to assure you that events are fast tending to the separation of these provinces from the mother-country. I have never been in favor of the annexation of the Canadas, but as a philanthropist I have long entertained the opinion that the independence of these provinces would serve to develop their own statesmen and promote the happiness of the people both of the mother-country and of the provinces. The change of opinion here has been most marked during the last six months. I intend placing a pamphlet copy of your Cooper Institute speech in the hands of the principal members of the Canadian Parliament.

Ever truly your friend,   JOSHUA R. GIDDINGS.

In addition to his regular consular duties, Giddings also devoted a portion of each day to the completion of his book, which he entitled a "History of the Rebellion: its Authors and Causes." He was most anxious to live long enough to finish it. In reference to this book he had written to his daughter Laura early in the year, —

"My mission has been performed; and when I shall have placed the story on paper and can see it in print, I shall feel that my work has been accomplished. I therefore devote my time and energies to that object, and intend to continue until it is finished. I shall then leave my vindication to posterity, though I think I have already been vindicated pretty well."

On the 15th of May, 1864, he was able to write to his wife: "I have employed a clerk. I think it best for my health to be rather indolent, and take the world easy. Since finishing my book I am quite a man of leisure." The book was then in the hands of his publishers, and it fortunately happened that the proof-sheets reached him on the day of his death, so that he was able to give them a hasty examination. It is mainly devoted to the Congressional debates on the slavery question and an exposition of the action of the Government relative thereto. It is not so much a history as a contribution to history, and as such it will be found valuable. Its compilation was a work of much labor and detail, and it is to be regretted that owing to his failing memory and the lack of a careful revision, occasional inaccuracies are to be found in the matter of dates and names. The work is in the public libraries of the country.

Our Reciprocity Treaty with Canada continued to be an exciting topic during the progress of the Civil War. Giddings recurred to it in a letter to Sumner, dated February 8, while on a visit to his home: —

MY DEAR SENATOR, — While in Washington I was told that the Colonial Secretary had transmitted to the Treasury Department certain statistics (not yet published) touching the Reciprocity Treaty. Of these statistics I cannot of course judge, not having seen them; but I shall not make my report on the subject until I can obtain the proper statistics.

But there are prominent facts, of which you and I are conscious. For instance, *coal* must constitute a large item of export to the Canadas. Most of this coal is of the anthracite kind, which gives out no smoke by which a steamer can be discovered at a great distance. Large quantities of this coal, on reaching Montreal or Quebec, are shipped to Nassau, and then sold to blockade-runners, to enable them to enter rebel ports with arms, ammunition, and clothing for the use of the rebels. One house in the city of Montreal furnished *four hundred tons* of this coal to a steamer bound to Nassau in September last, while she carried bituminous coal for her own use. This is but one case; yet I doubt not that the people of the United States were injured by this one cargo of coal more than they have been benefited by the whole of our Canadian commerce for the last year.

Another item. *Wheat* must form one of the principal articles of export. This is furnished by Ohio, Michigan, Indiana, Illinois, and Wisconsin, and is to some extent beneficial to those States. But the wheat is manufactured into flour mostly in Canada, while our own millers might as well enjoy the benefits of that process; and it is transported to Europe in British bottoms, while our own shipowners ought to have the benefit of transportation, — and this is done while the British pirates are driving our commerce from the ocean. Thus is almost the whole of our Canadian commerce benefiting our enemies and actually injuring ourselves. Very truly,

JOSHUA R. GIDDINGS.

His interest in the question of reciprocity seems never to have been intermitted. He resumed its discussion in the following letter, dated Montreal, April 5, in which the subject of annexation is also referred to: —

DEAR SUMNER, — The Canadas have no minister to represent them at Washington. Lord Lyons does not and cannot know their wants. If he did, he would be bound to act against them.

On reaching this city I at once found myself under more interesting circumstances than I expected. The feeling in favor of continuing the Reciprocity Treaty is far more intense than I expected. The new Ministry expects to retain power by continuing or renewing it. They are from the high Tory party, and are most bitter opponents, but are ready to bow low enough to obtain their objects.

I presume that you fully appreciate the object which as philanthropists and statesmen we have in view. Indeed, there would be the same propriety in a son's adhering to his father for counsel and direction at the age of forty that there is in Canada's looking to Great Britain for a governor and for advice. They are now constrained to look to us for favors. They are conscious of this fact, but have no idea that the more dependent they are on us, the sooner they must separate from England. But this I may not say to them. I therefore think we should cherish every measure which identifies their prosperity with ours. . . . That policy (annexation) is now openly talked of by business men, who declare they must have the *favor* of the *United States*, even if it be obtained by annexation. Such remarks two years ago would have been regarded as *treasonable*. But to-day if an end were put to the Reciprocity Treaty the whole business population of Canada here and west of this city would vote for annexation. I speak from what I see and hear and learn from others; but it were safe to say that such is the tendency of the business population. And we are now thrown into the position that in doing good to the people of Canada we are constrained to assume a position of *firmness*, and an apparent determination to deal out to them retributive justice.

I entertain no doubt as to the *ability* of your report on the Reciprocity Treaty; but I know you will excuse me for saying that I greatly desire that in it you will not be too delicately inclined. There are no statesmen in Canada, and never will be under her present position. They think the thoughts of England, and when Earl Russell takes snuff, they sneeze. I hope you will in your report presume that the provinces will *seek their best interest*, develop their own resources, protect their own labor, and elevate their own people. For they now live, move, and have their being for the benefit of Her Majesty and her minister. But I think it also prudent to say that Canada can and must do this for herself, without relying on the *United States* or *any other power*. This is one of the difficulties which we have to meet. They have an idea that we want them to be annexed to the United States. *I* do not think that best for them or for us. *Independence of thought, of action, of policy*, is the first step which I wish to see Canada take. I believe it better for them, for England, for us, that Canada should *govern herself*. I speak very freely to you, for it seems necessary that Canada should act on this subject, —

and indeed the Executive cannot act upon it, except secretly. I shall, however, communicate unofficially to the Department of State more fully. Very truly,

J. R. GIDDINGS.

During the spring of this year the letters of Mr. Giddings to different members of his family and to personal friends all breathe the most kindly and cheerful spirit, but they indicate the gradual weakening of his powers and the near approach of the end. On the 22d of May he wrote to his son:

"I find that I no longer possess that firmness and determination of purpose which once characterized my action. I am also well aware that when I give up business I shall die soon; yet I cannot find energy enough to withstand these infirmities. I write to say that you had better make your calculations to come here at a moment's notice and close up business. I hope I may continue here for the present quarter, but it is not certain that I shall remain a week. Indeed, if I continue in as much pain as I now suffer, I shall leave in less than a week."

His physician, Dr. Ross, became alarmed about him on May 21. Said he, —

"On that day Mr. Giddings sent for me about eight in the evening, and told me he felt that the end was rapidly approaching, and that he had written several letters, which he wished me to keep in my possession until his death, and that he was convinced it was close at hand. I did all I could to encourage him and rally him from his despondency. I left him about twelve, in seemingly better spirits. On Sunday and Monday he appeared to improve under the treatment I prescribed for him. On Wednesday he began to write an essay on private claims (at the urgent request of the Secretary of the Treasury) to the Hon. Mr. Washburne, of the House of Congress. After he had finished he wished me to read it to him; and what struck me very forcibly was that in several places he remarked that he felt convinced that his death was close at hand. He seemed to be fully impressed with the fact of his near departure. He often said to me that he had not the least fear of death, and was prepared for the change when it should come. He said he wished to die in harness, like his old friend John Quincy Adams."

On the evening of Friday, the 27th, he joined some friends at a game of billiards. This was his favorite mode of exercise, and, indeed, the only available one, in view of his growing infirmities and heavy frame. He had played one game, and while engaged in another, in good spirits, he was suddenly prostrated by another attack of heart trouble, and died in about eight minutes, at a little after ten o'clock. His elder daughter was with him, and arrangements were at once made for taking his remains to Jefferson. The newspapers of Montreal, in noticing the event, eulogized the character of Mr. Giddings and sketched his public career. A meeting of the most respectable and influential citizens of Montreal was held in Mechanics' Hall, presided over by the Mayor of the city, at which appropriate resolutions were adopted, expressive of their respect for the memory of Mr. Giddings, and tendering to his family their sincere sympathy. Similar resolutions were adopted by the New England Society of Montreal, while the Press of the Northern States, with remarkable unanimity, gave eloquent expression to the gratitude and love of the people for the veteran anti-slavery leader and champion of free speech in Congress.

His remains reached Ashtabula on Sunday afternoon, the 29th of May, where a large concourse of people were in waiting. A procession was formed, and proceeded to Jefferson the same evening. The funeral was on Monday, at one o'clock, when a brief discourse was delivered by the Rev. Mr. Conklin, of the Congregational Church; but owing to the unexpected detention of his daughter Laura and her husband on their journey from Washington, the burial did not occur till seven o'clock in the evening, just as the sun was sinking in the west.

CHAPTER XIII.

CHARACTERISTICS.

Personal Traits. — Devotion to Family. — Friendships. — Fondness for Athletic Sports. — Religious Principles. — Political Foresight. — Moral Earnestness. — Practical Qualities as a Reformer. — His Place in History.

THE story of the public life of Mr. Giddings, which I have endeavored to tell in the foregoing chapters, has afforded some glimpses of his private life and personal traits. These, however, demand a more particular notice in concluding my task.

The strong language so frequently found in his anti-slavery speeches led many to regard him as harsh and turbulent in his temper. This was a total misconception of his character. It was contradicted by the tones of his voice and the benignity of his face. His nature was singularly tender. His denunciations of slavery were severe, because his sense of justice was keen and his hatred of every form of oppression intense; but he was wholly free from malignity, and above the meanness of hating his fellow-men. The struggles and conflicts which generally impart a certain sadness and sternness to the character could not sour his temper or cloud the sunshine of his inborn kindliness. He was remarkable for the uniform buoyancy of his spirits, and his mind continued young in his old age. His cheerfulness was perennial. During the last months of his life, when his physician told him that the end was probable at any moment, he looked death in the face with serenity, and steadily prosecuted his daily task. His constitutional hopefulness has been referred to in previous chapters. It reinforced the courage and strength he needed in the great work of his life. His faith in the omnipotence of justice was absolute. He never despaired for a moment, even in the darkest days of the anti-slavery struggle, when others faltered or fell. He believed in God, and was filled with the enthusiasm of humanity.

His love of home was a passion, and his devotion to his family perfect. The burdens and cares of his public life were constantly aggravated by the necessity which compelled him to live apart from the household of his love. This is abundantly revealed in his correspondence with his family. In a letter to his wife in 1856 he says, —

"I want to be at home. I want to cheer you and the children, to make you all happy, and render the pathway of life pleasant and beautiful, so that in future we may not only meet the loved ones who have gone before us, but that we may all there constitute a family *circle*, where parting and gloom shall be no more."

His letters to different members of his family breathe the same spirit. They show a loneliness and longing for home which bordered on heart-sickness. In his correspondence with his younger children and his grandchildren, he took time from his other duties to print the letters in Roman text, in order that they might read them. The most trifling matters connected with the family interested him, not excepting his favorite Newfoundland dog, Rover, that had been taught to carry groceries and the mail for the family. In his letters from Canada he frequently inquired about the dog and his deportment, and was kept duly informed in regard to him. When he was at home Rover always went with him to the village church, and sometimes added his dissonant howl to the music of the organ, — for which he was promptly but quietly reproved.

Giddings was deeply interested in the political training of his boys, and in 1844, when the country was agitated by the question of the annexation of Texas, he wrote to one of them, —

"Let me beseech you not to play the craven. Although you are a boy, if you are ever at another public meeting where no one dares to speak of liberty and in contempt of slavery, speak yourself, with firmness, and with perfect sincerity and calmness."

He kept his family well informed of his part in the debates of the House, and found evident pleasure in reporting his successes, but was always careful to guard them against any apprehension of trouble on his account. When he had his encounter with Black of Georgia in 1845, he promptly wrote his son a detailed account of it, concluding, —

"Now, I suppose there will be all sorts of stories, as usual, and perhaps your mother may be alarmed; but you can assure her that I view the matter coolly, and that there is, in fact, no danger whatever. Do not let her know anything of it, unless it reaches her by the papers."

Nearly allied to the qualities I have named were his friendships. Nothing could have been more honorable to him than his relations to Adams and Sumner. His love for them was as perfect as ever existed between men, and it was fully reciprocated. His friendship for Hon. John A. Bingham of Ohio was equally admirable. They served together in Congress for years, and usually occupied the same quarters. Bingham was a most genial companion, a fascinating speaker, a lover of poetry, and an extensive reader of books. The tones of his voice, which were winning, became musical when he addressed "Father Giddings." He loved him as devotedly as any son could love his own father; and no one could witness the amenities of their intercourse without thinking better of his kind.

Giddings was remarkably fond of athletic sports, his favorite game being base-ball; and nothing but physical inability led him to discontinue it. The summer adjournment of Congress was always the signal at Jefferson for the opening of the base-ball season, and the ground was generally ready by the time he reached home. The first afternoon was sure to open the season. The game was then played with a soft ball, which was thrown at the player while on the run. Being left-handed, Giddings usually took the boys at a disadvantage, as they could not calculate upon his motions, and the ball often came where it was not looked for. He used to play with perfect abandon, and it was hard to tell which was the most boyish, he or those with whom he played, who generally ranged from fifteen to twenty-five, "without distinction as to race, color, or previous condition of servitude." When the game was over, he was the representative of his district till the next afternoon, when the Congressman again gave way to one of the nine. The habits of Mr. Giddings were almost Arcadian in this relation. He was also a great shot, and when there was game in the country, was no ordinary hunter. He was very fond of music. He purchased the first piano that came to Jefferson, and frequently joined his family in singing favorite selections.

Giddings had his religious training in the school of New England Congregationalism. For more than forty years he was a member of the Congregational Church; but as his zeal in the cause of freedom increased, and the indifference or hostility of nearly all religous denominations to the anti-slavery movement became more and more pronounced, his views respecting creeds and sectarian agencies were modified. He was not less religious, but his faith in ecclesiastical machinery was seriously impaired. In a letter to the "Anti-slavery Standard," published in 1857, he thus presents his views: —

"The Reformers struck at some of the prominent errors of the Church both in faith and practice, but they advanced no *fundamental* truths on which all men claiming Christianity must agree. The Reformers themselves held to the divine right of kings to bear civil rule over their fellow-men, to establish privileges for one class and impose heavy burdens on others; that the Church held the same rule over the conscience and the faith of mankind. They were intolerant, persecuted those who disagreed with them. Calvin himself advised, nay, caused, the burning of Servetus for uttering the honest sentiments of his own heart. No one then dared avow the right of all men to think for themselves, to decide upon their own form of faith, to proclaim the equal rights of all men to civil, religious, and spiritual freedom. Luther's ninety-five propositions were aimed at the sale of indulgences under the papal rule. Those propositions are of little interest to the present age. Calvin's five points of theology are far less interesting to the present generation than are the practical duties of *doing unto others as we would have them do unto us.* The Reformers of that age sought to control the thoughts, to guide the faith, of mankind by metaphysical theories and abstract dogmas but little understood by the people or divines. Hence the great number of sects of the present age, each holding to some doctrine, some article of faith, which distinguishes it from others. Yet all reflecting Christians now hold that the great object of human existence is the instruction, the elevation, the unfolding of each and every moral being, preparing him or her for usefulness here and for enjoyment here and hereafter, in just such degree as the moral faculties are developed."

After stating his well-known views respecting the equal rights of all men as derived from their Creator and the duty of the Government to protect them, he says, —

"I think the time has arrived when some modern Luther or Calvin should erect the standard of a higher, a purer theology, — a theology in harmony with the laws of justice, of God; a theology in harmony with the teachings of the gospel; a theology approved by the philosophy, the judgment, of enlightened men; a theology that acknowledges and proclaims the primal truths that life, that civil, religious, and spiritual freedom are the *gifts of God;* that every member of the human family has received from the Creator an equal and inalienable right to enjoy them; that such enjoyment is necessary to develop the intellect, elevate the soul, and prepare the individual for usefulness, for happiness here and hereafter; that every attempt to limit the sphere of human thought, or to hold the mind or the body of one man in subjection to the views or the will of another, or to prevent the enlargement of the immortal mind, or the full and perfect development of any human soul, constitutes a crime with which, by the laws of Nature and of Nature's God, the appropriate penalty is inseparably connected, while every act in harmony with those laws necessarily elevates the individual and prepares him for higher attainments.

"For the protection of these rights and the encouragement of these duties all governments and associations should be adapted. Of all the nations of the earth ours is the most favorably situated for carrying forward this great reformation. Our government was founded upon these truths, and most of our people believe them. The reformation has commenced, is in rapid progress. In all parts of the country men are awaking to the necessity of a more practical theology. The open and undisguised infidelity recently avowed in the Presbyterian General Assembly, that 'there is no such thing as eternal right and wrong,' has awakened the most thoughtless. Men see that mere theories, bald forms of sectarian faith, are impotent and useless. Our old organizations are becoming inert, inefficient, worn out. Men long to lay them aside, to disconnect themselves from these theoretical technicalities, which retard the union of hearts upon those great and vital truths which elevate mankind. Many of our ministers have caught the inspiration of these truths. They are giving utterance to the solemn convictions of their own judgment, unfettered by sectarian prejudices. The sea of human thought, which has remained quiet for a hundred and fifty years, is troubled. Its waters, nearly stagnant from long repose, are now ploughed by many keels. Discussion is stirring its deep foundations. The billows of agitation are rolling, and I trust the storm will continue until false theories and infidelity, the love of oppression, of tyranny, violence, polygamy, and slavery, shall be overwhelmed, and their broken wrecks cast upon the sterile coast of political and religious conservatism."

These extracts not only show the theological change of front of Mr. Giddings, as the result of his labors for the slave, but the general trend of thought among intelligent anti-slavery men. William Lloyd Garrison, Gerrit Smith, Beriah Green, and other anti-slavery leaders turned away from the Puritan doctrines in which they had been bred, when they found them proclaimed by churches and hierarchies which took the side of the oppressor. They were theologically reconstructed through their unselfish devotion to humanity and the recreancy of the churches to which they had been attached. They were less Orthodox, but more Christian. Their faith in the fatherhood of God and the brotherhood of man became a living principle, and compelled them to reject all dogmas which stood in its way. The venerable Dr. Furness, of Philadelphia, is credited with saying that the anti-slavery struggle in this country taught him more about the essential nature of the Gospel than he had learned in any other way. "It was felt to be something more than the attempt to apply the beatitudes and parables to a flagrant case of inhumanity,— it was regarded as a new interpretation of religion, a fresh declaration of the meaning of the Gospel, a living sign of the purely human character of a divine faith, an education in brotherly love and sacrifice."[1] It solemnized the marriage of ethics and religion, which thus became one.

In a letter to his wife, dated March 14, 1856, Mr. Giddings touchingly reveals the triumph of his humanity over the creed of his church:—

[1] Frothingham's Recollections and Impressions, p. 49.

"I am alone in my room. Bingham has gone home. I feel lonely. The House has adjourned over to Monday. I have labored hard, and almost brought up my correspondence. In my easy-chair I have thought back to the days of our youth, our early acquaintance, our more solemn association, our parents; the time when, in the innocence of youth and the ignorance of that day, we attended church and listened to sermons that uttered now would cause any hearer to recoil from them. What an age, and what a people! Yet all were sincere and honest; but oh, what thoughts of God, of heaven, of the relation between us and the Creator of the universe! Ah, pains and bitter regrets attended every thought of death, which now appears so comely and beautiful. What terrible thoughts of the danger of eternal fires! Who can paint the emotions I felt when I wept at the grave of a beloved sister, who was mild and lovely and virtuous and beautiful? What ideas then passed through my mind!"

These words voice the experience of many an earnest man and woman. In laboring for the emancipation of the slave, Giddings emancipated himself from the bondage of sectarian theology, and realized that Christianity does not consist in creeds or forms, but in uprightness of life and devotion to human welfare.

Giddings was gifted with unusual political foresight. He was a close student of facts, and knew how to penetrate their meaning. In dealing with the tactics of the slave-masters the truth of this statement was frequently illustrated. He mastered the philosophy of their movements. In a speech in the House of Representatives on July 14, 1846, he said, —

"We have seen the leading policy of the nation changed as often as the views of Southern men have altered. At the bidding of the slave-power we have fostered banks, and at the dictation of the same influence we have discarded and opposed them. When bidden by the potent voice of the South, we have imposed heavy duties upon imported manufactures in order to encourage domestic labor; and then again, under the same guidance, has our policy been changed so as to approximate free-trade. In short, sir, for fifty years we have constantly shifted our sails upon the ship of state in order to catch the changing Southern breeze."

It was in the light of these facts that he made his notable speech on the Oregon question. In referring to President Polk and his Cabinet, he said, —

"With the same degree of confidence that I have in my own existence, I declare that they will, before the nation and the world, back out from their avowed policy, and will surrender up all that portion of Oregon north of the forty-ninth parallel of latitude."

For this utterance he was ridiculed by some and denounced by others; but he was right. He knew that a war with England would threaten the life of slavery, and that the Democratic party would be compelled by the South to retreat from its position.

Again, on May 21, 1844, he warned the country that the annexation of Texas would result in the repeal of the tariff of 1842. He told the Democrats of Pennsylvania, who were deluded into the support of Polk, that "our tariff would be held at the will of Texan advocates of free trade." This statement was verified on July 2, 1846, when the tariff of 1842 was repealed by a vote of one majority in the Senate, both the Senators from Texas voting in the affirmative. Giddings claimed no gift of prophecy, but reasoned from the fact that slavery ruled the government, and would take counsel only of its own interest.

His foresight was also shown in his judgment of Winthrop, in December, 1847. In that judgment, as we have seen, he stood almost alone, and by it he invoked the relentless hostility of the party with which he had acted up to that time; but his forecast of Winthrop's action and his estimate of the latter's character were perfectly justified by facts. He took the true measure of the man, and saw clearly that while his party trusted him, Winthrop was not strong enough to face the emergency in which he was placed.

Still another illustration may be cited. In a speech in the House of Representatives nine years before Lincoln issued his Proclamation of Emancipation, Giddings uttered words which now seem prophetic. The champions of slavery then desired a war with Spain for the acquisition of Cuba and the more complete ascendency of their power over the government. Giddings reminded them that in such a struggle the enemy would strike at our weakest point, and might "bring the war into this American Africa, and rear the standard of freedom on our own soil." He warned them that in such a contest the war power of the government could interpose for the liberation of every slave in the Union. Said he, —

"When that contest shall come; when the thunder shall roll and the lightnings flash; when the slaves of the South shall rise in the spirit of freedom, actuated by the soul-stirring emotion that they are *men*, destined to immortality, entitled to the rights which God bestowed upon them; when the masters shall turn pale and tremble; when their dwellings shall smoke, and dismay sit on each countenance, — then, sir, I do not say we shall laugh at your calamity and mock when your fear cometh, but I do say, *the lovers of our race will then stand forth and exert the legitimate powers of this government of freedom. We shall then have constitutional power to act for the good of our country*, and *to do justice to the slave*. WE WILL THEN STRIKE OFF THE SHACKLES FROM HIS LIMBS. The Government will then have power to *act between slavery and freedom; and it can best make peace by giving liberty to the slaves*. And let me tell you, Mr. Speaker, *that time hastens;* the President is exerting a power that will hurry it on; and I shall hail it as the approaching dawn of that millennium which I know must come upon the earth."

These illustrations could readily be multiplied, and they show how his devotion to a great cause anointed his vision and made him a discerner of the signs of the times.

But the dominating fact in the life of Giddings was his moral earnestness. He was by no means wanting in other qualities which his anti-slavery leadership demanded. He had an abundance of pluck, pertinacity, and courage. He had readiness, prudence, vigilance, and self-possession. He had audacity when the occasion demanded it, and contempt for base personal assaults. But his earnestness was the master-key to his character, and the real source of his power. It inspired and invigorated all his faculties. The people saw that he had dedicated his life to the service of the truth, and therefore they trusted and followed him. They saw that he possessed the absolute courage of his convictions. He could say with Sumner, "The slave of principles, I call no party master," and he illustrated this by his solitary vote against a resolution of thanks to General Taylor for his services in the Mexican War. He defied all menaces, and spurned all suggestions of compromise. He faced political and social ostracism and personal violence without flinching. When Slade of Vermont and Gates of New York left Congress, and Adams was bending under the weight of years and infirmities, Giddings was obliged to bear the brunt of the unequal struggle, and he did it with an undaunted spirit. Whether standing alone or supported by allies, he never wearied in his warfare against slavery, nor lost an opportunity to smite it. When others faltered he pressed forward. He had a genius for persistency, and never relaxed his purpose to keep the great conflict at the front, whether it related to the horrors of the Florida War, the suppression of the freedom of debate, the demand of payment for slaves, the support of the internal slave-trade, the abolition of the traffic in the District of Columbia, or conspiracies for the extension of slavery. All obstacles yielded to his rare singleness of purpose. This was the secret of his power, and it entitles him to the foremost place in history among all the famous leaders of the anti-slavery cause in Congress.

The lesson of such a life is invaluable. He was wholly wanting in genius. He was deficient in imagination and the graces of rhetoric. There are passages in his speeches which rise to the height of eloquence, but as a rule they are merely the compact statements of a man of strong convictions and common-sense, whose ruling purpose was to impress others with his opinions, and whose profound earnestness made him indifferent to literary art. He was always bravely himself. He was well aware that his whole life had been handicapped by the trials and privations of his earlier years, while his native diffidence and love of peace would have lured him into the walks of private life; but his warfare with slavery was the travail of his soul, and he prosecuted it with unfaltering faith and unquenchable zeal. He could not do otherwise. It was sufficient for him that his conscience commanded him, and he succeeded by the strength of a great moral purpose which found an answering throb in the hearts of the people, and at last made him their prophet.

But the zeal of Giddings in the anti-slavery conflict was not without knowledge. No man was more clear-sighted respecting methods of action. He was eminently practical. His desire to serve the cause made him all the more anxious to find the most direct and effective way of doing it. When he first entered Congress he devoted himself to the mastery of the parliamentary manual. He knew the inestimable value of this knowledge, and how potent it had been in the practised hands of Southern members in securing the advantage over representatives from the Free States, who were generally retained in their places for a brief term only, and succeeded by men equally inexperienced. His continuance in Congress constantly added to his parliamentary resources, while no man in either House was so thoroughly equipped on the question of slavery. These were great advantages. They gave him confidence in himself, and commanded the respect of his fellow-members. In debating his favorite question he was perfectly at home, and was never disconcerted by questions. He invited them, and nothing pleased him better than the attempts of Southern members to badger him. They were always the losers in these encounters, as the Congressional Records will show; and this gradually led them to decline such ventures, and sometimes, as we have seen, to play the blackguard and the bully. The power of such a leader, resolutely exerted through many years, and combining perfect devotion to his cause with great ability to defend it, cannot be computed.

Giddings was not less practical and sensible in dealing with the relations of slavery to the Federal Government. He was not diverted from his work by any far-fetched constitutional theory, or any political vagaries, but always took counsel of his common-sense. In the matters of taxation, representation, and the return of fugitive slaves, the Federal Constitution involved the people of the Free States in the guilt of upholding slavery. Giddings made no denial of this, and admitted that the obvious remedy for it was an amendment of the Constitution; but this was wholly unattainable, as shown by Mr. Adams and himself in their masterly report on the subject in 1844. Equally futile was the hope of meeting the difficulty by the remedy of disunion. The people loved the Union more than they hated slavery, and could not be rallied under any revolutionary banner; moreover, the dissolution of the Union would leave the slave in his chains. The power of slavery had to be wrestled with by some other method, while the people of the Free States could only escape their complicity with the evil by leaving the country. Giddings did not feel called upon to do this, but believed it to be the duty of all good citizens to lay hold of such powers as they possessed in reforming the administration of the government. He therefore favored a plan of operations under the Constitution, and in strict conformity with its provisions.

When he entered Congress, in 1838, the people of the South, with great unanimity, avowed the principle that slavery was a State institution, with which the Federal Government had no rightful authority to intermeddle either to support or abolish it. As shown in a previous chapter, he proposed to hold the South to the logical consequences of this position. If slavery borrowed its life from State law, and could only exist within State boundaries, its existence in the District of Columbia was national slavery, and therefore forbidden by the Constitution; for Maryland and Virginia had relinquished their rights in the territory comprising this district by ceding it to the General Government. The same principle applied to the Act of Congress authorizing and regulating the coastwise slave-trade in vessels sailing under the national flag. It was legislation for the support of slavery, and therefore unwarranted by the Constitution. So all compensation for the loss of slaves captured by the enemy in a foreign war, or made free by landing on British soil, was likewise forbidden. The spread of slavery over our national Territories and the admission of new slaveholding States were of course unconstitutional, as finally declared in the resolution drafted by Giddings and incorporated into the Republican platform of 1856. In other words, while all the compromises of the Constitution were to be faithfully observed, the Federal Government, in all other respects, was bound to see to it that no man outside of the Slave States, and under its exclusive jurisdiction, should be deprived of life, liberty, or property without due process of law. Slavery was to have its pound of flesh, but not one drop of blood.

Such was the fundamental principle which was to be the starting point of organized political action against slavery, and the measure of its scope; and "to Giddings," says Von Holst, "more than to any other person belongs the credit of having, with full consciousness, made it the constitutional basis of his entire warfare against the slaveocracy, and of having applied it with a consistency never before attained to all questions to which it was pertinent." On this principle the Free-Soil party of 1848 planted itself, as did the Republican party eight years afterwards. On the lines indicated by this principle the political battle with slavery was to be fought, and Giddings foresaw the victory of the Free States, and that it would be final and decisive. He saw clearly that slavery could only maintain its ascendency and prolong its life by usurpation, as it had done in the past; and that without infringing any of its constitutional rights, and by strictly constitutional methods, this usurpation could be arrested and the curse driven into the last ditch. Time has amply vindicated his sagacity; and if any man can justly be singled out as the father of the Republican party, it is he. If his anti-slavery policy had been espoused by the people of the Northern States in season, the peaceful abolition of slavery would have been possible; and to him must be accorded the honor of having prosecuted this policy with such unflinching pertinacity and tireless zeal that the contagion of his example brought the people to his support before the absolute supremacy of slavery had been established on the ruins of the Constitution.

The great moral leaders of the anti-slavery struggle did their work outside of politics. They played their grand part in creating an anti-slavery public opinion, and to this extent they reinforced the work of legislation. But this was not enough. An anti-slavery public opinion could not execute itself. It needed some available method of action; and the lack of this was the great stumbling-block in the way of anti-slavery effort. The old question, "What has the North to *do* with slavery?" had to be answered; and the answer of Giddings inevitably made the conflict a political one. In the very nature of things it had to be fought out in Congress. It was here, indeed, that the work of moral agitation itself was largely carried on. "One good Congressman," said James G. Birney, "can do more for the cause than a hundred lecturers. He has almost daily occasion for agitation, and he speaks to the whole people. We can reach the South through no other means. The slaveholders gain their advantages in national politics and legislation, and should be met in every movement they make."

It was absolutely necessary thus to meet them. It was in Congress that the project was conceived and finally matured of transforming the government into a slave-owning and slave-trading oligarchy. It was here that cowardly and compromising statesmen of the Free States, during a period of more than forty years, surrendered the rights of free men at the bidding of their Southern overseers. It was here that Giddings and his faithful allies sounded the cry of danger in the ears of the nation, and made the Congressional debates the vehicle of anti-slavery truth in every section of the Union, and the seed-plot of a constantly growing anti-slavery opinion. And it was here that the slave-masters were at last overborne. It is true that anti-slavery action in Congress was half-hearted, reluctant, and compromising. No man saw this more clearly than Giddings, or labored more valiantly or effectively to inspire it with courage. It is also true that slavery perished by the madness of its champions in attempting to save its life by the destruction of the Union; but this madness was itself provoked by the victory of the Free States on the issue of "Freedom national, slavery sectional," which rang the knell of its ascendency and foreshadowed its doom. If political action was to be condemned on the score of its tardiness and inefficiency, the moral warfare against slavery could be assailed on the same ground. This victory was won in spite of the halting and reactionary element in the Republican party, and by it freedom made a very narrow escape; for if slavery had triumphed, its domination over the government would have been prolonged through indefinite years, if not permanently established. It is in the light of these facts that the labors of Giddings in Congress must be estimated.

The time has not yet come to write the final history of slavery in the United States. When we shall be farther from the thrilling events of the great struggle for its overthrow, and the passions and prejudices which it engendered shall have died away, the story will be told, and justice will be done to all. The chief actors in the world-famous movement will be assigned to their true positions; and whether they shall be judged by their fidelity to a great cause in the face of all dangers and temptations, or by the results of their labors in hastening the final consummation of their grand purpose, the rank of Giddings will be second to none. It will amply justify the prophetic lines of James Russell Lowell, written fifty years ago : —

> "Giddings, far rougher names than thine have grown
> Smoother than honey on the lips of men ;
> And thou shalt aye be honorably known,
> As one who bravely used his tongue and pen,
> As best befits a freeman, even for those
> To whom our Law's unblushing front denies
> A right to plead against the life-long woes
> Which are the negro's glimpse of freedom's skies.
> Fear nothing and hope all things, as the right
> Alone may do securely; every hour
> The thrones of ignorance and ancient Night
> Lose somewhat of their long-usurped power,
> And freedom's lightest word can make them shiver
> With a base dread that clings to them forever."

APPENDIX.

PACIFICUS:

THE RIGHTS AND PRIVILEGES OF THE SEVERAL STATES IN REGARD TO SLAVERY.

BEING A SERIES OF ESSAYS PUBLISHED IN "THE WESTERN RESERVE CHRONICLE" (OHIO), AFTER THE ELECTION OF 1842.

BY A WHIG OF OHIO.

INTRODUCTION.

To the Editor of the Chronicle, —

THE election is past, and our opponents have triumphed. They are now charged with the responsibility of administering our State government. This being the case, we may expect the election of a Senator to Congress who will vote to repeal the tariff and to abandon the protection of the free labor of the North. We must expect the election of such a man as will exert his influence against our harbor improvements and a completion of the Cumberland road, and who will oppose the distribution of the proceeds of the public lands. We must look for the election of a man who will vote for the annexation of Texas to this Union, and who will lend his influence generally to the slaveholding interests. The State will be so districted as to elect the greatest possible number of representatives in Congress who will sustain the same policy, and who will vote for John C. Calhoun to the office of President in 1844, should the election devolve upon the House of Representatives.

Had the friends of Northern rights united their political efforts at the recent election, these consequences would have been avoided; but we were divided, and of course were *conquered.* Crimination and recrimination will not extricate us from the difficulties into which our unhappy divisions have precipitated us. Future triumph can only be secured by future union; we should, therefore, profit by experience. Let us search out the rock on which we have split, that we may avoid it hereafter. If there be any political or moral principle involved in the controversy, let us understand what it is. Let it be developed and placed before the people, that we may all distinctly understand it. In order to do this, it is the intention of the writer to enter into an examination of this subject. He will endeavor to do so with such plainness and sincerity as the subject demands; no false delicacy shall deter him from a full, fair, and candid expression of truth, nor shall feelings of excitement induce him to use terms or epithets that may offend the sincere inquirer after truth, whether he lives in a Free or Slave State, or belongs to the Whig, the Democratic, or the Liberty party.

In order to be distinctly understood, your readers may expect an examination of the subject in the following order: —

1. He will inquire into the rights and privileges of the several States in regard to slavery.

2. The encroachments upon these rights, of which the anti-slavery men complain.

3. The remedy which I think all will agree should be adopted.

The whole will occupy several columns of your paper, and will be furnished as the writer finds leisure to communicate with your readers.

PACIFICUS.

November 1, 1842.

NUMBER I.

RIGHTS AND PRIVILEGES OF THE SEVERAL STATES CONCERNING SLAVERY.

MR. EDITOR, — For the purpose of fixing in the mind a definite idea of our rights and privileges respecting slavery it becomes necessary to look back to the time of forming the

Constitution. At that period the spirit of universal liberty pervaded the minds of our people generally, particularly those of New England and the Northern States. The sages and patriots of 1776 had put forth the undying truth *that man is born free*, as *a self-evident fact*. In obedience to this declaration, Massachusetts, ever forward in the cause of liberty, by a similar assertion of the rights of man had stricken the shackles from every slave within her territories. The soil of Vermont had never been contaminated with the footsteps of a slave. Pennsylvania, and indeed nearly all of the Northern States, had commenced a system of gradual emancipation. The delegates from the North carried with them a strong predisposition in favor of universal liberty. While in convention they spoke of slavery with deep abhorrence and the most irreconcilable hatred. Not so with the Southern States. They regarded slavery as necessary to their prosperity. They refused to enter into the constitutional compact upon any terms that would subject that institution to the control of the General Government. Up to this period each State had acted, in regard to slavery, according to the dictates of its own will. Each, for itself, held supreme, indisputable, and uncontrolled jurisdiction over that institution within its own limits. This entire power was reserved to itself by each State, and no portion of it was delegated to the General Government; and to place the subject in such plain and palpable light that it should never be questioned or disputed, Article 10 of the Amendments was subsequently adopted, by which it was declared that the powers not delegated by the Constitution were reserved to the several States. It is therefore plain that the General Government has now no more power over the institution of slavery than it had prior to the adoption of the Constitution. The people of the Southern States hold that institution as independently of the Federal Government as they did under the old Confederation.

Precisely to the same extent do the people of the Free States hold and enjoy the blessings of personal liberty. They delegated to the Federal Government no more power to involve them in slavery than the South did to involve *them* in its abolition. The rights of the States on this subject were mutual and perfectly reciprocal. Those States that desired to do so could continue the institution of slavery; and those that desired to be free, and entirely exempt from the expense, the disgrace, and the guilt of it, reserved to themselves the full and indisputable right to remain altogether separate from, and unconnected with, its evils. The sons of the Pilgrims regarded slavery as a violation of the will of Heaven and a flagrant transgression of the law of God. They would no sooner have been prevailed upon to involve themselves in its moral turpitude than they would in that of piracy or murder. The people of the Free States, therefore, secured to themselves the absolute right of remaining free from the guilt, the disgrace, and the expense of slavery, by withholding from the Federal Government all constitutional power in regard to that institution; while the Slave States secured to themselves an equal privilege to enjoy the benefits (as they supposed) resulting from a continuance of slavery.

These doctrines are not *new*, they are as old as the Constitution. They are not *local*, for they have been substantially asserted in Congress, and both in the North and the South. They are not *anti-slavery*, for they have been, for half a century, the declared doctrines of the *Slave States*. If any anti-slavery man claims for the Free States any further rights in regard to slavery than those expressed above, he is requested to make them known. If any Whig or Democrat of Ohio is willing to deny to the people of the Free States the rights above set forth, he is invited to express his views, in order that the public mind may be informed upon this important subject.

If these be the constitutional rights of the Free States, all will agree that they should be maintained and supported. On this point it would appear impossible that Whigs and anti-slavery men should disagree. I therefore submit the question to our editors, and the conductors of the public Press generally, whether they ought not to speak out boldly and temperately upon this subject? Ought they not to urge forward our State and national legislators to maintain and defend the rights of the Free States as assiduously as they do those of the Slave States? The question is also submitted to the members of our State Legislature, and to our members of Congress, whether they are not as much bound by their oath of office to preserve the Free States from all participation in the guilt, the disgrace, and the expense of slavery, as they are to preserve the Slave States from the abolition of that institution by Congress? Ought they not to put forth their influence to separate and wholly divorce the Federal Government from all support of slavery, and to bring it back to the position in which the Constitution placed it in relation to that institution?

Having thus stated, generally, the rights of the States, I shall, in my next communication, examine the subject of fugitive slaves, which has sometimes been urged as an exception to the general principle that we of the Free States are constitutionally unconnected with slavery.

PACIFICUS.

NUMBER II.

FUGITIVE SLAVES.

MR. EDITOR, — The convention that framed our Federal Constitution met with no trifling difficulty in fixing the rights of the people of the different States in regard to *fugitive slaves*. By the *common law* and the law of nations "*a slave became absolutely free by entering the territory of a free state or government*," whether he did so by consent of his master, or by escaping from his master's custody. It was foreseen that if this principle of the common law remained in force, *self-emancipation* would deprive the Slave States of an institution which they regarded as important to their prosperity. A member from South Carolina moved an amendment to the Constitution, requiring "*fugitive slaves and servants to be delivered up like criminals.*" This was objected to by members from Pennsylvania and Connecticut, for the reason that it would involve the people of the Free States in the expense of slavery. (*Vide* 3d volume Madison Papers, 1447.) An amendment was subsequently adopted, in the form in which it is now found in the last clause of the first section of the Fourth Article, which provides that " no person held to service or labor in one State, under the laws thereof, escaping into another, shall, in consequence of any law or regulation therein, *be discharged from such service or labor*," etc. By this provision the common law, as it then stood, was changed so far as the United States were concerned, so that a slave ESCAPING to a Free State did not thereby become *free*.

Under this provision Congress passed the law of 1793, requiring certain officers of the State and Federal Governments to act when fugitive slaves were brought before them; and it was supposed by our people generally that we were bound to aid the master in recapturing his fugitive slave. This has led many of our people to believe the subject of fugitive slaves to form an exception to the doctrine laid down in my first number. But the subject came before the Supreme Court of the United States at their last session, in the case of Prigg *vs.* The Commonwealth of Pennsylvania; and it was decided, on solemn argument, that no State officer was obliged to act in such case, and that so much of said law as required them to act was *unconstitutional*. In this manner the doctrine laid down in my last communication was confirmed by the Supreme Court of the United States in regard to *fugitive slaves*. There were many other important points decided in that case, from which the following principles are deduced: —

A slave by escaping to a Free State acquires certain important rights and privileges. When he reaches our territory we regard him as a *man*, not as property. If he work for me, or sell me property, he may sue me in his own name, and collect his pay. Neither I nor any other man, except his master, can take advantage of his having been a slave. If any person attempt to arrest him, as a slave, without process, he may defend himself with just so much force as becomes necessary to protect his person and his personal liberty. In this respect he enjoys the same rights and privileges which our citizens possess. He is liable to be arrested and taken back to slavery by his former master; *in all other respects* he is regarded in law as a *freeman*. While in a Slave State he may not resist the violence of his master by any act of self-defence; if he do so, he may be instantly slain by his master, or otherwise severely punished under the laws of such State. It is this law, declaring it criminal in him to defend his person against the violence of his master, which constitutes *slavery*. That law can have no operation in our State. The slave, therefore, by escaping from a Slave State, escapes from the operation of that law. Its penalties cannot be visited upon him for an act done in Ohio. There is no such law here, nor is it in the power of our Legislature to enact such a law. Our constitution forbids its existence.

The court, in the case referred to, expressly decided that the jurisdiction is vested *solely* in Congress; that the passing of a law upon the subject by Congress is conclusive that the master shall have the benefit conferred by the Act, and that no State law can be interposed to qualify or change the powers given by Congress. They further decided that it was equally plain that Congress intended that the master should have *no other or further facilities* for capturing his slave than those expressed in the law of Congress; and therefore, no State law can add to the powers conferred in the Act of 1793. It therefore follows that he may defend himself against his master while in this State, for the obvious reason that self-defence is a natural right, and there is no law having force within the State of Ohio which forbids its exercise. If his master attempt to arrest him, the slave may defend himself with so much force as may be necessary to protect his person and liberty. If the master press upon him, and it becomes necessary for his protection, he may kill his master, or the agents of his master, be they few or many, without inquiring whether they come from a Slave State or be citizens of Ohio. It is important that our citizens should distinctly understand that if they volunteer to arrest a fugitive slave they do so at their peril. I speak with confidence on this point. There is nothing in the Act of Congress forbidding the slave to exercise his natural right of self-defence, nor does it mention any penalty for so doing. The Act treats him as *property* merely, and visits upon him no more punishment for killing his master than it would upon a mule for the same act. The law of Congress settles the rights existing between the master and the people of the State to which the slave may flee, but it does not attempt to define the rights existing between the master and slave.

It follows, therefore, that the slave when he reaches our territory becomes at once reinstated in the enjoyment of all his natural rights which belonged to him while in Africa. It is true that we lend him no protection against his master, but we leave him to defend himself with all the means in his power.

He may, for this purpose, provide himself with weapons. If there be two or more of them together, they may unite their efforts to defend themselves, and in all respects put forth their physical powers to the same extent that they could were they on the soil of their native land. I am aware that many of our people think it wrong to do anything by which the slave shall learn his rights. With such I disagree. If it were in my power, every person should know his rights the moment he touches our soil. To withhold from him this knowledge would aid his master in regaining him. We are under no constitutional, legal, or moral obligation thus to aid the master; therefore every means we may use for that purpose makes us partakers of his guilt. On the contrary, we are under every moral obligation to use all our efforts and influence to the advancement of justice and liberty, so far as we can, without offending against the laws of our country. It is on this principle that every citizen of our State, whether he be a judge, justice of the peace, or any other State officer, incurs as much moral guilt when he assists a master in retaking a slave as he would were he to go with the master to Africa and aid him in capturing and bringing into slavery the inhabitants of that unhappy land. It must be a vitiated state of public opinion that regards the question in any other light. The offence against mankind is the same in either case, and I intend that no false delicacy shall deter me from an unreserved expression of our rights.

One of these rights is to inform every person within our borders of all his legal privileges. I would as soon take from a slave his physical powers of defence as I would rob him of his moral power. I would as soon bind his body with chains as I would bind his intellect in ignorance. But while the slave enjoys these natural rights, the master has his constitutional and legal privileges; and these we are bound also to respect and observe. The master may enter our State and pass through it in pursuit of his fugitive slave, and we have not the constitutional power to prohibit him. As individuals, we may refuse him admission to our dwellings, or we may deny him the rights of hospitality; we may regard him with horror, and teach our children to detest him; but he may, nevertheless, travel our roads, and may arrest his slave in our presence; and may bind him, if necessary, and transport him back to the State from whence he escaped. We have no right to interfere for the slave's protection, although our sympathies may be excited in his favor. On this subject our faith is pledged, and must not be violated.

But while we *permit* the master to do this, we do not *protect* him in doing it. Far from it. When he enters our State to arrest his fugitive slave, *so far as they two are concerned*, he does it at his own peril, as much as he would if he should go to Africa to kidnap a native of that country. He has no law to protect him, and must depend upon physical force; yet he must respect the rights of our people. He must not violate the sanctity of our private dwellings, nor must he violate the public peace. He may lay "*gentle hands*" upon the slave, — he may arrest and secure him; but we are under no obligations to furnish him the use of our prisons, or to guard his captive for him. If the slave defends himself, the master is not thereby authorized to shoot or kill him, as he would if in a Slave State. Should he do that, it would constitute murder under our law, for which he would be hanged, the same as though he had killed a free man. After he has arrested the slave, he cannot compel him to perform any menial service whatever, nor can he legally beat or chastise him. Should he do this, he may be arrested and punished for the assault and battery. The master's power extends so far as is necessary *to arrest and take back his slave;* beyond this he cannot go. But he may do everything to effect this object *peaceably*. Here his rights terminate. But this he does at his own peril; and if the slave, in defending himself, kill his master, it is a matter in which we have no concern. Yet he must not do it wantonly or unnecessarily. Should he beat off his master, and while the master is retreating shoot him, that too would be murder, and we should then hang the slave.

These are some of the rights of the master and of the slave while within our State; and it will be observed by every reader that it is a matter *entirely between themselves*. It is a subject in which our people are under no obligation to interfere. If the slave drive back the master when attempting to arrest him, there is no moral or legal duty resting upon us to step in to the master's aid. There is no such stipulation contained in our Constitution. The patriots who framed that charter of American liberty made no such degrading compromise for the people of the Free States. Yet by the Constitution our State is made the *race-ground* over which the master may pursue his slave, and may use every means to arrest him that an officer may use to arrest a citizen on legal process. There is this distinction, however, between the master and officer: we *protect* the officer, but not the master; for a person to resist an officer in the execution of process is criminal under our law.

Not so with the slave; he may defend himself precisely as he would in Africa, or as a citizen of our State may defend himself against a person who, without process, attempts to arrest him for crime. Nor are our people under any more obligation to assist a slaveholder to catch a slave here, than they are to go to Africa and aid in kidnapping. Indeed, if you will show me a man who, *knowing his rights*, will aid a master in catching a slave in this State, I will show you a man who would go to Africa and aid in kidnapping the people there, and bringing them into slavery, provided he could do so without incurring danger of the halter. Or if you will show me a judge, or justice of the peace, or other State officer, who, *knowing his rights*, will aid in sending a fugitive back into slavery, or in detaining one for further proof of his being a slave, I think I hazard little in saying that for the same fees he would send you or me into bondage, if he had the power to do so.

Yet it is a humiliating fact that in 1839 our Democratic Legislature attempted, by legal enactment, to make our State officers and citizens the catchpoles of Southern slaveholders. I say they *attempted* to do this, for by the decision of the Supreme Court above referred to, all such State laws are declared "UNCONSTITUTIONAL AND VOID." Notwithstanding they were then told that such Acts would be void, they gravely occupied their time, and expended the money of our citizens, in devising the best mode of *catching slaves*. They used all their power and influence to involve you and me, and our people generally, in the guilt, the disgrace, and the expense of slavery. In this they violated the Constitution of the United States, as well as that of our own State.

And now, Mr. Editor, anti-slavery men ask that the *party*, the *men*, who enacted this law should receive the full benefit of their servility. They desire that public sentiment should be expressed through our public papers; that this law be repealed, that our State be relieved from the disgraceful attitude in which it now stands; that the subject of fugitive slaves be left where the Constitution and laws of the United States have placed it. And can there be any difference of opinion on this subject between Whigs and anti-slavery men? Is there a Whig editor in our State who will hesitate to raise his voice against this disgraceful law, and to maintain the clear, absolute, and indisputable right of our people to be entirely free and exempt from the guilt, the disgrace and expense of catching fugitive slaves?

PACIFICUS.

NUMBER III.

SUPPRESSION OF DOMESTIC VIOLENCE.

Mr. Editor, — The framers of our Federal Constitution set forth, in the preamble of that instrument, the objects for which it was entered into. One of those objects is "TO SECURE TO OURSELVES AND OUR POSTERITY THE BLESSINGS OF LIBERTY." Mr. Webster, in his late letter to Lord Ashburton, says: "Slavery exists in the Southern States of this Union *under the guarantee of our Federal Constitution.*" The patriots who framed the Constitution declared their object was "*to secure the blessings of liberty.*" Mr. Webster affirms that they *guaranteed slavery*. Did Madison and Washington and Franklin *say* one thing, and *do* another, or is Mr. Webster mistaken in the assertion contained in his letter? If this doctrine of Mr. Webster be correct, it follows, of course, that the Free States are involved in all the *guilt, disgrace,* and *responsibility* of slavery; and the position assumed in my first communication, "that the Free States are no more liable to support slavery than the Slave States are to abolish it," is erroneous and unfounded. This doctrine of Mr. Webster is often asserted by Southern slaveholders, as well as by Northern men, who appear anxious to impress our people with the idea that the Free States are thus subsidiary to the Slave States, and involved in all the hateful consequences of slavery. I will not call such men *doughfaces*, — with *them* I have nothing to do; my business is with their *arguments*. Our country and posterity will hold them responsible for their attempts to induce our people to yield up their own constitutional rights and to become the voluntary supporters of slavery and the slave-trade. To arouse our people to the investigation of our constitutional rights in regard to this subject, and to inspire them to a patriotic and firm maintenance of our interests and honor, is the duty of the public Press and of public men.

To the people of Ohio and of the Free States I declare this doctrine unsupported by any clause in our Constitution. No such guarantee is found in that instrument. The patriots who framed that "bond of union" made no such degrading stipulation on the part of Northern freemen. If that instrument had contained any clause susceptible of a doubtful construction in this respect, all will agree that it would and ought to be so construed as *to secure the blessings of liberty*, rather than to *perpetuate slavery*. But there is no clause that can, in the opinion of the writer, be deemed *doubtful*, or that by any strained construction can be said to guarantee slavery. The fourth section of the Fourth Article is, however, quoted in support of the doctrine referred to. It reads as follows: "The United States shall *guarantee to every State in this Union a republican form of government*, and shall protect them against invasion, and on application of the Executive, when the Legislature cannot be convened, against domestic *violence*." The word " guarantee " is used in connection with a "*republican form of government*," and not with slavery. It can hardly be expected that any one will suppose these terms to be synonymous. It is believed, however, that those who adhere to the doctrine now contended against, rely upon the last clause, which pledges the protection of the United States against "*domestic violence*."

The history concerning the insertion of this provision is this: In 1786 the "Shays rebellion" broke out in the State of Massachusetts. This insurrection threatened the overthrow, not only of the government of that State, but portended the downfall of all the other State governments. While they were thus endangered, it was discovered that no authority existed in the old Articles of Confederation by which the troops of one State could be employed to suppress an insurrection in another. This difficulty gave rise to the adoption of this clause for suppressing domestic violence. Massachusetts was then the only State that had *abolished slavery*. In this history it is difficult to trace out any intention to *guarantee slavery*. It is impossible to see how any legal mind can torture this clause into such a guarantee. It is simply a provision for *suppressing insurrections*. It applies as much to the *Free* States as to *Slave* States, and would have been adopted had no slavery existed in any of the States. It has no relation to the character of the insurgents, whether they be *black* or *white*, *bondmen* or *freemen*, *masters* or *slaves*. If an insurrection actually take place, the power of the Federal Government must be employed to put it down, if milder measures will not effect that object. But the President, when called on for aid to suppress an insurrection, cannot stop to inquire into the cause from which it arose. He is entirely unauthorized to withhold such aid, in case it arise from the *abolition* of slavery. The truth is, the Federal Constitution considers slaves as *persons;* and draws no distinction in regard to the character of the insurgents. When the United States troops arrive upon the theatre of action, they must direct their efforts to suppressing the *violence*. It is their duty to slay all persons found in arms against the public tranquillity. The master and slave fighting side by side against the public authority must both be slain without distinction, and without inquiring into their relations to each other.

When the violence is suppressed, the duty of the troops will have been performed. If, then, every slave in the nation *peaceably leaves his master and starts for* CANADA, there is no power in the Federal Government to send our troops after them, or to set them as a guard to prevent their escape. The duty of the President and of the troops is to *suppress the violence*, and not to *support slavery*. Such escape of slaves would prove a total *abolition* of slavery. Where then would be the guarantee? But suppose the slaves engage in and continue the violence : it will then be the duty of our troops to *slay* them. Would such *killing of slaves be a support of slavery?* It would be so far an *abolition* of slavery, and if all the slaves be thus slain, slavery would be *abolished* (for no new importations can be made under our laws). Where, then, will be our guarantee? Again, if the slaves should stubbornly refuse to labor or to obey their masters, they would thereby work the abolition of slavery. But would such act obligate the Federal Government to furnish obedient servants? Or should they commit suicide, and thereby abolish the institution, would the United States become liable as guarantors? Or were they to pursue a course of secret destruction of their masters' property, and thus compel their owners to emancipate them, could the slaveholders demand indemnity of the Federal Government? Or should the slaves pursue any other course which would inevitably destroy that institution, would the Federal Government be held responsible? I apprehend but one answer can be given to these interrogatories.

But some politicians give a more loose and indefinite construction to this section. They hold that as Congress is bound to lend its protection when called on to suppress domestic violence, it is their duty, in time of peace, to provide arms, troops, and fortifications for that purpose, and to have them so distributed as to intimidate the slaves to obedience. If this construction be correct, it is certainly one that was not foreseen or intended by the framers of the Constitution. If it be correct, the freemen of the North may be taxed to erect a fortification on every plantation south of "Mason and Dixon's line," and to furnish a body-guard to every slaveholder and overseer in the United States. Indeed, such construction would render it the duty of our freemen of the North to go to the Slave States and act as life-guards to the slaveholders. But there is, in this section, no authority for the Federal Government to act on the subject until *actual violence takes place*. The President cannot order out the troops of the United States to suppress an insurrection, even when actual violence has occurred, unless his aid be invoked by the State authority. Every reader will see that two things are necessary to authorize the President to interfere, —

1. There must be actual violence.

2. There must be a demand of aid from the Federal Government by the State authorities.

Without these the President has no power to act. If violence arise, it is the privilege of the State Government to suppress it, and to enforce their own laws, if they please. In such case the President has no power to order the troops of the United States into the field. If the slaveholders anticipate violence from their slaves, they are at full liberty to remove all danger by emancipating them. But the President has no power to send our troops to the Slave States to guard the masters and overseers while they whip and scourge and torture their slaves, to compel them to labor for the support and to promote the luxury, of their owners. Yet such is, substantially, the doctrine avowed and inculcated by some Northern politicians, as well as Southern slaveholders; and the question comes home to our editors and public men whether such views shall be pressed upon the public mind without examination and contradiction.

I have now examined the only clause in our Constitution relied upon by those who urge that slavery exists in the Southern States under the *guarantee* of our Federal compact. The doctrine has no foundation except in the servile disposition of those who appear anxious to involve the people of the Free States in the guilt and dishonor of an institution with which we are constitutionally unconnected.

Mr. Webster, probably without deliberation or close examination of the subject, wrote his letter of directions to Mr. Everett, under the dictation of a slaveholding President, giving to that minister orders to exert our national influence to obtain indemnity for the slave-dealers who claimed the cargo of the "Creole." In this manner he involved the people of the Free States in the disgrace of that accursed traffic in human flesh. Having done this, it became necessary that he should sustain the doctrine in his correspondence with Lord Ashburton. In his letter addressed to that functionary, on the subject of the "Creole," he substantially declares the people of the Free States to be the guarantors of slavery and the supporters of the slave-trade, — which they execrate and detest. This saying of Mr. Webster will be quoted by thousands of Northern doughfaces to establish this unfounded doctrine. It is believed that every such effort to commit us to the support of slavery should be promptly met and exposed by our public Press. They are attempts to surrender up our constitutional rights, and should be discarded by every friend of liberty and by every lover of his country. On this point it would seem that no difference of sentiment could exist among our people, whether they belong to the Whig, the Democratic, or Liberty party. All are desirous that our Press and public men should speak forth, in plain and respectful language, our constitutional rights. They neither wish nor desire that language offensive to Southern men should be employed. On the contrary, they would have them treated with respect and kindness. It is proper that the public mind should be fully informed in regard to our rights, and that these rights should be respectfully and firmly maintained. Is there a Whig who would not do this? Is there an editor or elector in the Whig ranks who feels too *delicate* to assert our rights, or too *patriotic* to maintain them? I make these remarks in consequence of the feeling so often expressed, that the agitation of our rights is *impolitic*. The idea is one which should meet with universal disapprobation. We ought never to remain silent when our rights and interests are invaded.

Having examined the two paragraphs in our Constitution which are quoted to prove that we are involved in the support of slavery, I trust the reader will be prepared to say, with me, that the Federal Government and the Free States have the constitutional right to be separate and totally exempt from the support of slavery and the slave-trade, and that this right is as supreme, absolute, and unconditional as is the right of the Slave States to maintain them.

In my next I shall ask the attention of my readers to some of the instances in which their rights have been invaded.

PACIFICUS.

NUMBER IV.

VIOLATION OF THE CONSTITUTION FOR THE SUPPORT OF SLAVERY.

MR. EDITOR, — In my first communication I stated that, by our Federal Constitution, the Free States possessed "the absolute and unqualified right of being exempt and entirely free from the *expense*, the *guilt*, and the *disgrace* of slavery and of the slave-trade." To establish this principle beyond all doubt or cavil has been the object of my second and third numbers. Having thus disposed of that part of my subject, I shall now proceed to call the attention of my readers to some few of the instances in which the people of the Free States have been unconstitutionally involved in the *expense* of that institution; reserving for a future number all reference to the *guilt* and *disgrace* which have been forced upon us in order to sustain and encourage slavery.

This practice of sustaining slavery at the expense and inconvenience of the people of the Free States had its origin in the days of our Revolution. In 1780, the authorities of South Carolina sent a confidential agent to inform Congress that their State could furnish no troops to defend her territory against the British forces, as it was necessary that her men should all *remain at home to defend their families and friends against their slaves in case of insurrection.* (*Vide* Secret Journal of Congress.) Under these circumstances, troops were taken from the Northern States to defend them against the British, while they defended themselves against their slaves and compelled them to labor for the benefit of their masters. In this way Southern plantations were rendered productive, while those of the North were left destitute of laborers, and the burden of supporting slavery was thrown almost entirely upon the Northern States. By the subsequent adoption of the Constitution, slavery was made *strictly a State institution*, its burdens to be borne by such States as continued them; while those States which preferred to do so, had an equal right to be exempt from all its evils, by emancipating their slaves. Yet the practice of throwing the burden of supporting slavery upon the nation at large, thereby involving the Free States in its expense, has continued down to the present day.

These burdens have been cast upon the people of the Free States, — firstly, by appropriations made by Congress for the direct and avowed purpose of sustaining slavery and the slave-trade; and, secondly, by such action of the executive and legislative branches of government as was calculated eventually to produce that effect, and in some instances the *refusal* of Congress and the Executive to act, lest such action should relieve the people of the Free States from this burden.

To the first branch of this proposition I shall devote the present number.

Our first treaty, formed with the Creek Indians, was signed Aug. 7, 1790. It contained a stipulation on the part of the Indians *to surrender up all negroes then in their territory.*

The same stipulation was contained in nearly all our subsequent treaties with that savage nation. I regret that the limits prescribed to myself will not admit of detail, and I will here state that if any reader shall call for details on any point embraced in these essays, I will most cheerfully give them hereafter. This covenant of the Indians to surrender up negroes was connected with stipulations to perform other acts, and the exact amount paid for surrendering negroes is therefore unknown. For the violation of this clause of the treaty we compelled them to pay to the slaveholders of Georgia, at one time, two hundred and fifty thousand dollars. I think it a fair estimate to set down the sum paid to that nation, for the purpose of inducing them to return fugitive slaves, at three hundred thousand dollars. In our treaty with the Florida Indians, concluded at Camp Moultrie in 1823, we agreed to pay them six thousand dollars, and an annuity of five thousand dollars for twenty years. The Indians, on their part, stipulated "*to be active and vigilant in preventing fugitive slaves from passing through their country, and in apprehending and returning to their masters such as should seek an asylum among them.*" Official reports and documents, now on file in the War Department, show beyond contradiction that the Florida War was commenced and prosecuted for the purpose of regaining fugitive slaves, and to prevent further escapes of that class of people.

The expense of this war is estimated at *forty millions of dollars.*

After the close of the late war with Great Britain, our Government demanded of that nation compensation for the owners for such slaves as escaped to their army during hostilities. The demand was resisted, and years of diplomatic effort were employed in extorting from them the price of liberty thus gained by our fellow-men. After much effort and expense we obtained *fourteen hundred thousand dollars* for the slaveholders; but the people of the Free States were taxed to defray the expense of obtaining and distributing the money. In 1825, and for many years subsequent to that time, the efforts of our Government were put forth "*to prevent the abolition of slavery in the island of Cuba,* lest the example might affect the institution in our Southern States." And an agent was sent there to prevent the emancipation of slaves. Our people of the Free States were thus involved in the expense of opposing the liberty of mankind. In 1818, General Jackson marched his army into Florida; while there, his soldiers and the followers of his camp took many slaves from the people of that territory, and the people of the Free States have been taxed to pay for the negroes thus taken.[1] (*Vide* documents on file in the office of the Secretary of the Treasury.)

In 1816, certain fugitive slaves took refuge in the Territory of Florida and erected a fort upon the banks of the Appalachicola River. Here they made their gardens and cleared their fields and cultivated their farms. General Jackson sent orders to General Gaines to enter this territory of the king of Spain, to destroy the fort, and "*to arrest and return the fugitive slaves*

---

[1] In the last clause of the ninth article of our treaty with Spain, entered into in 1820, the United States agreed "to pay the Spanish officers and the private Spanish citizens for all *property lost by the movements of the late American army in Florida.*" On a reference of the question to the late Attorney-General, Felix Grundy, that officer gravely decided that slaves were *property,* and he substantially decided also that *stealing negroes* constituted a portion of the movements of our late army in Florida. Upon the authority of this opinion, Secretary Woodbury paid for the negroes, although no other secretary had ever entertained such an application.

to their masters." A gunboat was despatched for the purpose of effecting these objects. The fort was cannonaded with hot shot until the magazine was blown up, and two hundred and seventy men, women, and children were instantaneously murdered in cold blood, for no other crime than that of preferring *liberty to slavery.* A law was passed in February, 1838, to pay more than five thousand dollars to the officers and crew, as a bounty for this destruction of our fellow-beings. Our people of Ohio and the other Free States were thus involved in the expense of *murdering fugitive slaves* for the benefit of that institution.

The bill granting this sum, as a merited bounty for *killing slaves*, was reported by the chairman [1] of the Naval Committee, and, it is said, was passed upon their authority, without further examination in the House. Many of the Slave States have laws authorizing their officers to arrest and imprison free colored persons who enter their States, and to sell them as slaves unless the expense of imprisoning them be paid. Many free colored men, in the employ of the United States, have been thus imprisoned, and the expense paid by Government in order to release them. (*Vide* reports of committees made at the last session of Congress.) Much expense has also been incurred by Government in sending detachments of troops and of the marine corps to intimidate the slaves of the South to obedience. These instances have been frequent; so much so that officers commanding detachments do not even wait for orders from the War Department to march their forces into any region where appearances of insurrection are manifested.[2]

Every reader is aware that ships engaged in the slave-trade have been wrecked on or near the British West India islands, and the slaves, finding themselves at liberty, have refused to return. Our Government has espoused the cause of the slave-dealers, and for many years has involved the people of the Free States in the expense of obtaining from the British Government remuneration for the loss which the slave-merchants

[1] Hon. Isaac Toucey, a *Democratic* representative from Connecticut, was the author of the bill.
[2] Most appointments in the army and navy made by slaveholding Presidents are from the South.

sustained by the liberation of their slaves. Thus have we been taxed for the support of the slave-trade. I need not mention the particulars concerning the "Creole;" they will be recollected by every reader. More than a hundred thousand dollars have been appropriated for the erection of prisons in the District of Columbia. These prisons have been, and still are, used by slave-merchants to confine their slaves until their cargoes or coffles for Southern markets are completed. In a former number I referred to the fact that a *Democratic* Legislature of our own State appropriated the money of our fellow-citizens to pay themselves their *per diem* while they discussed the proper mode of *catching Southern slaves*. These are *some* of the instances in which the people of the Free States have been involved in the *direct* expense of sustaining and supporting slavery. The *amount* cannot be ascertained with precision. Many have estimated it at one hundred million dollars, or more than one eighth part of the whole sum expended by the United States since the adoption of our Federal Constitution, including the expense of the late war with Great Britain. They include in such estimate the expense of removing Southern Indians, and the amount paid for the purchase of Florida and Louisiana. The protection of slavery doubtless entered into and formed a part of the objects attained by these purchases and the removal of the Indians. But the writer is unwilling to bring forward, upon his own responsibility, any estimate that admits of dispute or argument. The amount is immense when viewed in the most favorable light. Yet the *abuse* consists in the clear and palpable violation of our constitutional rights, rather than in the number of dollars and cents taken from our pockets and appropriated to the support of slavery.

The Constitution has been violated, and these violations have become so frequent as to create alarm among our patriots and sages. (*Vide* Mr. Adams's late speech at Braintree.) The writer, however, considers the most alarming circumstance to be the perfect *silence* of our Northern Press, and our Northern statesmen and politicians, under the infliction of those abuses and violations of the Constitution, and of our rights and interests. We have submitted to them so long and so patiently that many of our people begin to entertain the opinion that we are constitutionally bound to contribute a portion of our substance, accumulated by our toil and labor, to enable the slaveholders of the South to keep their slaves in subjection. Sir, this supineness of the Northern Press and Northern men is unworthy of the descendants of our Revolutionary fathers. Further abuses should be resisted. While we pay all possible deference to the rights of the Slave States, we surely ought to maintain our own. We should stand upon the strict line of the Constitution. We ought not to permit our Southern brethren to invade our rights, while we should be equally careful not to encroach upon theirs.

PACIFICUS.

NUMBER V.

VIOLATIONS OF THE CONSTITUTION, CONTINUED.

MR. EDITOR, — In my last communication I referred to some of the instances in which the money, collected from our people of the Free States, had been appropriated *directly* to the support of slavery. It is now my purpose to refer to some instances in which the people of the Free States have been compelled to suffer pecuniary inconveniences and loss for the benefit of the slaveholding interests of the South.

It is more than forty years since the people of Hayti, following the example which we have set them, achieved their independence and established a government of their own. By their acts of valor and patriotism they became as much entitled to a rank among the governments of the earth as we did by our Revolution. This claim has been acknowledged by France and England, and, indeed, so far as I am informed, by all the civilized nations of the earth, *except the United States*. So far from recognizing the Government of Hayti, at an early day we passed a law to suppress all commercial intercourse between our people and the people of that island. (*Vide* Act of Congress approved 28th February, 1806.) This was done because the people had, most of them, been slaves; and it was designed to withhold from them our provisions in order to bring upon them famine and distress, lest their example might induce the slaves in our Southern States to assert their liberty. It is true that a hazardous and uncertain trade has existed between our people of New England and those of Hayti; but we have been virtually cut off from the *profits* and *advantages* of a commerce with that island, for the reason that intercourse with that people might affect the slaves of the Southern States and render them discontented in their chains of bondage. Most of this time we have been virtually excluded from the commerce of the British West India Islands. In the mean time Hayti has offered to our merchants golden temptations for their American produce. These temptations they were compelled to forego, in order that the Southern slaves might be held in ignorance of their rights. Our farmers of Ohio have been denied a market for their wheat, flour, beef, pork, and other produce, in order to maintain such a state of ignorance in the Slave States as would enable the masters to hold their slaves in subjection.

I have already alluded to the fact that by a law existing in most of the Slave States, colored seamen, when they arrive in port, are liable to be seized and imprisoned, lest their presence might create a desire for liberty among the slaves. If the persons thus imprisoned are found unable to pay the extravagant charges for their arrest and imprisonment, they are to be sold into slavery. These proceedings have operated as a tax upon the commerce of our Northern States. Thus have our interests been made to subserve the interests of slavery. In this way the Federal Government has extended its fostering care over that institution, at the expense of the people of the Free States. For forty years we have thus been rendered tributary to the Slave States. Our Government still refuses to enter into commercial relations with that of Hayti, and the interests of our shipowners, our sailors, our merchants, our mechanics and farmers, are depressed and discouraged, in order that ignorance and slavery may be prolonged in the South. And where are our statesmen or our editors, of either party, who boldly denounce this flagrant abuse of Northern interests and Northern rights? Nay, I appeal to every thinking, candid man to say whether a frank and temperate maintenance of our rights on this subject has not been regarded as unconstitutional and *dishonorable* by a portion of our people of the North? So long, so tamely and silently, have we been accustomed to yield up our interests for the benefits of slavery that an open assertion of our rights, and support of our interests, is regarded with distrust and jealousy.

In 1816 our people of the Free States were deeply engaged in commerce; our ships navigated every sea; our sailors were numerous; our merchants were enjoying a profitable commerce; our farmers were encouraged by a ready market for their products. The war, then but just closed, had left our nation in debt; a hundred millions of dollars were to be raised, besides the current expenses of government. Southern statesmen considered that the interests of the slaveholding States would be promoted by levying this vast sum upon the commerce of the Free States. The command was given and the blow was struck. Twelve thousand seamen were turned out of employ, commerce was crippled, and thousands of our shipowners and merchants were ruined, and the industry of the North was for a season paralyzed, for the purpose of relieving the Slave States of their due proportion of our public debt and the expenses of our government.

At length our people of the North gradually conformed to the tariff of 1816 and subsequent amendments. They vested their fortunes, accumulated by industry and economy, in the factories designed to supply our nation with such fabrics as were deemed necessary to the comfort of our people. Our laborers again found employment. Industry was encouraged. Our farmers of Ohio found a ready market for their produce; prosperity again cheered every department of society in the Free States. Our public revenues were ample. Our national debt was paid off, our harbor improvements, the improvement of our river navigation and our Cumberland road, were going forward with rapidity, when the slaveholding influence became dissatisfied, and threatened a dissolution of the Union. One of the Slave States arrayed its military forces to oppose this Northern prosperity and to reduce the Federal Government to the necessity of changing its policy for the fancied purpose of forcing prosperity upon the Slave States, in defiance of that law of Providence which has ordained that it shall never result from oppression and vice. The Compromise

Act of 1833 was nothing more nor less than the mandate of Southern statesmen, by which they directed that our harbor and river improvements should cease; that the sale of Ohio wheat, flour, pork, and beef in New England should stop, and that our farmers should be deprived of a home market for their produce; that the manufacturers of New England should be ruined; that hundreds of thousands of laborers should be turned out of employment; that the revenues of government should be struck down; that a national debt should be incurred, public credit impaired, and private credit ruined, — for the purpose of sustaining and encouraging the interests of the Slave States. The mandate was obeyed, and the people of the Free States have quietly, and almost silently, submitted to the loss of untold millions for the benefit of the Slave States. The writer would not be understood as saying these are violations of the *Constitution*, but that they were as clearly *violations of the rights of the Free States* as were the appropriations of money for the express purpose of capturing fugitive slaves. It is thus that our commerce with Hayti has been cut off, and our domestic labor has been left to compete with the pauper labor of Europe, in order that the interests of the Slave States might be protected, sustained, and upheld at the expense of Northern freemen.

Under the law distributing the proceeds of the public lands among the several States, a fund was provided by which all our Northern States would have extricated themselves from their present embarrassments, and would have been enabled to complete their internal improvements already commenced. Our canals and railroads would have given increased facilities to our internal commerce, stimulated our agricultural and mechanical laborers to greater effort by offering greater encouragement. They would have aided and increased our manufactures. They would, in a degree, have annihilated the space which now divides the people of New England from those of our Western States; our associations would have increased; refinement and taste would have been encouraged, intelligence more rapidly disseminated, and learning and science promoted. These advantages, though highly desirable to a free people, are dangerous to the interests of slavery, which must ever depend upon the ignorance and stupidity of the slave population in regard to their rights and the means of regaining them. All these results were clearly seen by that influence which is ever jealous of the progress of knowledge, which teaches man to know the rights that God has given him. Their sacrifice was deemed necessary to the interest of slavery. A slaveholding President became the willing instrument by which the object was effected. Consistency, self-respect, reason, and the rights of the Northern States presented but slight obstacles to the attainment of his purpose. These advantages to the Free States, increasing and expanding as we look forward to coming time, were sacrificed by the Federal Government for the purpose of preserving the slaveholding influence from all hazard. I am aware that a portion of our people consider these subjects of but little importance. They urge that all encroachments upon our rights in favor of the slaveholding interests are to be resisted, but deny that a protective tariff, the distribution of the proceeds of the public lands, the improvement of our harbors, our river navigation, or of the Cumberland road, are of such importance as to require their aid and support.

If these important interests be abandoned by those who make the " support of Northern rights " their motto, how can they expect the friends of internal improvements and of the tariff to unite with them in matters which they deem of far less pecuniary importance? If one class of our Northern men will tamely surrender our *pecuniary* interests, may we not expect that another portion will be as willing to yield up our *honor* to the demands of the Southern States? Is there an individual who is not perfectly conscious that such divisions must prove destructive to our sectional rights? If those whose minds dwell mostly on the moral influences of slavery, and who feel most deeply interested in removing the moral desolation it occasions, abandon all support of our pecuniary interests, separate from their political friends, and refuse to co-operate with them, can they expect by such separation to facilitate the accomplishment of their own purposes? Can any man of reflection suppose that we can extricate ourselves from the *moral* influence of slavery while it continues to control our pecuniary interests?

The safety of the Free States depends on preserving the

Constitution in its purity, and in the firm and temperate support of *all our rights*. If one of our important rights suffer, all must be affected. They will either stand or fall together. Division of our friends is itself a sacrifice of our rights. Union of our friends will secure our rights and our interests. I am aware that I shall be charged with speaking mostly in regard to the rights of the *North*, while I say but little of those of the *South*. But I beg my readers to understand that the South has not only *maintained* its *own rights*, but they have made our rights subservient to their interests; and it has therefore become necessary that public attention should be thus particularly called to the support of *the interests and the honor of the Free States*.

PACIFICUS.

NUMBER VI.

VIOLATIONS OF THE CONSTITUTION, CONTINUED.

MR. EDITOR, — Having in my last two numbers made some allusion to the manner in which the people of the Free States have been involved in the pecuniary expense of slavery, I will now proceed to examine some of the instances in which we have been involved in the moral guilt of that institution.

By Act of Congress approved Feb. 27, 1801, slavery and the slave-trade in the District of Columbia were re-established and continued. As some diversity of opinion exists in regard to the power of Congress over the subject of slavery in that District, it may be well to remark that the States of Maryland and Virginia, by deeds of cession bearing date in 1800, conveyed the territory embraced within the District of Columbia to the United States. These deeds of cession each contained a clause providing that the State laws should continue in force within the territory ceded, until Congress *should accept the grant*. Congress accepted the grant, and from that instant the State laws ceased to have any force or effect within the territory. It then came under the control of another sovereignty, and of course all former laws must cease. When I speak of former State laws, I refer to *all statute or munici-*

pal laws, including the laws of descent and distribution, and the laws for the collection of debts and punishing crimes, as well as the laws of slavery and the slave-trade. All these ceased to exist the moment Congress accepted the grants.

From that time to this, there has been no municipal law in existence within said District *except Acts of Congress.* In order that the people within the District shall suffer no inconvenience for the want of laws, Congress passed the Act above referred to. By this law, the statutes formerly in force were re-enacted, and became the *laws of Congress,* and have been in force since that time. In this way slavery was re-established, and by virtue of this Act of Congress the slave-trade is now continued in the city that bears the name of WASHINGTON. Repeal that *Act of Congress,* and the slave-trade will instantly be abolished, and slavery will be done away forever. Congress refuses to repeal this law of its own enacting, and by such refusal *upholds* the slave-trade, with all its horrors and its attendant guilt. By virtue of this law, parents are separated from their children, husbands from their wives, brothers from their sisters, and, chained to the coffle or placed on board the slave-ships, are destined for a Southern market. By virtue of this law of Congress, all the ties of domestic life are severed by the mercenary trader in human flesh. Here the father, in the presence of his wife and children, has been known to lay violent hands upon himself, and rush into the presence of his God, rather than meet the horrors of a separation about to be inflicted upon him, under the sanction of this *Congressional slave-code.* Here, within the walls of the prison, erected by funds drawn from the people of the Free States, the mother has been known, in the unutterable anguish of her soul, to murder the children of her own body, to prevent their otherwise inevitable doom of being exposed to a Southern slave-market; and with hands reeking with the blood of her offspring, to sever the thread of her own existence, rather than meet the tortures of that " execrable commerce," now carried on under the sanction of this law, passed and sustained by votes of *Northern representatives.*[1]

Petitions are forwarded every year to Congress, praying

[1] Every Democratic member from Ohio has for years opposed all attempts to repeal this law or to stop the traffic in slaves.

that body to repeal this law, and thereby release the people of the North from the soul-sickening guilt attendant upon this trade in suffering humanity. Yet these petitions are treated with contempt, and we are compelled to continue involved in this turpitude, fearing *that our release from it would affect the interest of the slave-dealers.* To prevent our release from this guilt, every Democratic member of Congress from Ohio has for years united his influence and efforts with the slaveholders of the South. Indeed, they have stood before the world as "*the Swiss Guards*" of the slave-dealers, ready on all occasions to fight the battles of those who follow a traffic condemned and execrated by the civilized world, cursed of God and hated by man. I will not occupy time by anything more than a mere reference to the fact that slavery and the slave-trade exist in the Territory of Florida under the sanction and approbation of the Congress of the United States.[1] In the guilt of thus sustaining and continuing the institution in that Territory the people of the Free States are deeply involved, while their petitions to be relieved from such guilt are indignantly scouted from the halls of legislation by their servants in the House of Representatives.

In a former number I referred to the fact that the Executive of the United States has put forth our national influence for many years "*to prevent the abolition of slavery in the Island of Cuba,*" *for the reason that* "*the sudden emancipation of a numerous population could not but be very sensibly felt upon the adjacent shores of the United States.*"[2] How far these efforts of our Government have involved us in the guilt of slavery and of the slave-trade as they have been carried on there for the last fifteen years, I am unable to determine. I refer to facts, and leave them for the consideration of the reader.

[1] Since the publication of this article, an attempt has been made in Congress to disapprove of a Territorial law of Florida which authorizes the sale into slavery of such free colored persons as come into any port of that Territory. The law was sustained by every Democratic member from Ohio, as well as most of those from the Free States, whose constituents will thereby become liable to be sold into interminable bondage. (*Vide* Journal of the House of Representatives of the 3d of January, 1842.)

[2] See letter of Mr. Van Buren, Secretary of State, to Mr. Van Ness, our Minister in Spain, Oct. 22, 1829.

The troops of the United States have often been called on to support the institution of slavery by the direct interposition of our arms. More than five hundred slaves were captured by our army in Florida, and returned to a state of interminable slavery. (*Vide* Ex. Doc. 45, of last session of Congress.) Thus the people of the Free States have been involved in all the guilt of enslaving our fellow-men in order that the slaveholders may have the benefit of their labor.

In my fourth number I referred to the manner in which a fort within the Territory of Florida was blown up, and two hundred and seventy men, women, and children were murdered by the crew of a gunboat detached from our naval force, for the sole purpose of robbing them of their lives, for no other reason than that they were unwilling to be robbed of their *liberty*. This murder, unparalleled in the history of any free and enlightened government on earth, was committed by persons in our employ, — by our agents, acting in our name and by our authority. We were thus involved in the guilt of violently sending two hundred and seventy of our fellow-beings to their final doom, in order that slavery may continue and prosper.

"The deep damnation of their taking off" rests upon us, — on the people of the Free States as well as on those of the Slave States.

In the general support which our Government has given to slavery they have involved our people of the Free States in the general guilt of that institution. The late census has given us some interesting data by which the number of lives annually *sacrificed* among the slaves may be estimated with an approximation to truth. It has been said by some intelligent slaveholders that the most profitable time in which "to use up a slave was seven years." By this it is understood that the slaveholder may make more profit from his slave by driving him so hard as to make the average length of life among his slaves no more than seven years after they reach maturity. By comparing the number of deaths between the ages of twenty and forty, among the slaves of the South and the laborers of the North, some opinion may be formed as to the number of murders by the abuse of slaves in the United States. The writer speaks from memory when he states that such comparisons show that four hundred thousand human lives have been sacrificed to the Moloch of slavery within the United States between 1830 and 1840. In the guilt of these wholesale murders the people of the Free States have been involved, in just such degree as they have lent their influence and aid in supporting that institution. Every man who uses his influence to withhold from our people a knowledge of these facts, and of their rights to be exempt from this inconceivable amount of guilt, becomes accessory to the murders thus committed. Our public men and editors who endeavor to suppress the agitation of our rights on this subject become voluntary participators in shedding this river of blood, the stains of which centuries will not wash from our national escutcheon.

I might refer to numerous instances in which the people of the Free States have been involved in the guilt of slavery and the slave-trade; but I have mentioned enough to serve as examples. My object has been to show my readers the manner in which their constitutional rights to remain free from the guilt and moral turpitude of slavery have been invaded. If the Federal Government had abolished slavery in every State of this Union, the outrage upon the Constitution would have been no greater than has been that of involving the people of the Free States in the base wickedness of slavery and of the slave-trade. Yet, Mr. Editor, our public Press and public men have not only remained supinely inactive under these positive violations of the Constitution and of our rights, but they have been absolutely *silent*.

One of our great political parties has constantly aided in the perpetration of those outrages upon the people, while it must be acknowledged that the other has exhibited entirely too much insensibility to our wrongs; although their votes and acts, for some years past, have demonstrated to the world an unwillingness entirely to yield up our blood-bought privileges. This servile yielding up of the Constitution, as well as the rights and interests of the Free States, will gain no favor among the people for either party. No *Southern patriot* will demand it; no *Northern patriot* will silently submit to it. If our Union be maintained, it will be by *supporting the Constitution*, not by *violating* it. By maintaining the rights both of the *North* and of the *South*, not by trampling upon those of either section. The South must be permitted to maintain their slavery while they wish to do so; the North must be permitted to enjoy its freedom uncontaminated and unpolluted by the *guilt of slavery*. The political party that throws its influence into the support of *all* these rights will be sustained by the people; while the party that either invades the rights of the South, or supinely surrenders up those of the North, will be found wanting, when weighed in the balance of public sentiment.

PACIFICUS.

NUMBER VII.

VIOLATIONS OF THE CONSTITUTION, CONTINUED.

MR. EDITOR, — I proceed to notice briefly some of the instances in which the people of the Free States have been involved in the *disgrace* of slavery. In my first number I alluded to the unanimous declaration by these States of the *self-evident truth* "THAT MAN IS BORN FREE, AND IS ENDOWED BY HIS CREATOR WITH THE INALIENABLE RIGHT OF LIFE, LIBERTY, AND THE PURSUIT OF HAPPINESS." Every act of our Federal Government which denies to our fellow-men these rights, exhibits to the world an inconsistency, and renders us obnoxious to the charge of hypocrisy. The first act of gross inconsistency on the part of the Federal Government was the Act of Congress, approved 27th February, 1801, by which slavery and the slave-trade were re-established, continued, and are now supported in the District of Columbia. Under that law the people of the Free States have for forty years been involved in the disgrace of the slave-trade, which, during that period, has been carried on in the city of Washington.

At an early day it was found that the slaves of the South escaped to the British West India Islands, to Mexico, and to Canada. Our Government espoused the cause of the slave-holders, and opened a correspondence with Great Britain and Mexico, in order to obtain an arrangement with those Governments for the return of such slaves; thus endeavoring to make the Federal Government and the Free States the protectors of slavery, and holding out to the world that it was a *national* institution, in palpable violation of the Constitution and of every dictate of justice. In 1835 the people of Florida sent a representation to General Jackson that the slaves of that Territory and of the adjoining States were in the habit of fleeing from their masters and taking refuge with the Seminole Indians. Our troops, paid by the Federal Government in money drawn from the people of the North, were ordered there, and were literally made the catchpolls of slaveholders, — thus making the capture of fugitive slaves the business of the *nation*, and involving the people of the Free States in its disgrace. I mentioned in a former number the fact that, by order of the War Department, a gunboat went up the Appalachicola River for the purpose of destroying a fort in which fugitive slaves had taken refuge, and that two hundred and seventy human beings were murdered in cold blood by the agents of our Government, paid by the freemen of the North.

In this extraordinary transaction our people of the Free States were involved in the disgrace of *murdering fugitive slaves*.

The efforts which our Government put forth to obtain indemnity for the owners of slaves who escaped to the British army during the late war, led that nation and the civilized world to believe that slavery was a *national* institution, sustained by the Free States as well as the Slave States; and we were consequently involved in all the odium of slavery. The exertions of our Government to prevent the abolition of slavery in Cuba, and thus to stop the progress of human liberty, involved the people of the Free States in all the disgrace attached to that extraordinary transaction. The spirited manner in which our Government espoused the cause of the slave-dealers who owned the cargoes of the "Comet" and "Encomium" brought upon the people of the Free States all the ignominy attached to the supporters of the slave-trade.

But the honor of the Free States has suffered most deeply from the restraints placed upon our people by the force of public sentiment among ourselves. This state of public opinion originated in the patriotism of the Northern States. Prior to the formation of our Constitution, our people felt the absolute necessity of a confederate government, with more ample powers than existed under the old Confederation. To obtain this, they were ready and willing to make sacrifices. Georgia and South Carolina would not adopt the Constitution unless they were permitted to follow the slave-trade for twenty years; to this the Northern States reluctantly consented, in order to bring them into the Union. The North also consented to permit the South to be represented in Congress in proportion to the number of their slaves, and to pursue their fugitive slaves into the Free States, and arrest and carry them back. These concessions were sacrifices of Northern sentiments and Northern interests, made for the purpose of obtaining a more efficient government, in order to strengthen and perpetuate the institutions of our country. In this manner the Constitution was *purchased* by the Free States. Since the adoption of the Constitution, we have been constantly called on to make further sacrifices to purchase its *continuance.* Thus, in 1820, the Slave States demanded an extension of the slaveholding influence, by the admission of Missouri as a Slave State, in order to check the increasing preponderance of the Free States. The Free States objected. The South threatened an immediate dissolution of the Union unless their demands were complied with. The North submitted for the purpose of *preserving the Union.* The sacrifice was declared an act of patriotism, and an example worthy to be imitated by statesmen and politicians. In 1833, South Carolina demanded a surrender of the tariff, and distinctly informed us that unless her demands were complied with she would dissolve the Union. The statesmen of the Free States hesitated, trembled, and submitted. The tariff was repealed, and the interests of the Free States yielded up in order to purchase a continuance of the Union. The act is yet quoted by some as an example of patriotism on the part of the Free States. Our Press, our statesmen and politicians treated it as such; and our people were thus led to believe that the sacrifice of Northern rights to the interest of the Slave States was, in fact, a duty and a virtue.

Whenever the interests of the North and the South came in conflict, Southern members were, for more than a quarter of a century, in the habit of threatening " a dissolution of the

Union," as the most effectual argument in favor of their measures; and it seldom failed to convince their opponents. This practice became so common that dictation appears to have been regarded as the *right* of the South, and *submission* was looked upon as the *duty* of the North. This feeling prevailed so long and to such an extent that any deviation from the accustomed submission was regarded as suspicious.

In our circles at home the agitation of any question which embraced the institution of slavery or the slave-trade was usually denounced as *abolition;* and without further examination was regarded as dishonorable to him who proposed it. Our public men became unwilling to raise any question that should affect slavery, lest they should thereby jeopardize their political standing; and the public Press discouraged every attempt to assert the rights of the Free States in opposition to the interests of the South. To support slavery it is absolutely necessary to suppress all knowledge of human rights among those held in bondage.

To the suppression of such knowledge our people of the Free States became accessory. In doing this, our own rights were lost sight of; we saw our money taken from our pockets and appropriated to the recapture, and even to the murder, of fugitive slaves, and were silent under the outrage. The spirit of independence and honor seemed to have fled from our people. We saw our Presidents, our heads of departments, our Speakers of the House of Representatives and of the Senate, our foreign ministers, our officers in the army and navy, mostly taken from the Slave States, and we meekly submitted to the abuse. We saw our respectful petitions to Congress treated with contempt; and our citizens, who dared thus to approach their servants, were insulted and abused by the supercilious advocates of slavery; while scarcely a solitary voice was heard in defence of Northern honor. Even such as dared to stand forth in defence of our rights and interests were generally condemned by the Press or "damned with faint praise." This was the point of our lowest degradation. History will mark the commencement of 1842 as the period of the deepest humiliation of the Free States. It was the time when the slave-power ruled triumphant, and, untrammelled by the Constutition, held the freemen of the North in almost willing subjection to its dictates; when the rights, the interests, and the honor of the Free States were regarded as of little importance, except as a means of promoting the interests of the Slave States. At this period, when all hope of supporting the rights of the North appeared about to expire, a most important incident transpired in the House of Representatives of the United States. John Quincy Adams presented a petition to *dissolve the Union*. I say nothing in favor of this petition; it was, however, a request that Congress would carry into effect the threats which for twenty-five years had been put forth by Southern statesmen. It was a request that those States which had assumed to themselves the control of the Federal Government might be left to take care of and protect themselves. The proposition horrified those who had so often menaced us with the consequences now prayed for by Northern men.

The effect produced by this petition was most important. Southern statesmen exhibited to the world a consciousness of *their entire dependence upon the Free States.* It was distinctly avowed by one of their ablest and most influential members that "*the dissolution of the Union would be the dissolution of slavery.*" It showed to the people of the Free States and to the world that our institutions and national independence must ever depend upon Northern freemen for support. From this moment Northern men felt more conscious of their power, and of the importance of our free institutions of the North. The sceptre of power then departed from the South, and must hereafter be swayed by the North, if our people prove themselves worthy of the high trust reposed in them. It is true, great efforts were subsequently made, and will continue to be made, by members from the Slave States, assisted by *Northern Democrats*, to stop the wheels of that revolution in the public mind which originated in the attempt to censure the venerable Adams. But their efforts have only served to awaken our people more fully to the maintenance of our rights.

PACIFICUS.

NUMBER VIII.

THE REMEDY.

MR. EDITOR, — I have now stated, generally, the constitutional rights of the people of the Free States concerning slavery, and have referred to some of the most prominent abuses to which those rights have been subjected. It remains for me to call the attention of my readers to the remedy. But this will at once suggest itself to the mind of every reader, and each will say that our remedy consists in a *united vindication of our rights;* that the real difficulty consists in our divisions, and our first efforts should be to unite the friends of Northern rights. In order to do this we must search out the cause of our division, and understand distinctly the point on which we separated. If I understand our Liberty men, they are anxious to maintain the rights of the Free States, and they ask for nothing more. I speak upon the authority of many leading men of that party. I have never met with an intelligent man who asked or demanded anything more than this; yet they say "the Whigs have neglected a portion of our most important rights," and they feel it their duty to separate from them and to form a distinct party, whose principal efforts are to be directed to the maintenance of such of our rights as have been neglected by the Whigs.

It was not my intention when I commenced these essays to throw censure upon any class of men, nor is such my present object; I may, however, be permitted to say that I think our Liberty friends did not well "define their position" before they separated from us. For the correctness of this remark I will refer to the recollection of the great mass of our people of all parties. At the time of separating from us they had not clearly set forth to the world our rights, which had been trampled upon; nor did they state with perspicuity the abuses which they sought to correct. Neither did they definitely mark the boundaries and limit the extent of the political reform which they were endeavoring to effect. On the contrary, there was a degree of obscurity pervading their objects. They professed opposition to slavery, and left the public to infer a design to invade the privileges of the Slave States, instead of maintaining our own. This idea has rested in the minds of a large portion of our people both in the Free and in the Slave States. It is true the charge was often denied, and it is equally true that the denial was not carried home to the minds of the great mass of our people, many of whom to this day really believe the object of the Liberty party to be an unconstitutional interference with the privileges of the Slave States. But so far as I have been able to learn their motives and to analyze their views, I understand them to be simply the *preservation of our own rights;* the repeal of all Acts of Congress passed for the support of slavery or the slave-trade ; to separate the Federal Government and the Free States from all unconstitutional connection with that institution ; and to leave it with the individual States where the Constitution placed it. This I believe to be the boundary and farthest extent of their *political* intentions. If they entertain any other or farther views, I hope Judge King (the candidate of the Liberty party for Governor of Ohio) will state to your readers, through the " Chronicle," the point on which I have failed to express their objects. I hope also that the editors of the " Philanthropist " and " Emancipator " will, through their respective papers, set forth definitely any error into which I may have fallen in regard to the designs and objects of their party.

But for the present, taking these to be the definite limits to which they aspire, I will respectfully ask the Whigs, as a party, and the Liberty men as a party, to show me the line of demarcation between them? Is there an individual in the whole Whig party of Ohio, or in the Free States, that is willing to surrender a single right of our people? If there be such a Whig, I have not met him. If there be a Whig editor north of Mason and Dixon's line who is willing to yield up any of the constitutional rights of the Free States, I hope he will favor the country with his views, and that he will inform us distinctly *which part* of the Constitution we ought first to surrender. I speak with great confidence when I say that I believe no such man can be found. Let the rights of the people of the Free States in regard to slavery be fairly and distinctly pointed out, and there will be no want of firmness nor of patriotism to maintain them. It is true, however, that many Whigs have and still do oppose the abolition of slavery in the District of Columbia; but they will assign to you as the reason that Congress *has not the constitutional power* to abolish it. If you then ask them if they are willing that Congress *should repeal its own laws,* for the support of slavery and the slave-trade in that District, they will at once answer you in the affirmative. If you inquire whether they are willing to lend their influence or their property to support slavery, they will answer you they detest the institution. If you interrogate them in regard to any other rights of the North, they will unhesitatingly assure you of their determination to sustain them.

If, then, our Whigs are willing to sustain *all* our rights, and our Liberty men have no further objects in view than the support of such rights, the question at once suggests itself, *Why do they divide?* What principle separates them from each other? And it is a question of high and solemn import, which the writer would repeat in the ear of every Whig, every anti-slavery man, and of every lover of our free institutions, *Why do you divide your political influence, and prostrate your political energies, while you agree in principle and are laboring for the same objects?*

We have the same interests to watch over, the same rights to maintain, and the same honor to protect. All these must receive our attention, or be left to those who as a party have uniformly lent themselves to the slaveholding influence. If we forget those rights, and spend our efforts in unmeaning contentions and useless quarrels with each other, will not our country hold us responsible? Our interests have been sacrificed, our rights have been trampled upon, our State has been disgraced, as I have heretofore shown. Yet we have divided our efforts, and separated from our political associates, and delivered the honor of our State to the keeping of a party who, forgetful of the dignity of freemen, have shown themselves willing to become the *catchers of slaves,* and to degrade themselves and their State by legislating for the sole purpose of robbing their fellow-men of that liberty with which the God of Nature has endowed them. But I desire to examine a little further the cause of our separation at the late election. The Whigs supported our tariff, our harbor improvements, the distribution of the proceeds of the public lands, with zeal and constancy. But our commerce with Hayti, the right of petition, the slave-trade in the District of Columbia, received from them, generally, much less attention, although they were not neglected by a portion of that party. These latter subjects were deemed of paramount importance by a portion of our political friends; on these they bestowed their principal thoughts, and treated the others with comparatively little attention. In this manner each party felt that they were exerting their efforts upon subjects of vital interest to our country, and each considered the other as laboring in behalf of interests that were not worthy of the attention paid to them.

In this way each party became dissatisfied with the other. Here, then, is the precise point of division among our friends, — not because either did *wrong*, but because each felt that the other was not sufficiently zealous in supporting *all* their interests. The division did not arise from any political sin of *commission*, but *for omitting some part of our duties*. The Democratic party has violently *opposed* those rights which Liberty men deemed sacred. The Whigs were lukewarm in supporting them, and on this account our Liberty friends withdrew from us, and thereby delivered over our interests to the disposal of those whose bitterness against the rights of man can scarcely find utterance in our language.[1] Having thus ascertained the cause and the precise point of our separation, the remedy is plain. It consists simply in *doing our duty*, — in maintaining our rights and interests and firmly resisting all abuses, in placing ourselves upon the exact line of the Constitution, and temperately, but resolutely, opposing all encroachments upon our interests, our honor, or our constitutional privileges.

I am aware that many of our editors and public men fear that the assertion and maintenance of our rights in regard to slavery would drive from us our Whig friends in the Slave States. If these fears were well grounded, they would form no good reason why we should surrender our constitutional rights in order to *purchase* their adherence. This is the

[1] *Vide* the late number of the "Ohio Statesmen."

policy of the opposite party. They appear anxious to surrender up our rights, our interests, and our honor for the purchase of Southern votes. If the Whigs attempt to rival that party in *servility*, they must fail. The independent spirit, the high sense of honor, the patriotic sentiment of our Whigs, will not permit them to become subservient to the slaveholding interest. But the argument is not well founded. Our Southern Whigs are generally men of liberal and patriotic sentiments. They will not ask of us the sacrifice of our constitutional rights. On the contrary, they will be as willing to grant us the enjoyment of *all* our rights as to demand the enjoyment of all their own. If they are not such men, they are unfit to be the associates of Northern Whigs. It is, however, true that they, as well as Northern men, have not heretofore fully understood our rights, for the reason that we ourselves *dared not assert them ;* and they, as well as Northern men, have unconsciously voted and acted in opposition to the rights of the Free States, under the impression that they were sustaining the Constitution. But when the attention of our Southern and Northern Whigs shall be directed to this subject, when they shall have fully investigated it, and shall understand the constitutional limits of slavery, I apprehend there will be no difference between them. It is, therefore, all important that public attention should be directed to this matter. Indeed, intelligence in regard to Northern rights cannot be longer suppressed. A spirit of inquiry is abroad among the people, and it is increasing daily, and becoming stronger and stronger.

A marked and palpable change has taken place in the public mind within the past year. In February last almost the entire Press united in the opinion that we were bound to support the coastwise slave-trade of the South. At this time who is willing to hazard his reputation by advocating such doctrine? Yet, with such examples before us, a portion of our Press and of our public men exhibit much timidity as to asserting and maintaining our constitutional rights. So long have the people of the North been accustomed to silent submission when our rights have been invaded that many of our editors, our statesmen and politicians, still appear to doubt the *safety* of an open, frank, and manly defence of our interests and our honor. It however needs no spirit of prophecy to foretell the downfall of any party which has not the moral and political courage to maintain the rights and interests of the North. If the Whigs come forth to the defence of these interests and maintenance of these rights, their success is not less certain than the continuance of time ; and if the opposite party continue to *oppose* these rights and interests, their defeat is inevitable.

PACIFICUS.

NUMBER IX.

BJECTIONS ANSWERED.

MR. EDITOR, — In this, my closing number, it is my intention to answer some objections that have been urged against a union of the friends of Northern rights. The first and most important objection urged by the "Liberty men" is, that "Henry Clay is the Whig candidate for President, and they cannot vote for him because he is a slaveholder." My first answer to this objection is that Mr. Clay is *not* the candidate of the Whig party at present ; and whether he will be is quite uncertain. Nor can I admit it to be good or sound policy for me to withdraw from the support of good men, *at this time*, for the reason that I think a bad man may be a candidate two years hence for another office. Again, should Mr. Clay die before the next Presidential election, or should he not be a candidate, how can they justify their withdrawal at the late election from the support of men who openly avow and support every principle which they do themselves? My next answer is that Mr. Clay, under the laws of Kentucky, is permitted to hold slaves. By the Constitution of the United States that is made no disqualification for office. It is an objection unknown to the Constitution, and we ought to be careful how we attempt innovations upon that instrument, unless they be made in the mode pointed out for its amendment.

The first President under the Constitution was a slaveholder ; and the slaveholders of those States have an equal right to hold office that gentlemen who reside in the Free

States have. For us, at this day, to establish such a rule as a test for office would be a violation of the rights of the people of the Slave States. This is, in my opinion, highly objectionable. It would show us willing to *invade* their rights, while we profess to maintain our own. This would be inconsistent. Our inquiry should be, *Will he maintain the Constitution, and will he support the constitutional rights of all parts of the Union?* If we are satisfied that he will do this, we ought not to throw away our political influence, and suffer our interests, our honor, and our constitutional rights to be trampled under foot by a party who appear anxious to bring us under the subjection of the South. I would, in all candor, ask our Liberty men whether they would not prefer the support of our rights by a slaveholding President rather than their destruction by "a Northern man with Southern principles"? I certainly prefer that our candidates should not be slaveholders; for I believe slaveholding, even in a Slave State, to be immoral and wrong, and must detract from the moral character of those who practise it. Like all other vices, it should have its due weight in our estimate of character; but it is entitled to nothing more. Should Mr. Clay or his friends satisfy me that, if elected President, he will, in good faith, support all these rights to which I have alluded, and which have been so often and so long trampled upon, and he be the only candidate who, in my opinion, will sustain those rights, and who at the same time has a reasonable chance for election, I could not justify myself to my conscience were I to withhold my support from him. Were I to do so, and thereby elect a man who I believed would violate our Constitution and disregard our rights, I should thereby become accessory to his acts.

In order to satisfy myself in regard to Mr. Clay's views on this subject, I, as one of the sovereign people, may propound to him any and all questions that I may deem important on this subject; and if he be worthy of that high office, he will not hesitate to answer them fully and frankly. If I then become satisfied that he will, if elected, disregard those constitutional rights of the North, I cannot support him, — it would be wrong for me to do so; for I should become accessory to the violation of our Constitution and the subversion of the rights of the Free States. Questions of *policy* constantly require of us mutual concessions of opinion; but no circumstances can justify the yielding up of any portion of the Constitution. When that shall be done, society will be resolved into its original elements.

Another objection is, that slaveholders when in office do injustice to the Free States. This assertion has proven too true in many cases, but is not correct in all instances. I quote the example of the present Speaker of the House of Representatives, the Hon. John White. No Northern man has condemned his official acts. He has discharged his duties honorably, and is as much entitled to confidence as though he lived in a Free State. Here I would caution our anti-slavery men not to permit their lofty principles of human rights to dwindle down to mere local jealousies. We should no more invade the *spirit* of the Constitution by making the holding of slaves a test for office, than we should permit our Southern friends to invade its *letter*.

Again, it is said that the Whigs have done nothing in favor of those rights which anti-slavery men consider so important. Is the assertion correct? Have not J. Q. Adams, William Slade, Seth M. Gates, and other Whigs done what they could for the defence and support of Northern rights? But it is said these are *individuals*. Yet they belong to the Whig party, and constitute a part of it; and surely their acts cannot be placed to the credit of the *other party*. But do not our friends, who make this objection, charge over to the Whig party the acts of individuals belonging to that political sect when they oppose the cause of human rights? The great body of the Whig party in Congress voted to repeal the obnoxious Twenty-first Rule. A few individuals, joining with the opposite party, prevented its repeal. Our Liberty papers and their party charged this as the act of the *Whig party*, while they deny to that party any credit for the efforts of Mr. Adams and others. This practice is unjust, and ought to cease. But have not the Whig party (and when I speak of the party, I mean the *majority* of the party) voted in support of these rights for the last two years? Have they not voted against the odious *gag* and in favor of the right of petition when these questions came before them? Did they not sustain Mr. Adams when an attempt was made to censure him? Did they not sustain Mr. Giddings when censured? Did not the Whig party in his district sustain him? I ask in what instance, for the last two years, have the Whigs in the House of Representatives failed to sustain these rights when agitated upon the floor of Congress? I will not say that they have at all times maintained our rights; but I do not hesitate in saying that I know of no instances when the question of Northern rights has been brought distinctly before them, for the last two years, in which a majority of the members of the Whig party present have not sustained those rights.

Yet it is asserted by some that "the two great political parties have been equally opposed to the rights of mankind and to the interests of the people of the Free States." I can hardly believe that any intelligent man would make such statement while under the exercise of a suitable regard to candor. It is well known that for the last two years in every instance in which those rights so dear to our friends have come before Congress, every Democratic member from this State has opposed them, and that every Whig member from this State has sustained them; and such, too, has been substantially true of the two parties generally, though not to the same extent. A Whig member from this State introduced resolutions declaring the rights of the Free States as set forth in my second number, and was sustained by every Whig colleague; while one of his Democratic colleagues moved a resolution to *censure* him for thus presuming to assert our rights, and every Democratic member voted for the resolution of censure. And is it possible that any man can now be sincere in saying that the two parties are *alike* subservient to the interests of the South?[1]

But it is said that the Whigs *have been* subservient to Southern dictation; and their acts, in former years, are quoted to prove the fact. This charge is too true. Up to a certain time both parties appear to have been submissive to the demands of the Slave States. Such, too, was the case generally with the men who now make this charge. Their attention had

---

[1] The votes in Congress for suppressing the slave-trade in the District of Columbia, and for repealing the Territorial law of Florida which authorizes selling freemen into slavery, were given since the above was published. On these questions the representatives from the Free States were divided almost entirely by party lines.

not been aroused to the subject. They, with the Whigs and Democrats, were equally unconscious of the encroachments upon our rights; and the Whigs or the Democrats may now make this charge against the "Liberty party" with the same propriety that the latter can urge it against the others. The truth is, the abuse of Northern rights has but just begun to attract attention. But whatever has been done in Congress has been done by the *Whigs*. Up to this time there has been no Liberty man in that body or in our State Legislature. But such has been the revolution in public opinion that if it continues to progress as it has for the last year, it will be completed, our rights secured, and the Constitution will be vindicated before that party will get any members elected to either body. Would it not be far better for the cause of Northern rights if our Liberty men were to deal justly and candidly with both of the great political parties, and to approve as frankly that which is praiseworthy, as they condemn that which is wrong?

But it is said that the present political parties have become *corrupt*, and it is therefore necessary to form a new party that shall be free from such political corruptions. But I ask from whence are we to find the men for this new party? Must they not come from the present parties? And will they be more pure, more honest, and more patriotic when transferred to a new party than they now are? Are there any regenerating influences to act upon such as join the new party? Are their political transgressions to be washed out? Will the Whig who has always acted honestly, and been guided by a sincere desire for his country's good, be more likely to leave his party than the demagogue and the office-seeker? I would not by any means be understood as impugning the motives of those who now constitute the Liberty party; on the contrary, I believe them as honest and patriotic as any other class of men. But I ask them if the formation of a new party will not be likely to draw to them the profligate and the unprincipled from both of the other parties?

Again, it is said to have become necessary to form a party whose *principal* object shall be the maintenance of those rights which our anti-slavery men may deem important. If by this form of expression it be understood that those who unite with that party are, in any degree, to neglect the protection of free labor by a proper tariff of duties; or if they intend to abandon the improvement of our lake harbors, and our river navigation, and other Northern interests which the Whigs deem important, — then I, for one, cannot unite with them, nor can I believe their prospect of success very flattering. Our people may easily be persuaded to *maintain* our rights when their attention is called to them; but it will be difficult to convince them that it has become their duty to *neglect* either their *rights* or their *interests*.

But if a portion of our friends form a distinct party for the support of the right of petition and to maintain the freedom of debate, and for that purpose they should oppose those who are engaged for the protection of the free labor of the North, while another portion turn their attention to this latter object, and oppose their influence to the former, is it not perfectly clear that *both must fail;* while a union in support of both would inevitably secure the triumph of each?

But I have not time to pursue the subject further; I have already occupied more of your paper and more of the attention of your readers, than I designed when I commenced these essays. It has been my object to call public attention to what I believe the true points in issue. I have intended to speak with such plainness that no man, nor party, nor editor, should say that I feared to state the *whole* truth, or that Whig papers dare not publish arguments touching *all* our rights. And if I have fallen short of this, I again call upon the editors of the "Philanthropist" and the "Emancipator" to show wherein. And, on the other hand, if there be a Whig editor who is unwilling to support *all* our rights, or who thinks the assertion and support of all our rights and interests impolitic or imprudent, I desire him to place his objections before the public. It is surely time that our papers and our people had ceased to contend about *names* and *terms*, and that they should search out some *principle*, or some constitutional or political right, as the foundation of their quarrels.

Again, the writer would say to his readers that he has put forth no opinion upon the constitutional rights of the several States without mature investigation, or on which he entertains any doubt. Yet he claims for himself no infallibility. And if any man desire explanations, or authorities on any point, he will most cheerfully furnish them.

In taking leave of my readers I wish to say that I was induced to appear before the public on this subject from the most thorough conviction that no fixed and established policy will be framed by the General Government while the rights of the Free States remain unsettled concerning slavery. Looking at Ohio, New York, and all of New England, and considering the result of our late elections, and the divisions which distract and divide the friends of the North and of liberty in those States, we must all acknowledge that we have little hope of seeing our interests, our honor, or our rights protected until *union* shall characterize our political efforts. Since the commencement of these essays many things have transpired to rivet this conviction more thoroughly upon the mind. I refer, among other things, to the Latimer case at Boston, and the absorbing interest now felt on the subject in Massachusetts and in Virginia.[1] Feeling desirous to call the attention of our people, as well as that of our politicians and statesmen, to the importance of a speedy settlement of those questions which involve the most vital interests of the Free States, I have seized upon such moments as I could spare from other employments to place some of my views before the public. I have done this under the strong conviction that every true patriot should put forth his influence to sustain our rights and to unite our people in the protection of our interests, our honor, and the Constitution of our common country.

PACIFICUS.

[1] Since this article was published, the Norfolk meeting in Virginia have passed resolutions recommending to their Legislature the "arming and disciplining of their militia," preparatory to the coming conflict between the Slave and Free States. Yet while Virginia is thus urged to arm her militia in support of slavery, some Northern editors feel it their duty to remain silent in regard to Northern rights.

INDEX.

A.

ABBOTT, A., 231, 260.
Abolitionists, the, 45, 73, 87, 97, 136, 157, 212, 214, 287, 311, 377, 383; Henry Clay's famous speech against, 65-66, 159; divided between support of Birney and Harrison for the Presidency, 88; alarm the slaveholders by organized political action, 91; many support Clay for President, 158.
Adams, Charles Francis, 210, 214, 269; correspondence with Giddings, 199-200, 213-214, 228-229, 278; a "Conscience Whig," 206; an intimate friend of Giddings, 208; editor of the "Boston Whig," 232; supported Giddings in his controversy with Winthrop, 232.
Adams, John Quincy, 44, 54, 56, 57-58, 64, 75, 92-93, 97, 122-123, 124, 125, 128, 131, 133, 141, 145, 147, 150, 173, 178, 190, 212, 214, 245, 248-249, 258, 355, 357, 359, 360, 381, 384, 385, 390, 406; representative to Congress, 48; his friendship for Giddings, 48, 169-170, 208, 398; his position in the House, 48; independent in politics, 49. 79; occasions dissension among the Whigs, 49; champion of the right of petition, 49, 91-92, 102, 103 *et seq.*, 140, 148-149, 380; disregard of legislative rules, 51-52; his position on the slavery question, 61-63; counsel for the anti-slavery men in the "Amistad" case, 76-77; his service in the Twenty-sixth Congress. 78-79; memorable action in the New Jersey delegation contest, 78-79; chairman of the Committee on Foreign Affairs, 102; presents a petition for the dissolution of the Union, 103-104, 332; his trial and punishment demanded by Southern members, 104-105, 105-106; zeal of his friends to assist him, 105; replies to the Southern leader, H. Marshall, 106; insulted by Southern members, 106-107; his defence of his actions, 107-110; effect of his triumph on the anti-slavery movement, 110-111; his action in the case of the "Creole," 118, 119-120; maintained the right of the Federal Government to abolish slavery in the States, 119-120; claims of the West Florida slaveholders, 142; failing in health, 148; appointed chairman of a committee to provide rules for the House, 148; introduces memorial of the Massachusetts Legislature, 151-152; chairman of a committee to report on the memorial, 151; his report, 151-152; loss of friends through devotion to anti-slavery cause, 168-169; obtains the repeal of the "gag-rule," 171; his position on the Oregon question, 189; votes against the Mexican War Bill, 192; supports Winthrop for Speaker, 217, 222; his death, 239-240; Giddings's lectures on, 371.
"Alabama," the, 390.
Alford, J. C., of Georgia, threatens Giddings, 98.
Allen, Charles, 206, 252, 258, 271, 274, 283.
Allen, William, of Ohio, 83, 188, 190.
American Anti-Slavery Society, the, foundation of, 87; Arthur Tappan its first president, 89.
"Amistad," case of the, 73-77, 153-155, 205, 256, 309-310.
Andrews, S. J., 33, 128, 147.
Arnold, T. D., of Tenn., 146.
Ashburton, Lord, 129.
Ashmun, George, 192, 206, 260, 274, 276, 283, 373.
Atchison, D, R., of Mo., 308.
Atherton, C. G., of N. H., his gag resolutions, 51.

B.

BAILEY, Dr. Gamaliel, 90; editor of the "Philanthropist" and "National Era," 88; an ardent anti-slavery man, 88; letter to Giddings, 88-89; his house the rendezvous of reformers, 284, 346.
Baldwin, Judge, 76.
Banks, Nathaniel P., 322, 336; elected Speaker, 325-326.
Barringer, D. M., of N. C,. 277.
Barrow. Senator, 114.
Bayly, T. H., 274, 310, 316.
Bell, John, 283, 344, 377.
Benezett, Anthony, 37.
Benton, Thomas H., 83, 183, 283, 384, 385.
Berrien, J. M., of Georgia, 152.
Bingham, John A., a warm friend of Giddings, 398-399.
Birdseye, Victory, 147.
Birney, James G., 62, 91, 131, 157, 160, 411; Abolitionist candidate for President in 1840, 88; nominated by the Liberty party for President in 1844, 158.
Black, E. J., 97-98, 172-173, 398.
"Black Warrior," case of the, 314-315.

Blair, Francis P., 346.
Blair, Francis, P., Jr., 373.
Borden, Nathaniel B., 147.
"Boston Atlas," 226-227, 229.
"Boston Whig," 229, 232.
Botts, J. M., 109; his motion to censure Giddings for his action in the "Creole" affair, 121-122; condemned Giddings's resolutions as ill-timed, 126.
Bowditch, H. I., Dr., 188, 189.
Brainerd, Lawrence, 242.
Brengle, Francis, 156.
Briggs, George N., 98, 147.
Briggs, J. A., 188.
Bronson, David, 147.
Brooks, James, 295, 297; speech on joint resolution in honor of Kossuth, 291-293.
Brooks, Preston S., his assault on Sumner, and subsequent trial by the House, 332-334.
Brougham, Lord, 147.
Brown, John, letters to Giddings, 327-328; assisted by Giddings, 370; his Virginia raid, 370.
Brown, Milton, 182.
Brown, William J., his attempt to obtain the Speakership, 273-275; rage of Southern members against, 275.
Buchanan, James, 83, 339; nomination and election to the Presidency, 337; favored the admission of Kansas as a Slave State, 341.
Buffum, Arnold, 352.
Burke, Edmund, 151, 201, 239.
Burlingame, Anson, 334.
Burritt, Elihu, 282.
Burt, A., 262.
Butler, General, 387.

C.

CALHOUN, JOHN C., 65, 80, 114, 116, 120, 127, 128, 283; his action in the "Enterprise" affair, 81-84; offers resolutions to nationalize slavery, 82-83, 126-127, 160; Secretary of State, 157; his treaty for the annexation of Texas, 178-182; position on the Oregon question, 189-190; opposed Polk's call for additional troops for Mexican War, 198; his address to the South in support of slavery, 268.
Calhoun, William B., 105, 145, 147.
California, 257, 269-270, 281, 310.
Campbell, Lewis D., 322, 348.
Campbell, Mr., 217.
Cartter, David K., 372, 373.
Cass, General, 185, 190, 271, 278, 283, 306; minister to France, 117; candidate for President, 251; his "Nicholson Letters," 251.
Chase, Salmon P., organizer of the Liberty party in Ohio, 130; correspondence with Giddings, 130-133; elected to the Senate, 257, 266-268, 271; his election distasteful to the Whigs, 267; his connection with the Free-Soil address regarding the Missouri Compromise, 311, 312.
Chatham, Lord. *See* William Pitt.
Cherokee Indians, the, 175, 367.

Chittenden, Thomas C., 105, 147.
Choate, Rufus, 11.
Cilley, J., 58, 108.
Clark, Mr., 329.
Clarke, Staley N., 147.
Clay, Cassius M., 165.
Clay, Henry, 13, 54, 57, 83, 90, 140, 213, 214, 219, 271, 282, 347, 381; speech against the Abolitionists, 65-66; defends the Whigs for favoring Abolitionism, 80; his sympathy with Giddings because of the House censure, 125; nominated for President, 157; position on the annexation of Texas and slavery, 157 *et seq.*; his friendship with Giddings, 158-159, 208, 299; Giddings's confidence in, 159, 160; he causes the Whigs great anxiety, 161 *et seq.*; correspondence with Giddings, 161-163, 164-165, 208-210; his Alabama letter, 163-164; his vacillation costs him his election, 165-168; his gratitude to Giddings, 167; opposed to the Mexican War Bill, 193; sacrificed by the Whigs in 1848, 252; his admirers unite with the Free-Soil party, 253; connection with the "Monroe Doctrine," 295-296; death of, 299.
"Cleveland Daily Herald," the, 223.
Clifford, Nathan, 92.
Clinton, General, 201.
Cobb, Howell, 177, 178, 272, 276.
Coe, Rev. Harvey, 20.
Colcock, W. F., of S. C., 309.
Coleman, Nathaniel, 21.
Collamer, Jacob, of Vt., 277.
"Comet," the, 113, 120, 142.
Conklin, Rev. Mr., 395.
Cooper, James, 142.
Cooper, Mark A., 97, 123, 125.
Corwin, Thomas, 13, 47, 131, 255, 383; his speech opposing the Mexican War, 199-200; proposed as a Presidential candidate, 199, 200, 207; his attitude on slavery unsatisfactory to anti-slavery Whigs, 210-213; disappoints his anti-slavery supporters, 214-215; Secretary of the Treasury, 215; approves the Compromise Measures of 1850, 215.
Colton, Captain, 18.
Cox, J. D., opposes Giddings's renomination to Congress, 355.
Cranston, Henry T., 192.
Crawford, W. H., Secretary of the Treasury, 141.
Creek Indians, the, 175-177, 196, 299, 361, 366-368.
"Creole," case of the, 114 *et seq.*, 160, 359.
Crittenden, John J., his amendment to the Lecompton Bill, 341 *et seq.*
Crocket, David, 46.
Cuba, its annexation to the United States desired by the Democrats, 315-317, 405.
Culver, Erastus, 192, 229, 230, 231, 235.
Curtis, George T., 228.
Curtis, George William, delegate to the Republican Convention in 1860, 373; his efforts to embody the principles of the Declaration of Independence in the Republican platform, 373-374.
Cushing, Caleb, 121.

INDEX. 465

D.

DADE, Major, 262.
Dana, Richard H., Jr., 206.
Davis, Garrett, 80, 151.
Davis, Mr., of Massachusetts, 83, 90.
Davis, Jefferson, of Mississippi, 244.
Davis, Henry Winter, of Maryland, 347.
Dawson, J. B., of Louisiana, insults and threatens Giddings in the House, 145-146, 174.
Declaration of Independence, 340, 377, 380; infidelity to, by politicians North and South, 336; efforts to embody its principles in the Republican platform of 1860, 372-376.
Delano, Columbus, 192, 229, 230, 231-232; defends Giddings's action regarding the Mexican War, 203 204.
Democrats, their status in the Twenty-sixth Congress, 77-78; control all the departments of government, 77; ascendency in the House dependent on admission of New Jersey members, 77-79; charge the Whigs with sympathy with Abolitionism, 80; themselves in sympathy with slavery, 137; nominate Polk for President, 158; defeated in Ohio, 167; profit by the Plaquemine frauds in Louisiana, 168; Oregon question divides them, 189-191; adverse effects of Van Buren's defeat, 207, 251; some of them vote for Winthrop as Speaker, 222; nominate Cass for President, 231; anti-slavery members unite in forming a third party, 253; forced to show their position on slavery, 259-260; support Chase for Senator from Ohio, 267; shaken by the question of prohibition of slavery in national Territories, 279; elect Cobb as Speaker in the Thirty-first Congress, 272; try to suppress the discussion of slavery, 286-291; nominate Pierce for President, 302; their platform favors the suppression of freedom of speech, 302; Giddings's arraignment of, 302-305; control a majority of the State Legislatures and both Houses of Congress in 1853, 309; denounce Giddings for agitating the slavery question, 310; desire the annexation of Cuba, 315-317; willing to subordinate the slavery issue to political success, 318; in a minority in the House in the Thirty-fourth Congress, 321; united in support of Buchanan in 1856, 337; attempt to involve the Republicans in Brown's Virginia raid, 370-371; forewarned by Giddings of the effects of the annexation of Texas, 404.
Dennison, Governor, 378, 382.
DeWitt, Alexander, 311.
Dickey, Mr., of Penn., 263.
Dix, John A., 306.
Dixon, N. F., of R. I., 83.
Douglas, Stephen A., 190, 283, 298, 307, 380; first asserts his doctrine of popular sovereignty, 184; favors the repeal of the Missouri Compromise, 310-312; leader of the Northern Democrats in 1856, 236; opposes the admission of Kansas with Lecompton constitution, 342 *et seq.*; measures which led to his debate with Lincoln, 351.
Downing, Charles, of Fla., 98, 99.
Drayton, Captain, 241-243.
Duncan, Alex., of Ohio, 183.
Duncan, J. H., 309.
Dunlap, James, 165.
Durkee, Charles, 271, 274, 341.

E.

EDWARDS, Jonathan, 38.
Emerson, Benjamin, 103.
"Encomium," the, 113, 120, 142.
English, W. H., of Indiana, 350.
"Enterprise," case of the, 81-84, 114, 116, 120, 160.
Everett, Edward, Chairman of the Committee on Foreign Affairs, 141.
Everett, H., of Vermont, 120, 121.
Ewing, Thomas, 13, 255, 283; his criticism of the Republican party, 377-378; supports Lincoln for President, 377; arraigns the Legislature and Governor of Ohio, 378; Giddings's reply to, in defence of the Republican party, 378-383.
"Exiles of Florida," the, 360, 365-369.

F.

FASSETT, Henry, 137-138, 279.
Fessenden, W. P., 121.
Ficklin, O. B., 270.
Field, David Dudley, 306.
Fillmore, Millard, 33, 121, 122, 282, 302; nominated by the Know-Nothings for President in 1856, 337.
Florida, purchase of, 43; admission to the Union, 43, 184; Indian wars in, 43, 80, 92-96, 135, 175-178, 262; slavery in its constitution, 184.
Floyd, C. A., of N. Y., 121.
Foote, H. S., of Mississippi, 244, 288, 291.
Foote, Solomon, of Vermont, 174.
Fox, Charles James, 201, 202, 239.
Franklin, Benjamin, 39, 41.
Frasier, Major, 17.
Free-Soil Party, the, 44-45, 207, 252, 261, 272, 284; its convention in Massachusetts addressed by Giddings, 247; Buffalo convention of, 253; nominates Van Buren for President, 254; bitterness of the Whigs towards, 254-255; effect of its action in 1848, 257; helps elect Chase Senator from Ohio, 266-267; favors Thaddeus Stevens for Speaker of the House in the Thirty-first Congress, 272; charged with causing the defeat of Winthrop for the Speakership, 272, 276; its opposition to Winthrop vindicated by his subsequent career, 272; its attempt to elect W. J. Brown Speaker, 273-275; defence of, by Giddings, 276-277; enduring work of its leaders, 284-285; helps elect Wade Senator from Ohio, 287; its prophecies regarding the Whigs verified, 302; its political outlook in 1852, 306; its address in reference to the Missouri Compromise, 311-

312; its rapid advance in public favor, 320; unites forces with the Republicans in the Speakership contest of 1855, 322; based on the principle that slavery was a State institution, 410.
Frémont John C., Republican candidate for President in 1856, 257, 335.
Fugitive Slave Law, 282, 283, 284, 286, 288, 301, 302, 304, 324, 379.
Furness, Rev. W. H., 402.

G.

GAG-RULE, known as the Twenty-first rule of the House, 91; efforts of J. Q. Adams to repeal, 91-92, 102, 140, 148-149; repeal of 171.
Gaines, General, 176, 299.
Garner, Margaret, 328.
Garnet, Rev. Hiram, 364.
Garrison, William Lloyd, opposes the formation of a political anti-slavery party, 89; his religious principles, 402.
Gates, Seth M., 105, 142; member of Congress, 79-80; high moral character of, 79; an ardent sympathizer with the anti-slavery movement, 80, 103; opposes the annexation of Texas, 146-147; retires from public life, 148, 406.
Gedney, Lieutenant, 74.
Ghent, treaty of, 112, 115, 361.
Giddings, Comfort Pease, 25.
Giddings, George, 12.
Giddings, Grotius Reed, 25; began the practice of law in 1860, 25; his distinguished action in the Rebellion, 26; injured in the New York riots, 26; his death, 26.
Giddings, John, 12.
Giddings, Joseph Addison, 25; practises law, later judge of the Probate Court, 25; editor of "The Ashtabula Sentinel," 25.
Giddings, Joshua, 12.
Giddings, Joshua, Jr., 12; fought in the Revolution, 12; married twice, 12; moves to western New York, 12; moves to Ohio, 13.
Giddings, Joshua Reed, 27, 76-77, 88, 105, 108, 111, 116, 129, 141, 147, 190, 230, 260, 271, 272, 274, 281, 283; ancestry, 11-12; birth, 12; his Ohio home, 13; youth, 15-20; education, 16-17, 19-20; in the War of 1812, 17-18; teaches school, 19-20; studies law, 21-22; first essay in public speaking, 22; admitted to the Bar, 23-24; marriage, 24; begins practice of law, 25; his children, 25-26; moves to Jefferson, 28; early practice in court, 29-30; the Williams vs. Hawley case, 30-32; great success in criminal cases, 32-33; elected to the State Legislature, 33-34; chairman of the Committee on Military Affairs, 34; defeated for the State Senate, 34; forms a partnership with B. F. Wade, 34; dissolution of partnership and retirement from practice, 35; suffers financial losses, 35; fails in health, 35; travels, 35-36; engages again in law practice, 36; enters Congress as a member of the Whig party, 36-37, 44-45; first becomes interested in the slavery question, 45; extracts from his private journal, 46-72; tedious journey to Washington, 46; warm friendship for J. Q. Adams, 48, 168-170, 208, 398; visits Van Buren, 50; a fearless opponent of slavery, 52-53; makes his first regular speech in the House, 58-60; action for the abolition of slavery in the District of Columbia, 64-65; makes his first anti-slavery speech, 67-70; steadfastness of purpose in the face of sectional opposition, 70-71; action in the "Amistad" case, 77, 153-155, 205, 309-310; first defection from the Whig party, 79; speech on the Calhoun resolutions in the "Enterprise" affair, 84-85; supports General Harrison for President in 1840, 91; action regarding the Florida War, 92-96, 177-178, 380; incurs the odium of the slaveholders, 97-99; insulted in the House by Southern members, 97-98; timely service in rousing the Free States to an appreciation of the encroachments of slavery, 99-100; letter from William Jay, 100; President Harrison's displeasure with, 100; chairman of the Committee on Claims, 102-103; presents petition for dissolution of the Union, 110; letter to his wife describing J. Q. Adams's trial in the House, 110-111; action in the "Creole" affair, 118 et seq.; his resolutions on the "Creole" case, 118-120, 384; withdraws these resolutions, 121; his censure demanded, 121-122; preparations for his defence, 122-123; denied the privilege of defending himself, 123-124; censured by the House, 124; his note of protest to the "National Intelligencer," 124-125; resigns his office as representative, 125; sympathy of Mr. Clay, 125; his resolutions condemned as ill-timed, 126, 127; his position justified by law and precedent, 126-127; re-elected to the House, and instructed to re-assert his principles, 128, 129; letter to his son, 128; vindicates his position in a public speech, 129-130; his firmness results in re-establishing freedom of debate in the House, 130; letters from Salmon P. Chase, 130-133; considers a third-party movement unwise in 1842, 133; his "Pacificus" essays, 133-137, 158, 159; to establish the principle of Federal non-intervention with slavery, the aim of his public life, 136, 409-411; effect of his essays, 136-137; mistake in exhorting the opponents of slavery to support the Whig party, 137; determines to retire from public life, 137; declines a re-election to Congress, 137-138; prevailed upon to remain in office, 138; letters to his wife, 138-139, 158-159, 198, 245-246, 389, 397; commended on all sides for his firmness in maintaining his doctrines, 139; attempt to deprive him of the chairmanship of the Committee on Claims, 140; opposes the claims of the West Florida Slaveholders, 142; speaks on the "Comet" and "Encomium" claims, 143-144; insulted and threatened in the House by Dawson, 145-146; denounced as an "Abolitionist" and "agitator," 148; removed from the

chairmanship of the Committee on Claims, 148, 177; assigned to the Committee on Revolutionary Pensions, 148; assists J. Q. Adams in fighting for the repeal of the gag-rule, 149; exposes the home squadron as the tool of slavery, 150-151; member of the committee to consider the Massachusetts memorial, 151, 152; letter to his daughter, 155; his first speech in opposition to the annexation of Texas, 156-157; friendship with Henry Clay, 158-159, 208; confidence in Clay's anti-slavery character, 159, 160; his active support of the Whig cause, 160, 161-167; correspondence with Clay, 161-163, 164-165, 208-210; charged by the Liberty party with having sold himself to Clay, 166-167; untiring efforts in the Ohio State election in 1844, 167; mistaken opinion of Clay and the Whigs, 168; insulted and threatened by Southern members, 172-175; speech on Calhoun's treaty for the annexation of Texas, 178-182; his feelings on the final vote for annexation, 183; speech on the Oregon question, 186-188, 317; receives letters regarding the Oregon question, 188-189; opposes the Mexican War Bill, 192; denounces Polk for declaring war with Mexico, 195-196; speech on the Indian Appropriation Bill, 196-197; series of public speeches in Maine, 197-198; correspondence with Charles Sumner, 199; 202-203, 205, 208, 210-213, 214, 216-217, 222, 227, 258, 260-261, 267-268, 277-278, 287, 334-335, 357-358, 384-385, 386-387, 388-389, 390, 391-394; correspondence with C. F. Adams, 199-200, 213-214, 228-229, 278; arraignment of Polk's Mexican War policy, 200; action in opposing the Mexican War based on British precedents, 200-201; position attacked by Mr. Winthrop, 201-202; defended by Mr. Delano, 203-204; leader of the liberal Whigs in the West, 206; chief representative of the anti-slavery cause in Congress, 207; warm friendship for C. F. Adams and Charles Sumner, 208, 398; disapproved of Clay's nomination in 1847, 208; steadfast in his faith in Corwin, 214; letter to Horace Greeley, 215-216; opposition to Winthrop for Speaker, 216 *et seq.*; reluctant to oppose his party friends, 218, 219-220; abused by the Whigs for his opposition to the party, 222 *et seq.*; letter to the "Cleveland Daily Herald," 223-226; controversy with Mr. Winthrop, 226 *et seq.*; 276-277, 280-281; his statement answered by the "Boston Atlas," 226-227, 229, 232; his defence in the "Boston Atlas" and "Boston Whig," 229; supported by C. F. Adams and Sumner, 232; vindicated in his refusal to support Winthrop, 235-238, 241; appointed to the Committee on Indian Affairs, 236; his solitary vote against thanking Generals Scott and Taylor, 238-239, 406; slighted by Winthrop in the appointment of a committee to attend J. Q Adams's funeral, 240; predicts the disbandment of the Whig party, 241;

ridicules the claims of General Taylor as a Whig, 241; brave action in the case of the "Pearl," 241-244; series of public speeches in Massachusetts, 245-247; a recognized authority on slavery matters, 247-249; speech on indemnities for lost slaves, 249-251; activity in the Presidential campaign of 1848, 255-256; charges against, by Elisha Whittlesey and Truman Smith, 255-256; his answer to Smith, 256-257; under the social ban, 258, 284; action in the Pacheco case, 263-266; extracts from his diary, 263-264, 267, 269-270, 344-349; a candidate for Senator from Ohio, 266-268; replies to Calhoun's address to the South, 268-269; opposed to the admission of California and New Mexico as Slave States, 269-270; letter from Rev. Joshua Leavitt, 275; defends the Free Soilers against the charges of the Whigs, 276-277; attacked by the Whig Press, 278-280; letter to Henry Fassett, 279; charged with purloining papers from the General Post-Office, 279-280; speech on the Texas Boundary Bill, 281-282; disapproves of armed defence of the Union, 282; denounces the Fugitive Slave Law, 282, 283; speech on "the agitation of the Slavery Question," 282-283; speech on the Fugitive Slave Law, 288-289; Stanly's reply to, 289-291; charged with a design of involving the nation in war, 291; 293, 294; attends a meeting of the Pennsylvania Anti-Slavery Society. 294-295; letter to his son, 294-295; speech in defence of foreign intervention in Hungary, 295-298; criticises Webster's foreign policy, 296-297; visits Clay shortly before the latter's death, 299; speech on the compromise measures, 300-301; arraignment of the Whigs and Democrats, 301, 302-305; declares civil war to be imminent, 304; sonnet dedicated to, 305; unsuccessful attempt to defeat his re-election, 306-307; a member of the Committee on Territories, 307; opposes the claim of W. H Wigg, 308; denounced by the Democrats for agitating the slavery question, 310; connection with the Free-Soil address regarding the Missouri Compromise, 311; speech on the Kansas-Nebraska Bill, 313-314; speech on the Homestead Bill, 314; action in the case of the "Black Warrior," 314-318; rebukes President Pierce, 316-317; not in sympathy with the Know-Nothing movement, 318; opposed to the restoration of the Missouri Compromise, 318-319; vigilance in the matter of slavery, 319; his resolution submitted at the Speakership conference of Republicans and Free Soilers, 322-324; his activity in the Speakership contest, 324-325; administers the oath of office to Speaker Banks, 325; his satisfaction at the election of Banks as Speaker, 326, 327; attends the Republican Convention at Pittsburg in 1856, 326-327; letters from John Brown to, 327-328; speech on the Deficiency Bill, 328-332; defence of the Indians, 329-330; denounces the action of

United States troops in Kansas, 330-331; arraignment of the slave-code of Kansas, 331-332; vigorous protest in regard to the Brooks assault on Sumner, 332-335; delegate to the first nominating convention of the Republican party, 335; his part in the preparation of the Republican platform, 335; his satisfaction at the indorsement of his principles by the Republicans, 336; activity in the Presidential campaign of 1856, 337; speech on the Kansas policy of Buchanan, 337-338; prostrated by heart-trouble, 338; letter from J. P. Hale, 338-339; letters to Chief-Justice Taney regarding the Dred Scott decision, 340; opposes the Lecompton Bill, 341; his perplexity regarding the Crittenden Amendment, 343 *et seq*.; speech on "The Conflict between Religious Truths and American Infidelity," 351-352; speech on English right of visitation, 352; prostrated a second time by heart-trouble, 353; defeated for renomination to Congress, 353 *et seq.*; his serenity over his defeat, 352; messages of sympathy from his friends, 356-358; universal regret at his retirement from public life, 358-360; his "Exiles of Florida," 360, 365-369; farewell speech in Congress, 361-363; testimonials from his friends, 363-364; assists in raising funds for the relief of John Brown, 370; charged with being accessory to Brown's Virginia raid, 370-371; leaves Congress a poor man, 371; delivers a course of lectures on J. Q. Adams, 371; a delegate to the Republican Convention of 1860, 371-376; his efforts to embody in the Republican platform the principles of the Declaration of Independence, 372-376; his congratulation to Lincoln on his nomination for President, 376; activity in the Presidential campaign of 1860, 376; his "History of the Rebellion," 384, 386, 391; accepts the position of Consul-general to Canada, 384; his anxiety to be in Washington, 385-386; his interest in reciprocity with Canada, 386-387, 391-394; letter from Horace Greeley, 387-388; health rapidly failing, 388-389, 391, 394; completion of his book, 391; death, 394-395; eulogized by the Press of Montreal and the Northern States, 395; funeral, 395; personal traits, 396-397; devotion to his family, 397-398; his friendships, 398-399; his fondness for athletic sports and music, 399; his religious principles, 399-403; his political foresight, 403-405; moral earnestness his dominating characteristic, 405-407; his practical qualities as a reformer, 407-412; the father of the Republican party, 411; his place in history, 412-413; Lowell's lines in praise of, 413.

Giddings, Laura, 26; marries George W. Julian, 26; her death, 26; letter from her father, 391.

Giddings, Lura Maria, 25; among the early workers in the anti-slavery reform, 25; with her father in Montreal at time of his death, 25, 395; her part in the erection of a monument to her father, 25.

Giddings, Mrs. J. R., 24, 26; letters from her husband, 138-139, 158-159, 198, 245-246, 389, 397.

Giddings, Thomas, 12.
Gilmer, T. W., of Va., 103, 105, 109, 151.
Gott, Daniel, 259, 260, 277, 278.
Granger, Ralph, 37.
Greeley, Horace, 215, 252, 263; his belief in the right of the Slave States to secede, 282; attends the Republican Convention at Pittsburg in 1856, 326.
Green, Beriah, 402.
Grinnell, Joseph, 192, 231, 260.

H.

HABERSHAM, R. W., of Georgia, 93.
Hale, John P., 271, 283, 288, 337; candidate of the Liberty party in 1847 for President, 207, 212; solitary vote in the Senate against thanking Generals Scott and Taylor, 238-239; proposes a bill to prevent riots in Washington, 243; Free-Soil candidate for President in 1852, 306; letter to Giddings, 338-339; charged with being accessory to Brown's Virginia raid, 371.
Halleck, General, 388.
Halsted, Murat, *quoted*, 374.
Hamlin, E. S., of Ohio, 242.
Hamlin, Hannibal, Republican candidate for Vice-President in 1860, 371.
Hammet, W. J., 173, 178.
Hannegan, Senator E. A., rupture with President Polk on the Oregon question, 190; reconciliation, and appointment as minister to Russia, 191.
Haralson, H. A., 259.
Harney, Lieutenant-Colonel, 96; General, 329.
Harrison, William Henry, 54-55, 88-89, 90, 131, 378, 380, 381; Whig candidate for President in 1840, 84-86; a pro-slavery Virginian, 86-87; elected President in 1840, 91; charged with encouraging Abolitionists, 97; displeased with Giddings's speech on the Seminole War, 100; disappoints the anti-slavery men, 100-101.
Haskell, W. T., of Tenn., 243.
Hawley, Dr., 30-32.
Hawthorne, Nathaniel, 11.
Hayes, General, 17.
Henry, T., of Penn., 105.
"Hermosa," the, 113, 114.
Hewell, a slave-dealer, 114.
Hillyer, Junius, of Ga, 300.
Hinsdale, Mr., *quoted* 14, *note* 1.
Hoar, E. R., 206.
Hoar, Samuel, 206.
Hodges, Mr., 250, 256.
Holmes, Isaac E., 103, 121, 122, 142, 222, 242, 261.
Hopkins. Dr. Samuel, 38.
Hopkins, G. W., of Va., 104, 108.
Howard, Jacob M., 142, 147.
Howe, John W., 271, 307.
Hubbard, Henry, of N. H., 83.
Hudson, Charles, 147, 174, 192, 231.
Hull, General, 17.
Hunter, R. M. T., Speaker of the House in the Twenty-sixth Congress, 79.

INDEX. 469

Hutchins, John, defeats Giddings for the nomination to Congress, 353-354; an ardent anti-slavery man, 354.

I.

INGERSOLL, Charles J., 77, 153.
Ingersoll, J. R., 151.
Iowa, admitted to the Union, 184.
Irwin, Alexander, 277.

J.

JACKSON, Andrew, 55, 81, 86, 99, 113, 141, 142, 144, 176, 180, 249, 314.
Jackson, J., of Georgia, 288.
James, Francis, 295.
Jay, John, 39, 202, 203, 204.
Jay, William, letter to Giddings, 100, 247-248; a contributor to anti-slavery literature, 249.
Jefferson, Thomas, 39, 144, 157, 243; Lincoln's tribute to, 375.
Jessup, General, commander of the United States army in the Florida wars, 92, 94, 95, 175-177, 262, 265, 299.
Jones, Anson, 21.
Jones, Mr., of Wisconsin, 58-59.
Jones, G. W., Senator from Iowa, 288.
Jones, Submit, 12.
Jones, William, case of, 149-150.
Julian, George W., 271, 295; marries the daughter of Giddings, 26; opposed to W. J. Brown for Speaker in 1849, 273, 275.

K.

KANSAS, 325, 326, 337, 370; effort to establish slavery in, 312-313, 320, 327-328, 330-332, 340 et seq.; bill for organizing the Territory of, 313; slave-code of, 331; Lecompton Bill for its admission as a State, 341 et seq.
Kansas-Nebraska Bill, 307, 313, 323.
King, Daniel P., 192.
King, Judge, of Ohio, 132.
King, Preston, 212, 252, 271, 273, 306.
Knight, N. P., 83.
Know-Nothing party, 319, 322; the policy and organization of, 318; controlled by demagogues, 318; divided on the slavery issue, 321; its phenomenal success, 321; puts forward two candidates for the Speakership in 1855, 322; nominates Fillmore for President in 1856, 337.
Kossuth, Louis, invited to visit the United States, 291; resolutions of sympathy with, 291, 294; his doctrine of foreign intervention, 295, 297.

L.

LAWRENCE, Joseph, of Penn., 105.
Lay, Benjamin, 37.
Leavitt, Rev. Joshua, 105, 275.
Lecompton constitution, 341.
Letcher, John, of Va., 322, 323.
Levin, L. C., of Penn., 283.

Lewis, Mr., 329.
Liberty party, the, 44-45, 91, 160, 218; organized in Ohio, 130-133; failed to rally the people, 137; nominates James G. Birney for President in 1844, 158; joined by many anti-slavery Whigs, 166; controversy with Giddings, 166-167; John P. Hale its Presidential candidate in 1847, 207; withdraws its candidate, 253; unites in a third-party movement, 253-254.
Lincoln, Abraham, 13, 14, 63, 257, 343, 377, 378, 379, 380; voted against the abolition of the slave-trade in the District of Columbia, 261; a moderate Wilmot-Proviso man, 261; measures which led to his debate with Douglas, 351; Republican nominee for President in 1860, 371, 376; his tribute to Jefferson, 375; replies to Giddings's congratulatory letter, 376; his Proclamation of Emancipation, 405.
Lincoln, Levi, 206.
Linn, Archibald L., 147.
Louisiana, importance of its acquisition, 40, 43.
Lovejoy, Elijah P., 45.
Lovejoy, Owen, 326.
Lowell, James Russell, editor of the "Atlantic Monthly," 368; his favorable notice of Giddings's "Exiles in Florida." 368-369; his lines in praise of Giddings, 413.

M.

MADISON, James, 40, 117, 265.
Mann, Horace, 236, 264.
Marsh, George P., 231, 277.
Marshall, Humphrey, prosecutes the trial of J. Q. Adams in the House, 105-106; his charges against Mr. Adams, 106, 107; Mr. Adams's chastisement of, 108-109; the Southern Know-Nothing candidate for Speaker in 1855, 322.
Mason, General, 59.
Mason, J. M., Senator from Virginia, 372; charges Giddings with conspiracy in Brown's Virginia raid, 370.
Mattocks, John, 147.
McClellan, General, 237, 388.
McDowell, James, of Va., 283.
McIlvaine, A. R., 229, 230, 231.
McLean, Judge, 207, 208.
McMullen, Fayette, of Va., 324.
Medill, Joseph, 338.
Mexico, 190, 248; cause of war with the United States, 147, 184, 195; United States declares war with, 191; General Taylor's invasion of, 193; sufferings of the United States army in, 198; unpopularity in United States of war with, 198-199; success of United States armies in, 206.
Miles, General, 329.
Miller, J. W., Senator, 288.
Missouri, 43, 307, 330.
Missouri Compromise, the, 283, 307, 308, 324, 352; repeal of, 310-313; its restoration favored by the Whigs, 320-321; effect of its repeal, 325, 377, 380; popular cry for its restoration, 318.

Monroe, James, his first proclamation of the "Monroe Doctrine," 295.
Montez, P., 73-77, 153.
Montgomery, William, of Penn., his amendment to the Lecompton Bill, 342.
Moore, John, of La., 145.
Morgan, Christopher, 147.
Morrill, Justin S., 302.
Morse (of Maine), 151.
Morse (of Ohio), 266, 267.

N.

NEBRASKA, 320; bill for organizing a government of, 307, 313; conflict over the slavery question in, 312-313.
New Mexico, 269-270, 311.
Newton, Eben, of Ohio, 307.
Nowell, Senator from Michigan, 83.

O.

OGLETHORPE, General, 37.
Ohio, admitted to the Union, 13; character of its settlers, 14-15; state of its society, 28.
Oregon, 329, 404; question of its annexation, 183-191; saved from slavery, 257.
Oyler, Mr., 372.

P.

PACHECO, Antonio, 262-266.
"Pacificus" Essays. See Appendix.
Paine, Thomas, 38.
Palfrey, John G., 210, 213, 214, 217, 219, 225, 259, 264, 267, 269, 272, 281, 321; a "Conscience Whig," 206; representative to Congress, 220; personal characteristics, 220; opposed to Winthrop for Speaker, 221-222; abused by the Whigs for opposing Winthrop, 222; ill-feeling of Winthrop towards, 232; appointed to the Committee on Agriculture, 236; vindicated in his refusal to support Winthrop, 238; his action in the case of the "Pearl," 243; letter to Giddings, 356-357.
Palmerston, Lord, 387.
Parker, Theodore. letters to Giddings, 248-249; contributed to anti-slavery literature, 249.
Payne, W. W., of Ala., 172.
Peabody, Dr. Andrew P., 220.
"Pearl," the, case of, 241-244.
Pease, Elizabeth, 12.
Pease, John, 12.
Pennsylvania Abolition Society, 39, 294.
Phillips, P., of Alabama, 315.
Phillips, Stephen C., 206, 210, 217.
Phillips, Wendell, 245.
Pickering, Timothy, 202.
Pierce, Franklin, 83; Democratic nominee for President, 302; elected President, 305-306; approves the compromise measures, 309; recommends payment of indemnity in the "Amistad" case, 309; his action in the case of the "Black Warrior," 315-317; rebuked by Giddings, 316-317.
Pitt William (Lord Chatham), 201, 202, 239.
Polk, James K., 65, 129; nominated by Democrats for President in 1844, 158; committed to the policy of the annexation of Texas, 158; supported by the worst classes of society, 160-161; his Kane letter, 167-168; his election hastened the advent of the Civil War, 168; violated his promises to his party, 183; his inauguration, 184; his position on the Oregon question, 184, 185, 187; message on the Oregon dispute with England, 185; charges of Democratic leaders against, 190; his settlement of the Oregon question, 190; reconciliation with Democratic leaders, 191; orders General Taylor to Corpus Christi, 191; denounced by the Whigs for causing the Mexican War, 194; Giddings's charges against, 195-196; his call for additional troops for the Mexican War, 198; his action on the Oregon question prophesied by Giddings, 404.
Pomeroy, General, 327.
Porter, A. S., of Michigan, 83.
Prentiss, S. S., 54, 56.
Preston, W. B., 277.
Proclamation of Emancipation, 405.

Q.

QUAKERS, their hostility to slavery in the colonies, 37.
Quincy, Josiah P., praises Giddings's "Exiles in Florida," 369.

R.

RANNEY, Rufus P., 35.
Rantoul, Robert, Jr., 306.
Raymond, Henry J., 290.
Raynor, Kenneth, 173.
Republican party, the, first organized, 321; joins forces with the Free Soilers in the Speakership contest of 1855, 322; elects N. P. Banks Speaker, 325; call for a National Convention of, 326-327; nominates John C. Frémont for President in 1856, 335; indorses Giddings's resolution in their platform, 236; coalition with the Douglas Democrats and Southern Whigs to defeat the Lecompton Bill, 342 et seq.; disastrous results of this coalition, 350-351; its disruption arrested by the Illinois Republicans, 351; charged with being accessory to Brown's Virginia raid, 370; disposition to abandon its position of 1856, 371-372; nominates Lincoln and Hamlin for President and Vice-President in 1860, 371; criticised by Thomas Ewing, 377-378; Giddings's defence of, 378-383; founded on the principle that slavery was a State institution, 410; Giddings the father of, 411.
Rhett, R. B., 79, 151.

INDEX.

Richardson, William A., the Democratic candidate for Speaker in 1855, 322.
Robinson, Governor of Kansas, 346.
Robinson, J. M., of Illinois, 83.
Rockwell, Julius, 264, 276.
Root, Joseph M., 192, 199, 245, 269, 271, 273, 281.
Ross, Dr., 394.
Ross, John, 175.
Ruiz, I., 73-77, 153.
Ruggles, Senator John, 83.

S.

SAMPLE, S. C., of Indiana, 151.
Sandiford, Ralph, 37.
Saunders, R. M., of N. C., 150.
Sayres, Mr., 241-243.
Schenck, Robert C., 229, 230, 276, 283.
Schouler, James, his "History of the United States," 126, note 1.
Scott, Dred, case of, 351, 352; repudiated the principles of the Declaration of Independence, 339-340; political significance of, 340.
Scott, General Winfield, 233, 238; advocated the right of Slave States to secede, 282; the Whig nominee for President in 1852, 301; defeated for the Presidency, 305.
Seminole Indians, the, war with, 43, 80, 92-96, 175-176, 196, 262, 366-368.
Severance, Luther, 192, 229, 231.
Seward, William H., 131, 283, 356.
Sharpe, Granville, 40.
Simonton, William, of Penn., 105.
Skelton, Charles, 309.
Slade, William, 64, 105, 142, 147, 406; an ardent anti-slavery man, 61, 79, 103; retired from public life, 148; letter to Giddings, 189.
Slatter, Hope H., 244.
Slavery, its early history in America, 37-45; repugnant to most of the colonies, 37-39; efforts of the Quakers to prohibit, 37; the slave-trade forbidden by the Continental Congress, 38; Thomas Paine's anti-slavery articles, 38; the champions of independence its chief foes, 38-40; formation of Abolition societies, 39; the churches anti-slavery, 39; forbidden in the territory under National Government, 39; abolished in seven of the States, 39; foreign slave-trade forbidden in the new Constitution, 39; concessions of the Constitution to, 39-40, 44; a State institution, 40, 409-410; considered a temporary evil, 40; the idea of property in man avoided in the Constitution, 40, 265; its rise to great political power, 40-45; stimulated by invention of the cotton-gin and acquisition of Louisiana, 40, 43; effect of Franklin's anti-slavery petition to Congress, 41; treaty with Cherokee Indians for recovery of fugitive slaves, 41-42; fugitive-slave law of 1793, 42; first threats of dissolving the Union, 42; nationalized in the District of Columbia, 42-43, 62-63, 135; the regulation by Congress of the coastwise slave-trade unconstitutional, 43, 112, 135; subserviency of the National Government to its methods, 43-44, 135; Florida purchased in the interest of, 43; the Missouri struggle in 1820, 43; the Florida wars carried on in its behalf, 43, 80, 92-96, 135, 175-178, 365-368; the churches its bulwarks, 44; dangers of opposing it, 44; right of petition and freedom of debate on, forbidden in the House, 45, 80, 118; Lovejoy murdered for his opposition to, 45; prostitutes the mail service, 45; its supremacy during the first session of the Twenty-sixth Congress, 80-84; submission of public men to its demands, 84; not a prominent issue in the Presidential campaign of 1840, 86, 88; foundation of the American Anti-Slavery Society, 87; the people of the Free States aroused to an appreciation of its evils, 99-100, 103, 127-128, 206; questions arising from, cause serious complications with England, 112 et seq.; the Senate a unit in the service of, 118; its power illustrated in the treatment of Giddings, 125; the "Pacificus" papers on, 133-134, 141; its extension sought by the annexation of Texas, 146-147, 161; the home squadron employed in the interests of, 150-151; the memorial of the Massachusetts Legislature, 151-153; the Georgia resolutions, 152-153; strengthened by the annexation of Texas, 186; its prohibition in newly acquired Mexican territory a vital issue, 206; in the District of Columbia, 259-262; Calhoun's address to the South in support of, 268; attempts to secure its territorial extension, 269-270; the most important question which confronted the Thirty-first Congress, 270, 271; Giddings speaks on, 282-283; the compromise measures of the Thirty-first Congress regarding, 283-284; efforts of Whigs and Democrats to prevent discussion of, 286-291; subserviency of Whigs and Democrats to, 302; efforts to establish it in Kansas, 312-313, 320, 327-328, 330-332, 340 et seq.; logically opposed to the Declaration of Independence, 336; Giddings's manner of dealing with, 407-412; principal cause of its overthrow, 412.
Slicer, Rev. Henry, 244-245.
Slidell, John, 168, 173.
Smith, Caleb B., 260, 277.
Smith, Gerrit, his connection with the Free-Soil proclamation regarding the Missouri Compromise, 311; charged with being accessory to Brown's Virginia raid, 371; his religious principles, 402.
Smith, O. H., Senator from Indiana, 47.
Smith, Truman, 83, 147, 250-251, 260, 277; abuses Giddings, 255; Giddings's reply to, 255-256.
Southard, S. L., 83.
Stanly, Edward, of N. C., 54, 143, 294, 295, 297; his scurrilous attack on Giddings, 289-291.
Stephens, Alexander H., 178, 198-199, 283, 338.
Stevens, Thaddeus, 272, 283.

Stevenson, Andrew, his action on the slavery question while minister to England, 113, 142.
Stiles, W. H., of Georgia, 174.
Strahan, John, 192.
Stuart, A. H. H., 124.
Sturgeon, Daniel, of Penn., 83.
Sumner, Charles, 214, 215, 235, 236, 271, 282, 406; correspondence with Giddings, 199, 202-203, 205, 210-213, 214, 216-217, 222, 227, 258, 260-261, 267-268, 277-278, 287, 291, 334-335, 357-358, 384-385, 386-387, 388-389, 390, 391-394; a "Conscience Whig," 206; his friendship with Giddings, 208, 398; enters the Senate, 208, 287; supported Giddings in his controversy with Winthrop, 232; urges Giddings to speak in Massachusetts, 245; his account of Giddings's visit to Massachusetts, 247; indignant at the attacks of the Whig Press on Giddings, 278; his connection with the Free-Soil address regarding the Missouri Compromise, 311, 312; assaulted by P. S. Brooks, 332.
Sutliff, Flavel, forms a law partnership with Giddings, 36.
Sutliff, Milton, opposes the renomination of Giddings to Congress, 355.

T.

TEXAS, General Taylor ordered to guard the southern boundary of, 191; hostilities with Mexico regarding the boundaries of, 191; Boundary Bill, 281, 283.
Texas, annexation of, a vital issue, 146; the slaveocracy secretly plotting for, 146; J. Q. Adams first to sound the alarm against, 146; its undesirability, 146-147; the cause of war with Mexico, 147, 185, 195; action of the Mexican government regarding, 147; Giddings makes the first speech in opposition to, 156-157; an important issue in the Presidential election of 1844, 157 *et seq.*; Calhoun's treaty for, 178-182; achieved by the joint resolution of Congress, 182-183; 191; gave the Slave States a majority in the Senate, 186; effects of on the tariff of 1842, 404.
Tallmadge, Senator N. P, 83.
Taney, Chief-Justice, 340.
Tappan, Arthur, first president of the American Anti-Slavery Society, 89.
Tappan, Benjamin, senator from Ohio, 83.
Tappan, Lewis, a pioneer in the anti-slavery cause, 89; letter to Giddings, 89-90.
Taylor, General, 176-177, 215, 219, 229, 238, 256, 261, 271, 278, 287, 302, 378, 406; ordered to Corpus Christi, 191; invades Mexico, 193; the Mexican War makes him a prospective candidate for President, 207; his non-committal attitude in politics, 241; nominated by the Whigs for President, 252; his political principles, 252; elected President, 258; appointments to office, 277; death of, 281.
Thayer, Eli, 372.
Thompson, Waddy, 51-52, 92, 98, 100.
Tilden, Daniel R., 192.
Tilden, Samuel J., 306.
Tomlinson, Thomas, 147.
Tompkins, P. W., 222.
Toombs, Robert, 263, 281.
Townshend, Dr., 266, 267.
Triplett, Philip, of Ky., 124.
Tuck, Amos, 271.
Tyler, John, 102, 115, 116, 129, 147.

U.

UPSHUR, A. P., Secretary of State, 157.
Utah, 311.

V.

VALLANDIGHAM, C. L., charges Giddings with conspiring in Brown's Virginia raid, 370.
Van Buren, Martin (President), 36, 50, 51, 66, 89, 99, 113, 143, 144, 212, 213, 214, 271, 306; his attempt to shelter the slave-trade under the national flag, 74-77; "a Northern man with Southern principles," 86; his anti-Texas letter, 158; a possible anti-slavery candidate for President in 1847, 207; his followers unite in a third-party movement, 253; nominated for President by the Free-Soil convention, 254.
Vance, Joseph, 177, 192, 230.
Venable, A. W., of N. C., 259.
Vinton, S. F., of Ohio, 261, 276, 277.
Von Holst, Dr., his "Constitutional History of the United States" quoted, 194.

W.

WADE, Benjamin F., 34-35, 45, 211, 256, 307, 311, 348; Senator from Ohio, 287.
Wade, Edward, 311, 348; elected to Congress, 307.
Walker, Senator from Mississippi, 182.
Wall, G. D., Senator from N. J., 83.
Wallace, Governor, 128.
Walsh, Mike, of N. Y., 309.
Ward, General, 120.
Warren, Lott, of Ga., 92.
Washburne, E. B., of Illinois, 394.
Washington, George, 42, 298.
Waters, Abner, 24.
Waters, Laura, 24.
Watson, James C., 176-177, 299-300.
Webster, Daniel, 83, 90, 127, 128, 129, 283; Secretary of State, 116; his action in the "Creole" affair, 116-118, 120; retired from the State Department, 157; considered by anti-slavery men as a candidate for President, 207; nominated for President by the Massachusetts Whig convention, 210; in favor of the Wilmot Proviso, 210; claimed Free Soil as a Whig doctrine, 254; Secretary of State, 281, 287; criticism of his foreign policy, in 1842, 296-297.
Weed, Thurlow, 188.
Weld, Theodore, 11, 45, 105.
Weller, John B., 122, 123.
Wesley, John, 37.

Whigs, 91, 97, 131, 132, 213, 229, 274, 282, 301, 307, 380; their power in the Twenty-sixth Congress, 78; their majority in the House depends on the admission of New Jersey members, 78-79; charged by the Democrats with favoring Abolitionism, 80; defended by Henry Clay, 80; Harrison their candidate for President in 1840, 85; their sole issue, 85-86; in a majority in the Twenty-seventh Congress, 102; divided into warring factions, 102; choose John White Speaker of the House, 102; credited with anti-slavery tendencies, 137; nominate Clay for President in 1844, 157; represented the best elements of society in the campaign of 1844, 160; many of their anti-slavery members join the Liberty party, 166; their success in Ohio due to the efforts of Giddings, 167; foreign-born citizens the bitter opponents of, 168; not a trustworthy agency in combating the South, 168; their cowardice leads them to vote for the Mexican War Bill, 192-194; unworthy of their leader, Henry Clay, 193; denounce President Polk for bringing on the Mexican War, 194; threatened with disruption, 206-207; "Conscience" and "Cotton," 206, 253; their attitude in 1847 stated by Giddings, 215-216; in Massachusetts, 219; their abuse of Giddings and Palfrey for refusing to support Winthrop for the Speakership, 222 *et seq.*; their disbandment predicted by Giddings, 241; nominate General Taylor for President in 1848, 252; their readiness to sacrifice principle for success, 252, 318; their treachery to Clay, 252; many members withdraw from the party, 252-253, 254; their bitterness towards the Free Soilers, 254-255; their treatment of Giddings, 258; forced to show their position on slavery, 259-260; defeat Giddings for the Ohio Senatorship, 267; seriously divided, 270-271; nominate R. C. Winthrop for Speaker of the House in the Thirty-first Congress, 272; move the "plurality rule" to govern the election of Speaker, 272, 276; charge Winthrop's defeat to the Free Soilers, 272, 276; their efforts to suppress the discussion of slavery, 286-291; General Scott their nominee for President in 1852, 301; deprecate in their platform the agitation of the slavery question, 301-302; demoralization of, 302; Giddings's arraignment of, 302-305; overwhelming defeat in 1852, 305-306; disruption of, 306, 318, 320; maintain their party organization in New York, 321; conservative members of, a discordant element in the Republican party, 372.

White, John, Speaker of the House of Representatives, 102.
Whitefield, George, 37.
Whitney, Eli, 41.
Whittlesey, Elisha, 21, 23, 24, 34, 37, 255.

Whittlesey, William A., 22, 23.
Wickliffe, C. A., Postmaster-general, 173, note.
Wigg, William Hazzard, 308.
Wilder, Horace, 37.
Williams, of North Carolina, 79.
Williams *vs.* Hawley, case of, 30-32.
Wilmot, David, 271, 273, 275.
Wilmot Proviso, 210, 211, 212, 214, 219, 220, 236, 237, 252, 256, 263, 281, 284, 311.
Wilson, Henry, 206, 252, 334, 384; letter to Giddings, 356.
Winthrop, Robert C., 211, 213, 217, 220, 276, 277, 278, 283; criticises Giddings for voting to withhold supplies for the Mexican War, 201-202; Delano's reply to, in defence of Giddings, 203-204; a "Cotton Whig," 206; elected Speaker of the House of Representatives, 216, 222; his election opposed by Giddings, 216 *et seq.*, 274; personal characteristics, 218; his famous toast, 218-219; opposes the anti-slavery spirit of Massachusetts, 219; desires General Taylor's nomination for President, 219, 237; favors the Mexican War, 219 224, 233-234; questioned as to his organization of the House if chosen Speaker, 221-222; elected Speaker by the aid of Democratic votes, 222; supported for Speakership by J. Q. Adams, 222; controversy with Giddings, 226 *et seq.*; his feelings towards C. F. Adams and Sumner, 232; Giddings justified in refusing to support him, 235-238; his hostility to the Free-Soil movement, 237; declines to vote for the Wilmot Proviso, 237; espouses the policy of Congressional "non-action" with slavery in the Territories, 237; opposes the formation of the Republican party in 1856, 237; opposes the election of Lincoln in 1860, 237; supports General McClellan in 1864, 237; slights Giddings, 240, 257; Whig nominee for Speaker of the House in the Thirty-first Congress, 272; his defeat charged to the Free Soilers, 272, 276; withdraws from the Speakership contest, 273; correctness of Giddings's prophecies regarding, 404.

Wise, H. A., his abuse of J. Q. Adams, 106-107.
Woodbury, Levi, 141.
Woods, Mr., of Ohio, 307.
Wool, General, 330.
Woolman, John, 37.
Wright, John C., 30-31.
Wright, H. B., of Penn, 314.

Y.

YOUNG, R. M., of Illinois, 83.
Young, Augustus, of Vermont, 105.

Z.

ZOLLICOFFER, F K., 325.